D0777494

The World Beat Series

WILLIAM H. BEEZLEY, University of Arizona
DAVID E. LOREY, The Hewlett Foundation
Series Editors

The World Beat Series consists of books designed for use in under-graduate courses in the social sciences. The general focus is social issues and social change, with many selections highlighting the stories of individuals and communities. All volumes include readings drawn from around the world, presenting a global offering of perspectives and information. Each book provides a mix of previously published articles, unpublished pieces (some of them commissioned specifically for the volume), and primary documents on a particular topic. An introduction by the volume editor places the general topic and the individual selections in their broader contexts. Texts in this series are an easy way for professors to "globalize" their courses in one stroke. World Beat books easily replace outdated course readers and old supplementary texts for undergraduate classes at both the introductory and advanced levels.

Volumes Published

David E. Lorey and William H. Beezley, editors. *Genocide, Collective Violence, and Popular Memory: The Politics of Remembrance in the Twentieth Century* (2002). Cloth ISBN 0-8420-2981-8 Paper ISBN 0-8420-2982-6

Wendy F. Kasinec and Michael A. Polushin, editors. *Expanding Empires: Cultural Interaction and Exchange in World Societies from Ancient to Early Modern Times* (2002). Cloth ISBN 0-8420-2730-0 Paper ISBN 0-8420-2731-9

David E. Lorey, editor. *Global Environmental Challenges of the Twenty-first Century: Resources, Consumption, and Sustainable Solutions* (2003). Cloth ISBN 0-8420-5048-5 Paper ISBN 0-8420-5049-3

Global Environmental Challenges of the Twenty-first Century

Global Environmental Challenges of the Twenty-first Century

Resources, Consumption, and Sustainable Solutions

THE

WORLD BEAT SERIES

No. 3

Edited by

David E. Lorey

SR BOOKS

A Scholarly Resources Inc. Imprint
Wilmington, Delaware

Scholarly Resources Inc.
104 Greenhill Avenue
Wilmington, DE 19805-1897
www.scholarly.com

Library of Congress Cataloging-in-Publication Data

Global environmental challenges of the twenty-first century : resources,
consumption, and sustainable solutions / edited by David E. Lorey.
    p. cm. — (The world beat series)
    Includes bibliographical references.
    ISBN 0-8420-5048-5 (cloth : alk. paper) — ISBN 0-8420-5049-3 (pbk.)
    1. Global environmental change. 2. Sustainable development. 3. Nature
—Effect of human beings on. I. Lorey, David E. II. Series.

GE149 .G547 2002
363.738'74—dc21   2002072688

∞ The paper used in this publication meets the minimum requirements of
the American National Standard for permanence of paper for printed library
materials, Z39.48, 1984.

To Michael Fischer,

friend, companion in the field,

and fellow poetry reader

About the Editor

David E. Lorey received his B.A. in history from Wesleyan University and his M.A. and Ph.D. in Latin American social and economic history from the University of California, Los Angeles. From 1989 to 1997 he directed the program on Mexico and was Visiting Professor of History at UCLA. Since 1997, Lorey has directed the U.S.-Latin American Relations Program at the Hewlett Foundation. There, Lorey has developed several new grant programs, one of which is an initiative in environment and sustainable development in Mexico, Chile, Argentina, and Brazil. His publications include *The U.S.-Mexican Border Region in the Twentieth Century* (1999).

Contents

Introduction

As most readers of this book will already be well aware, humankind currently faces mounting environmental challenges that make continued development along its current path both undesirable and ultimately unsustainable. We have most of the scientific knowledge and the technology to confront these challenges; what we lack is broad understanding, political will, and individual empowerment. Rather than attempting to convince or frighten readers, this book provides them with the tools they need to understand the most pressing environmental issues of our day and gives them practical insights on how they can make a real difference.

Environmental problems in this new century range from dealing with toxic wastes produced by industrialization, pollution of air and water, contamination from agricultural pesticides and synthetic fertilizers to responding to human-induced climate change, biodiversity loss, and unsustainable use of natural resources. The most daunting of these problems are those that have the potential to alter the course of life on the planet and lead to the irreversible decline of natural ecosystems; those challenges are the focus of this collection of essays and articles.

Scientists and activists who work in the area of environmental studies and action sometimes divide environmental issues into "brown" and "green." Brown issues are the negative side effects produced by industrial development and by such modern activities as driving cars and mass consumption of goods, services, and energy. Green issues, in contrast, are those that relate to the preservation, restoration, and sustainable use of natural resources, biodiversity, and habitat. While brown issues are of great importance in the everyday life of most of the people in the world, it is green issues that will most crucially shape our lives in the current century and life for humans and other living things on the planet far into the future.[1]

The principal purpose of this book is to present state-of-the-art information and analyses on each of five "green" environmental issues that will be crucial in the coming century. The selections are intended to provide a window on current understanding of human interactions with the natural world in these five areas and on how the future impacts of such interactions—both predictable and unpredictable—will shape this century. Although we remain amazingly ignorant of a great deal having to do with life on Earth, we now know enough to be able to describe accurately the significant environmental changes going on around us and caused by us. We have also developed sophisticated tools for predicting future trends. It seems clear that many of the human-caused changes under way in the natural world will become increasingly dangerous to us if current trends are not dramatically changed, halted, or reversed.

Another important purpose of the book is thus to raise awareness of the dangers of not addressing green environmental issues in a timely fashion. As the following chapters demonstrate, some of the coming threats can already be identified and others can be reasonably predicted from current knowledge. Other future outcomes of current environmental trends, however, can simply not be predicted reliably given our current understanding of the way we affect our surroundings. Unpredictable long-term impacts of forces already set in motion are perhaps the most challenging of all. One example comes from studies of likely outcomes of global warming: scientists cannot predict accurately whether the continuation of the current warming trend will lead to the disruption and reordering of ocean currents like the Gulf Stream that are crucial to human civilization as we know it. To further complicate the picture, humans may find it impossible to reverse changes that have already been set in motion, particularly those associated with the loss of biodiversity around the globe and of worldwide climate change. Thus, substantial and lasting modifications in human behavior in these areas are particularly important now.

A final purpose of the book is to suggest ways that we can take action—to give hope that sustainable solutions do exist, even if we do not fully understand them at present. It is easy to feel overwhelmed in the face of great environmental threats—as in the face of the forces of the natural world—but individuals, as well as nations and multinational organizations (including businesses), can make significant contributions to solutions. The first step is to gain useful knowledge about the problems to be faced; the second step is to know where it is most useful to act. The message of this book is that the reader can make a difference readily and easily without making some huge personal sacrifice.

The chapters that follow address five specific issues: the implications of continuing human population growth, the emerging global fresh-water crisis, the challenge of climate change, biodiversity loss, and debates over sustainable development. In all five areas, I have selected articles that give a sense of the complexity of the issues. None of the selections offers easy solutions or allows us to believe that we know enough to develop easy solutions in the near future. While there is considerable scientific consensus about trends, causes, and consequences in the five areas, in none of them are there clear answers to the question of how high standards of living can be achieved for 10 billion humans while the natural foundation of those standards of living is at the same time wisely and creatively used. Achieving this goal, or other developmental aims substantially like it in spirit, will tax human inventiveness and imagination like no previous social or political challenge.

Each of these five issues is integrally bound up with the others, of course. To give just one example, the continued warming of global climate is expected to have, by midcentury, the effect of reducing rainfall in certain key watersheds in the United States. It is estimated, for example, that surface flows in the Colorado and Rio Grande basins could be reduced by between 10 and 40 percent by midcentury, which would have far-reaching impacts on populations in the arid southwest portion of the United States and in the far north of Mexico. A reduction of this sort would force significant changes in human water-use patterns in both Mexico and the United States. Reductions in surface water flow would also have significant impacts on biodiversity in these watersheds. As to solutions, sustainable use of surface water and groundwater resources will be extremely difficult to institute, given the tangle of social, legal, and historical constraints that inevitably accompany the allocation of water among users—issues that are complicated in the case of the Colorado and Rio Grande by a maze of interstate and international issues.

The first set of selections in this book deals with driving forces: human population, agricultural production, and global "carrying capacity." In the astounding success of our species in populating the world there is an extremely important context for the understanding of green environmental issues for the twenty-first century. After tens of thousands of years during which the human population grew slowly from fewer than 250 million people in Julius Caesar's time to roughly 1 billion in 1776, it has increased in the last two centuries to 6 billion and is expected to increase to 10 billion by midcentury. The central issue derives from the likely consumption patterns of those 10 billion humans and the carrying capacity of the natural environment. Can 10 billion humans use the natural resources of the planet in a way that provides a reasonable level of security and income for the majority of people and can also adequately protect natural resources for use by future generations? Or is there a definable limit to the amount of food and other goods that can be sustainably produced for those humans?

The interaction of population growth, consumption, and environment is taken up in the first three chapters. Joseph Speidel lays out trends in population growth and explains the various factors that will drive the increase in human numbers over the next several decades. Speidel notes that people in developed countries consume 67 percent of resources and generate 75 percent of waste and pollution, although they represent only 20 percent of the world's population. Paul and Anne Ehrlich and Gretchen Daily address the issue of the carrying capacity of Earth and its natural resources, summarizing and extending arguments that they first made thirty years ago. They conclude that food security is essential for environmental security (because hungry people are in no position to consider the long-term health of Earth's life-support systems) and thus call for significant reductions in human fertility. In his selection, Robert Kates explores the relationship between population, technology, and consumption and describes various ways of estimating the environmental degradation stemming from the interaction of these factors.

The second section of the book focuses on the emerging crisis in fresh-water around the globe. Water is the single most important resource sustaining human life—and it is almost everywhere threatened. Threats range from contamination with industrial wastes and sewage to increasingly severe problems with supply and shortages for millions of humans in both the developed and the developing worlds. Water scarcity is already changing the pattern of the international grain trade as countries facing water shortages import grain rather than water, given the lesser weight of grain, each pound of which requires 1,000 pounds of water to irrigate. Millions of people joining the developed world will expect to eat meat as part of their modern lifestyle, and this demand will put added pressure on freshwater supplies; each pound of beef requires eight pounds of grain, which in turn requires 1,000 gallons of water to grow (to put that in simpler terms, a McDonald's quarter-pounder requires 250 gallons of water to irrigate the grain to feed the cow).[2]

The social and political importance of water will become ever more apparent in the twenty-first century as its relative scarcity increases. Sandra Postel argues in her selection that water availability will be a serious constraint to achieving human food requirements by 2025. According to Postel, several factors, including overuse of groundwater and reallocation of water from agriculture to cities, will combine to limit crop production in many important growing regions. At the same time, more and more countries will see their populations exceed the level they can be fully sustained by their available water supplies. Many observers even believe that freshwater will be the source of violent conflict among communities and nation-states in the not-too-distant future. I have included two selections that discuss conflict over freshwater, present and future. Joyce Starr considers the case of the Middle East, where several rival states are severely water-short; Paul Smith and Charles Gross of the Asia-Pacific Center for Security Studies present information on water issues and potential conflict in Asia. Of course, there are also non-human issues at stake: the more freshwater that we remove from natural waterways for human use, the more we disrupt a set of crucial freshwater habitats—in many cases, habitats that humans too depend upon for their survival. The case of the slow death of the Salton Sea, which began life as a freshwater lake, is addressed by Robert Boyle.

The third set of selections focuses on global climate and atmosphere. Our planet enjoys a benign climate because of the miraculous existence of a thin layer of gases that maintains a temperature conducive to life and also makes possible the existence of resources such as water from which life evolved and upon which it depends. The fragility of the atmosphere is rarely appreciated: to put it in perspective, the distance from the ground to the top of the sky is no farther than an hour-long cross-country run.[3] The much-discussed ozone layer, which shields all living things from harmful ultraviolet radiation, is so thin in the stratosphere that if it were brought down to sea level and subjected there to normal atmospheric pressure, it would be only three millimeters thick. Yet the atmosphere, because of the greenhouse effect, maintains Earth at a temperature about 33 degrees centigrade warmer than it would be if it had no blanket of air.

There is little doubt that global climate is changing. Scientists have reached a striking measure of consensus both about the nature of global warming and about the role of humans in the change. It is universally accepted among scientists, for example, that the twentieth century witnessed a 1-degree Fahrenheit increase in global temperatures. Further, it is commonly estimated that by the middle of the twenty-first century global climate may be from 5 to 9 degrees Fahrenheit warmer. Although such a change in environment may not appear to be large enough to cause great concern, scientists agree that the consequences of such change will be dramatic and may well be devastating for humans. Scientists point out that, at its height 18,000 years ago, the most recent Ice Age was only from 5 to 9 degrees Fahrenheit cooler than present-day temperatures. Warming at the current rate will take temperatures on Earth higher than anything experienced for over 100,000 years. As to the human contribution to global warming, there exists a broad consensus that the significant increases in greenhouse gases caused by the use of fossil fuels during global industrialization over the last 200 years (gases and materials that reflect solar warmth back to the surface of Earth such as carbon dioxide, methane, nitrogen oxides, and CFCs) have increased the rate of warming.[4]

What scientists do not agree on are the sorts of changes in daily life and perhaps in the future viability of human development that will follow from what seem at first glance to be modest changes in climate conditions. The one sign that many people have witnessed in the last decade is the apparently increasing incidence of extreme weather events: storms, floods, droughts, harvest failures, and the like. These episodes may give a sense of the speed at which these changes will be upon us. Whereas in previous epochs this sort of climate change happened over tens of thousands of years—to produce an Ice Age, for example—now the trends are greatly increased, with similar rates of climate change occurring over a period of mere decades. The lead selection on climate change is a recent review of the science on global warming conducted by the Intergovernmental Panel on Climate Change (IPCC). The IPCC was established in 1988 by the World Meteorological Organization and the United Nations Environmental Programme with the mission of providing state-of-the-art scientific, technical, and socio-economic information on climate change. Stephen Schneider, in his speculative piece about how a warmer Earth might affect the daily activities of humans, shares some of his preoccupations with global warming. In a selection that considers another angle on human-caused changes in soil and atmosphere, Peter Vitousek and his colleagues discuss the causes and consequences of human alteration of the global nitrogen cycle.

The fourth section of this book addresses the issue of biodiversity. The continuing loss of biodiversity all around us, in almost every major ecosystem, and everywhere in the world, will undoubtedly be a cause of major concern in the twenty-first century. The world's forests, for example, which harbor more than half of all species on Earth and provide natural services such as flood control and climate regulation, are steadily shrinking as human numbers and the global economy expand.[5] Nearly half of the forests that once covered Earth have been lost. What is particularly frightening to scientists about biodiversity loss is that we really have little understanding of what the loss, in large part caused by human modification of natural habitat, might mean for the survival of life on the planet. The rate of extinction taking place all around us appears to exceed the rate of extinction at the end of the Cretaceous period, during which the dinosaurs and about 70 percent of all living things disappeared from the world.[6]

The chapters gathered here on biodiversity provide a sense of the interconnectedness of life on the globe and of the importance of that interconnectedness to human survival. It is not commonly appreciated how little we know about the biodiversity of the natural world around us. Of the estimated 15-40 million species in the world, scientists have studied only 1.8 million.[7] Nor is it commonly recognized that biodiversity gave rise to and remains essential to human life; without a high degree of biodiversity we may find ourselves much less resilient to other environmental changes. Just two examples suffice to give a sense of the centrality of biodiversity to human life: first, the vast majority of what we eat depends ultimately on tiny insect pollinators to reproduce; and second, at least one-quarter of the medications that we use are derived from naturally occurring plants and animals. John Tuxill and Chris Bright focus on the big picture, reviewing our current understanding of the process and implications of the loss of biodiversity in the modern world. In his chapter, Chris Wille discusses ongoing attempts in Costa Rica to measure biodiversity even as it disappears. Anne Platt McGinn offers an overview of the impacts of human activity on the marine environments that are crucial to the maintenance of Earth's biodiversity.

The final group of selections in this volume address the concept of sustainable development, an idea which is frequently advanced as the only possible solution to the environmental challenges that human development has created. Sustainable development is commonly understood to be a pattern of development that uses natural resources in a way that protects natural capital for the use of future generations, to "meet the needs of the present without compromising the ability of future generations to meet their own needs," as defined by the World Commission on Environment and Development in 1987. Pundits observe that, in fact, there are only two kinds of development: sustainable and unsustainable. Either we draw from the natural capital of the surrounding world in ways that protects that capital or we diminish it in ways that ultimately weaken us.

There are many examples of entire civilizations that outgrew their ability to develop in a sustainable fashion: one thinks, for example, of the disappearance of the great Maya cities, the collapse of the ancient Mesopotamian world, or the end of the advanced civilization that raised the mysterious heads on Easter Island (see Chapter 14 in this volume by Jared Diamond). That development can be unsustainable is abundantly clear.[8] Many scientists now think our present civilization and the natural environment are on a similar "collision course," as 102 Nobel laureates and many others put it in the World Scientists' Warning to Humanity in 1992.

A great deal of work remains to be done, however, to make sustainable development a reasonable response and a realistic option to the environmental challenges that we face in the new century. Some of the possible paths are suggested here by the work of Daniel Janzen, who focuses on balancing human and ecosystem needs in the tropics. The concept of ecosystem services, discussed by Gretchen Daily, Charles Petersen, and Jane Lubchenco in their articles, provides a novel way to think about human relations with the natural world that may encourage sustainable development.

An extremely important context for efforts to find sustainable ways of developing is the functioning of the global private sector as it expands to meet the consumption needs and desires of an ever larger number of people. Corporate social responsibility, which includes protecting and enhancing the natural environment, is a rapidly growing movement for addressing environmental ills. That the practices of companies can make big differences is borne out by the example of Chiquita, which in 2000 received certification from the Rainforest Alliance for all 127 of the banana farms it owns in Latin America. Chiquita cut its use of agricultural chemicals, reduced waste, promoted wildlife conservation, recycled plastics, and reforested; now 60 percent of the Chiquita bananas sold in the United States and 90 percent of those sold in Europe are grown on its certified farms. Chiquita benefited directly from reduced costs for pesticides and herbicides and indirectly from its improved image.[9] The Forest Stewardship Council, based in Oaxaca, Mexico, has certified timber operations in 241 forests (covering 45 million acres) that produce wood products for IKEA and Home Depot, among others.[10] One of the leading organizations promoting corporate social responsibility in the United States is Business for Social Responsibility (BSR), which describes in the document included here what environmentally sustainable business practice looks like, with examples from some of the private firms that are leading the field.

An increasingly important player in the field of developing and implementing sustainable solutions is the nongovernmental organization, or NGO. Sheila Jasanoff details three principal ways that NGOs can help advance sustainable solutions: by serving as important critical voices, helping to shake up accepted environment knowledge and policy; by bringing knowledge into the realm of practice; and by disseminating new information to the public and to policymakers. In addition, for many individuals concerned about environmental issues, NGOs provide a convenient and direct way of taking action and seeing tangible outcomes result. NGOs have been extremely effective in promoting sustainable development in Europe. There, their activities have led to the adoption of major innovations by governments and the private sector: extended producer responsibility (where producers are liable for the environmental consequences of products from assembly to disposal); reducing and recycling packaging waste (in Germany, responsibility for disposal of packaging waste now lies with manufacturers and retailers rather than with consumers and municipalities); vehicle and other equipment takebacks (making it possible for the final owner of an old vehicle to return it to a facility where is dismantled and reused); eco-labeling programs (which allow consumers to know precisely how the goods they use were produced); and environmental covenants between government and industry (which in many cases obviate the need for complex and inefficient regulation of industry by government).[11]

Finally, and at the other extreme from the activities of large corporations, are the values and practices of individuals—expressed in both consumption and political-action patterns. One of the reasons it is so hard to understand the relevance of environmental issues is that they are frequently invisible to individuals on a day-to-day basis; our choices have seemingly very little to do with causing or redressing environmental problems. But it is the combination of individual decisions big and small—how long to leave a light on, whether to take the car, the train, or a bicycle to work, whether to recycle or throw away, whether to vote for incentives for continued urban sprawl, whether to purchase one product or invest in one firm rather than another—that ultimately leads to pressures on natural resources. It has been convincingly demonstrated that consumer choice makes a very big difference in environmental outcomes. The most important choices that we as consumers make are how we get to class or work (for most Americans, this means the kind of cars we drive), the size of the houses we live in (and thus our requirements for heating, lighting, and freshwater), and the food we eat. As Michael Brower and Warren Leon show in the final selection, making changes in just these three areas of everyday life—a goal well within our ability—has important repercussions for the health of the planet.

As noted at the beginning of this introduction, it is hoped that this book will encourage focused action as well as inform readers. The environmental challenges we face are tremendous and the solutions of which we are capable are not obvious or easy, yet good, positive responses are within our grasp. While readers of this book in their fifties may not live to see the consequences of current development choices, readers in their late teens, twenties, and thirties will directly confront them. Doing nothing—that most common of human responses to complex and daunting challenges—is tantamount to continuing or accelerating environmental destruction and its dire consequences.[12] Doing something, individually and socially, is within our power.

I see two principal reasons for developing sustainable answers to the problems analyzed in the essays gathered here. The first has to do with the survival of the human species. There is little doubt among scholars that global warming or the continuing loss of biodiversity alone will make the survival of the human species increasingly difficult if it continues at current rates for another century. We all share an interest in—and perhaps a responsibility for—preserving the world for future generations. This first motivation is a hard-nosed, realistic rationale for changing the way we interact with the natural world; it calls upon us in many capacities, but principally as producers and consumers, to take environmental issues seriously, to take actions to remedy damage already done, and to avoid future unsustainable use of natural capital.

The second reason for informed action in the area of green environmental issues, although related to the first, is of a more spiritual nature. Humans are members of a vast and only partially understood web of life. We have no explicit mandate from a higher power to wantonly destroy that web for our short-term benefit. The responsibility to protect the natural world that sustains human life should be a central part of our sense of place in the universe. As practical as we become about addressing environmental issues, we should not lose the humility that comes with knowing that we do not fully understand all of the consequences of our interactions with the natural world. That same humility should guide us in making use of the natural world with gratitude, respect, and caution.

The following chapters are intended both to inform and to raise hope: we can indeed do something about big environmental issues, as individuals and as societies. Doing something begins with understanding the impending crisis—grasping both the parameters of what we currently know and sensing how dimly we understand some of the undergirding forces of the natural world. Once we understand the outlines of the challenges we face, I think we will find that the greatest challenge in moving forward is how to balance individual needs and desires for better lives with the social and environmental requirements for sustainable living. I believe we can achieve this balance.

The selections gathered here indicate that we can take action on two basic levels—the individual and the social. As individual consumers, voters, and firms, we can assume responsibility for the inescapable impact our everyday choices have on our surroundings and take small, practical steps to reduce that impact to sustainable proportions. Ironically, problems that seem to overwhelm the individual scale of our lives can be effectively addressed with routine, day-to-day decisions. As societies, we must work together with determination and good faith to address global issues that will take decades to resolve. We must involve both public and private actors; and we must seek to equitably distribute the burdens of more sustainable decisionmaking. Working as both individuals and as a global community-of-interest, we can place future human development on a sustainable path.

Notes

1. Another, similar division is made by Albert Gore in his *Earth in Balance: Ecology and the Human Spirit* (Boston: Houghton Mifflin, 1992), 7. Gore draws a distinction between environmental issues that are fundamentally local in nature, like hazardous waste, and those that represent threats to the entire globe.

2. Hillary French, *Vanishing Borders: Protecting the Planet in the Age of Globalization* (New York: Norton, 2000), 53.

3. Gore, *Earth in Balance*, 83.

4. Stephen H. Schneider, *Global Warming: Are We Entering the Greenhouse Century?* (San Francisco: Sierra Club Books, 1989), 18–29. See also Intergovernmental Panel of Climate Change, *Climate Change 2001: Third Assessment Report* (in three volumes: *The Scientific Basis; Impacts, Adaptation, and Vulnerability*; and *Mitigation*), available online at www.IPCC.ch.

5. French, *Vanishing Borders*, 19.

6. Kevin Shear McCann, "The *diversity*-stability debate," *Nature* 405 (May 11, 2000): 228–33. See also Simon A. Levin, *Fragile Dominion: Complexity and the Commons* (Reading, MA: Helix Books, 1999).

7. Data are taken from the chapter in this volume by John Tuxill and Chris Bright.

8. See Clive Ponting, *A Green History of the World: The Environment and the Collapse of Great Civilizations* (New York: St. Martin's Press, 1991).

9. *EcoAméricas*, December 2000, 3.

10. *Business Week* (November 20, 2000): 62–63. See *Newsweek* (August 27, 2001), for a brief analysis of business's growing interest in tradable allowances for greenhouse gases.

11. Edith Brown Weiss, "European Innovations in Environmental Law and Policy," in *The Convergence of U.S. National Security and the Global Environment*, The Aspen Institute Congressional Program, vol. 16, no. 3 (June 2001): 43–51.

12. Gore, *Earth in Balance*, 37.

1

Environment and Health
Population, Consumption, and Human Health

J. Joseph Speidel

In this first chapter, Joseph Speidel addresses a series of framing issues that affect both our understanding of environmental problems and our ideas about possible solutions. After growing slowly for thousands of years, human population has expanded exceedingly rapidly in the last two centuries and is expected to reach 10 billion by midcentury. Twenty percent of those people—those of us living in the developed world—consume two-thirds of Earth's resources and generate three-quarters of its waste and pollution, including greenhouse gases. What will be the environmental impacts of modern consumption practices if those practices are gradually adopted by the other 80 percent of the globe's human population?

J. Joseph Speidel, who holds an M.D. from Harvard, served as vice president of Population Action International from 1983 to 1994. Currently, he directs the Population Program at the Hewlett Foundation.

There is strong evidence that the growth of the world population poses serious threats to human health, socioeconomic development and the environment.[1,2] In 1992 the Union of Concerned Scientists issued a World Scientists' Warning to Humanity, signed by 1600 prominent scientists, that called attention to threats to life-sustaining natural resources.[3] In 1993 a Population Summit of 58 of the world's scientific academies voiced concern about the

From J. Joseph Speidel, "Environment and Health: Population, Consumption, and Human Health," *Canadian Medical Association Journal* 5, no. 163 (September 5, 2000): 551–56. © 2002 Canadian Medical Association (www.cma.ca/cmaj/index.asp). Reprinted by permission of J. Joseph Speidel and the Canadian Medical Association.

intertwined problems of rapid population growth, wasteful resource consumption, environmental degradation and poverty.[4] These reports share the view that, without stabilization of both population and consumption, good health for many people will remain elusive, developing countries will find it impossible to escape poverty, and environmental degradation will worsen.

Population Growth

It has taken only 12 years for the world population to grow from 5 billion to today's 6 billion. This is the shortest time ever to add 1 billion people—a number equivalent to the population of India or the combined population of the United States and Europe.

Over the 17 centuries ending in 1800, the world population grew slowly, from an estimated 250 million to about 1 billion. Over the past 2 centuries, and especially after 1950, declining death rates brought about rapid growth. By 1950 the world population had reached 2.5 billion, the world total fertility rate (TFR: the mean lifetime number of children borne by each woman) was 5.3, and the population was growing by about 40 million per year.[5,6] Since 1950 the world TFR has declined to 2.9, but continued declines in death rates and the growth of the population to 6 billion have combined to bring about a doubling of annual growth to 84 million in the world population.[7]

Over the past 200 years Western nations have made a gradual demographic move from high to low birth rates and death rates. These countries are now growing by only 0.1% annually.[7] Over the past 50 years public health measures and improved nutrition in developing countries have rapidly lowered death rates. Although use of family planning in these countries has increased substantially (from about 10% of couples to over 50%), greater use of contraception is hampered by poverty, lack of education and inadequate access to family planning information and services.[8,9] As a result, declines in birth rates in developing countries have been uneven and have usually lagged behind declines in death rates. Therefore, growth rates have remained relatively high.[5–7,9] Currently, more than 97% of population growth is occurring in developing countries, which between 1987 and 1999 grew by 1 billion people.[7,10]

The United Nations recently presented 3 demographic projections for the next 100 years that, although rapid declines in fertility are expected, still see substantial increases in the world population.[11,12] Because population projections are extremely sensitive to fertility rates, the accuracy of long-range projections is uncertain.[12,13]

The UN's medium-fertility projection suggests a decline from the current world TFR of 2.9 to 2.1 by 2050, with a resulting population size of 8.9 billion that will continue to grow slowly to 9.5 billion by 2100. The U.S.

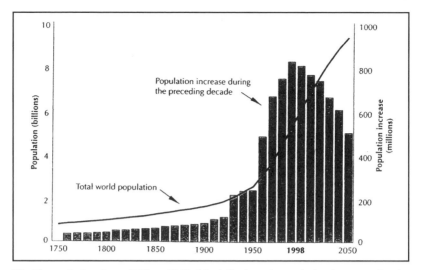

World population from 1750 to 2050 (black line), and population increases by decade (black bars).[14]

Census Bureau projects a slightly higher total world population in 2050 of 9.3 billion (Fig. 1).[14]

The UN's high-fertility model assumes that, in countries with high fertility rates (TFRs above replacement level), the TFRs will stabilize at 2.6 and that, in countries with low fertility rates (TFRs currently below 2.1), the TFRs will increase and stabilize at between 2.1 and 2.3. This model projects that the world population will continue to grow rapidly, reaching 10.7 billion by 2050 and 16.2 billion by 2100.

The UN's low-fertility model, which assumes worldwide TFRs of less than 2.1, projects an initial increase in population size followed by a slow decline to 7.3 billion in 2050 and 5.1 billion in 2100.[11,12] In part because support for international family planning programs remains inadequate, the low-fertility projection seems unlikely. Without greatly strengthened efforts to provide family planning services, even the medium projection is in doubt.[15-17]

The fertility of the world's developed countries is now at a TFR of 1.5,[7] so low that gradual population decline can be expected in most of these countries.[11] The fertility rates of some 25 developing countries, including those in East Asia and China, are already at or are likely to soon decline to or go below replacement level. Some 44% of the world's people now live in low-fertility countries (20% in developed countries, 20% in China and 4% in other developing countries), and UN population projections suggest that more developing countries will reach fertility levels below replacement level.[11,12]

However, high fertility persists in much of the world. The current TFR for the 3.6 billion people living in poor countries outside of China is estimated to be 3.7 and their annual population growth rate 1.9%. At this rate, their population would double in just 36 years. Despite projected declines in fertility, the number of annual births worldwide are expected to remain at over 130 million for the next 25 years.[14] This is because past high fertility rates in most poor countries have left these countries with large and still increasing numbers of women of reproductive age; their number is projected to increase from 1.2 to 1.7 billion between 1998 and 2025.[14] In China, for example, although the TFR is estimated to be below the replacement level of 2.1, the large number of couples of reproductive age have kept China's population growing by more than 11 million annually.[7,11]

Even though Europe and Japan are densely populated and have high levels of consumption, the prospect of gradual population decline in these countries has raised concerns related to immigration, the ethnic composition of countries, the size of the labour force and the ability of workers to support elderly people as the share of population over retirement age increases.

The United States and Canada are, to some extent, exceptions among Western nations. Because of high levels of immigration their populations are still growing relatively rapidly. The U.S. population is projected to increase from 275 million to 394 million by 2050.[18,19] The arrival of about a million people per year (800 000 legal and 200 000 illegal immigrants) and the high fertility rate among the 26 million foreign-born residents is fuelling this growth.[18,19] Similar projections for Canada suggest an increase from the current 31 million to over 42 million in 2050, with over half of this growth the result of immigration.[20,21] Considering the high level of individual consumption in the United States and Canada, this 43% increase in population will have profound implications for land, air and water resources.

Interactions between Population, Consumption, the Environment, and Health

Some 10 000 years ago, when only about 5 million people inhabited the Earth, few biological systems were seriously damaged by human activity. Today, however, the world faces an environmental dilemma. Current demands are depleting many of the Earth's natural resources and ecological services.[22–24] Within the next 50 years, it is likely that those life-supporting systems will somehow have to accommodate 3 billion more people as well as support desperately needed advances in living standards for those in poverty, particularly the 3 billion people now living on about $2 a day.[11,25,26]

The impact of humans on their environment is related to population size, per capita consumption and the environmental damage caused by the technology used to produce what is consumed. The exploitation of technology and the high consumption pattern of people in Japan, Europe, the United States and Canada have a greater adverse impact per capita on the world's environment than that of a subsistence farmer in Bangladesh, for example. Although they represent 20% of the world's population, the 1.2 billion people living in developed countries consume an estimated 67% of all resources and generate 75% of all waste and pollution.[22–24]

Between 1950 and 1997 the world's population doubled and the global economy expanded 6-fold, from $5 trillion to $29 trillion of annual output.[27] A further modest 2% annual growth in incomes and consumption per capita worldwide could result in a doubling of consumption every 35 years, or about an 8-fold increase by the year 2100. This increased consumption per capita, on top of a projected population increase of 1.6 times, from 6 to 9.5 billion,[11] would require economic production to increase 13-fold. To achieve this without substantial degradation of important ecosystems presents a daunting challenge.

There are many important interactions between population growth, consumption, environmental degradation and health. Human activity has already transformed an estimated 10% of the Earth's surface from forest or rangeland into desert. The productive capacity of 25% of all agricultural lands, an area equal to the size of India and China combined, has already been degraded.[24,28] Unproductive land and food scarcity currently contribute to malnutrition among 1 billion people, with infants and children suffering the most serious health consequences.[29,30]

Projected population growth in Africa, South Asia and other developing countries, together with declining availability of water from aquifers, threatens the food security of more than 1 billion people in developing countries. Recent studies have indicated that depletion of aquifers threatens India with a 25% decline in grain production, at a time when over half of the country's children are malnourished and the population is projected to increase by some 500 million over the next 50 years.[31,32] Other large countries where rapid population growth and declining cropland per person threaten food security include Nigeria and Pakistan. If Nigeria's population increases from the current 111 million to a projected 244 million in 2050, grainland per capita will decline from 0.15 to 0.07 hectares. The corresponding projection for Pakistan is an increase in population from 146 million to 345 million and a shrinkage of grainland per person from 0.08 to 0.03 hectares.[33] Countries with these levels of grainland typically import over half of their grain, an expensive prospect for these impoverished countries.[31,32]

Water scarcity also impairs health as fresh water supplies for human use become polluted with toxic materials and pathogens. Proper treatment of human waste is currently not available for about 2 billion people, and 1.3

billion people are at risk of waterborne diseases because they lack access to pure drinking water.[22,24,34]

There is growing evidence that global warming is occurring, increasing the prospect of flooded coastal areas and cities, disruptions of agriculture, increasingly severe storm damage[35–37] and significant extension of the range of insects and other vectors of diseases.[38]

Environmental degradation, declining food security and uncontrolled epidemics of communicable diseases have slowed, and even reversed, the demographic transition to low death rates in some poor countries. In contrast to developed countries, where cardiovascular diseases and cancer are the leading causes of death, in poor countries infectious diseases cause 45% of all deaths.[39] Ninety percent of annual worldwide deaths from communicable diseases are caused by 6 infectious diseases: acute respiratory infections (3.5 million deaths), AIDS (2.3 million), diarrheal diseases (2.2 million), tuberculosis (1.5 million), malaria (1.1 million) and measles (0.9 million).[39] As a consequence of the AIDS epidemic, some 29 African countries have experienced substantial increases in death rates and substantial declines in average life span. By 2010–2015 life expectancy is projected to decline by 17 years on average in the 9 hardest hit countries.[40,41] In Botswana and Zimbabwe over 20% of the adult population is HIV positive.[40]

Poverty, lack of education, and social and economic factors are powerful, if indirect, correlates of health status. Wealthy nations provide environments that offer protection against infectious diseases through preventive measures such as vaccination, water purification, sanitary sewage disposal and control of insect vectors. Wealthier nations and individuals can better afford to pay for needed preventive and curative health services. Higher levels of education, especially among women, are also associated with low fertility and good health—the well educated are better equipped to stay healthy and obtain needed health care services.[42–46] It is reasonably well established that the families in developing countries with the smallest number of children usually have the highest incomes and the healthiest and best-educated children. Therefore, to the extent that rapid population growth and large family size hamper economic development by perpetuating poverty, high growth rates also contribute to poor health.[25,47–49]

Developing countries that have established strong family planning programs and have successfully slowed rapid population growth have fared much better economically than countries that have neglected the population issue. The Asian economic "tigers"—South Korea, Thailand, Malaysia and Taiwan—have a 30-year history of supporting family planning and an average of about 2 children per family. This has benefitted the health of their people both by fostering economic development and establishing a healthy pattern of reproduction.[48–50]

Facing the Challenges of Poor Health, Rapid Population Growth, and High Consumption Levels

In 1994 demographer John Bongaarts[51] disaggregated the sources of future population growth in developing countries into 3 categories: 49% will come from momentum caused by the population's young age structure (the result of previous high fertility), 33% will come from unwanted fertility (i.e., births to those who wish to stop child-bearing but who are not using contraception), and only 18% will come from high desired family size (i.e., desiring more than an average of 2 children). The fact that most couples in developing countries want small families[51] bodes well for the success of family planning programs in those countries. However, family planning must be accessible. Meeting the family planning needs of the 100–120 million women in developing countries who wish to limit their child-bearing but lack access to adequate information and services would lower the TFR from the current 3.2 half-way to the TFR of 2.1 needed for population stabilization.[9,51]

Participants at the 1994 United Nations International Conference on Population and Development made a collective commitment to improve women's status and to make family planning and a limited array of reproductive health services universally available in developing countries by the year 2015.[2] Their emphasis on reproductive health recognized the reality that, in developing countries, 25% to over 50% of treatable or preventable diseases among women aged 15–49 years are related to reproduction. Typically the largest share is associated with pregnancy, unsafe abortion and childbirth. In some countries AIDS and other STDs predominate.[52–54] Over a woman's lifetime, the risk of dying from pregnancy-related causes is about 1 in 16 in Africa, 1 in 65 in Asia, 1 in 130 in Latin America, but only 1 in 6000 in the United States and 1 in 10 000 in northern Europe. A broader array of reproductive health care services, including safe abortion, prenatal care and the ability to deal with the complications of childbirth, could prevent many deaths.[55–59]

Family planning is necessary to allow a pattern of healthy child-bearing. Eliminating child-bearing among teenagers, women over 35 and women who have already had 4 children, and increasing intervals between births to at least 2 years, would avoid about 25% of the 585 000 maternal deaths each year. If women in poor countries bore only 2 children, the annual number of maternal deaths would be reduced by close to 50%.[42,55,57–59]

The safe pattern of child-bearing that reduces risk among women also lowers the risk of death among infants and children. Currently each year in developing countries some 11 million children do not survive their first 5 years of life.[61] Establishing a healthy pattern of child-bearing could be expected to reduce infant and child mortality by about 20% to 25%.[42] For example, in Kenya, a typical developing country, an interval of 18 months or less between births results in a risk of infant death that is twice the risk associated with a longer interval.[47,60–64]

Reproductive health programs that include but also go beyond family planning and safe childbirth services are needed to address domestic violence, which occurs in up to 1 in 3 women,[65] and STDs, which are responsible for 333 million new cases of infection throughout the world each year.[66] Family planning and maternity care programs can serve as a starting point for services that address these problems because they serve the same population of young, sexually active women who are most at risk of exposure to STDs and domestic violence.[64–66]

The cost of family planning and reproductive health services recommended for developing countries at the United Nations International Conference on Population and Development was estimated to be $17 billion annually by the year 2000.[2] It was agreed that two-thirds of this total cost should come from developing countries—an expenditure of less than 5¢ weekly per person living in these countries—and that one-third should come from donor countries—an expenditure of less than 10¢ weekly per person living in developed countries. Unfortunately, developing countries are spending only about $5 billion annually, less than 50% of their financial target of $11.3 billion, and donor nations are spending only about $1.4 billion, less than 25% of their $5.7 billion goal.[16,17]

If we are able to summon the political will to make good reproductive health care, including family planning and safe abortion, widely available, and if we make reasonable progress in educating women and improving their status, population growth is likely to decline to manageable levels.[55,67,68] In Thailand between 1970 and 1987, a voluntary family planning program, stressing cooperation between the public and private sectors, brought about an increase in contraceptive use from about 10% to 67% of couples.[67] As a result, the average number of children per woman fell from 6.2 to 2.2. Important reasons for the program's success included use of the injectable contraceptive Depo-Provera, the distribution of oral contraceptives by non-physicians and strong government support of the program.

Better reproductive health care in poor countries, however, will not be enough to save our natural systems. Both developed and developing countries must introduce economic systems and new technologies that are more efficient, generate less waste and require less consumption of natural resources.[22,23,69–72] With the world increasingly seeking economic development through market-based policies, it is imperative that governments and the private sector integrate strategies into economic life that will protect the environment. The way forward to economic progress with more efficiency and less consumption is clear in many sectors, and research can bring additional advances.[73]

The limitation of greenhouse gas emissions, critical to climactic stabilization, can be addressed by less reliance on, and more efficient use of, fossil fuels. Further development of wind, geothermal, photovoltaic and other eco-friendly sources of energy is needed. Carbon emissions can be reduced by preserving forest resources through increased use of recycled paper and wood substitutes. These and other measures to slow the rapid decline in biodiversity are needed. The protection of habitats in ecologically threatened "hot spots" is one promising approach.[70–72]

Governments and international development agencies should eliminate environmentally unsound development projects and subsidies for a large array of ecologically unsound practices and products. Policies needing reform include those related to tobacco, mineral production, logging, transportation, agriculture, fisheries, livestock, energy use, waste disposal, control of pesticides and other toxic substances, air quality, and use of land and water resources.[74]

Efforts to address the environmental impact of consumption must give attention to the damage and waste caused by conflict and worldwide outlays for military activities, estimated at $700 billion annually.[75]

Of crucial importance is the path of economic development that is traversed by poor countries. China, with a population of 1.2 billion, has experienced an economic expansion of two-thirds since 1990 and a corresponding increase in consumption of many resources.[76] It has surpassed the United States in consumption of grain, meat, fertilizer, steel and coal. If China's per capita oil consumption equalled that of the United States, the Chinese would consume 80 million barrels a day, far outstripping the daily world production of 60 million barrels. Social and economic progress in China and other developing countries is necessary, but, according to Brown and colleagues,[76] these countries must bypass what the West has done and show how to build environmentally sustainable economies. Unfortunately, many rapidly industrializing countries are proceeding with little regard for the environment.[76]

Reforming our economies and industries will be technically difficult, costly and time-consuming. Measures that will help slow population growth are relatively less expensive. Our future well-being depends on increased access to family planning and reproductive health services in developing countries and decreased consumption by people in wealthy countries. We must develop and adopt more efficient technology for industrial production in all countries. Our governments, the private sector and individuals must work together to devise and adopt new patterns of sustainable economic behaviour and to support and enable voluntary and responsible family planning. The challenge is to meet the needs of today's populations without compromising the welfare of future generations.

Notes

1. *United Nations Conference on Environment and Development*; 1992 June 1–12; Rio de Janeiro. Washington: Council on Environmental Quality; 1992.

2. *Reproductive rights and reproductive health. International Conference on Population and Development*; 1994 Sept 5–13; Cairo. New York: United Nations; 1995.

3. *World scientists' warning to humanity.* Cambridge (MA): Union of Concerned Scientists; Nov 1992.

4. *Population Summit of the World's Scientific Academies.* Washington: National Academy Press; 1994.

5. Mazur LA, editor. *Beyond the numbers: a reader on population, consumption and the environment.* Washington: Island Press; 1994.

6. Cohen JE. *How many people can the earth support?* New York: WW Norton; 1995. p. 400–1.

7. *2000 world population data sheet.* Washington: Population Reference Bureau; 2000. Available: www.prb.org/pubs/wpds2000 (accessed 2000 Aug 4).

8. Freedman R, Blanc AK. Fertility transition: an update. In: Blanc AK, editor. *Demographic and Health Surveys World Conference*; 1991 Aug 5–7; Washington, DC. Vol. I. Columbia (MD): IRD/Macro International; 1991. p. 5–38.

9. Bongaarts J, Mauldin WP, Phillips JF. The demographic impact of family planning programs. *Stud Farm Plann* 1990; 21:299–310.

10. *1987 world population data sheet.* Washington: Population Reference Bureau; 1987.

11. *World population prospects: the 1998 revision.* New York: United Nations; 1999.

12. *World population projections to 2150.* New York: United Nations; 1998.

13. Bongaarts J. Demographic consequences of declining fertility. *Science* 1998; 282:419–20.

14. McDevitt TM. *World population profile: 1998.* Washington: US Census Bureau; 1999. p. 9,17. Available: www.census.gov/ipc/www/wp98.html (accessed 2000 July 31).

15. Conly SR, Chaya N, Helsing K. *Contraceptive choice: worldwide access to family planning [Progress Towards World Population Stabilization series].* Washington: Population Action International; 1997. Available: www.populationaction.org/programs/rc97.htm (accessed 2000 July 31).

16. Conly SR, Speidel JJ. *Global population assistance: a report card on the major donor countries.* Washington: Population Action International; 1993.

17. Conly SR, De Silva S. *Paying their fair share? Donor countries and international population assistance.* Washington: Population Action International; 1999. Available: www.populationaction.org/programs/dac98/dac_download.htm (accessed 2000 July 31).

18. *Population projections of the United States by age, sex, race, and Hispanic origin: 1995 to 2050 [Current Population Reports no P25–1130].* Washington: US Census Bureau; 1996. Available: www.census.gov/prod/1/pop/p25–1130 (accessed 2000 July 31).

19. *Annual demographic survey* [suppl to *Current Population Survey*]. Washington: US Census Bureau; Mar 1997.

20. *The world at six billion.* New York: Population Division, United Nations; 1999, p. 13, 154. Available: www.un.org/esa/population/sixbillion.htm (accessed 2000 July 31).

21. *Components of population growth: Canada, the provinces and territories, July 1, 1998–June 30, 1999.* Ottawa: Statistics Canada. Available: www.statcan.ca / english/Pgdb/People/Population/demo33a.htm (accessed 2000 Mar 22).

22. Ehrlich PR, Ehrlich AH. *The population explosion.* New York: Simon and Schuster; 1990.

23. Green C. *Population reports: the environment and population growth: decade for action* [series M, no 10]. Baltimore: Johns Hopkins School of Hygiene and Public Health; 1992.

24. World Resources Institute. *World resources 1998–99. A guide to the global environment: environmental change and human health.* New York: Oxford University Press; 1998. Available: www.wristore.com/worres19.html (accessed 2000 July 31).

25. Ahlburg DA. Population growth and poverty. In: Ahlburg DA, Kelley AC, Mason KD, editors. *The impact of population growth on well-being in developing countries.* New York: Springer-Verlag; 1996.

26. *Why population matters.* Washington: Population Action International; 1998. Available: www.populationaction.org/why_pop/whypop.htm (accessed 2000 Aug 7).

27. Brown LR, Renner M, Flavin C. *Vital signs, 1998.* Washington: Worldwatch Institute; 1998. p. 74, 102.

28. World Resources Institute. *World resources 1994–95. People and the environment.* New York: Oxford University Press; 1994. Available: www.wristore.com / worresrep19p.html (accessed 2000 Aug 1).

29. Bender W, Smith M. Population, food and nutrition. *Popul Bull* 1997;51:4.

30. Brown LR, Flavin C, French H. *State of the world 1998.* Washington: Worldwatch Institute; 1998. p. 79–95.

31. *Our demographically divided world: rising mortality joins falling fertility to slow population growth* [press release]. Washington: Worldwatch Institute; 1999 Apr 10. Available: www.worldwatch.org/alerts/990408.html (accessed 2000 Aug 1).

32. Brown LR, Flavin C, French H. *State of the world 2000.* Washington: Worldwatch Institute; 2000. p. 39–58.

33. Brown LR, Gardner G, Halweil B. *Beyond Malthus; nineteen dimensions of the population challenge [Worldwatch Environmental Alert series].* New York: WW Norton; 1999. p. 17–40, 61–4.

34. World Bank. *World development report 1993: investing in health.* New York: Oxford University Press; 1993; p. 90.

35. Brown LR, Flavin C, French H. *State of the world 1998.* Washington: Worldwatch Institute; 1998. p. 113–30.

36. Brown LR, Abramovits J, Bright C, Flavin C, Gardner G, Kane H, et al. *State of the World 1996.* Washington: Worldwatch Institute; 1996. p. 21–39.

37. *Climate change, state of knowledge.* Washington: Office of Science and Technology; 1997.

38. Paltz JM, Epstein PR, Burke TA, Balbus JM. Global climate change and emerging infectious diseases. *JAMA* 1996;275(3):217–23.

39. *Removing obstacles to healthy development: World Health Organization report on infectious diseases.* Geneva: World Health Organization; 1999. p. 6–9. Available: www.who.int/infectious-disease-report/index-rpt99.html (accessed 2000 Aug 1).

40. *The world at six billion.* New York: Population Division, United Nations; 1999. p. 37–8. Available: www.un.org/esa/population/sixbillion.htm (accessed 2000 July 31).

41. *The UN AIDS report.* Geneva: UNAIDS; 1999. p. 17–41. Available: www.unaids.org/publications/documents/unaids/index.html (accessed 2000 Aug 1).

42. Healthier mothers and children through family planning. *Popul Rep J* 1984; May–Jun (27):J657–96.

43. *The health rationale for family planning: timing of births and child survival.* New York: Population Division, Department for Economic and Social Information and Policy Analysis, United Nations; 1994.

44. *Human development report 1996.* New York: United Nations Development Programme; 1996. Overview available: www.undp.org/hdro/96.htm (accessed 2000 Aug 1).

45. *The world health report 1999.* Geneva: World Health Organization; 1999. p. 5–7. Available: www.who.int/whr/1999/en/report.htm (accessed 2000 Aug 2).

46. World Bank. *World development report 1993: investing in health.* New York: Oxford University Press; 1993; p. 37–71, 108–133.

47. Pappas G, Queen S, Hadden W, Fisher G. The increasing disparity in mortality between socioeconomic groups in the United States, 1960 and 1986. *N Engl J Med* 1993;329:103–9.

48. Population Crisis Committee. Population growth and economic development: the new policy debate. *Population* [Washington] 1985;Feb(14):1–8.

49. Knodel J, Havanon N, Sittitrai W. *Family size and the education of children in the context of rapid fertility decline.* Ann Arbor (MI): Population Studies Center, University of Michigan; 1989. Rep no 89-155.

50. Bloom DE, Williamson JG. Demographic transitions and economic miracles in emerging Asia. *World Bank Econ Rev* 1998;12(3):419–55. Available: www.worldbank.org/research/journals/wber/revsep98/demo.htm (accessed 2000 Aug 2).

51. Bongaarts J. Population policy options in the developing world. *Science* 1994;263:771–6.

52. World Bank. *World development report 1993: investing in health.* New York: Oxford University Press; 1993; p. 82–6.

53. Duke RC, Speidel JJ. The 1991 Albert Lasker Public Service Award. Women's reproductive health: a chronic crisis. *JAMA* 1991;266:1846–7.

54. Speidel JJ. Population: What does it mean to health? *Physicians for Social Responsibility Quarterly* 1993;3(4):155–65.

55. Starrs A. *Preventing the tragedy of maternal deaths: a report on the International Safe Motherhood Conference, Nairobi, Kenya, February 1987.* Washington: World Bank; 1987. p. 13.

56. *Maternal mortality rates: a tabulation of available information.* Geneva: World Health Organization; 1986.

57. *Revised 1990 estimates of maternal mortality: a new approach by WHO and UNICEF.* Geneva: World Health Organization; 1996.

58. Winikoff B, Sullivan M. Assessing the role of family planning in reducing maternal mortality. *Stud Fam Plann* 1987;18:128–43.

59. Alan Guttmacher Institute. *Sharing responsibility: women, society and abortion worldwide.* New York: The Institute; 1999.

60. Conly SR. *Family planning and child survival. The role of reproductive factors in infant and child mortality: an analysis.* Washington: Population Crisis Committee; 1991.

61. Grant JP. *The state of the world's children.* New York: Oxford University Press for UNICEF; 1991. p. 5.

62. Acsadi GT, Johnson-Acsadi G. *Optimum conditions for childbearing.* London (UK): International Planned Parenthood Federation; 1986.

63. Shane B. *Family planning saves lives.* 3rd ed. Washington: Population Reference Bureau; 1997.

64. Khanna J, Van Look PFA, Griffin PD, editors. *Reproductive health: a key to a brighter future: biennial report 1990–1991.* Geneva: World Health Organization; 1992.

65. Heise L, Ellsberg M, Gottemoeller M. Ending violence against women. *Popul Rep L* 1999;Dec(11):1–43.

66. Murray CJL, Lopez AD, editors. *Health dimensions of sex and reproduction: the global burden of sexually transmitted diseases, HIV, maternal conditions, perinatal disorders, and congenital anomalies.* Vol 3 of *Global burden of disease and injury series.* Boston: Harvard School of Public Health on behalf of the World Health Organization and the World Bank; 1998.

67. Bennett A, Frisen C, Kamnuansilpa P, McWilliam J. *How Thailand's Family Planning Program reached replacement level fertility: lessons learned* [Population technical assistance project, occasional paper no 4]. Washington: US Agency for International Development; 1990.

68. *High stakes: the United States, global population and our common future. A report to the American people from the Rockefeller Foundation.* New York: Rockefeller Foundation; 1997.

69. Cohen JE. *How many people can the earth support?* New York: WW Norton; 1995.

70. Brown LR, Flavin C, French H. *State of the world 1998.* Washington: Worldwatch Institute; 1998.

71. Brown LR, Flavin C, French H. *State of the world 1999.* Washington: Worldwatch Institute; 1999.

72. Brown LR, Flavin C, French H. *State of the world 2000.* Washington: Worldwatch Institute; 2000.

73. Brown LR, Flavin C, French H. *State of the world 1998.* Washington: Worldwatch Institute; 1998. p. 149–87.

74. Brown LR, Flavin C, French H. *State of the world 1997.* Washington: Worldwatch Institute; 1997. p. 132–50.

75. Brown LR, Renner M, Flavin C. *Vital signs, 1998.* Washington: Worldwatch Institute; 1998. p. 114–5

76. Brown LR, Flavin C, French H. *State of the world 1998.* Washington: Worldwatch Institute; 1998. p. 13–4.

2

Food Security, Population, and Environment

Paul R. Ehrlich, Anne H. Ehrlich, and Gretchen C. Daily

Thirty years ago Paul and Anne Ehrlich developed the notion that Earth has a finite carrying capacity for human development, or at least for development of the present sort. In this selection, the authors return to the idea of carrying capacity, summarizing and extending their earlier arguments. These experts question whether it will be possible to feed, clothe, and house 10 billion humans. It is almost certainly the case that most people will be unable to eat the kinds of meals that most U.S. readers of this book now eat— and the situation will be due not to problems of distribution but to the inability of agricultural innovations to keep up with population growth. Without suggesting a looming Malthusian crisis, we do want to raise the key issue of how the planet's finite environment can satisfactorily and equitably sustain ever larger human populations. The authors conclude that food security is essential for environmental security because hungry people are in no position to consider the long-term health of Earth's life-support systems. Following on the first chapter, this second chapter calls for significant reductions in population growth.

Paul Ehrlich is Bing Professor of Population Studies and director of the Center for Conservation Biology at Stanford University. Anne Ehrlich is associate director and policy coordinator at the Center for Conservation Biology. Gretchen Daily is Bing Interdisciplinary Research Scientist in the Department of Biological Sciences at Stanford.

Whether the expansion of food production can keep pace with population growth over the long term remains the crux of the sustainability debate precipitated by Malthus almost two centuries ago. The success of food production

From Paul R. Erhlich, Anne H. Erhlich, and Gretchen C. Daily, "Food Security, Population, and Environment," *Population and Development Review* 19, no. 1 (March 1993): 1–11, 21–32. Reprinted by permission of the Population Council.

and distribution systems in meeting human needs at the present time is relatively easy to evaluate; no index so plainly measures failure as the extent of hunger and hunger-related disease and death. Yet the lack of ambiguity in assessing current access to food belies the staggering complexity inherent in the biophysical, social, and economic dimensions of humanity's most important enterprise—the production and distribution of food. This article outlines the complex of issues that are critical to humanity's ultimate success in what is, arguably, the greatest challenge of the coming century—maintaining growth in global food production to match or exceed the projected doubling (at least) of the human population.

Now that the global community is no longer transfixed by the Cold War, the severity of threats to environmental and food security is becoming more apparent. These forms of security are closely intertwined, since food production is highly sensitive to environmental conditions, and conversion of natural land for agriculture is a major cause of the deterioration of Earth's life support systems. Furthermore, both environmental and nutritional security are to a significant degree international problems, as reflected in the global trade in commodities, the global environmental commons, and the famine and mass migrations of people that can be provoked by regional food scarcity.

Doubts about humanity's ability to continue an exponential expansion of food production in the near future stem from two basic observations. The first is that the extraordinary expansion of food production since Malthus's time has been achieved at a heavy cost—the depletion of a one-time inheritance of natural capital crucial to agriculture. That cost now amounts to an annual loss of roughly 24 billion tons of topsoil (Brown and Wolfe, 1984), trillions of gallons of groundwater (e.g., Reisner, 1986), and millions of populations and species of other organisms (all involved in supplying ecosystem services crucial to food production—Ehrlich and Daily, 1993). The loss is permanent on any time scale of interest to humanity.

The second observation is that while agricultural output grew faster in the last four decades than even some optimists had predicted,[1] past expectations that a population of 5 billion could easily be fed have not been met, largely because hungry people have not had the means to purchase food. In fact, 200 million or more people have starved to death or died of hunger-related disease in the past two decades (UNICEF, 1992) and as many as a billion people are chronically undernourished today, about half of them seriously so (UN Population Fund, 1992).[2] In several major developing regions, including Africa and Latin America, the numbers of hungry people have continued to increase (FAO, 1992b; Stone, 1992), despite the impressive gains in food production.

The nutritional carrying capacity of Earth is the maximum number of people that could be provided with adequate diets at any given time without undermining the planet's capacity to support people in the future. Cultural and technological innovation may increase nutritional carrying capacity, just as irreversible (over a time scale relevant to society) depletion of essential, nonsubstitutable resources may reduce it. While biophysical factors impose the ultimate limits on nutritional carrying capacity, social, political, and economic constraints determine the extent to which that potential capacity is actually realized. These constraints are rooted in inequity in the ownership of arable land, in the frequent choice of low-nutrition over high-nutrition crops and perishable over easy-to-store farm products, in access to inputs and farm credit, in the availability of jobs, in the world food market, and in political neglect of the agricultural sector in many poor economies.

Nutritional Security

A nutritionally secure society has the ability to provide all of its people with diets adequate to sustain work and other normal daily activities. Today this security can be achieved through domestic food production or the ability to purchase or trade for foodstuffs produced in surplus elsewhere. True nutritional security includes buffers against inadequate harvests due to regional drought or other climatic events, as well as against difficulties in obtaining food through international trade. Some such buffers exist, in that food trade today is truly global, and most of the time shortages in one region can be made up by surpluses in another through trade. For very poor countries that lack foreign exchange to buy food on the world market in times of crop failure, the World Food Programme and several private agencies can provide emergency supplies.

Even so, it should be no surprise that most nations see it in their own interest to maintain some degree of self-sufficiency in food production, no matter how well integrated the world food market and distribution system may be. In years when worldwide food production falls significantly short of consumption (as it did in 1988 and perhaps 1991), higher global market prices may prevent some countries from making up food deficits with imports. Similarly, the World Food Programme at such times has more than the usual difficulty in marshaling supplies for famine-stricken poor countries.

If the next century were guaranteed to be one of food abundance, nations might be well advised to live entirely by the principles of comparative advantage in their food trade policies. On the other hand, if food shortages increase in frequency and severity in the decades ahead, as seems far more likely, then nations may be wise to take steps to preserve food production capacity at home. In an extreme situation, formerly dependable granaries may be reluctant to export food.

Norman Borlaug, when receiving the Nobel Prize in 1970 as a founder of the green revolution, cautioned that, at best, the new technology could buy humanity 30 years to solve the population problem. When he spoke, there were still fewer than 4 billion people. More than two-thirds of that 30 years have now passed, and the human population has passed 5.5 billion and is still growing at 1.7 percent per year, adding some 95 million people annually. Demographic projections now indicate that, barring catastrophe, the human population may reach 12 billion before growth stops, and might go higher (UN Population Fund, 1991, 1992).

Despite warnings by Borlaug and many others, a general impression remains that the green revolution has more or less permanently solved the problem of feeding the growing population and that famine has been largely banished, except for local disasters traceable to political conflicts (Swaminathan and Sinha, 1986). Indeed, it is often asserted that the persisting widespread chronic undernourishment results from maldistribution of otherwise abundant food supplies, and that better distribution would solve the hunger problem (e.g., Lappé and Collins, 1977).

There is some truth in this view. Outright starvation today is primarily a problem of food distribution failures, often precipitated by political turmoil in an already vulnerable, poorly nourished population, as in the tragic situation in Somalia and a few years ago in Ethiopia and Sudan (Drèze and Sen, 1991). But, while these acute cases gain much public attention, they are a tiny tip of the iceberg of widespread hunger, mostly in developing countries, whose causes are more complicated.

Maldistribution and Absolute Shortage

In the strictest sense, the widespread chronic food shortages in many developing regions can be attributed largely to maldistribution resulting from poverty and related economic factors, including inequities in the world trade system. Even so, an assessment by Robert Kates, Robert Chen, and colleagues of the Alan Shawn Feinstein World Hunger Program at Brown University suggests that the present food supply is not as abundant relative to needs as is often assumed. Recent world harvests, if equitably distributed and with no grain diverted to feeding livestock, could supply a vegetarian diet to about 6 billion people. A diet more typical of South America, with some 15 percent of its calories derived from animal sources, could be supplied to about 4 billion people. A "full but healthy diet" (about 30 percent of calories from animal sources) of the sort eaten by many people in rich countries could be supplied to less than half the 1992 population of 5.5 billion (Chen, 1990).

These numbers are not exact, of course, and they are based on assumptions that may somewhat overstate the amount of postharvest food wastage.[3] They nonetheless put in perspective the notion that hunger is "just a problem of distribution." Even if it were possible to transform most human beings into strict vegetarians willing to share equally, the sheer size and growth rate of the population would still be increasingly important factors in providing everyone with a minimal diet because of growing population-related stresses on the world's finite food production systems. This is not to say that a smaller population today would necessarily be better fed; economic, political, and social factors are not only important determinants of food production and distribution patterns, but also may inhibit or stimulate cultural and technological innovations that improve production capacities.[4] But agronomically and ecologically, it certainly would be easier to feed all people well if there were fewer of them.

Even now, when much talk still is of food "gluts," hunger remains one of the most serious elements of the human predicament. Low grain prices are not an indicator of nutritional security, but of the inability of poor people to generate demand for food. The United Nations Children's Fund (UNICEF) estimates that one in three children under five years old in developing countries is malnourished, and that each year in recent decades on the order of 10 million people (the vast majority of them young children) have died of hunger or hunger-related diseases (UNICEF, 1992). Other international agencies calculate that up to a billion people are unable to obtain sufficient energy from their food to carry on normal activities (Kates and Haarmann, 1992).

Even if those estimates were overstated by a factor of two,[5] the human nutritional situation would constitute a vast tragedy that has grave implications. In addition to causing direct suffering, hunger has negative effects on the economies of developing countries by, among other things, reducing the productivity of the work force. It decreases the educational potential of tens of millions of children, increases the vulnerability of the human population to epidemics such as AIDS, Ebola virus, new influenza strains, and drug-resistant tuberculosis, and threatens the political stability of the nations most affected.

Complacency about the security and abundance of the world food supply even in the near future, moreover, is unjustified, especially if the environmental dimensions of the agricultural enterprise are carefully considered. Indeed, the expansion of global grain production (the basis of the human food supply), which kept well ahead of population growth between 1950 and 1984, has failed to do so since then.[6] The 1990 harvest, the largest in history, was lower on a per capita basis than that of 1984.

Providing sufficient food both for people now undernourished and for the projected additions to the population during the next half-century (assuming the population does not by then exceed 10 billion) would require nearly tripling food production by 2040—a task that rivals even the remarkable achievements of the period 1950–84. But most of the readily available opportunities for substantial expansion of world food production (e.g., opening of new fertile lands, developing the first fertilizer-sensitive "miracle" strains of major crops, and applying the first doses of synthetic fertilizer) have been taken, and agriculture is now faced with a series of problems and potential difficulties that agricultural scientists realize will not be easily overcome (Plucknett and Horne, 1990).

Food from the Sea

The prospects for humanity's other major food source, oceanic fisheries, are also problematic. Provision of food from the sea is one of the most important services that natural ecosystems perform for *Homo sapiens*. The roughly 80 million metric tons of fishes now extracted from the sea annually are a small factor in the human feeding base compared with about 1,800 million (1.8 billion) metric tons of grains. Nonetheless, seafood provides an important protein supplement for the diets of many people; over half of all human beings get the majority of their animal protein from fishes, and for many poor people it is the only animal protein in their diets (McGoodwin, 1990).

Of many free services provided by natural ecosystems, supplying food from the sea is one that is clearly under stress. The theoretical maximum sustainable yield of marine fishes is generally agreed to be about 100 million metric tons (Ryther, 1969; World Resources Institute, 1992)—only about 15 percent above the level reached in the late 1980s (FAO, 1991). Policy failures exacerbate production problems; maintaining even 80 million tons sustainably will depend upon careful fisheries management, protection and restoration of coastal wetlands, and abatement of ocean pollution—none of which seems in prospect at the moment. Indeed, the current pattern is one of overexploitation of stocks to the point of collapse, followed by shifts to exploitation of new stocks, generally in more remote regions or of less desirable species. The rising costs of harvesting fishes are reflected in the prices of seafood, which have doubled in real terms since 1965 (World Resources Institute, 1992).

The only bright spot in the fisheries picture has been a rapid rise in production from aquaculture, which accounted for about 5 million tons of the marine catch and another 7 million tons from inland waters. Aquaculture also carries environmental costs and risks (World Resources Institute, 1992). Pollution problems have plagued many fish-farming ventures, and, like crop monocultures, fish monocultures are vulnerable to diseases.

Indeed, the overfishing and degradation of the marine environment may have reduced potential harvests from the sea for the foreseeable future. Experience, though limited, indicates that, once depressed to small numbers, many fish populations recover very slowly if at all. The structures of the biological communities of which they are members may be permanently altered to ones less favorable to humanity.

Constraints on Food Production

Continuing to expand harvests is likely to prove difficult because the inherent constraints of a finite world will increasingly come into play.[7] Among the constraints to increasing food production, those best categorized as "biophysical," include: (1) *losses of farmland* to other uses because of population pressures and limits to the amount of suitable new land that can be brought into production (Brown et al., 1990; World Resources Institute, 1992); (2) diminishing opportunities to irrigate additional farmland, associated in part with *limits to freshwater supplies* (Postel, 1990; Falkenmark and Widstrand, 1992); (3) *erosion and degradation of soils* (Brown and Wolfe, 1984; Oldeman, Van Engelen, and Pulles, 1990; Aber and Melillo, 1991; World Resources Institute, 1992); (4) biological limits to yield (production per hectare) increases, already seen in little-understood *"caps" on yield* in rice and possibly other crops (but not yet in corn or potatoes) (Bugbee and Monje, 1992; Walsh, 1991); (5) limits to or diminishing marginal returns from the application of *fertilizers* (Brown, 1991; Brown et al., 1990; Smil, 1991); (6) a complex of problems associated with chemical control of *pests* (Francis, Flora, and King, 1990; Ehrlich and Ehrlich, 1991); (7) *declining genetic diversity* of crops themselves and of their wild relatives (National Research Council, 1991; Plucknett et al., 1987); (8) the possibility of depressed yields from *increased ultraviolet-B radiation* (Worrest and Grant, 1989); (9) reduced yields from a variety of *air pollutants* (including those causing acid precipitation) that are toxic to crops (World Resources Institute, 1986); (10) the substantial possibility of agricultural disruptions and reduced production due to rapid *climate change and sea-level rise* (Parry, 1990; Schneider, 1989); and (11) a general *decline in the free services* supplied to agriculture by natural ecosystems (Ehrlich and Ehrlich, 1991). We now examine each of these constraints.

Land

Earth's 5.5 billion people now occupy or use some 90 percent of the land surface that is not desert (receiving less than 250 mm of rain per year) or under permanent ice cover. About 17 percent of that potentially productive land is planted in crops; the rest is urban or otherwise built on, used as pasture, or covered by forests that are exploited to one degree or another. The remaining uncultivated land that could be planted in crops is almost all marginal, as is indicated by the small fraction of the increase in food production since 1950 that is attributable to an expansion of cropland. In 1950, 593 million hectares were planted in grains; by 1990, that had increased by 21 percent to 720 million hectares, but production had increased by 139 percent due to more than a doubling of average yield, from about one ton per hectare per year to about 2.3 tons per hectare per year (Brown, 1988).

Furthermore, much of the land that might be converted to crops now, especially that under tropical moist forests, is still occupied by natural ecosystems that are playing important roles in supporting the human enterprise, such as storing carbon and controlling the hydrologic cycle (which supplies fresh water). Repeated attempts to clear and farm tropical moist forest land have demonstrated that much of it is unsuitable for conventional farming and quickly degrades to wasteland if put to the plow (Ehrlich, 1988; Sanchez, 1976; Tivy, 1990).

Fertile farmland is often sacrificed to meet the growing demands of urbanization. Population growth, urban migration, and industrialization are driving the expansion of cities over the rich agricultural land on which they typically were founded. This loss of farmland has occurred in places as disparate from each other as California, where urban sprawl has obliterated several important fruit-growing areas, and East Asia, where some 5,000 kilometers are lost to urbanization annually.[8]

The competition between cropland and living space is not limited to city margins. NASA scientist Marc Imhoff and his colleagues (Imhoff et al., 1986) have analyzed that competition in rural Bangladesh, where people live on bulwarks raised above the water level of the countryside, which is flooded annually by rainfall and runoff. During the dry season, soil for the bulwarks is dug from the centers of the paddies. The area of the bulwarks increases at the expense of paddy area as the population grows, and the water in the excavated paddies deepens to the point where the highest-yielding rice strains can no longer be planted, leading to a decline in rice production (Imhoff, personal communication). Ongoing research on deep-water rice cultivars may ameliorate the latter problem, but the need for more living space is sure to continue.

Imhoff proposes that such losses of paddy area are widespread in South and East Asia, undetected largely because of the "noise" in statistics created by fluctuations in harvests related to weather and economic factors, and because they are partly offset by increased yields from better agricultural technologies and intensified cultivation.

Potential for further conflict over land use arises from the need to move toward a sustainable global energy economy. Currently, about 75 percent of the world's energy is supplied by fossil fuel combustion (Hall et al., 1992). The associated release of greenhouse gases and the consequent threat of global warming have spurred research into other options, one of the most attractive of which appears to be energy from processed biomass (plant matter). Using biomass fuels for a substantial part of the future energy budget would, however, require dedicating the equivalent of approximately 15 percent of the land now in forests and 40 percent of that in croplands to biomass energy crop production (Hall, Mynick, and Williams, 1991). Though the tradeoffs are difficult to evaluate (Braunstein et al., 1981; Pimentel et al., 1984), it appears certain that the competition for fertile land will intensify.

Soil

Soil is a precious element of the natural "capital" that humanity has inherited but is now rapidly depleting. Soil is generated by ecosystems on a time scale of centimeters per millennium (Hillel, 1991). In many areas, because of human activities, it is eroding at rates up to centimeters per decade. As was noted above, globally some 24 billion tons of soil are lost annually in excess of the natural rate of soil regeneration, and it has been estimated that the remaining topsoil on Earth's cropland is being lost at an average rate of 7 percent per decade (Brown and Wolfe, 1984). Even if this estimate were several times too high, current agricultural practices would still be unsustainable in the long term (Daily and Ehrlich, 1992).

Soil itself is a complex ecosystem, and its fertility is tightly tied to the diversity of life it contains—billions of tiny organisms per gram in rich agricultural soils (Overgaard-Nielsen, 1955). Those organisms are involved in maintaining soil quality and transferring nutrients from soil to crops. They are also prime actors in the recycling and mobilization of nutrients, functions that are utterly indispensable not only for healthy ecosystems but for crop production. Yet these obscure organisms are threatened by many aspects of modern industrial agriculture (Hillel, 1991; Pimentel et al., 1992).

Just since 1945, according to a study sponsored by the United Nations Environment Programme (UNEP), nearly 11 percent of the world's vegetated land has suffered moderate to extreme degradation and another 6 percent has been lightly damaged (Oldeman, Van Engelen, and Pulles, 1990; World Resources Institute, 1992). The productivity of the 7 percent of land that is moderately damaged (by UNEP's definition) has been substantially reduced, and the soil's biotic functions have been seriously impaired. Restoration of full productivity is possible but would require considerable expenditure of labor and other resources. The biotic functions of severely degraded land (3 percent) have been largely destroyed, and their restoration seems problematic. Extremely degraded soils (less than 1 percent) are essentially unreclaimable. The fraction of land that is degraded varies considerably among continents; in North America, only about 5 percent of the land is estimated to be moderately degraded or worse; in Europe the fraction is 17 percent; and in Mexico and Central America it rises to 24 percent.[9] The principal human activities that have caused this degradation are agriculture, overgrazing, and deforestation. Such rapid deterioration of the world's productive land is not an encouraging sign, especially since the activities causing land degradation will surely be intensified in the decades ahead. . . .

Biotic Diversity

Biotic diversity is the most irreplaceable component of our resource capital and the least understood and appreciated. It is also vitally important to agricultural productivity (Pimentel et al., 1992). Plants, animals, and microorganisms are organized, along with the physical elements of the environment with which they interact, into ecosystems. These provide indispensable services that support human civilization. Many of these services are essential to agriculture, including: maintenance of the gaseous composition of the atmosphere; moderation of climate; control of the hydrologic cycle; recycling of nutrients; control of the great majority of insects that might attack crops; pollination; and maintenance of a vast "genetic library" containing many millions of kinds of organisms, from which humanity has "withdrawn" the crop and livestock species on which civilization was built, and which potentially could (if preserved) provide enormous benefits in the future (Ehrlich and Ehrlich, 1981, 1991). Indeed, that library holds the raw materials with which plant geneticists work.

Yet biodiversity resources are being lost at an accelerating rate that may cause the disappearance by 2025 of one-quarter of all the species now existing on Earth (Wilson and Peter, 1988; Ehrlich and Wilson, 1991; Wilson, 1992). Every species and genetically distinct population that disappears is a marvel gone forever—often without humanity ever knowing what potential direct economic value it might have possessed, much less its role in providing ecosystem services (Ehrlich and Daily, 1993). Even if the evolutionary process that creates diversity continued at rates comparable to those in the geologic past, it would take tens of millions of years for today's level of diversity, once seriously depleted, to be restored.

Of particular concern for feeding the growing human population, the great potential for developing new crops and domestic animals from the world's vast storehouse of biodiversity is being compromised by the global extinction episode now under way. Only a score or so of plant species are really important as crops today; at most a few hundred supply humanity with significant quantities of food. There are at least a quarter-million species of higher plants, many with substantial untapped potential as crops. About 75,000 are known to have edible parts, and 7,500 or so have been used by human societies as food (Wilson, 1989). Furthermore, selection can sometimes create cultivated strains that are edible even if their wild ancestors are not. The current wholesale destruction of populations and species of wild plants, however, is rapidly foreclosing the potential for developing new food sources.

Loss of Genetic Diversity

High-yield agriculture is primarily a product of evolutionary plant genetics, the scientific discipline that has taken traditional crop varieties and, through selective breeding, produced new varieties with enhanced amounts of the structures (e.g., nutrient-rich seeds in grains) desired by humanity while eliminating undesirable aspects (bitter flavors, toxins, poor storage quality). The basic resource that permitted the selection process to accomplish this goal is a subset of biodiversity: genetic diversity. Maintaining genetic diversity is vital for the continuation of high-yield agriculture. That diversity, basically a storehouse of different genes, makes it possible to create new crop strains by recombining their genes in new ways. New strains are continually needed to meet ever-changing conditions: the evolution of new varieties of pests and diseases that attack crops, changing climatic conditions, exposure to novel air pollutants, and so on.

The genetic diversity of crops has been threatened in two ways. First, as farmers around the world rapidly adopted a few, genetically similar green revolution crop varieties, a host of traditional ones have been displaced, causing a loss of genetic variability within the crop species being grown. Second, the destruction of natural habitat is steadily eliminating populations of wild crop relatives, another reservoir of genes that could be critical to maintaining productivity (Hoyt, 1988; Vaughan and Chang, 1993). For example, the important "miracle" rice strain IR36 was developed at the International Rice Research Institute (IRRI) by a team under the direction of the eminent rice breeder Gurdev Khush. Two critical attributes contributing to the strain's success, resistance to blast (a fungus disease) and to grassy stunt (a virus), were derived from a wild species of rice (Plucknett et al., 1987). The situation with respect to farm animals is, if anything, worse. While some programs have been organized to save the genetic diversity of crops, no similar efforts have been made to preserve diversity of animals (National Research Council, 1991; Cohen et al., 1991; Plucknett et al., 1987).

Genetic diversity is likely to be an especially crucial resource if the next few decades become, as expected, an era of unprecedentedly rapid intensification of stresses on agriculture. The challenge for plant geneticists would be daunting even if a maximum amount of genetic variability were available; the loss of that variability in many crops exacerbates their difficulties. The problems will be greatest in the poorest countries, where populations are hungriest and agricultural sectors are least robust and most lacking in research and development capability. . . .

Why the Lack of Concern?

In the light of these many difficulties, why is there so little concern among political leaders and in much of the American agricultural community about the prospects for feeding the rapidly expanding human population and about the environmental costs that almost inevitably will be associated with the attempt? Why do these attitudes stand in such stark contrast to those of, say, scientists at the International Rice Research Institute, who are now deeply engaged in an effort to avert nutritional disaster in Asia? Perhaps some of the blame can be laid on educational systems in general and on ecologists in particular. Most people, even those educated in first-rate universities, are given virtually no understanding of agricultural systems and still less of the eco-logical factors that govern them.

In addition, for decades the training of agronomists has lacked adequate contact with modern ecological science, partly because of the historical sepa-ration in universities of agriculture departments from those specializing in "pure" biology. This isolation can be traced to a traditional view, now fortu-nately breaking down, that pure scientists demean themselves by dirtying their hands with applied research. As a result of these educational failures, many of the potential biological constraints on agriculture are little appreci-ated by agricultural scientists and especially by agricultural economists.

A second problem is traceable to widespread misinterpretation of the practical implications of a thought exercise by Revelle (1976), evaluating the world's theoretical agricultural potential. Glib references to his speculation that the planet could feed 40 billion people[10] ignore the absurdity of the se-quence of assumptions compounded in the calculation. Revelle assumed, among other things, that the amount of cultivated land could be increased more than twofold (when actually most of the world's suitable land is already under cultivation and much prime farmland is now being degraded or lost); that losses to pests would be minimized to 10 percent (perhaps a third of their present level); that postharvest wastage of food would be negligible (when it may be as high as 40 percent: Chen, 1990); that the present impact of agricul-ture on environmental systems could be greatly increased without penalty (although today's impact is not sustainable); and that food would be perfectly equitably distributed among people with no grain diverted to livestock. In addition, Revelle's calculations did not include the possibility that global change could reduce productivity.

This leads us to a third problem that pervades optimistic assessments of the state of the environment in general and of the prospects for eliminating world hunger in particular (e.g., National Research Council, 1986): blind faith in the effectiveness of present market systems in sensing and respond-ing to an accelerating, complex process of environmental deterioration. That faith is clearly misplaced. Interaction between economists and natural and physical scientists is essential for designing new market-based and other policy incentives to help price, internalize, and allocate the myriad elements of our poorly understood life-support systems. It is encouraging that interaction and collaboration between economists and ecologists is growing rapidly. None-theless, it would be folly to count on the success of this very difficult enter-prise in planning for human nutritional security.

We strongly concur with the view expressed by Nathan Keyfitz (1991): "If we have one point of empirically backed knowledge, it is that bad policies are widespread and persistent. Social science has to take account of them" (p. 15). This point seems especially applicable to agricultural policy.

Finally, man does not live by bread alone; food production is not the only constraint to consider when contemplating maximum desirable population size and the health of the environment. The present agricultural system is still sufficiently far from theoretical biophysical limits (Revelle, 1976; Bugbee and Monje, 1992) that, were all humanity to cooperate in a global effort to maximize food production, it could probably increase agricultural output severalfold on a one-time basis. Even if such a feat could be accomplished, it is likely that the endeavor would cause the irreversible depletion of substantial natural capital. It would also compromise achievement of a truly high standard of living.

To be sure, the complexities of agricultural economics tend to obscure the basic food situation from the perspective of many in the agricultural community and outside of it. It is naturally difficult for, say, an Australian wheat farmer or a New Zealand sheep rancher to worry about a world with too little food when prices for wheat and lamb are very low and the European Community and the United States are "dumping" surplus food at subsidized prices on the world market.

It is not, of course, that there are not people who need such commodities; instead, those people are very poor and, in the language of economics, they do not generate "demand" for food. People also have trouble envisioning how hunger can be widespread in countries that export agricultural commodities. But to earn foreign exchange, needed to finance development, many poor countries with meager natural resources have little alternative but to export crops.

Most serious of all, it is very difficult for human beings to grasp slowly evolving trends like those that are leading toward a food-environment crisis. Neither our biological nor our cultural evolution has prepared us to readily perceive changes taking place on a time scale of decades (Ornstein and Ehrlich, 1989). Furthermore, ignoring the food problem is easy for the rich, since by far the largest part of it occurs in the form of a steady attrition from undernourishment and disease rather than as spectacular famines. Yet the price of largely neglecting population growth and the maldistribution of food for the last two decades has been high: at least 200 million people have died of hunger and poverty; tens of millions more people are chronically hungry today than were so 20 years ago (World Bank, 1990, 1992; UN Population Fund, 1992); and the few decades "bought" by the green revolution have nearly expired with no encore in sight. Humanity can ill afford to continue making the same mistakes.

Prospects for the Future

Rather than surging ahead of population growth again in the coming decades, it must be considered at least as likely that agricultural production will increasingly fall behind. The generally lackluster performance of agriculture in most regions since 1984 lends credence to this possibility, along with other factors that will, at the least, make further large increases problematic. One prediction (Brown, 1988) had global agricultural production increasing only by an annual average of 0.9 percent in the 1990s (about the rate achieved by Japanese rice farmers in the past two decades), while population continues growing by some 1.7 percent per year. Nothing yet has happened to contradict that gloomy prediction.

Indeed, the future world food situation may be better represented by Rwanda than by Iowa. James Gasana (1991), Minister of Agriculture, Livestock, and Forests of that Central African nation, wrote that Rwanda's agricultural problems were

> . . . high population pressure and decreasing agricultural productivity due to soil erosion. Population pressure has made us intensify our agriculture and by doing that we have experienced significant soil losses. So we have a high level of population relative to food output. . . . Our problem is that we have no more new areas that we can colonize. And we have to stop land being lost. We estimate that our arable lands are diminishing each year by about 8000 hectares. . . . We can produce enough food for 5 million people—but we have 7.3 million people. . . . I am afraid that if the rate of population growth continues, we might have serious difficulties.[11]

Even if enough food is produced, many areas may lack the fuelwood needed to cook it—and cooking is necessary to get the nutritional value out of many staple foods. In the tropics, rural populations depend almost entirely on fuelwood for energy; fuelwood supplies roughly 90 percent of energy use in Zambia and Kenya and 95 percent in Nepal, Sri Lanka, and Thailand (El-Hinnawi and Hashimi, 1982). In many if not most developing areas, this level of fuelwood harvest is unsustainable. The UN Food and Agriculture Organization estimated in the mid-1980s that 1.5 billion of the 2 billion people who depended largely on fuelwood were cutting at rates exceeding regrowth, and that 125 million people living in 23 countries could not find enough wood to satisfy their needs (Repetto, 1987). This overharvesting leads to deforestation and deterioration of soil, which in turn tends to reduce agricultural productivity by disrupting the hydrologic cycle and changing local climates.

While we have concentrated here on the ecological constraints on agricultural production, in no way is this emphasis intended to slight the severe economic, political, and social dimensions of the world food problem. These have been dealt with extensively by others, most recently in an excellent study by the World Institute for Development Economics Research (WIDER) (Drèze and Sen, 1990, 1991). We only wish to emphasize that ways must be found both to feed all of humanity and to maintain the integrity of Earth's life-support systems despite the problems pervading social (and agricultural) policy that seem endemic to our species.

It may be even more difficult to formulate the needed kinds of international policies if the post-Cold War "new world order" means returning to a nineteenth-century style of balance-of-power maneuvering among increasing numbers of nations, as some analysts feel it might (*The Economist,* 1991–92). Still, nations today are given incentives to cooperate by an unprecedented interdependence in trade and commerce. And the power any nation can attain is limited in part by the plethora of organizations that increasingly regulate international affairs.

What Should Be Done?

It is impossible to avoid the conclusion that the prudent course for humanity, facing the population-food-environment trap, must above all be to reduce human fertility and halt population growth as soon as humanely possible. While it is necessary to raise demand for food by reducing poverty, it is crucial also to decrease the need for food by limiting the annual increment of new mouths to feed. We will not deal further with issues of population control here, but success in this area remains a sine qua non for a sustainable future. On the supply side, expanding food production to support the growing population must be moved much higher on the political agenda.

Since the most rapid population growth and the largest deficits in food production per person are both found in developing countries, their agricultural sectors must be the chief focus of efforts to address food shortages. Particular attention must be given to finding ecologically sound ways of increasing production of food for domestic consumption and for reducing crop losses to pests and spoilage. Careful attention should be given to substituting more productive crops for less productive ones, as China has done in switching from rice to potatoes and corn in the north and in areas of higher altitude. Similarly, the use of amaranths and other neglected traditional crops for increasing food production in tropical and subtropical (often the hungriest) regions should be pursued vigorously. In general, one of the best opportunities for increasing incomes and hence food demand is through more productive, labor-intensive agricultural technologies.

Further disturbance and destruction of natural ecosystems must be avoided to the greatest degree possible, in order to preserve biodiversity and maintain ecosystem services. Conservation of soil and water must become a top priority in agricultural systems worldwide. And enormous efforts must be made to restore the productivity of degraded lands. In the Tammin area of Western Australia, for example, local farmers have been reclaiming salinized wheatfields by replanting local vegetation, which lowers water tables and permits rain to flush salt below the root zone of the wheat (Saunders, Hobbs, and Ehrlich, 1993). But even in Australia, rates of ecosystem degradation still greatly outpace those of ecosystem restoration. Restoration ecology seems certain to become a central discipline of the future, especially if crops are to be grown for biomass fuels as well as for food. Finally, establishing more integrated pest management systems should be promoted wherever the technical ability to do so can be mobilized (Holl et al., 1990).

To achieve these goals, much more attention and assistance must be given to strengthening the agricultural sectors of developing nations, economically and politically (Timmer, Falcon, and Pearson, 1983). A major, relatively inexpensive step would be to increase support for the institutions in the Consultative Group on International Agricultural Research (CGIAR). The International Rice Research Institute, CIMMYT (Centro Internacional de Mejoramiento de Maíz y Trigo, the equivalent of IRRI for corn and wheat), and other international agricultural research institutes are severely constrained in their activities by lack of money. (The total budget of those institutions in 1988 was only $243 million, well under one-thousandth of the U.S. military budget or about a third of the cost of a B-2 bomber.) A few additional tens of millions of dollars annually allocated to the 13 institutions in CGIAR could pay huge benefits. Consider that the relatively small amount, slightly over one billion dollars, spent for IRRI and CIMMYT since their establishment can reasonably be claimed to have saved the lives of countless millions by generating the green revolution. The hundreds of millions of dollars that will be spent on the famine relief operations begun in late 1992 by the U.S. military in Somalia, by contrast, cannot possibly help to solve the basic food problem even in that country.

Extremely important, though complex and politically daunting, is an overhaul of the world trade system for food, including abolition of many counterproductive agricultural subsidies. In the wake of the patent failure of the communist experiment, it is likely that government intervention in domestic food markets in developing countries will decline. This could prove a great benefit in the numerous instances where policies of keeping food prices low in the cities have discouraged agricultural production. Nevertheless, all governments have a responsibility to ensure that their people are fed and to avoid political instability caused by hunger. Such instability could threaten world peace, an especially grim prospect as nuclear weapons technologies continue to spread. The importance of agriculture and of food distribution systems in this regard has been made very clear in the wake of the collapse of the Soviet Union.

Food security is essential for environmental security; hungry people are in no position to consider the long-term health of Earth's life-support systems. Nutritional security of all peoples requires negotiations and agreements among governments at least as much as does military security. While these arrangements should utilize market mechanisms where possible, this does not mean that totally unregulated "free trade" in food is ideal. Efficient as markets can be, government interventions (including international agreements) are required when significant costs and benefits are not privately borne. In such cases, mechanisms are needed that place an appropriate value on preserving ecosystem services and that allocate the costs of doing so among the people who can both afford them and benefit most from them. Somehow, for instance, developing countries must receive fair compensation for preserving tropical forests, just as a citizen of the United States is compensated when his or her land is taken for a nature reserve.

In theory, much could be done to reduce the maldistribution of food, although doing so is certain to be very difficult in practice. In any event, far more effort is called for. One should not conclude that simply increasing per capita food production will enable the poor to eat well. Experience in the United States and elsewhere certainly bears this out. Unhappily, one of the most recalcitrant elements with respect to world food distribution, as we have already indicated, is lack of effective demand. Hungry people are poor and do not have the buying power to reward farmers for their efforts by driving prices up. Thus malnutrition exists side by side with food prices that are "too low," a situation compounded by food "surpluses" and complex systems of agricultural subsidies in rich nations.

Alleviating poverty is therefore an essential ingredient for providing all of humanity with food security. Indeed, unless progress is made in that direction, and unless the food supply grows significantly faster than the population (unlikely from both economic and ecological perspectives), the numbers of the hungry will increase further. If an absolute global shortage of food materializes in the next couple of decades, as it well might (Daily and Ehrlich, 1990), distributional problems could be expected to increase disproportionately as food prices rise beyond the reach of the poorest groups. Prudent policymaking demands that both supply and distribution problems be tackled simultaneously.

Conclusion

Were society to concentrate its efforts on improving agricultural production and distribution systems worldwide, substantially more food could be grown than is grown today—for a while. It is doubtful, however, whether food security could be achieved indefinitely for a global population of 10 or 12 billion people. Rather, it seems likely that a sustainable population, one comfortably below Earth's nutritional carrying capacity, will number far fewer than today's 5.5 billion people; how many fewer will depend in part on how seriously Earth's carrying capacity will have been degraded in the process of supporting the population overshoot. Moreover, we are convinced that 10 billion people cannot be nourished even temporarily unless far greater attention and resources are directed to developing a more productive, environmentally sound agriculture and to improving food distribution. We must educate all people about this need and bring agriculture into the center of the world stage. Aside from dealing with the complementary population issue, nothing could be more critical to the human future.

Notes

1. See the interesting discussion by M. K. Bennett, "Population and food supply: The current scare" (*Scientific Monthly,* vol. 68, no. 1, January 1949), reprinted in the "Archives" section of *Population and Development Review* 18, no. 2: 341–358. Bennett was misled by demographic projections indicating a world population of 3.3 billion in the year 2000, and appears to have been unaware of the ecological dimensions of the agricultural situation. But he also underestimated (as did many others) the success of what became known as the "green revolution."

2. International agencies differ in their estimates of the numbers of undernourished people because, among other reasons, they use somewhat different criteria for their calculations. The Food and Agriculture Organization of the United Nations (FAO) estimated that about 786 million people in developing regions were chronically undernourished in the period 1988–90 (FAO, 1992a, 1992b). The World Bank estimated that in the mid-1980s some 920 million people in developing regions outside China were underfed, nearly half of them getting too little food to prevent stunting of growth or threats to health (cited in World Resources Institute, 1988, chapter 4). Kates and Haarmann (1992) cite a figure of over a billion for "energy deficient for work" derived from assessments made by the World Hunger Program, based on World Bank estimates.

3. The estimates include a 40 percent overall loss between production and consumption, including a 10–15 percent loss after food leaves retail outlets, based on FAO and other sources. Other estimates are more conservative, but not strictly comparable (e.g., Greely, 1991).

4. A good, brief discussion of these social factors, although one that tends to underestimate the contribution of population growth to the problem, is Murdoch, 1990.

5. Some analysts claim that estimates of undernourishment in sub-Saharan Africa are exaggerated (see Svedberg, 1991).

6. See Brown, 1988; Brown et al., 1990; Brown et al., 1992. Recent information also comes from U.S. Department of Agriculture reports (e.g., USDA, 1992). Some of the slowness of increase in grain production in the late 1980s can be traced to land withheld from production for policy reasons in rich nations (perhaps 5 percent of grain land).

7. Perhaps the ultimate limit is the finite amount of available energy that is "fixed" annually from sunlight by green plants and other producer organisms in the process of photosynthesis. The technical term for that photosynthetic product—the energy produced by photosynthesizers, less the energy used for their own life processes—is *net primary production* or NPP. Humanity is already directly consuming over 5 percent of the NPP on Earth's land surfaces and is co-opting (by diverting it into altered ecosystems containing different sets of organisms than would otherwise be present) about 30 percent of the total. If one takes into account loss of potential productivity,

due to ecosystem conversion and land degradation, the human diversion of the world's terrestrial NPP rises to about 40 percent, with a much smaller effect, so far, on the NPP of oceanic systems (Vitousek et al., 1986). Given the dimensions of the human takeover of land for farming, grazing, and forest exploitation, as well as for habitation and infrastructure, it is not hard to see why the impact is so large. This situation also illuminates why biologists are not sanguine about the prospect of a doubling or tripling of the human population within the next century.

8. FAO estimate cited in Brown et al. (1990: 65). One need only visit the outskirts of New Delhi or Manila to see this loss occurring at dramatic rates.

9. Like many published estimates (e.g., extent of hunger, rates of soil erosion) related to the world food situation, these numbers have an illusory precision. There is, for example, wide disagreement about UNEP estimates of desertification (Pearce, 1992). What is indisputable is that substantial portions of Earth's surface critical to agriculture have been degraded and that degradation is continuing at a time when substantially increased food production will be needed.

10. Statement of Catholic Bishops, reported in *The Washington Post*, 19 November 1988.

11. The 1992 population growth rate in Rwanda was about 3.4 percent, giving a doubling time of about 20 years (Population Reference Bureau, 1992).

References

Aber, J., and J. Melillo. 1991. *Terrestrial Ecosystems*. Philadelphia: Saunders.

Braunstein, H., et al. 1981. *Biomass Energy Systems and the Environment*. New York: Pergamon Press.

Brown, L. 1988. "The changing world food prospect: The nineties and beyond," *Worldwatch Paper* 85. Worldwatch Institute, Washington, D.C.

_____. 1991. "Fertilizer engine losing steam," *World Watch* 4, no. 5: 32–33.

_____, and E. Wolfe. 1984. "Soil erosion: Quiet crisis in the world economy," *Worldwatch Paper* 60. Worldwatch Institute, Washington, D.C.

_____, et al. 1990. *State of the World 1990*. New York: W. W. Norton.

_____, C. Flavin, and H. Kane. 1992. *Vital Signs 1992*. New York: W. W. Norton.

Bugbee, B., and O. Monje. 1992. "The limits of crop productivity," *BioScience* 42, no. 7: 494–502.

Chen, R. (ed.). 1990. *The Hunger Report: 1990*. The Alan Shawn Feinstein World Hunger Program, Brown University.

Cohen, J., et al. 1991. "Ex-situ conservation of plant genetic resources: Global development and environmental concerns," *Science* 253: 866–872.

Daily, G., and P. Ehrlich. 1992. "Population, sustainability, and Earth's carrying capacity," *BioScience* 42, no. 10: 761–771.

Drèze, J., and A. Sen (eds.). 1990 and 1991. *The Political Economy of Hunger*: Vol I: *Entitlement and Well-being,* 1990; Vol II: *Famine Prevention,* 1990: Vol. III: *Endemic Hunger,* 1991. Oxford: Oxford University Press.

The Economist. 1991–92. "A multi-power world," 21 December–3 January.

Ehrlich, A. 1988. "Development and agriculture," in P. R. Ehrlich and J. P. Holdren (eds.), *The Cassandra Conference*. College Station, Texas: Texas A & M University Press.

_____, and G. Daily. 1993. "Population extinction and saving biodiversity," *Ambio.*

Ehrlich, P., and A. Ehrlich. 1981. *Extinction: The Causes and Consequences of the Disappearance of Species.* New York: Random House.

_____, and A. Ehrlich. 1991. *Healing the Planet.* Boston: Addison-Wesley.

_____, and E. Wilson. 1991. "Biodiversity studies: Science and policy," *Science* 253: 758–762.

El-Hinnawi, E., and M. Hashimi. 1982. *Environmental Issues.* UNEP. Dublin: Tycooly International Publishing.

Falkenmark, M., and C. Widstrand. 1992. "Population and water resources: A delicate balance," *Population Bulletin* 47, no. 3.

Food and Agriculture Organization (FAO). 1992a. *Food and Nutrition: Creating a Well-fed World.* Rome: FAO.

_____. 1992b. *World Food Supplies and Prevalence of Chronic Undernutrition in Developing Regions as Assessed in 1992.* Rome: FAO.

Francis, C., C. Flora, and L. King. 1990. *Sustainable Agriculture in Temperate Zones.* New York: Wiley-Interscience.

Gasana, J. 1991. "A very tough challenge for us," *International Agricultural Development* (September/October) 11, no. 5: 8.

Greely, M. 1991. "Postharvest losses—the real picture," *International Agricultural Development* (September/October) 11, no. 5: 9–11.

Hall, D., H. Mynick, and R. Williams. 1991. "Alternative roles for biomass in coping with greenhouse warming," *Science and Global Security* 2: 1–39.

_____, et al. 1992. "Biomass for energy: Supply prospects," in T. B. Johansson et al. (eds.), *Renewable Energy: Sources for Fuels and Electricity.* Washington, D.C.: Island Press, pp. 593–652.

Hillel, D. 1991. *Out of the Earth: Civilization and the Life of the Soil.* New York: The Free Press (Macmillan).

Holl, K., G. Daily, and P. Ehrlich. 1990. "Integrated pest management in Latin America," *Environmental Conservation* 17: 341–350.

Hoyt, E. 1988. *Conserving the Wild Relatives of Crops,* International Board for Plant Genetic Resources, International Union for the Conservation of Nature and Natural Resources (IUCN), and Worldwide Fund for Nature (WWF), Rome and Gland.

Imhoff, M., et al. 1986. "Monsoon flood boundary delineation and damage assessment using space-borne imaging radar and Landsat data," *Photogrammetric Engineering and Remote Sensing* 53: 405–413.

Kates, R., and V. Haarmann. 1992. "Where the poor live: Are the assumptions correct?" *Environment* 34, no. 4: 5–11, 25–28.

Keyfitz, N. 1991. "Population and development within the ecosphere: One view of the literature," *Population Index* 57, no. 5: 5–22.

Lappé, F., and J. Collins. 1977. *Food First.* Boston: Houghton Mifflin.

McGoodwin, J. 1990. *Crisis in the World's Fisheries.* Stanford: Stanford University Press.

Murdoch, W. 1990. "World hunger and population," in C. Carroll, J. Vandermeer, and P. Rosset (eds.), *Agroecology.* New York: McGraw-Hill, pp. 3–20.

National Research Council, Committee on Population, Working Group on Population Growth and Economic Development. 1986. *Population Growth and Economic Development: Policy Questions.* Washington, D.C.: National Academy Press.

National Research Council, Board on Agriculture. 1991. *Managing Global Genetic Resources.* Washington, D.C.: National Academy Press.

Oldeman, L., V. Van Engelen, and J. Pulles. 1990. "The extent of human-induced soil degradation," Annex 5 of L. Oldeman et al., *World Map of the Status of Human-Induced Soil Degradation: An Explanatory Note.* rev. 2nd ed. International Soil Reference and Information Centre (ISRIC). Waginengen, Netherlands.

Ornstein, R., and P. Ehrlich. 1989. *New World/New Mind.* New York: Doubleday.

Overgaard-Nielsen, C. 1955. "Studies on enchyfraeidae 2: Field studies," *Natura Jutlandica* 4: 5–58.

Parry, M. 1990. *Climate Change and World Agriculture.* London: Earthscan Publications.

Pearce, F. 1992. "Mirage of the shifting sands," *New Scientist* (12 December): 38–42.

Pimentel, D., et al. 1984. "Environmental and social costs of biomass energy," *BioScience* 34, no. 2: 89–94.

_____, et al. 1992. "Conserving biological diversity in agricultural/forestry systems," *BioScience* 42, no. 5: 354–362.

Plucknett, D., and M. Horne. 1990. "The Consultative Group on International Agriculture Research—goals, accomplishments, and current activities," *Food Reviews International* 6: 67–89.

_____, et al. 1987. *Gene Banks and the World's Food.* Princeton: Princeton University Press.

Population Reference Bureau (PRB). 1992. *1992 World Population Data Sheet.* Washington, D.C.: PRB.

Postel, S. 1990, "Water for agriculture: Facing the limits," *Worldwatch Paper* 93, Worldwatch Institute, Washington, D.C.

Reisner, M. 1986. *Cadillac Desert: The American West and Its Disappearing Water.* New York: Viking.

Repetto, R. 1987. "Population, resources, environment: An uncertain future," *Population Bulletin* 42, no. 2.

Revelle, R. 1976. "The resources available for agriculture," *Scientific American* 235, no. 3: 164–178

Ryther, J. 1969. "Photosynthesis and fish production in the sea," *Science* 166: 72–76.

Sanchez, P. 1976. *Properties and Management of Soils in the Tropics.* New York: Wiley-Interscience.

Saunders, D., R. Hobbs, and P. Ehrlich (eds.). 1993. *Reconstruction of Fragmented Ecosystems: Global and Regional Perspectives.* Sydney: Surrey Beauty.

Schneider, S. 1989. *Global Warming: Entering the Greenhouse Century.* San Francisco: Sierra Club Books.

Smil, V. 1991. "Population growth and nitrogen: An exploration of a critical existential link," *Population and Development Review* 17, no. 4: 569–601.

Stone, R. 1992. "A snapshot of world hunger," *Science* 257: 876.

Svedberg, P. 1991. "Undernutrition in sub-Saharan Africa: A critical assessment of the evidence," in Drèze and Sen (1991). Vol. III, pp. 155–193.

Swaminathan, M., and S. Sinha (eds.). 1986. *Global Aspects of Food Production.* Riverton, N.J.: Tycooly International.

Timmer. C., W. Falcon, and S. Pearson. 1983. *Food Policy Analysis.* Baltimore: Johns Hopkins University Press.

Tivy, J. 1990. *Agricultural Ecology.* Essex: Longman, Harlow.

United Nations Children's Fund (UNICEF). 1992. *State of the World's Children.* New York: United Nations.

United Nations Population Fund (UNFPA). 1991. *Population and the Environment: The Challenges Ahead.* New York: UNFPA.

_____. 1992. *State of the World's Population.* New York: UNFPA.

United States Department of Agriculture (USDA), Foreign Agriculture Service. 1992. *World Agriculture Production.* Circular Series WAP 11–92 (November).

Vaughan, D., and T. Chang. 1993. "In situ conservation of rice genetic resources," *Economic Botany* 46.

Vitousek, P., et al. 1986. "Human appropriation of the products of photosynthesis," *BioScience* 36, no. 6:368–373.

Walsh, J. 1991. "Preserving the options: Food productivity and sustainability," Consultative Group on International Agricultural Research (CGIAR), Issues in Agriculture no. 2.

Wilson, E. 1989. "Threats to biodiversity," *Scientific American* (September): 108–116.

_____. 1992. *The Diversity of Life.* Cambridge: Harvard University Press.

_____, and F. Peter (eds.). 1988. *Biodiversity.* Washington, D.C.: National Academy Press.

World Bank. 1990. *World Development Report 1990.* New York: Oxford University Press.

_____. 1992. *World Development Report 1992.* New York: Oxford University Press.

World Resources Institute. 1986. *World Resources 1986.* New York: Basic Books.

_____. 1988. *World Resources 1988–89.* New York: Basic Books.

_____. 1992. *World Resources 1992–93.* New York: Oxford University Press.

Worrest, R., and L. Grant. 1989. "Effects of ultraviolet-B radiation on terrestrial plants and marine organisms," in R. Jones and T. Wigley (eds.), *Ozone Depletion: Health and Environmental Consequences.* New York: Wiley, pp. 197–206.

3

Population and Consumption
What We Know,
What We Need to Know

Robert W. Kates

In this selection, Robert Kates explores the relationship between population, technology, and consumption, describing various ways of estimating the environmental degradation stemming from the interaction of these three factors. He discusses debates over how to define consumption and looks at different consumption patterns in the developed and in the developing worlds. He focuses his analysis around an updating of the so-called IPAT formula, an attempt by scientists to link resource impacts (I), population (P), affluence (A), and technology (T). In his conclusions, Kates draws attention to additional factors that we still only dimly understand, particularly the human desire to consume—issues such as satisfaction, satiation, and sublimation.

A member of the National Academy of Sciences, Kates teaches at Brown University; in his research, he addresses long-term population dynamics, global environmental change, and the prevalence and persistence of hunger.

Thirty years ago, as Earth Day dawned, three wise men recognized three proximate causes of environmental degradation yet spent half a decade or more arguing their relative importance. In this classic environmentalist feud between Barry Commoner on one side and Paul Ehrlich and John Holdren on the other, all three recognized that growth in population, affluence, and technology were jointly responsible for environmental problems, but they strongly differed about their relative importance. Commoner asserted that technology and the economic system that produced it were primarily responsible.[1] Ehrlich and Holdren asserted the importance of all three drivers: population, affluence,

From Robert W. Kates, "Population and Consumption: What We Know, What We Need to Know," *Environment* (April 2000), 10, 12–19. © 2000 Robert W. Kates. Reprinted by permission of Robert W. Kates.

and technology. But given Ehrlich's writings on population,[2] the differences were often, albeit incorrectly, described as an argument over whether population or technology was responsible for the environmental crisis.

Now, 30 years later, a general consensus among scientists posits that growth in population, affluence, and technology are jointly responsible for environmental problems. This has become enshrined in a useful, albeit overly simplified, identity known as IPAT, first published by Ehrlich and Holdren in *Environment* in 1972[3] in response to the more limited version by Commoner that had appeared earlier in *Environment* and in his famous book *The Closing Circle*.[4] In this identity, various forms of environmental or resource impacts (I) equals population (P) times affluence (A) (usually income per capita) times the impacts per unit of income as determined by technology (T) and the institutions that use it. Academic debate has now shifted from the greater or lesser importance of each of these driving forces of environmental degradation or resource depletion to debate about their interaction and the ultimate forces that drive them.

However, in the wider global realm, the debate about who or what is responsible for environmental degradation lives on. Today, many Earth Days later, international debates over such major concerns as biodiversity, climate change, or sustainable development address the population and the affluence terms of Holdren's and Ehrlich's identity, specifically focusing on the character of consumption that affluence permits. The concern with technology is more complicated because it is now widely recognized that while technology can be a problem, it can be a solution as well. The development and use of more environmentally benign and friendly technologies in industrialized countries have slowed the growth of many of the most pernicious forms of pollution that originally drew Commoner's attention and still dominate Earth Day concerns.

A recent report from the National Research Council captures one view of the current public debate, and it begins as follows:

> For over two decades, the same frustrating exchange has been repeated countless times in international policy circles. A government official or scientist from a wealthy country would make the following argument: The world is threatened with environmental disaster because of the depletion of natural resources (or climate change or the loss of biodiversity), and it cannot continue for long to support its rapidly growing population. To preserve the environment for future generations, we need to move quickly to control global population growth, and we must concentrate the effort on the world's poorer countries, where the vast majority of population growth is occurring.

Government officials and scientists from low-income countries would typically respond:

If the world is facing environmental disaster, it is not the fault of the poor, who use few resources. The fault must lie with the world's wealthy countries, where people consume the great bulk of the world's natural resources and energy and cause the great bulk of its environmental degradation. We need to curtail overconsumption in the rich countries which use far more than their fair share, both to preserve the environment and to allow the poorest people on Earth to achieve an acceptable standard of living.[5]

It would be helpful, as in all such classic disputes, to begin by laying out what is known about the relative responsibilities of both population and consumption for the environmental crisis, and what might need to be known to address them. However, there is a profound asymmetry that must fuel the frustration of the developing countries' politicians and scientists: namely, how much people know about population and how little they know about consumption. Thus, this article begins by examining these differences in knowledge and action and concludes with the alternative actions needed to go from more to enough in both population and consumption.[6]

Population

What population is and how it grows is well understood even if all the forces driving it are not. Population begins with people and their key events of birth, death, and location. At the margins, there is some debate over when life begins and ends or whether residence is temporary or permanent, but little debate in between. Thus, change in the world's population or any place is the simple arithmetic of adding births, subtracting deaths, adding immigrants, and subtracting outmigrants. While whole subfields of demography are devoted to the arcane details of these additions and subtractions, the error in estimates of population for almost all places is probably within 20 percent and for countries with modern statistical services, under 3 percent—better estimates than for any other living things and for most other environmental concerns.

Current world population is more than six billion people, growing at a rate of 1.3 percent per year. The peak annual growth rate in all history—about 2.1 percent—occurred in the early 1960s, and the peak population increase of around 87 million per year occurred in the late 1980s. About 80 percent or 4.8 billion people live in the less developed areas of the world, with 1.2 billion living in industrialized countries. Population is now projected by the United Nations (UN) to be 8.9 billion in 2050, according to its medium fertility assumption, the one usually considered most likely, or as high as 10.6 billion or as low as 7.3 billion.[7]

A general description of how birth rates and death rates are changing over time is a process called the demographic transition.[8] It was first studied in the context of Europe, where in the space of two centuries, societies went from a condition of high births and high deaths to the current situation of low births and low deaths. In such a transition, deaths decline more rapidly than births, and in that gap, population grows rapidly but eventually stabilizes as the birth decline matches or even exceeds the death decline. Although the general description of the transition is widely accepted, much is debated about its cause and details.

The world is now in the midst of a global transition that, unlike the European transition, is much more rapid. Both births and deaths have dropped faster than experts expected and history foreshadowed. It took 100 years for deaths to drop in Europe compared to the drop in 30 years in the developing world. Three is the current global average of births per woman of reproductive age. This number is more than halfway between the average of five children born to each woman at the post-World War II peak of population growth and the average of 2.1 births required to achieve eventual zero population growth.[9] The death transition is more advanced, with life expectancy currently at 64 years. This represents three-quarters of the transition between a life expectancy of 40 years to one of 75 years. The current rates of decline in births outpace the estimates of the demographers, the UN having reduced its latest medium expectation of global population in 2050 to 8.9 billion, a reduction of almost 10 percent from its projection in 1994.

Demographers debate the causes of this rapid birth decline. But even with such differences, it is possible to break down the projected growth of the next century and to identify policies that would reduce projected populations even further. John Bongaarts of the Population Council has decomposed the projected developing country growth into three parts and, with his colleague Judith Bruce, has envisioned policies that would encourage further and more rapid decline.[10] The first part is unwanted fertility, making available the methods and materials for contraception to the 120 million married women (and the many more unmarried women) in developing countries who in survey research say they either want fewer children or want to space them better. A basic strategy for doing so links voluntary family planning with other reproductive and child health services.

Yet in many parts of the world, the desired number of children is too high for a stabilized population. Bongaarts would reduce this desire for large families by changing the costs and benefits of childrearing so that more parents would recognize the value of smaller families while simultaneously increasing their investment in children. A basic strategy for doing so accelerates three trends that have been shown to lead to lower desired family size: the survival of children, their education, and improvement in the economic, social, and legal status for girls and women.

However, even if fertility could immediately be brought down to the replacement level of two surviving children per woman, population growth would continue for many years in most developing countries because so many more young people of reproductive age exist. So Bongaarts would slow this momentum of population growth by increasing the age of childbearing, primarily by improving secondary education opportunity for girls and by addressing such neglected issues as adolescent sexuality and reproductive behavior.

How much further could population be reduced? Bongaarts provides the outer limits. The population of the developing world (using older projections) was expected to reach 10.2 billion by 2100. In theory, Bongaarts found that meeting the unmet need for contraception could reduce this total by about 2 billion. Bringing down desired family size to replacement fertility would reduce the population a billion more, with the remaining growth—from 4.5 billion today to 7.3 billion in 2100—due to population momentum. In practice, however, a recent U.S. National Academy of Sciences report concluded that a 10 percent reduction is both realistic and attainable and could lead to a lessening in projected population numbers by 2050 of upwards of a billion fewer people.[11]

Consumption

In contrast to population, where people and their births and deaths are relatively well-defined biological events. there is no consensus as to what consumption includes. Paul Stern of the National Research Council has described the different ways physics, economics, ecology, and sociology view consumption.[12] For physicists, matter and energy cannot be consumed, so consumption is conceived as transformations of matter and energy with increased entropy. For economists, consumption is spending on consumer goods and services and thus distinguished from their production and distribution. For ecologists, consumption is obtaining energy and nutrients by eating something else, mostly green plants or other consumers of green plants. And for some sociologists, consumption is a status symbol—keeping up with the Joneses—when individuals and households use their incomes to increase their social status through certain kinds of purchases.

In 1977 the councils of the Royal Society of London and the U.S. National Academy of Sciences issued a joint statement on consumption, having previously done so on population. They chose a variant of the physicist's definition:

> Consumption is the human transformation of materials and energy. Consumption is of concern to the extent that it makes the transformed materials or energy less available for future use, or negatively impacts biophysical systems in such a way as to threaten human health, welfare, or other things people value.[13]

On the one hand, this society/academy view is more holistic and funda-mental than the other definitions; on the other hand, it is more focused, turn-ing attention to the environmentally damaging. This article uses it as a working definition with one modification, *the addition of information to energy and matter, thus completing the triad of the biophysical and ecological basics that support life.*

In contrast to population, only limited data and concepts on the transfor-mation of energy, materials, and information exist.[14] There is relatively good global knowledge of energy transformations due in part to the common units of conversion between different technologies. Between 1950 and today, glo-bal energy production and use increased more than fourfold.[15] For material transformations, there are no aggregate data in common units on a global basis, only for some specific classes of materials including materials for en-ergy production, construction, industrial minerals and metals, agricultural crops, and water.[16] Calculations of material use by volume, mass, or value lead to different trends.

Trend data for per capita use of physical structure materials (construc-tion and industrial minerals, metals, and forestry products) in the United States are relatively complete. They show an inverted S shaped (logistic) growth pattern: modest doubling between 1900 and the depression of the 1930s (from two to four metric tons), followed by a steep quintupling with economic re-covery until the early 1970s (from two to eleven tons), followed by a leveling off since then with fluctuations related to economic downturns.[17] An aggre-gate analysis of all current material production and consumption in the United States averages more than 60 kilos per person per day (excluding water). Most of this material flow is split between energy and related products (38 percent) and minerals for construction (37 percent), with the remainder as industrial minerals (5 percent), metals (2 percent), products of fields (12 per-cent) and forest (5 percent).[18]

A massive effort is under way to catalog biological (genetic) informa-tion and to sequence the genomes of microbes, worms, plants, mice, and people. In contrast to the molecular detail, the number and diversity of or-ganisms is unknown, but a conservative estimate places the number of spe-cies on the order of 10 million, of which only one-tenth have been described.[19] Although there is much interest and many anecdotes, neither concepts nor data are available on most cultural information. For example, the number of languages in the world continues to decline while the number of messages expands exponentially.

Trends and projections in agriculture, energy, and economy can serve as surrogates for more detailed data on energy and material transformation.[20] From 1950 to the early 1990s, world population more than doubled (2.2 times), food as measured by grain production almost tripled (2.7 times), energy more than quadrupled (4.4 times), and the economy quintupled (5.1 times). This

43-year record is similar to a current 55-year projection (1995–2050) that assumes the continuation of current trends or, as some would note, "business as usual." In this 55-year projection, growth in half again of population (1.6 times) finds almost a doubling of agriculture (1.8 times), more than twice as much energy used (2.4 times), and a quadrupling of the economy (4.3 times).[21]

Thus, both history and future scenarios predict growth rates of consumption well beyond population. An attractive similarity exists between a demographic transition that moves over time from high births and high deaths to low births and low deaths with an energy, materials, and information transition. In this transition, societies will use increasing amounts of energy and materials as consumption increases, but over time the energy and materials input per unit of consumption decrease and information substitutes for more material and energy inputs.

Some encouraging signs surface for such a transition in both energy and materials, and these have been variously labeled as decarbonization and dematerialization.[22] For more than a century, the amount of carbon per unit of energy produced has been decreasing. Over a shorter period, the amount of energy used to produce a unit of production has also steadily declined. There is also evidence for dematerialization, using fewer materials for a unit of production, but only for industrialized countries and for some specific materials. Overall, improvements in technology and substitution of information for energy and materials will continue to increase energy efficiency (including decarbonization) and dematerialization per unit of product or service. Thus, over time, less energy and materials will be needed to make specific things. At the same time, the demand for products and services continues to increase, and the overall consumption of energy and most materials more than offsets these efficiency and productivity gains.

What to Do about Consumption

While quantitative analysis of consumption is just beginning, three questions suggest a direction for reducing environmentally damaging and resource-depleting consumption. The first asks: *When is more too much for the life-support systems of the natural world and the social infrastructure of human society?* Not all the projected growth in consumption may be resource-depleting—"less available for future use"—or environmentally damaging in a way that "negatively impacts biophysical systems to threaten human health, welfare, or other things people value."[23] Yet almost any human-induced transformations turn out to be either or both resource-depleting or damaging to some valued environmental component. For example, a few years ago, a series of eight energy controversies in Maine were related to coal, nuclear, natural gas, hydroelectric, biomass, and wind generating sources, as well as to various energy policies. In all the controversies, competing sides, often more than two, emphasized environmental benefits to support their choice and attributed environmental damage to the other alternatives.

Despite this complexity, it is possible to rank energy sources by the varied and multiple risks they pose and, for those concerned, to choose which risks they wish to minimize and which they are more willing to accept. There is now almost 30 years of experience with the theory and methods of risk assessment and 10 years of experience with the identification and setting of environmental priorities. While there is still no readily accepted methodology for separating resource-depleting or environmentally damaging consumption from general consumption or for identifying harmful transformations from those that are benign, one can separate consumption into more or less damaging and depleting classes and *shift* consumption to the less harmful class. It is possible to *substitute* less damaging and depleting energy and materials for more damaging ones. There is growing experience with encouraging substitution and its difficulties: renewables for nonrenewables, toxics with fewer toxics, ozone-depleting chemicals for more benign substitutes, natural gas for coal, and so forth.

The second question, *Can we do more with less?*, addresses the supply side of consumption. Beyond substitution, shrinking the energy and material transformations required per unit of consumption is probably the most effective current means for reducing environmentally damaging consumption. In the 1997 book, *Stuff: The Secret Lives of Everyday Things,* John Ryan and Alan Durning of Northwest Environment Watch trace the complex origins, materials, production, and transport of such everyday things as coffee, newspapers, cars, and computers and highlight the complexity of reengineering such products and reorganizing their production and distribution.[24]

Yet there is growing experience with the three Rs of consumption shrinkage: reduce, recycle, reuse. These have now been strengthened by a growing science, technology, and practice of industrial ecology that seeks to learn from nature's ecology to reuse everything. These efforts will only increase the existing favorable trends in the efficiency of energy and material usage. Such a potential led the Intergovernmental Panel on Climate Change to conclude that it was possible, using current best practice technology, to reduce energy use by 30 percent in the short run and 50–60 percent in the long run.[25] Perhaps most important in the long run, but possibly least studied, is the potential for and value of substituting information for energy and materials. Energy and materials per unit of consumption are going down, in part because more and more consumption consists of information.

The third question addresses the demand side of consumption: *When is more enough?* [26] Is it possible to reduce consumption by more satisfaction with what people already have, by *satiation,* no more needing more because there is enough, and by *sublimation,* having more satisfaction with less to achieve some greater good? This is the least explored area of consumption and the most difficult. There are, of course, many signs of *satiation* for some goods. For example, people in the industrialized world no longer buy additional refrigerators (except in newly formed households) but only replace them. Moreover, the quality of refrigerators has so improved that a 20-year or more life span is commonplace. The financial pages include frequent stories of the plight of this industry or corporation whose markets are saturated and whose products no longer show the annual growth equated with profits and progress. Such enterprises are frequently viewed as failures of marketing or entrepreneurship rather than successes in meeting human needs sufficiently and efficiently. Is it possible to reverse such views, to create a standard of satiation, a satisfaction in a need well met?

Can people have more satisfaction with what they already have by using it more intensely and having the time to do so? Economist Juliet Schor tells of some overworked Americans who would willingly exchange time for money, time to spend with family and using what they already have, but who are constrained by an uncooperative employment structure.[27] Proposed U.S. legislation would permit the trading of overtime for such compensatory time off, a step in this direction. *Sublimation,* according to the dictionary, is the diversion of energy from an immediate goal to a higher social, moral, or aesthetic purpose. Can people be more satisfied with less satisfaction derived from the diversion of immediate consumption for the satisfaction of a smaller ecological footprint?[28] An emergent research field grapples with how to encourage consumer behavior that will lead to change in environmentally damaging consumption.[29]

A small but growing "simplicity" movement tries to fashion new images of "living the good life."[30] Such movements may never much reduce the burdens of consumption, but they facilitate by example and experiment other less-demanding alternatives. Peter Menzel's remarkable photo essay of the material goods of some 30 households from around the world is powerful testimony to the great variety and inequality of possessions amidst the existence of alternative lifestyles.[31] Can a standard of "more is enough" be linked to an ethic of "enough for all"? One of the great discoveries of childhood is that eating lunch does not feed the starving children of some far-off place. But increasingly, in sharing the global commons, people flirt with mechanisms that hint at such—a rationing system for the remaining chlorofluorocarbons, trading systems for reducing emissions, rewards for preserving species, or allowances for using available resources.

A recent compilation of essays, *Consuming Desires: Consumption, Culture, and the Pursuit of Happiness,*[32] explores many of these essential issues. These elegant essays by 14 well-known writers and academics ask the fundamental question of why more never seems to be enough and why satiation and sublimation are so difficult in a culture of consumption. Indeed, how is the culture of consumption different for mainstream America, women, inner-city children, South Asian immigrants, or newly industrializing countries?

Why We Know and Don't Know

In an imagined dialog between rich and poor countries, with each side listening carefully to the other, they might ask themselves just what they actually know about population and consumption. Struck with the asymmetry described above, they might then ask: "Why do we know so much more about population than consumption?"

The answer would be that population is simpler, easier to study, and a consensus exists about terms, trends, even policies. Consumption is harder, with no consensus as to what it is, and with few studies except in the fields of marketing and advertising. But the consensus that exists about population comes from substantial research and study, much of it funded by governments and groups in rich countries, whose asymmetric concern readily identifies the troubling fertility behavior of others and only reluctantly considers their own consumption behavior. So while consumption is harder, it is surely studied less.

A Comparison of Population and Consumption	
Population	**Consumption**
Simpler, easier to study	More complex
Well-funded research	Unfunded, except marketing
Consensus terms, trends	Uncertain terms, trends
Consensus policies	Threatening policies
SOURCE: Robert W. Kates	

The asymmetry of concern is not very flattering to people in developing countries. Anglo-Saxon tradition has a long history of dominant thought holding the poor responsible for their condition—they have too many children—and an even longer tradition of urban civilization feeling besieged by the barbarians at their gates. But whatever the origins of the asymmetry, its persistence does no one a service. Indeed, the stylized debate of population versus consumption reflects neither popular understanding nor scientific insight. Yet lurking somewhere beneath the surface concerns lies a deeper fear.

Consumption is more threatening, and despite the North-South rhetoric, it is threatening to all. In both rich and poor countries alike, making and selling things to each other, including unnecessary things, is the essence of the economic system. No longer challenged by socialism, global capitalism seems inherently based on growth—growth of both consumers and their consumption. To study consumption in this light is to risk concluding that a transition to sustainability might require profound changes in the making and selling of things and in the opportunities that this provides. To draw such conclusions, in the absence of convincing alternative visions, is fearful and to be avoided.

What We Need to Know and Do

In conclusion, returning to the 30-year-old IPAT identity—a variant of which might be called the Population/Consumption (PC) version—and restating that identity in terms of population and consumption, it would be: $I = P*C/P*I/C$, where I equals environmental degradation and/or resource depletion; P equals the number of people or households; and C equals the transformation of energy, materials, and information.

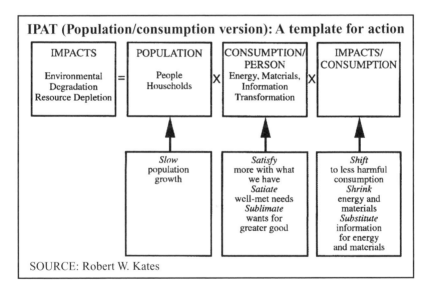

IPAT (Population/consumption version): A template for action

IMPACTS	POPULATION	CONSUMPTION/ PERSON	IMPACTS/ CONSUMPTION
Environmental Degradation Resource Depletion	= People Households	X Energy, Materials, Information Transformation	X
	Slow population growth	*Satisfy* more with what we have *Satiate* well-met needs *Sublimate* wants for greater good	*Shift* to less harmful consumption *Shrink* energy and materials *Substitute* information for energy and materials

SOURCE: Robert W. Kates

With such an identity as a template, and with the goal of reducing environmentally degrading and resource-depleting influences, there are at least seven major directions for research and policy. To reduce the level of impacts per unit of consumption, it is necessary to separate out more damaging consumption and *shift* to less harmful forms, *shrink* the amounts of environmentally damaging energy and materials per unit of consumption, and *substitute* information for energy and materials. To reduce consumption per person or household, it is necessary to *satisfy* more with what is already had, *satiate* well-met consumption needs, and *sublimate* wants for a greater good. Finally, it is possible to *slow* population growth and then to *stabilize* population numbers as indicated above.

However, as with all versions of the IPAT identity, population and consumption in the PC version are only proximate driving forces, and the ultimate forces that drive consumption, the consuming desires, are poorly understood, as are many of the major interventions needed to reduce these proximate driving forces. People know most about slowing population growth, more about shrinking and substituting environmentally damaging consumption, much about shifting to less damaging consumption, and least about satisfaction, satiation, and sublimation. Thus the determinants of consumption and its alternative patterns have been identified as a key understudied topic for an emerging sustainability science by the recent U.S. National Academy of Sciences study.[33]

But people and society do not need to know more in order to act. They can readily begin to separate out the most serious problems of consumption, shrink its energy and material throughputs, substitute information for energy and materials, create a standard for satiation, sublimate the possession of things for that of the global commons, as well as slow and stabilize population. To go from more to enough is more than enough to do for 30 more Earth Days.

Notes

1. B. Commoner, M. Corr, and P. Stamler, "The Causes of Pollution," *Environment,* April 1971, 2–19.

2. P. Ehrlich, *The Population Bomb* (New York: Ballantine, 1966).

3. P. Ehrlich and J. Holdren, "Review of the Closing Circle," *Environment,* April 1972, 24–39.

4. B. Commoner, *The Closing Circle* (New York: Knopf, 1971).

5. P. Stern, T. Dietz, V. Ruttan, R. H. Socolow, and J. L. Sweeney, eds., *Environmentally Significant Consumption: Research Direction* (Washington, D.C.: National Academy Press, 1997), 1.

6. This article draws in part upon a presentation for the 1997 De Lange-Woodlands Conference, an expanded version of which will appear as: R. W. Kates, "Population and Consumption: From More to Enough," in *In Sustainable Development: The Challenge of Transition,* J. Schmandt and C.H. Wards, eds. (Cambridge, U.K.: Cambridge University Press, 2000), 79–99.

7. United Nations, Population Division, *World Population Prospects. The 1998 Revision* (New York: United Nations, 1999).

8. K. Davis, "Population and Resources: Fact and Interpretation," K. Davis and M. S. Bernstam, eds., in *Resources, Environment and Population: Present Knowledge, Future Options,* supplement to *Population and Development Review,* 1990: 1–21.

9. Population Reference Bureau, *1997 World Population Data Sheet of the Population Reference Bureau* (Washington, D.C.: Population Reference Bureau, 1997).

10. J. Bongaarts, "Population Policy Options in the Developing World," *Science,* 263: (1994), 771–776; and J. Bongaarts and J. Bruce, "What Can Be Done to Address Population Growth?" (unpublished background paper for The Rockefeller Foundation, 1997).

11. National Research Council, Board on Sustainable Development, *Our Common Journey: A Transition Toward Sustainability* (Washington, D.C.: National Academy Press, 1999).

12. See Stern et al., note 5 above.

13. Royal Society of London and the U.S. National Academy of Sciences, "Towards Sustainable Consumption," reprinted in *Population and Development Review,* 1977, 23 (3): 683–686.

14. For the available data and concepts, I have drawn heavily from J. H. Ausubel and H. D. Langford, eds., *Technological Trajectories and the Human Environment* (Washington, D.C.: National Academy Press, 1997).

15. L. R. Brown, H. Kane, and D. M. Roodman, *Vital Signs, 1994: The Trends That Are Shaping Our Future* (New York: W. W. Norton and Co., 1994).

16. World Resources Institute, United Nations Environment Programme, United Nations Development Programme, World Bank, *World Resources, 1996–97* (New York: Oxford University Press, 1996); and A Gruebler, *Technology and Global Change* (Cambridge, Mass.: Cambridge University Press, 1998).

17. I. Wernick, "Consuming Materials: The American Way," *Technological Forecasting and Social Change,* 53 (1996): 111–122.

18. I. Wernick and J. H. Ausubel, "National Materials Flow and the Environment," *Annual Review of Energy and Environment,* 20 (1995): 463–492.

19. S. Pimm, G. Russell, J. Gittelman, and T Brooks, "The Future of Biodiversity," *Science,* 269 (1995): 347–350.

20. Historic data from L. R. Brown, H. Kane, and D. M. Roodman, note 15 above.

21. One of several projections from P. Raskin, G. Gallopin, P. Gutman, A. Hammond, and R. Swart, *Bending the Curve: Toward Global Sustainability,* a report of the Global Scenario Group, Polestar Series, report no. 8 (Boston: Stockholm Environmental Institute, 1995).

22. N. Nakicénovíc, "Freeing Energy from Carbon," in *Technological Trajectories and the Human Environment,* ed. J. H. Ausubel and H. D. Langford (Washington, D.C.: National Academy Press, 1997); I. Wernick, R. Herman, S. Govind, and J. H. Ausubel, "Materialization and Dematerialization: Measures and Trends," in J. H. Ausubel and H. D. Langford, eds., *Technological Trajectories and the Human Environment* (Washington, D.C.: National Academy Press, 1997), 135–156; and see A. Gruebler, note 16 above.

23. Royal Society of London and the U.S. National Academy of Sciences, note 13 above.

24. J. Ryan and A. Durning, *Stuff: The Secret Lives of Everyday Things* (Seattle, Wash.: Northwest Environment Watch, 1997).

25. R. T. Watson, M. C. Zinyowera, and R. H. Moss, eds., *Climate Change, 1995: Impacts, Adaptations, and Mitigation of Climate Change—Scientific-Technical Analyses* (Cambridge, U.K.: Cambridge University Press, 1996).

26. A sampling of similar queries includes: A. Durning, *How Much Is Enough?* (New York: W. W. Norton and Co., 1992); Center for a New American Dream, *Enough! A Quarterly Report on Consumption, Quality of Life and the Environment* (Burlington, Vt., The Center for a New American Dream, 1997); and N. Myers, "Consumption in Relation to Population, Environment, and Development," *The Environmentalist,* 17 (1997): 33–44.

27. J. Schor, *The Overworked American* (New York: Basic Books, 1991).

28. A. Durning, *How Much Is Enough? The Consumer Society and the Future of the Earth* (New York: W. W. Norton and Co., 1992); Center for a New American Dream, note 26 above; and M. Wackernagel and W. Ress, *Our Ecological Footprint: Reducing Human Impact on the Earth* (Philadelphia, Pa.: New Society Publishers, 1996).

29. W. Jager, M. van Asselt, J. Rotmans, C. Vlek, and P. Costerman Boodt, *Consumer Behavior: A Modeling Perspective in the Context of Integrated Assessment of Global Change,* RIVM report no. 461502017 (Bilthoven, the Netherlands: National Institute for Public Health and the Environment, 1997); and P. Vellinga, S. de Bryn, R. Heintz, and P. Mulder, eds., *Industrial Transformation: An Inventory of Research,* IHDP-IT no. 8 (Amsterdam, the Netherlands: Institute for Environmental Studies, 1997).

30. H. Nearing and S. Nearing, *The Good Life: Helen and Scott Nearing's Sixty Years of Self-Sufficient Living* (New York: Schocken, 1990); and D. Elgin, *Voluntary Simplicity: Toward a Way of Life That Is Outwardly Simple, Inwardly Rich* (New York: William Morrow, 1993).

31. P. Menzel, *Material World: A Global Family Portrait* (San Francisco: Sierra Club Books, 1994).

32. R. Rosenblatt, ed., *Consuming Desires: Consumption, Culture, and the Pursuit of Happiness* (Washington, D.C.: Island Press, 1999).

33. National Research Council, Board on Sustainable Development, *Our Common Journey: A Transition Toward Sustainability* (Washington, D.C.: National Academy Press, 1999).

4

Water for Food Production
Will There Be Enough in 2025?

Sandra L. Postel

Water is essential for almost all life on the planet, including human life—we can thus think of it as the first resource. For the 10 billion humans who will populate the globe at midcentury, perhaps the most important use of water will be in producing crops for food. Yet, as Sandra Postel shows in this chapter, freshwater resources are already being overexploited in practically all regions of the world. Because agriculture uses 1,000 pounds of water to irrigate each 1,000 pounds of grain, the issues of food production and food security are intimately tied to freshwater management. The eating of red meat, a practice frequently associated with a modern lifestyle, has significant implications for freshwater use. Each pound of beef, for example, requires eight pounds of grain to produce, and thus one pound of beef represents 1,000 gallons of water used to irrigate the grain to feed the cow.

Postel is director of the Global Water Policy Project in Amherst, Massachusetts, where her research focuses on international water issues and strategies.

This year marks the 200th anniversary of the publication of Thomas Malthus's famous essay postulating that human population growth would outstrip the earth's food-producing capabilities. His writing sparked a debate that has waxed and waned over the last two centuries but has never disappeared completely. Stated simply, Malthus's proposition was that because population grows exponentially while food supplies expand linearly, the former would eventually outpace the latter. He predicted that hunger, disease, and famine would result, leading to higher death rates.

From Sandra L. Postel, "Water for Food Production: Will There Be Enough in 2025?" *BioScience* 48, no. 8 (August 1998): 629–35. © 1998 American Institute of Biological Sciences. Reprinted by permission of *BioScience*.

One of the missing pieces in Malthus's analysis was the power of science and technology to boost land productivity and thereby push back the limits imposed by a finite amount of cropland. It was only in the twentieth century that scientific research led to marked increases in agricultural productivity. Major advances, such as the large-scale production of nitrogen fertilizers and the breeding of high-yielding wheat and rice varieties, have boosted crop yields and enabled food production to rise along with the world population (Dyson 1996). Between 1950 and 1995, human numbers increased by 122% (U.S. Bureau of the Census 1996), while the area planted in grain expanded by only 17% (USDA 1996, 1997c). It was a 141% increase in grainland productivity, supplemented with greater fish harvests and larger livestock herds, that allowed food supplies to keep pace with population and diets for a significant portion of humanity to improve.

Despite this remarkable success, concern about future food prospects has risen in recent years because of a marked slowdown in the growth of world grain yields, combined with an anticipated doubling of global food demand between 1995 and 2025 (McCalla 1994, FAO 1996b). Whereas annual grain yields (expressed as three-year averages) rose 2–2.5% per year during every decade since 1950, they registered growth of only 0.7% per year during the first half of the 1990s (Brown 1997, USDA 1997a, 1997b). Excluding the former Soviet Union, where the political breakup and economic reforms led to large drops in productivity, global grain yields increased an average of 1.1% per year from 1990 to 1995, approximately one-half the rate of the previous four decades (Brown 1997). Today, the principal difference between those analysts projecting adequate food supplies in 2025 and those anticipating significant shortfalls is the assumed level of productivity growth—specifically, whether annual productivity over the next three decades is likely to grow at closer to the 1% rate of the 1990s or the 2–2.5% rate of the previous four decades.

Water—along with climate, soil fertility, the choice of crops grown, and the genetic potential of those crops—is a key determinant of land productivity. Adequate moisture in the root zone of crops is essential to achieving both maximum yield and production stability from season to season. A growing body of evidence suggests that lack of water is already constraining agricultural output in many parts of the world (Postel 1996, UNCSD 1997). Yet, to date, I am aware of no global food assessment that systematically addresses how much water will be required to produce the food supplies of 2025 and whether that water will be available where and when it is needed. As a result, the nature and severity of water constraints remain ill defined, which, in turn, is hampering the development of appropriate water and agricultural strategies.

In this article, I estimate the volume of water currently consumed in producing the world's food, how much additional water it will take to satisfy new food demands in 2025, and how much of this water will likely need to come from irrigation. I then place this expected irrigation demand in the context of global and regional water availability and trends. Finally, I discuss the policy and investment implications that emerge from the analysis.

Table 1. Estimated water consumption by crops worldwide, 1995.[a]

Crop	Global production (x 1000 t)	Water-use efficiency of harvested yield[b] (kg/m^3)	Estimated water requirement (km^3/yr)
Wheat	541,120	0.8–1.0	601
Rice	550,193[c]	0.7–1.1	611
Maize	514,506	0.8–1.6	429
Other grains	290,236	~ 0.6–1.2	323
Roots and tubers	609,488	~ 4.0–7.0	111
Pulses	55,997	~ 0.2–0.6	140
Soybeans	125,930	0.4–0.7	229
Other oilseeds	125,749	~ 0.2–0.6	314
Ground nuts	27,990	0.6–0.8	40
Vegetables and melons[d]	487,287	~ 10.0	49
Fruits (except melons)[d]	396,873	~ 3.5	113
Sugar cane[e]	1,147,992	5.0–8.0	177
Sugar beets[e]	265,963	6.0–9.0	36
Tobacco	6,447	0.4–0.6	13
Other[f]			21
Total			3207

[a]Data from FAO (1996a) and Doorenbos and Kassam (1979).

[b]The midpoints of these ranges are used to calculate the crop water requirement. Water-use efficiency values were not available for all crops, so where necessary I have attempted to make a reasonable assumption based on available information; these assumed values are denoted by a tilde (~).

[c]Rough rice; to calculate milled-rice production, multiply by 0.7.

[d]Statistics on fruit and vegetable production in many countries are unavailable, and much of the reported data excludes production from small household and community gardens, which can be substantial in some countries. The United Nations Food and Agriculture Organization (FAO 1996a) has attempted to estimate total production of fruits and vegetables but does not break down these estimates by crop type. Thus, I have applied a reasonable water-use efficiency value based on known values for crops in these categories. Nevertheless, the margin of error for the estimated water requirements of fruits and vegetables is larger than that for the other crops.

[e]Values are for production of cane and beets, not for the raw sugar derived from them; per unit of sugar, beets are significantly more water efficient than cane.

[f]Coconuts, olives, tree nuts, coffee, cocoa beans, tea, and hops; the water requirements for these crops are little better than informed guesses, but this high margin of error does not significantly affect the global total.

Total Water Consumed in Food Production

The volume of water consumed in producing current food supplies is much larger than estimates of agricultural water use typically suggest. These estimates have focused almost exclusively on the volume of water removed from rivers, lakes, and underground aquifers for irrigation. They typically neglect the soil moisture derived directly from rainfall that is consumed by agricultural cropping systems, pastures, and grazing lands. This omission is perhaps understandable, given that such rainfed lands do not require investments in dams, canals, and other water infrastructure and do not figure into projected demands on regional water supplies. Yet it results in an incomplete and misleading picture of the volume of water actually used to produce the world's food—and, by extension, of future water requirements for food production.

Water Consumed by Crops and Croplands

In general, there is a linear relationship between a crop's water consumption and its dry matter yield up to the point at which water is no longer limiting (Sinclair et al. 1984). The amount of dry matter produced per unit of water transpired—which is known variously as a crop's water-use efficiency or transpiration ratio—is the slope of this linear relationship, and it varies by crop, climate, and other factors. For example, climatic and other conditions being equal, C_4 crops, such as maize, tend to use water more efficiently than other grains because of their special anatomical and biochemical characteristics. A crop grown in a drier climate will transpire faster than the same crop grown in a more humid climate because of the larger vapor pressure gradient between the plant's stomata and the atmosphere. Thus, the volume of water a given crop uses will vary by crop type, climate, season, and other factors, but the basic linear relationship between dry matter production and transpiration generally holds for all crops and growing environments (Kramer and Boyer 1995).

In determining the amount of water consumed in producing the global food supply, several additional factors must be taken into account. Water is consumed not only through transpiration but also through evaporation from the soil and leaf surfaces. Under field conditions, evaporation is difficult to measure separately from transpiration, so the processes are typically referred to jointly as evapotranspiration. In addition, because only the edible portion of a crop contributes to food supplies, the portion of a crop's dry matter that is actually harvested (known as the harvest index) must also be taken into account. The water-use efficiency of the harvested yield is expressed as the harvested crop yield per unit of water evapotranspired and is often denoted by Ey. These values are shown in Table 1, along with the total 1995 production of each crop or crop category. Lacking detailed regional data, the estimated global crop water requirements shown in Table 1 were derived by multiplying the inverse of the midpoint of the Ey value for each crop or crop category by the 1995 global production of that crop. This calculation results in an estimated minimum water requirement for the 1995 global harvest of crops of approximately 3200 km³ (3200 billion cubic meters).

Not surprisingly, wheat, rice, maize, and other grains—the staples of the human diet and also sources of feed for livestock—account for more than 60% of the total crop evapotranspiration requirement. Soybeans and other oilseed crops account for 17% of this requirement, and sugar cane alone accounts for approximately 6%. It is important to emphasize that the values in Table 1 do not reflect how much water is *actually* consumed in crop production but rather the *minimum required* for that production. Inefficiencies in irrigation that result in evaporative losses, for example, are not taken into account; I address such additional consumptive uses of water in a later section.

The plants from which the world's food commodities are harvested represent only a portion of total cropland biomass. The net photosynthetic product of the world's croplands has been estimated at 15×10^9 t/yr (Ajtay et al. 1979, Vitousek et al. 1986). Assuming that an average of 2 g biomass is produced per 1 L of water evapotranspired (Monteith 1990, Postel et al. 1996), a total of 7500 km³ would be consumed through evapotranspiration in cropland ecosystems—more than twice the estimated evapotranspiration of the crop plants themselves (Table 2). Because crop production depends on the productivity of the supporting ecosystem, this higher figure may more accurately reflect the total amount of water consumed through evapotranspiration on the world's croplands.

Water Consumed by Converted Pasture and Grazing Land

The world's domesticated animals—including 1.3 billion cattle, 900 million pigs, and more than 12 billion chickens (FAO 1996a)—contribute meat, milk, eggs, and other items to the human diet. Of the 2700 kilocalories available per capita per day on average worldwide (FAO 1995b), approximately 16% comes from animal products. However, this share varies greatly by country and region: For example, 32% of the estimated 3410 calories per capita per day available in Europe comes from animal products, compared with just 7% of the average 2282 kilocalories per capita per day available in Africa (FAO 1995a).

Livestock variously eat grass, hay, feed grain, and food waste. Although the feed grain and food waste are included in the crop production figures in Table 1, a separate calculation needs to be made to account for evapotranspiration on converted pasture and grazing land. Again, assuming an average biomass production rate of 2 g/L of water, the estimated water consumption occurring on pasture- and rangeland totals 5800 km³/yr (Table 2; Vitousek et al. 1986, Postel et al. 1996).

Non-beneficial Evapotranspiration of Irrigation Water and from Aquaculture Ponds

Irrigated lands—those receiving artificial water applications to supplement natural rainfall—totaled 249.5 x 10⁶ ha in 1994, the most recent year for which data are available (FAO 1996a). Because irrigation makes possible more than one harvest a year on the same parcel of land and allows farmers greater control over the watering of their crops, these lands are dispropor- tionately important in global food production; they represent just 17% of the world's total cropland area but yield on the order of 40% of the world's food (Rangeley 1987, Yudelman 1994).

Table 2. Total water consumed in food production, 1995.[a]

Activity	Estimated water consumption (km³/yr)
Water consumed directly by crops and associated cropland biomass	7500
Water consumed by converted pasture and natural grazing land used by livestock	5800
Non-beneficial evapotranspiration of irrigation water[b]	500
Water consumed in aquaculture production	0[c]
Total	13,800

[a]Calculations based on information in Doorenbos and Kassam (1979), FAO (1996a), Postel et al. (1996).
[b]See text for explanation.
[c]Negligible on a global basis.

Shiklomanov (1996) estimated that in 1995 a total of approximately 2500 km³ was withdrawn from rivers, lakes, and aquifers for irrigation. However, a portion of this water never benefits a crop. Some of it is lost to evapotranspi- ration as the water is stored in ponds or reservoirs, transported by canals, and applied to farmers' fields. Water percolating into the soil through unlined canals or running off the end of a farmer's field also represents inefficiency and can degrade both land and water quality. But because this water is not evapotranspired, it is theoretically available to be used again and so is not counted as a loss. No good global estimate of non-beneficial irrigation water losses exists, but they may amount to approximately 20% of the volume with- drawn (Perry 1996). Applying this figure to the 1995 estimate of irrigation withdrawals suggests unproductive evapotranspiration losses of 500 km³, as shown in Table 2.

Water also evaporates from ponds used in fish farming, an increasing source of protein worldwide. These evaporation losses are difficult to estimate because aquaculture production can occur in coastal bays or estuaries, indoor tanks, or artificial ponds. Currently, evaporation from ponds is negligible relative to the total water consumed in food production. Yet fish farming is growing rapidly: Aquaculture production tripled between 1984 and 1995, from 7 x 10^6 t/yr to 21 x 10^6 t/yr, and in 1995 it accounted for 19% of the global fish harvest (McGinn 1997). As aquaculture expands, pond evaporation will increase and may factor significantly into the water budgets of water-short areas.

Summing the estimated volumes of water consumed by cropping systems, grasslands and pasture, and non-beneficial evaporation of irrigation supplies yields an estimate of total water consumption for food production in 1995 of 13,800 km^3/yr—or nearly 20% of the total annual evapotranspiration occurring on the earth's land surface. For the 1995 population of 5.7 billion (PRB 1995), this global total translates to an annual average of approximately 2420 m^3 per capita.

Changing Structure of Global Food Sources

The structure and sources of the global food supply in 2025 will not be simply an extrapolation of past trends. Serious constraints exist on the expansion of grazing land, fisheries, and cropland, which suggests that most of the additional food required in the future will need to come from higher productivity on existing cropland. This shift has important implications for the volume and sources of water that will be required to satisfy future food needs.

Rangeland Constraints

According to a global assessment of soil degradation (Oldeman et al. 1991), over-grazing has degraded some 680 x 10^6 ha of the world's rangelands since midcentury. This finding suggests that 20% of the world's pasture and range is losing productivity and will continue to do so unless herd sizes are reduced or more sustainable livestock practices are put into place. With the global ruminant livestock herd, now numbering about 3.3 billion, unlikely to increase appreciably, most of the increase in meat production will need to come from grain-fed livestock.

Fisheries Constraints

The wild fish catch from marine and inland waters totaled 91 x 10^6t in 1995, little more than in the late 1980s. On a per capita basis, the 1995 global fish catch was down nearly 8% from the 1988 peak (McGinn 1997). With the

United Nations Food and Agriculture Organization (FAO 1993) reporting that all 17 of the world's major fishing areas have either reached or exceeded their natural limits, no growth can be expected in the oceanic catch. Aquaculture, the most rapidly growing source of fish, now accounts for one of every five fish consumed, a share that is expected to increase (McGinn 1997). Although fish is a more water-efficient source of animal protein than virtually any other grain-fed source, the expansion of aquaculture will increase pressures on both cropland and water supplies in the future.

Cropland Constraints

With production from both rangelands and fisheries reaching natural limits, most of the increased food supply in 2025 will need to come from cropland. However, on a net basis, cropland area is unlikely to increase appreciably. As much as 10^7 ha may be lost each year due to erosion, other forms of degradation, or conversion to nonfarm uses (Leach 1995, Pimentel et al. 1995). Because such losses are often not fully counted in official statistics—which show that cropland expanded an average of 1.6×10^6 ha/yr between 1979 and 1994 (FAO 1996a)—net cropland expansion could well be close to zero or even negative. Moreover, possibilities for opening up new cropland are mostly in areas in which the long-term crop production potential is relatively low and the biodiversity and other ecological costs are very high, such as in Brazil and central Africa.

Implications for Future Water Requirements

By definition, the water requirements of rain-fed crops are met by rainfall, which is supplied freely by nature and rarely counted in estimates of global agricultural water use. With net cropland area unlikely to expand much if at all, the potential for increased use of direct rainfall to meet crop evapotranspiration requirements is limited largely to improving the productivity of rainwater on existing croplands, both irrigated and rain-fed. Terracing, mulching, contour bunding (placing stones or vegetation along contours), and other methods of capturing rainwater to enhance soil moisture have proven effective at increasing yields of rain-fed crops (Unger and Stewart 1983, Critchley 1991, Reij 1991). Rain-fed production may also benefit from greater focus on boosting total crop output from the land—for example, through agroforestry and synergistic intercropping—as opposed to boosting the yields of single crops.

Globally, the volume of water available for crop evapotranspiration will need to roughly double by 2025 if total crop production is to double. Although actual crop water requirements in 2025 will depend on the crop mix, the climate under which crops are grown, changes in the harvest index, and other factors, a doubling is a reasonable assumption. Because net cropland area is likely to expand minimally if at all, I assume no increase in the water use of related cropland biomass and focus on the direct evapotranspiration requirements of crops, an estimated 6400 km^3 in 2025.

How this additional water for crop evapotranspiration will be partitioned between rainfall and irrigation is impossible to project, especially given that the current partitioning of the crop water supply can be approximated only roughly. However, if 40% of the global harvest currently comes from irrigated land and if, on average, 70% of the soil moisture on this irrigated land comes from irrigation water (the other 30% comes directly from rainfall), then irrigation water would account for about 900 km^3 of the 3200 km^3 required for crop evapotranspiration in 1995; the other 2300 km^3 would have been supplied directly from rainfall (Table 3). It seems reasonable to assume that modest cropland expansion and enhanced rainwater productivity might allow productive use of rainfall for crop evapotranspiration to increase by 50% between 1995 and 2025. To satisfy the global crop water requirement in 2025, the volume of irrigation water consumed by crops would thus need to more than triple—from an estimated 900 km^3 in 1995 to 2950 km^3—and irrigation's share of total crop water consumption would rise from 28% to 46%. The volume of irrigation water annually available to crops as soil moisture would need to expand by 2050 km^3—equivalent to the annual flow of 24 Nile Rivers or 110 Colorado Rivers.

Table 3. Estimated 1995 crop consumption of rainwater and irrigation water and projections for 2025.

Year	Projected global crop evapo-transpiration requirement (km^3/yr)	Supply directly from rainfall (km^3/yr)	Supply from irrigation (km^3/yr)	Irrigation share of global crop evapo-transpiration requirement (%)
1995	3200	2300	900	28
2025	6400	3450	2950	46
Increase	100%	50%	227%	

Prospects for Supplying the Needed Irrigation Water

Current trends in water use and availability strongly suggest that supplying an *additional* 2050 km^3 per year for consumptive agricultural use on a sustainable basis will be extremely difficult. A variety of trends and indicators signal that water constraints on agriculture are already emerging, both globally and regionally.

The Global Demand-Supply Outlook

Of the 40,700 km^3 that run to the sea each year in rivers and aquifers, only an estimated 12,500 km^3 are actually accessible for human use, of which human activities already appropriate an estimated 54% (Postel et al. 1996). By 2025, water withdrawals for irrigation could approach 4600 km^3/yr, assuming 3500 km^3/yr of consumptive use (both beneficial and non-beneficial) and somewhat higher irrigation efficiency than at present. In addition, estimates by the Russian hydrologist Igor Shiklomanov (1993) suggest that worldwide household, municipal, and industrial water uses currently average approximately 240 m^3/yr per capita. Greater use of more efficient household and industrial technologies could reduce this per capita requirement substantially (Postel 1992), but the resulting savings would be partially offset by the water needed to meet minimum drinking and household requirements of the more than 1 billion people now lacking them (Gleick 1996).

Assuming an average global per capita household, municipal, and industrial water use of 200 m^3/yr, the combined demand in these sectors would total some 1640 km^3 in 2025. Adding this amount to estimated irrigation withdrawals and reservoir losses suggests that global withdrawals in 2025 could total 6515 km^3. This estimate exceeds by 26% that of Shiklomanov (1996), in large part because of the higher global irrigation water requirement that emerges from the more detailed crop-water analysis carried out in this study.

Adding in greater instream flow needs to dilute pollution, human appropriation of accessible runoff in 2025 could exceed 70%, up from just over 50% at present, even with fairly optimistic assumptions about supply expansion (Postel et al. 1996). Both the dams and other infrastructure built to meet the higher demand, as well as the high level of human co-option of the supplies available, would cause much greater loss of valuable freshwater ecosystem services (Postel and Carpenter 1997), further decline of fisheries, and more rapid extinction of species that depend on aquatic ecosystems.

Global Irrigation Trends

Worldwide growth of irrigated area has dropped from an average of 2% per year between 1970 and 1982 to 1.3% per year between 1982 and 1994 and shows no sign of picking up speed. Rising construction costs for new irrigation projects and the declining number of ecologically and socially sound sites for the construction of dams and river diversions have led international donor institutions and governments to reduce irrigation investments. Irrigation lending by the four major donors—the World Bank, the Asian Development Bank, the U.S. Agency for International Development, and the Japanese Overseas Economic Cooperation Fund—peaked in the late 1970s and dropped by nearly half over the next decade (Rosegrant 1997). Governments in many Asian countries—including China, the Philippines, Bangladesh, India, Indonesia, and Thailand—also cut back irrigation investments substantially during the 1980s. Although private investment has countered this trend somewhat, irrigation worldwide has been growing at a slower pace than population: Per capita irrigated area peaked in 1978 and fell 7% by 1994, the latest year for which data are available (Gardner 1997).

At the same time, the steady buildup of salts in irrigated soils is leading to a decline in the productivity of a portion of the existing irrigation base. Estimates suggest that salinization affects 20% of irrigated lands worldwide (Ghassemi et al. 1995) and may be severe enough on 10% of these lands to be reducing crop yields. Spreading at a rate of up to 2×10^6 ha annually (Umali 1993), salinization is offsetting a portion of the gains achieved by bringing new lands under irrigation. Together, spreading soil salinization and the declining rate in the expansion of irrigation have contributed significantly to the decline in grain yield growth witnessed during the first half of the 1990s.

Regional Signs of Water Depletion and Unsustainable Use

Groundwater overpumping and aquifer depletion now plague many of the world's most important food-producing regions, including the north plain of China, the Punjab of India, portions of Southeast Asia, large areas of north Africa and the Middle East, and much of the western United States (Postel 1996). Falling water tables not only signal limits on the ability to expand future groundwater use but also indicate that a portion of the world's current food supply depends on water that is used unsustainably—and therefore cannot be counted as a reliable portion of the world's long-term food supply. Saudi Arabia, which as recently as 1994 was producing nearly 5×10^6 t of wheat by mining nonrenewable groundwater, illustrates this point well: When fiscal problems led the government to reduce the subsidies that had propped up this unsustainable wheat production, Saudi grain output plummeted 62% in two years, falling to 1.9×10^6 t in 1996 (USDA 1997a).

Many of the planet's major rivers are showing signs of overexploitation as well, adding to the evidence that it will be difficult to greatly increase agricultural water supplies. In Asia, where the majority of world population growth and additional food needs will be centered, many rivers are completely tapped out during the drier part of the year, when irrigation is so essential. According to a World Bank study (Frederiksen et al. 1993), essentially no water is released to the sea during a large portion of the dry season in many basins in Asia. These include the Ganges and most rivers in India, China's Huang He (Yellow River), Thailand's Chao Phraya, and the Amu Dar'ya and Syr Dar'ya in central Asia's Aral Sea basin. The Nile River in northeast

Africa and the Colorado River in southwestern North America discharge little or no freshwater to the sea in most years (Postel 1996).

Increasing Competition for Water

Even as limits to tapping additional water supplies are appearing, agriculture is losing some of its existing water supplies to cities as population growth and urbanization push up urban water demands. The number of urban dwellers worldwide is likely to double to 5 billion by 2025. This trend will increase pressure to shift water out of agriculture to supply drinking water to growing cities, as is already happening in China, the western United States, parts of India, and other water-short areas.

In addition, rising public concern about the loss of fisheries, the extinction of aquatic species, and the overall decline of freshwater ecosystems is generating political pressure to shift water from agriculture to the natural environment, particularly in wealthier countries. In the United States, for example, the U.S. Congress passed legislation in 1992 that dedicates 987×10^6 m^3 of water annually from the Central Valley Project in California, one of the nation's largest federal irrigation projects, to maintaining fish and wildlife habitat and other ecosystem functions. Among the objectives of the Central Valley Project Improvement Act is restoring the natural production of salmon and other anadromous fish to twice their average levels over the past 25 years (Gray 1994).

Further evidence of heightened competition for irrigation water comes from a county-level analysis of the 17 western U.S. states (Moore et al. 1996), which found agricultural activities to be a factor in the decline of 50 fish species listed under the Endangered Species Act (ESA). This analysis also found that 235 counties contained irrigated land that drew water supplies from rivers harboring ESA-listed fish species. These findings suggest that U.S. irrigated agriculture may face more widespread water losses because of legal obligations to protect species at risk.

Water, Population, and the Global Grain Trade

Finally, a growing imbalance between population size and available water supplies is eliminating the option of food self-sufficiency in more and more countries. As annual runoff levels drop below $1700 m^3$ per person, food self-sufficiency becomes difficult, if not impossible, in most countries. Below this level, there is typically not enough water available to meet the demands of industries, cities, and households; to dilute pollution; to satisfy other ecological functions; and to grow sufficient food for the entire population. Thus, countries begin to import water indirectly, in the form of grain.

Table 4. Grain import dependence of African, Asian, and Middle Eastern countries with per capita runoff of less than 1700 m³/yr.[a]

Country	Internal runoff per capita, 1995 (m³/yr)[b]	Net grain imports as share of consumption (%)[c]
Kuwait	0	100
United Arab Emirates	158	100
Singapore	200	100
Djibouti	500	100
Oman	909	100
Lebanon	1297	95
Jordan	249	91
Israel	309	87
Libya	115	85
South Korea	1473	77
Algeria	489	70
Yemen	189	66
Armenia	1673	60
Mauritania	174	58
Cape Verde	750	55
Tunisia	393	55
Saudi Arabia	119	50
Uzbekistan	418	42
Egypt	29	40
Azerbaijan	1066	34
Turkmenistan	251	27
Morocco	1027	26
Somalia	645	26
Rwanda	808	20
Iraq	1650	19
Kenya	714	15
Sudan	1246	4
Burkina Faso	1683	2
Burundi	563	2
Zimbabwe	1248	2
Niger	380	1
South Africa	1030	-3
Syria	517	-4
Eritrea	800	Not available

[a]From WRI (1994), FAO (1995a), and USDA (1997a).

[b]Runoff figures do not include river inflow from other countries, in part to avoid double-counting. Only Armenia, Azerbaijan, Djibouti, Iraq, Mauritania, Sudan, Turkmenistan, and Uzbekistan would have more than 1700 m³ per capita in 1995 and 2025 if current inflow from other countries were included.

[c]Ratio of annual net grain imports to grain consumption averaged over the period 1994–1996.

Of the 34 countries in Africa, Asia, and the Middle East that have annual per capita runoff levels below 1700m^3, all but two (South Africa and Syria) are net grain importers; 24 (70%) of these countries already import at least 20% of their grain (Table 4). Collectively, their annual net grain imports, averaged over 1994–1996, totaled 48 x 10^{6}t, which suggests that water scarcity is to some degree driving about one-fourth of the global grain trade. With approximately 1500m^3 of water required to grow 1t of grain in these countries (higher than the global average because of the higher evapotranspiration rates in drier climates; FAO 1997), these annual grain imports represent 72km^3 of water.

As populations grow, per capita water supplies will drop below 1700m^3 per year in more countries, and countries that are already on the list of so-called water-stressed countries will acquire more people. By 2025, 10 more African countries will join the list, as will India, Pakistan, and several other Asian nations; China will only narrowly miss doing so. Given current population projections (PRB 1997), the total number of people living in water-stressed African, Asian, and Middle Eastern countries will climb 6.5-fold by 2025, from approximately 470 million to more than 3 billion. With nearly 40% of the projected 2025 population living in countries whose water supplies are too limited for food self-sufficiency, dependence on grain imports is bound to deepen and spread.

Conclusions and Implications

Water availability will be a serious constraint to achieving the food requirements projected for 2025. The need for irrigation water is likely to be greater than currently anticipated, and the available supply of it less than anticipated. Groundwater overdrafting, salinization of soils, and re-allocation of water from agriculture to cities and aquatic ecosystems will combine to limit irrigated crop production in many important food-producing regions. At the same time, more and more countries will see their populations exceed the level that can be fully sustained by available water supplies.

The common presumption that international trade will fill emerging food gaps deserves more careful scrutiny. With each 1 t of grain representing approximately 1000 t of water, water-stressed countries will increasingly turn to grain imports to balance their water budgets. The majority of people living in water-stressed countries in 2025 will be in Africa and South Asia, home to most of the 1 billion people who are currently living in acute poverty (UNDP 1996) and the 840 million people who are currently malnourished (FAO 1996b). It is questionable whether exportable food surpluses will be both sufficient and affordable for poor food-importing countries.

Given the limited potential for sustainable increases in cropland area and the mounting barriers to expanding irrigated area, measures are urgently needed to ensure that the best rain-fed land now in production remains in production. Rain-fed land does not compete directly with urban and industrial uses for water in the way that irrigated land does. In a world of deepening water scarcity, rain-fed land will thus become increasingly important to global food security. Whether through land-use zoning or other means, it deserves premium protection.

Clearly, greater efforts are needed to raise the water productivity of the global crop base, both rain fed and irrigated. Boosting by half the productive use of rainwater for crop evapotranspiration, as assumed in this analysis, will be difficult. Small-scale water harvesting, terracing, bunding, and other means of channeling and storing rainwater to increase soil moisture will be crucial. Successful examples of these types of projects in Africa (Critchley 1991), India (Centre for Science and Environment 1997), and elsewhere suggest greater potential for drought-proofing and increased rain-fed production than has been realized to date.

Improving irrigation efficiency can also increase agricultural water productivity. The estimated $500km^3$ of unproductive evaporation of irrigation water theoretically represents potential water savings sufficient to grow 450 x 10^6t of wheat, although only a portion of these losses could realistically and economically be captured. These savings increase the effective water supply without the need to build additional reservoirs or extract more groundwater. For example, researchers at the Sri Lanka-based International Irrigation Management Institute found that eliminating the flooding of rice fields prior to planting reduced water use by 25% (Seckler 1996). The portion of this reduction resulting from lower evaporative losses represents true water savings and effectively increases the available supply.

Efficient sprinklers, drip systems, and other methods of delivering irrigation water more directly to the roots of crops can also reduce unproductive evaporation. Research in the Texas High Plains has shown substantial water savings with low-pressure sprinklers that deliver water close to the soil surface rather than in a high-pressure spray (High Plains Underground Water Conservation District 1996). Water productivity gains of 20–30% or more are not uncommon when farmers shift to more efficient irrigation practices. Worldwide, however, such efficiency measures have spread slowly relative to their potential because of high upfront capital costs, relatively low crop prices, and heavy government subsidies that artificially lower irrigation water prices.

Improving the water-use efficiency of crops, shifting the mix of crops, and breeding crop varieties that are more salt tolerant and drought resistant may also increase agricultural water productivity. These gains do not come easily, however, because drawbacks can negate the potential benefits. For example, crop varieties that perform well under cooler temperatures may produce higher yields per unit of water consumed but have a lower harvest-index potential (Sinclair et al. 1984). Moreover, a good portion of the potential for improving crop water-use efficiency may already have been exploited. For example, breeders have already shortened the maturation time for irrigated rice varieties from 150 days to 110 days, substantially increasing that crop's water efficiency (IRRI 1995).

Finally, more equitable distribution of food may be necessary to satisfy the basic nutritional needs of all people as water constraints on agriculture increase. For the past three decades, the share of the world's grain supply fed to livestock has consistently ranged between 38% and 40% (Brown 1996). This large amount of grain—and, indirectly, water—could be used more productively to satisfy human nutritional requirements. For example, the diet of a typical U.S. adult, with a relatively high percentage of calories derived from grain-fed livestock, includes enough grain to support the diets of four typical Indians.

Although it may be tempting to assert that the prospective shortage of water for crop production calls for stepped-up construction of large dams and river diversions to increase supplies, this conclusion is not sound. The aquatic environment is showing numerous signs of declining health, even at today's level of water use. Large dams and river diversions have proven to be primary destroyers of aquatic habitat, contributing substantially to the destruction of fisheries, the extinction of species, and the overall loss of the ecosystem services on which the human economy depends. Their social and economic costs have also risen markedly over the past two decades. Along with efforts to slow both population and consumption growth, measures to use rainwater and irrigation water more productively, to use food supplies more efficiently, and to alter the crop mix to better match the quantity and quality of water available offer more ecologically sound and sustainable ways of satisfying the nutritional needs of the global population.

References

Ajtay GL, Ketner P, Duvigneaud P. 1979. Terrestrial primary production and phytomass. Pages 129-182 in Bolin B, Degens ET, Kempe S, Ketner P, eds. *The Global Carbon Cycle*. New York: John Wiley & Sons.

Brown LR. 1996. Worldwide feedgrain use drops. Pages 34-35 in Brown LR, Flavin C, Kane H. *Vital Signs, 1996*. New York: W. W. Norton.

_____. 1997. *The Agricultural Link: How Environmental Deterioration Could Disrupt Economic Progress*. Washington (DC): Worldwatch Institute.

Centre for Science and Environment. 1997. *Dying Wisdom*. New Delhi (India): Centre for Science and Environment.

Critchley W. 1991. *Looking after Our Land: Soil and Water Conservation in Dryland Africa*. Oxford (UK): Oxfam.

Doorenbos J, Kassam AH. 1979. *Yield Response to Water*. Rome: Food and Agriculture Organization of the United Nations.

Dyson T. 1996. *Population and Food: Global Trends and Future Prospects*. London: Routledge.

[FAO] Food and Agriculture Organization of the United Nations. 1993. *World Review of High Seas and Highly Migratory Fish Species and Straddling Stocks*. Rome: Food and Agriculture Organization. Fisheries Circular no. 858.

———. 1995a. *Irrigation in Africa in Figures*. Rome: Food and Agriculture Organization. Water Report no. 7.

———. 1995b. *Production Yearbook 1994*. Rome: Food and Agriculture Organization.

———. 1996a. *Production Yearbook 1995*. Rome: Food and Agriculture Organization.

———. 1996b. *Food for All*. Rome: Food and Agriculture Organization.

———. 1997. *Water Resources of the Near East Region: A Review*. Rome: Food and Agriculture Organization.

Frederiksen H, Berkoff J, Barber W. 1993. *Water Resources Management in Asia*. Washington (DC): World Bank.

Gardner G. 1997. Irrigated area up slightly. Pages 42-43 in Brown LR, Renner M, Flavin C. *Vital Signs, 1997*. New York: W. W. Norton.

Ghassemi F, Jakeman AJ, Nix, HA. 1995. *Salinisation of Land and Water Resources*. Sydney (Australia): University of New South Wales Press.

Gleick PH. 1996. Basic water requirements for human activities: Meeting basic needs. *Water International* 21: 83-92.

Gray B. 1994. The modern era in California water law. *Hastings Law Journal* January: 249-308.

High Plains Underground Water Conservation District. 1996. *November: The Cross Section*. Lubbock (TX): High Plains Underground Water Conservation District.

[IRRI] International Rice Research Institute 1995. *Water: A Looming Crisis*. Manila (The Philippines): International Rice Research Institute.

Kramer PJ, Boyer JS. 1995. *Water Relations of Plants and Soils*. San Diego: Academic Press.

Leach G. 1995. *Global Land and Food in the 21st Century: Trends & Issues for Sustainability*. Stockholm (Sweden): Stockholm Environment Institute.

McCalla AF. 1994. *Agriculture and Food Needs to 2025: Why We Should Be Concerned*. Washington (DC): Consultative Group on International Agricultural Research.

McGinn A. 1997. Global fish catch remains steady. Pages 32-33 in Brown LR, Renner M, Flavin C. 1997. *Vital Signs, 1997*. New York: W. W. Norton.

Monteith JL. 1990. Conservative behaviour in the response of crops to water and light. Pages 3-16 in Rabbinge R, Goudriaan J, Van Keulen H, Penning de Vries FWT, Van Laar HH, eds. *Theoretical Production Ecology: Reflections and Prospects.* Wageningen (The Netherlands): Simulation Monographs 34, Pudoc.

Moore MR, Mulville A, Weinberg M. 1996. Water allocation in the American West: Endangered fish versus irrigated agriculture. *Natural Resources Journal* 36:319-357.

Oldeman LR, van Engelen VWP, Pulles JHM. 1991. The extent of human-induced soil degradation. Annex 5 of Oldeman LR, Hakkeling RTA, Sombroek WG. *World Map of the Status of Human-Induced Soil Degradation: An Explanatory Note*. Wageningen (The Netherlands): International Soil Reference and Information Centre.

Perry CJ. 1996. *The IIMI Water Balance Framework: A Model for Project Level Analysis*. Colombo (Sri Lanka): International Irrigation Management Institute. Research Report no. 5.

Pimentel D, et al. 1995. Environmental and economic costs of soil erosion and conservation benefits. *Science* 267: 1117-1123.

Postel S. 1992. *Last Oasis: Facing Water Scarcity*. New York: W. W. Norton.

_____. 1996. *Dividing the Waters: Food Security, Ecosystem Health, and the New Politics of Scarcity*. Washington (DC): Worldwatch Institute.

Postel S, Carpenter S. 1997. Freshwater ecosystem services. Pages 195-214 in Daily GC, ed. *Nature's Services: Societal Dependence on Natural Ecosystems*. Washington (DC): Island Press.

Postel SL, Daily GC, Ehrlich PR. 1996. Human appropriation of renewable freshwater. *Science* 271: 785-788.

[PRB] Population Reference Bureau. 1995. *1995 World Population Data Sheet*. Washington (DC): Population Reference Bureau.

_____. 1997. *1997 World Population Data Sheet*. Washington (DC): Population Reference Bureau.

Rangeley WR. 1987. Irrigation and drainage in the world. Pages 29-35 in Jordan WR, ed. *Water and Water Policy in World Food Supplies*. College Station (TX): Texas A&M University Press.

Reij C. 1991. *Indigenous Soil and Water Conservation in Africa*. London: International Institute for Environment and Development.

Rosegrant MW. 1997. *Water Resources in the Twenty-First Century: Challenges and Implications for Action*. Washington (DC): International Food Policy Research Institute.

Seckler D. 1996. *The New Era of Water Resources Management: From "Dry" to "Wet" Water Savings*. Washington (DC): Consultative Group on International Agricultural Research.

Shiklomanov IA. 1993. World fresh water resources. Pages 13-24 in Gleick PH, ed. *Water in Crisis*. New York: Oxford University Press.

_____. 1996. *Assessment of Water Resources and Water Availability in the World*. St. Petersburg (Russia): State Hydrological Institute.

Sinclair TR, Tanner CB, Bennett JM. 1984. Water-use efficiency in crop production. *BioScience* 34: 36-40.

Umali DL. 1993. *Irrigation-Induced Salinity*. Washington (DC): World Bank.

[UNCSD] United Nations Commission on Sustainable Development. 1997. *Comprehensive Assessment of the Freshwater Resources of the World*. New York: United Nations Economic and Social Council.

[UNDP] United Nations Development Programme. 1996. *Human Development Report, 1996*. New York: Oxford University Press.

Unger PW, Stewart BA. 1983. Soil management for efficient water use: An overview. Pages 419-460 in Taylor HM, Jordan WR, Sinclair TR, eds. *Limi-*

tations to Efficient Water Use in Crop Production. Madison (WI): American Society of Agronomy, Crop Science Society of America, Soil Science Society of America.

U.S. Bureau of the Census 1996. International electronic database. Suitland (MD): U.S. Bureau of the Census.

[USDA] United States Department of Agriculture. 1996, 1997a. Production, supply, and distribution (electronic database). Washington (DC): United States Department of Agriculture.

_____. 1997b. *World Agricultural Production*. Washington (DC): United States Department of Agriculture.

_____. 1997c. *Grain: World Markets and Trade*. Washington (DC): United States Department of Agriculture.

Vitousek PM, Ehrlich PR, Ehrlich AH, Matson PA. 1986. Human appropriation of the products of photosynthesis. *BioScience* 36: 368-373.

[WRI] World Resources Institute. 1994. *World Resources, 1994–95*. New York: Oxford University Press.

Yudelman M. 1994. The future role of irrigation in meeting the world's food supply. In *Soil and Water Science: Key to Understanding Our Global Environment.* Madison (WI): Soil Science Society of America.

5

Water Wars

Joyce R. Starr

Given the importance of freshwater to food security outlined in the previous chapter, it is not surprising that many observers believe that freshwater will be the cause of violent conflict among communities and nations in the future. Such conflict may be particularly likely in regions already afflicted by serious, ongoing disputes. The focus of the present chapter is the Middle East, where problems of water supply have been a semi-permanent feature of human habitation for hundreds, if not thousands, of years. Several traditionally rival states are already severely water short. Joyce Starr speculates on what this situation may imply for the region as well as for the West.

A frequent radio and television commentator, Starr has made regular appearances on CNN, ABC, NBC, CBS, and the BBC. She is the author of numerous popular non-fiction works, including Covenant over Middle East Waters: Water Is the Soul of Peace.

The Middle East water crisis is a strategic orphan that no country or international body seems ready to adopt. Despite irrefutable evidence that the region is approaching dangerous water shortages and contamination, Western leaders have so far failed to treat the issue as a strategic priority. Yet when the current Persian Gulf war ends, the water crisis could erupt. This intensifying security issue requires sustained policy actions as well as new bureaucratic and consultative structures.

As early as the mid-1980s, U.S. government intelligence services estimated that there were at least 10 places in the world where war could break out over dwindling shared water—the majority in the Middle East. Jordan, Israel, Cyprus, Malta, and the countries of the Arabian Peninsula are sliding into the perilous zone where all available fresh surface and groundwater supplies will be fully utilized.

From Joyce R. Starr, "Water Wars," *Foreign Policy* 82 (Spring 1991): 17–36. © 1991 by The Carnegie Endowment for International Peace. Reprinted by permission of *Foreign Policy*.

Algeria, Egypt, Morocco, and Tunisia face similar prospects in 10 to 20 years. Morocco has made serious efforts in the water and sanitation sectors. Still, that country faces the prospect of a declining water supply beyond the year 2000, when its population is projected to grow to 31 million.

Algeria, Israel, the West Bank, Gaza, Jordan, Tunisia, and Yemen are already facing a "water barrier" requiring accelerated efforts, investments, regulations, and controls just to keep apace of spiraling populations. Middle Eastern and North African countries combined will absorb 80 million people by the close of the 1990s, pitting the Davidian capacity of existing water and sanitation services against the Goliath of demand.

The human toll translates into tragic statistics. The United Nations International Children's Emergency Fund (UNICEF) reports, for example, that 40,000 children worldwide—a majority of them on the African continent —are dying daily from hunger or disease caused by lack of water or contaminated water. At the turn of this century, almost 40 percent of the African population will be at risk of death or disease from water scarcity or contamination.

Yet the Middle East and North Africa are failing to confront overall water shortages. Water consumption for all uses is still less than available water, although fresh water is increasingly scarce throughout the region. The challenges are to make water available at an acceptable cost in places where it is most needed and to dramatically improve the management of existing water resources.

According to the World Bank, the Middle East has the highest median cost of water supply and sanitation in the world. Capital costs of water reached a median of $300 per capita in 1985, about twice those on the American continent and more than five times those in Southeast Asia. Given its burdensome population growth rates, the region cannot afford to expand water supplies at current exorbitant prices.

Israel, Egypt, Jordan, Syria, Tunisia, and Turkey are the only countries in the region that have instituted tariff systems for municipal and industrial water use. Minimal fees for irrigation levied by Middle East nations, however, do not recover even the costs of operation and maintenance. The Gulf states are also exhausting strategic groundwater reserves for the production of crops that could be imported at a lower price.

But efficient pricing and internal management alone, without effective cooperation among countries, will still not resolve the Middle East water puzzle. The Gulf states, for example, use natural gas by-products from oil drilling to distill water even though waters in neighboring countries flow freely into the ocean. These states could rechannel oil funds to pay poorer countries for available water, while saving their energy and the resulting environmental degradation.

Moreover, with Middle East population growth averaging a staggering 3 percent annually, the mere prospect of overflowing sewage could bring

Middle Easterners to loggerheads. The annual waste-water collection from the Greater Cairo area alone is equivalent to the total amount of water used yearly for domestic, industrial, and irrigation purposes in the entire country of Jordan. Without regional cooperation over water and waste management, sewage could eventually become a catalyst for armed conflict in the Middle East.

Middle Eastern leaders are acutely conscious of the potential for conflict stemming from chronic water shortages. "The only matter that could take Egypt to war again is water," declared President Anwar Sadat in the spring of 1979, only days after signing the historic peace treaty with Israel. His unveiled threat was not directed at Israel, but at Ethiopia, the upstream neighbor that controls 85 percent of the headwaters of Egypt's life line, the Nile River. In 1990 Jordan's King Hussein issued similar warlike declarations.

Most countries in the Middle East are linked to one another by common aquifers subject to overwithdrawal or overcontamination. Iraqi leader Saddam Hussein's rationale for invading Kuwait in August 1990 was the latter's overpumping of shared oil reserves. How long will it be before aquifer conflict becomes common terminology in the lexicon of Middle East specialists?

Water security will soon rank with military security in the war rooms of defense ministries. Strategic coordination of Saudi Arabia's water supplies is clearly crucial for the defense of the kingdom. Sixty percent of the world's desalination capacity is in the Persian Gulf countries. Saudi Arabia's desalinated water alone exceeds 30 percent of global production, while Kuwait and all the other Gulf states are almost totally dependent on their desalting plants for their fresh water supply. The Saudis' private worries that their immense desalination plants, the size of small cities, would become targets for aggression have suddenly become a global nightmare. Indeed, every one of the Gulf states is strategically vulnerable to full attack or sabotage on their desalting capability.

Saudi Arabia's concerns over water became a priority for the U.S. government when it was faced with maintaining several hundred thousand thirsty American troops in the Saudi desert. The Defense Department has so far relied on bottled water plants in Saudi Arabia and the United Arab Emirates (UAE). Reportedly, the Water Resources Management Action Group, an interagency group under the direction of the Department of Defense, has plans for the provision of potable water to troops in the field in the event Saudi and UAE supplies are disrupted. Yet the price the United States would have to pay to ship water to its troops could be much greater than the price of oil.

The United States also shipped portable desalination units to Saudi Arabia. Water tankers were allegedly given as high a priority on military aircraft as armor and weaponry, a special reserve unit dealing with water supply was activated, and American experts were assigned to identify water sources in unpopulated areas close to the Kuwaiti and Iraqi borders. Nevertheless, according to Edward Badolato, former deputy assistant secretary for energy emergencies at the Department of Energy, the U.S. government "is doing almost nothing" to anticipate sabotage of pumping stations, treatment plants, pipelines, or dams in the Middle East. More than a thousand terrorist attacks were directed against energy targets around the world in 1990. The U.S. Corps of Engineers, which built a camp for 4,000 airmen in Saudi Arabia with state-of-the-art engineering, has developed defensive security plans to protect U.S. domestic water facilities, but not facilities overseas. "We're not equipped to deal with it," said Badolato. "We haven't focused on the water problem. We're barely capable of focusing on oil."

Water, communication, and transportation are fundamental to economic survival, with energy as the common denominator. Leon Awerbuch, manager for power and desalination at the Bechtel Corporation, points out that almost all of the desalting plants in Saudi Arabia and Kuwait are dual-purpose power/desalination facilities. Moreover, the majority of water used for Gulf petrochemical production comes from desalination facilities. The more important works in Saudi Arabia, as in other Middle East countries, are loosely ringed by troops and checkpoints—and even equipped with a few missiles—but the overall level of protection, insists Badolato, is no more than the security provided to postal or telephone systems.

Sharing the Nile

A decade of drought in East Africa has depleted the Nile waters on which Egypt depends. The river provides 55.5 billion cubic meters of water—more than 86 percent of the total used in Egypt each year. During the summer of 1988, the Nile dropped to its lowest point in a century, forcing Egyptian authorities to dip into Lake Nasser reserves.

The crisis underscored the life-or-death implications for Egypt's economy of a continuing decline in Nile waters. Tourism revenues will be threatened as hotels are unable to obtain water for drinking and sanitary services, and leisure vessels will not be able to navigate the river. Oil export revenues could dry up as oil is diverted to generate the 28 percent of the country's power normally produced by the Nile. Moreover, Egypt's food production could be crippled because almost all its farming depends on Nile flood irrigation. Egypt already imports approximately 50 percent of its food requirements, and an increase in imports would further burden its strained economy. Relaxing state subsidies on food prices is hardly a politically attractive choice, given the food riots President Anwar Sadat faced when he tried to comply with International Monetary Fund austerity measures in February 1977.

Yet, while regional supplies are falling, Egypt's water needs are increasing at an alarming rate because of the country's astonishing population growth, projected to reach 75 million by the year 2000. The last country along the path of the Nile, Egypt has little control over the actions of eight upstream governments. Foreign Minister Boutros Ghali maintains that the "national security of Egypt is . . . a question of water."

In September 1989 Ghali sounded the water alarm to members of the U.S. Congress. He forecast that if current circumstances persist, Egypt and the Sudan will experience a severe deficit in water resources by the year 2010, both requiring 5 billion cubic meters per year. Egypt has almost no rain—about three inches a year—and only 50 percent of the Sudan's agriculture is irrigated by rainfall. The countries bordering Lake Victoria—Kenya, Tanzania, Uganda, and to some extent Rwanda—will require a similar amount of water—at least 10 billion cubic meters per year—in the next two decades. "What is worse is that each Nile country expects different benefits from the control and management of water resources," Ghali stated, adding:

> The other African countries . . . have not reached the level of agriculture through irrigation that we have, and therefore are not as interested in the problem of water scarcity. It is the classic difference in attitudes found among upstream and downstream countries which are on the same international river.

Even in the best of circumstances, most of the Nile countries will be unable to generate sufficient capital to finance critically needed water storage and management projects without massive assistance from donor nations and lending institutions. Africa's foreign debt is approximately $260 billion, with Nile basin countries sharing at least $80 billion of that burden. As Ghali noted, assistance from international organizations and donor countries will be impossible to get "unless we have not only stability, but also a consensus among us." Despite years of effort, however, no formal protocol yet exists among all riparians for a Nile water-sharing plan. Ethiopia is torn by internal insurgency, as is the Sudan. The Ethiopians also have enduring fears that Egypt will misuse the waters of the Nile.

Nevertheless, the framework for a comprehensive Nile basin plan does exist. Egypt succeeded in forming a consultative group comprising all the Nile countries, called the *Undugu* Group, or "fraternity" in Swahili. In recent *Undugu* planning meetings, the Egyptians presented a promising long-range scheme for tapping the Nile to generate massive electric power for export to other regions in exchange for hard currency, which in turn would be used for water and irrigation projects in the Nile countries.

According to the Egyptian plan, the electricity produced by the upstream Inga Dam in Uganda and the Aswan Dam in Egypt would be linked by transmission lines to the downstream countries, including Egypt, and beyond to Jordan, Syria, Turkey, and the European Community. Additional hydroelectric dams are envisioned in the Sudan, on Lake Mobutu in Zaire, and on Lake

Albert in Uganda, all of which would feed into the intercontinental grid. Pollution-free energy would be sold to the north, as a quid pro quo for capital development funds. A plan of such scope and vision may be the only way to finally bring a water-sharing agreement to these nations.

By invading Kuwait, Iraq also forged a link between Egypt's water security concerns as an African state and its Middle East national security agenda. The Kuwait Fund for Arab Economic Development and other Gulf financial institutions expressed intentions in July 1990 to underwrite Egypt's North Sinai agriculture project estimated at more than $1.3 billion. The project was designed by the U.N.'s Food and Agriculture Organization to expand Egyptian settlement in the Sinai and increase agricultural production. Ninety-seven percent of Egyptian territory is barren desert, with 52 million Egyptians concentrated on 3 percent of the land. Egypt's population also gains an additional 1 million people every 10 months. The loss of Kuwaiti and Gulf potential assistance to make the desert bloom was perhaps another fear rallying Egypt to the American side in the current crisis.

Farther east, water sharing between Israel and Jordan has remained relatively stable for the last several decades, albeit with occasional flare-ups. Thus Israeli government authorities initially dismissed King Hussein's 1990 suggestions that water disputes could lead to war as a ploy to open up the pipeline of desperately needed Arab aid. Still, there was a sense of foreboding that the king would resort to the water issue to inflame public opinion.

It appears, however, that Hussein's wrath may have been directed less at water sharing than at Israeli reluctance to assent to World Bank funding for the Wahda (Unity) Dam on the upper Yarmuk River. The dam will regulate the water supply, ensuring sorely needed water for the Jordan Valley and vital municipal and industrial water for the Amman-Zarqa urban complex. But the World Bank will not proceed with financial support for international water projects unless all riparians to a particular project signal their agreement. Israel has withheld its approval, contingent on being assured of what it deems a fair share of the waters. Because the Yarmuk contributes some 3 percent of Israel's national water supply, the Israelis contend that the Yarmuk project could seriously affect their ability to meet growing water demands. Fears and counter-fears have resulted in the loss of valuable time in a race against a common crisis, whereas a resolution could benefit all riparians—Israel, Jordan, and Syria.

One of Israel's strategic concerns in granting territory to the Palestinians is the future of the Yarkon/Taninim mountain aquifer that lies beneath both pre-1967 ("Green Line") Israel and the West Bank. However, a variety of Israeli, Palestinian, and foreign experts contend that 80, 60, 40, or 20 percent of the aquifer lies under the West Bank—depending on the expert speaking. There may be more than one truth. Theoretically, 70 to 80 percent of the aquifer could be in the West Bank, as well as 70 to 80 percent of the waters recharged by rain. However, all of these recharged waters flow westward toward the coastal plain and the Mediterranean Sea. Israel pumps the majority of the naturally recharged waters, which it has done since the mid-1960s, to sustain its agricultural, industrial, and population growth. The West Bank aquifer supplies 25–40 percent of Israel's waters, while underground resources, waste-water reclamation, catchments, saline springs, and other sources provide the remainder.

Palestinian experts generally acknowledge that Israel provides requisite water to the West Bank for domestic and industrial use. They nevertheless claim that Israel refuses sufficient water for agricultural expansion, which is viewed as the life-force of economic viability for the territories. Israeli authorities respond that agriculture has been the primary culprit draining the aquifer's resources.

Both Israeli Jews and Israeli Arabs use more water per capita for domestic purposes than do West Bank and Gaza Strip Palestinians. Domestic and industrial uses combined, however, account for less than 30 percent of Israel's supply, while agriculture uses the most water—not only in Israel, but throughout the Middle East. Water-absorbing crops like Israeli cotton or Jordanian bananas contribute to export income while ravaging the water supply.

The agricultural sector supplies 5 percent of Israel's gross national product but drains more than 70 percent of the country's water. Israeli farmers have been forced to accept a 37 percent reduction in water over the last year for certain crops, while Israelis living in the West Bank are prohibited from engaging in extensive farming. Already exploited to dangerous limits, the aquifer will become increasingly saline and sustain irreparable damage through overuse or free drilling by either side.

Israel alone is currently using its water resources at between 15 and 20 percent beyond their natural replenishment rate, causing water table levels to drop and shallow wells to go dry. The Sea of Galilee, or Lake Kinneret, which has been supplying almost one-third of Israel's requirements, is at its lowest level in 60 years. The Israeli government intends to declare a state of emergency over the country's waters if the drought continues. State Comptroller Miriam Ben Porat issued a special report in January 1991, confirming that "in practical terms, Israel has no water reserves in its reservoirs." Ben Porat blamed the Agriculture Ministry for allocating too much water to farmers while ignoring warnings of shortages. "Today, there is a real danger that it will be impossible to provide water in enough quantity and quality even in the short-term," she stated.

The Gaza Strip, which is semiarid, claims only one aquifer. Contamination has reached a critical level because of the heavy local use of pesticides and fertilizers and the lack of services to remove or treat raw sewage in many towns and villages. Heavy pumping has also caused seawater intrusion. Gaza's water will be unusable by the year 2000, when its population will approach 1 million.

Israel is laying pipes to pump water to the Gaza Strip from its own reserves. But with an expected 1 to 2 million Soviet Jews arriving in the coming decade—added to an estimated 5.4 million other Israelis by the year 2000—there is simply no way that Israel, the West Bank, or Gaza can meet their water requirements unless Israel reclaims sewage at a faster pace, desalinates water at an accelerated rate and cost, or imports water. In addition, Israel had almost no rain over the past year. A prolonged drought could easily turn a critical situation into a catastrophe.

West Bank Palestinians obtain their water through pre-1967 wells at no charge and through the Israeli water carrier for a fee. Some Israeli authorities claim that Israeli settlers and Palestinians in the territories pay the Israeli government equal rates for water. Palestinians charge that the Israeli government subsidizes water for the settlers, who use more than their fair share.

Volumes of articles have been written on this subject, and yet there is no common pool of reliable, neutral data to draw upon. All parties to the conflict —including academics—have thus far tended to present facts, interpret figures, and recycle newspaper reporting according to their own political preferences. The one fact that is indisputable, however, is that the Palestinians have no decision-making power in their own water future. Yet, ironically, without a comprehensive water-sharing agreement or understanding between Israel, the West Bank, Jordan, and Syria, on the one hand, and Israel and the Gaza Strip, on the other, there can be no policy road map to a just allocation scheme.

The parties to the conflict are simply quibbling about numbers that may or may not be true. The reality is that Israel, the West Bank and Gaza, and Jordan are facing a combined water deficit of at least 300–400 million cubic meters per year (and some estimate the figures to be as high as 500–600 million cubic meters). This is aggravated by drought conditions. A way must be found to meet this deficit at a cost the parties can afford, through either technological applications or importation of water.

As Israel searches farther afield for water, negotiations with private Turkish firms become increasingly attractive. One potential scheme would transport water from Turkey in flexible barges or floating bags. The cost of associated infrastructure including special terminals and additional pipelines could add $200 million alone to the cost of the water. Although Agriculture Minister Rafael Eitan said in November 1990 that the Israeli government would not import water, he encouraged developing private importing arrangements.

Fact-finding talks between the Israeli Water Commission and Turkish companies are still in the preliminary stages. "If the cost of water is too high," said one Israeli authority, "there will be no deal." Meanwhile, adverse publicity and political démarches in the Arab world have also slowed the discussions.

The Jordan and Yarmuk River basins are well suited to integrated development, but all joint schemes proposed have been victim to Arab-Israeli or Syrian-Jordanian enmity. The proposed Wahda Dam, which would store and utilize Yarmuk River water otherwise discharged into the Jordan River and ultimately the Dead Sea, may in fact buy Jordan less than a five-year respite from shortages, given the country's yearly population growth rate of 3.8 percent—one of the world's highest.

Consequently, to meet its growing water needs, Jordan is relying on incremental solutions, including deeper drilling for groundwater sources and relatively expensive technologies like drip irrigation. One promising approach is solar-powered pumping and desalination of brackish groundwater in the Jordan River valley south of the Dead Sea; but the initial costs of such a scheme are prohibitive for a country in Jordan's economic straits. Technology and engineering can help redress Jordan's water problems, but regional political cooperation among the local river-sharing states must be achieved first to jointly develop and make use of the area's surface water sources.

Compared with its neighbors, Lebanon has plentiful water resources, which could be shared. Its numerous rivers and underground systems are reliably recharged from ample precipitation, especially snow in the mountains. A national water-shortage engineering and management system could turn Lebanon into a lucrative Middle East water haven, were there the vision and stability to realize it. Instead, the country is crippled by severe water shortages in Beirut, seawater intrusion in the coastal aquifer, farm lands neglected by lack of irrigation water, and pipelines and aquifers severely damaged by civil war.

Turkey's Water Plan

Turkey, with its abundance of water, is in a position to serve as a balancing force in the Middle East. Since the mid-1980s, current President and former Prime Minister Turgut Ozal has been championing the concept of a Turkish water "peace pipeline" to serve both Gulf and Near East countries. The proposal is to take water from two rivers, the Seyhan and Ceyhan, that empty into the Mediterranean, and transport it southward through Syria, Jordan, and Saudi Arabia to the Gulf. Two massive pipelines would supply water to these countries—one to Jordanian and Syrian cities, and the other to Bahrain, Kuwait, Oman, Qatar, Saudi Arabia, and the UAE. Altogether the project could bring potable water to more than 15 million people at a construction cost of more than $20 billion. Local fabrication of prestressed concrete cylinder pipes and other components would generate numerous industries and jobs in the region.

But the "peace pipeline," if it can be financed, would take at least eight to ten years to construct, and the financing itself depends upon all the states involved working out a joint water-sharing agreement, which has not been attainable for even individual projects in the past. The Saudis and Kuwaitis have not accepted Ozal's request for both approval and investment, on political grounds as well as arguments that the price of water delivered through the pipeline would be too high compared to local desalination.

Senior Kuwaiti and Saudi Arabian officials have also feared giving the Turks a role in and possible control over their water sovereignty. The pipeline could attract more favorable attention once the Kuwaiti crisis subsides, although a water carrier that passes through several countries would be vulnerable to attack. Regardless of the constraints, Ozal has taken the Middle East water issue to a new level of public diplomacy.

Although Turkey, which controls the headwaters of the Tigris and Euphrates Rivers, is generously endowed with water, 40 percent of its arable land is in southeastern Anatolia, which suffers from a general shortage of water. To alleviate this shortage, Turkey in 1983 initiated the South East Anatolia Development Project, also known by its Turkish acronym GAP, a series of 13 subprojects comprising irrigation and hydroelectric dam sites, including the massive Ataturk Dam. Seven of these sites are located on the Euphrates River and the other six are on the Tigris.

Upon completion, the project will supply approximately 24 billion kilowatt-hours of energy (almost half of Turkey's current energy needs) and open 1.6 million hectares of land to irrigated cultivation. The Turkish government hopes to sell the additional food production to Europe and the Middle East, which is expected to import $20 billion worth of foodstuffs by the end of the century. However, at present levels of investment, it could take the Turkish government more than 50 years to complete the total program.

GAP has raised Syrian and Iraqi anxieties over the availability of water for their own agricultural and industrial projects. Syria and Iraq fear that the Ataturk Dam could divert most of the Euphrates' flow into Turkey's Urfa Plain, forcing Iraqi and Syrian dependence on Turkish water. Iraq, long concerned about the effects of Syrian development schemes on the Euphrates, is now arguing that Turkey's dam construction could reduce the river's annual flow into Iraq of 22 billion cubic meters anywhere from 50 to 75 percent. Turkish officials contend that this is technically impossible and that Turkey would also be injured in any attempt to store water over a prolonged period. Once again, the lack of shared technical data and neutral analysis feeds fear and mistrust.

Turkey contributed to its downstream neighbor's fear in November 1989 by announcing that it would hold back the flow of the Euphrates for one month, starting in January 1990, in order to begin filling the Ataturk Dam. Some Middle East sources suggest that Saddam Hussein read the action as part of a U.S. plot against Iraq. To allay concerns, the Turkish government did provide "detailed technical information" to both Syria and Iraq on this water diversion. In addition, Turkey offered to compensate her neighbors for the month-long loss of Euphrates water by boosting the river's flow between November and January.

During the height of the tension, Ozal emphasized his commitment to resolve water disputes with Iraq and Syria, acknowledging their concerns. "I appreciate their fears," he said, "but we will not harm them. To the contrary, Turkey will more than make up for the water shortage. I have tried to convince Iraq and Syria of our positive intentions." As would be expected, however, Iraq and Syria reacted to the impoundment of Euphrates water with a surge of diplomatic cables, visits, and warnings.

These problems have been exacerbated by the current drought. This past year was one of the region's driest in half a century, resulting in a significant drop in the level of the Euphrates. In an average year, the Euphrates' capacity is an estimated 31,820 million cubic meters, a quantity that can satisfy the demands of Turkey, Syria, and Iraq. However, in 1989 the level fell to 16,870 million cubic meters, causing serious water shortages in all three countries.

The drought depressed Turkey's economy; but Syria's situation is even worse. The low level of the Euphrates, combined with pollution from Syrian pesticides, chemicals, and salt, has forced the government to cut back on the supply of drinking water and electricity to Damascus, Aleppo, and several other cities. Damascus is without water most nights, and is estimated to lose as much as 30 percent of its water from old, leaking pipes.

Unlike Syria, Iraq is fortunate in having access to the less-exploited Tigris. Before the Kuwaiti crisis, Iraq was planning to invest over $300 million in more than 20 flood control, hydroelectric, water storage, and irrigation projects on the Tigris, its tributaries, and Lake Tharther. A major scheme is intended to divert water from the Tigris into Lake Tharther, and then into the Euphrates if Euphrates water is insufficient to irrigate Iraqi croplands.

The past record of disputes over water is evident. In 1975 Iraq and Syria came to the brink of war over Syria's reduction of the flow of the Euphrates to fill the Ath-Thawrah Dam, which Iraq claimed had adversely affected 3 million Iraqi farmers. Turkey also reportedly uncovered an alleged Syrian plot to blow up the Ataturk Dam, which Syria views as a threat to its farmers. In 1987 Ankara allegedly hinted at a cut in the flow of Euphrates water to Syria over Syrian support for Kurdish terrorists, an enduring source of tension between the two countries. In October 1989, Syrian MiGs on a "training mission" shot down a Turkish survey plane well within Turkey's borders. Five people were killed in the incident, which was reportedly linked to Syrian-Turkish tensions over water.

The friction between Iraq, Syria, and Turkey over water access can only be defused through an explicit agreement among the three countries covering water allocations in the Tigris and Euphrates basins. But discussions have dragged on inconclusively since the 1960s. For example, the Trilateral Commission on the Euphrates has met periodically, but has discussed only technical matters such as river flow rates and rainfall data. In the absence of a formal protocol on water-basin management and apportionment among riparians, the World Bank and other multilateral lending agencies have been unable to offer a financing package for GAP and related infrastructure development projects.

Meanwhile, the downstream riparians are suffering from acute salinity, and none of the parties can meet their development goals. A comprehensive management plan would eliminate Iraqi and Syrian fears, while increasing the generated benefits for all three countries. Continued stalemate and the unilateral construction of new dams, by contrast, could lead to escalating disputes and armed confrontation.

Responding to the Emergency

The United States could play a leading role in bringing together the parties to Middle East water problems, ending a period of sluggish progress toward a common appreciation of a common threat. The United States also has unique expertise on water to assist the Middle East with the emerging crisis. The U.S. government, through its many departments and agencies, has undertaken extensive technical water assistance programs throughout the world. The quiet pool of dedicated water-related talent, hidden in the recesses of the U.S. government, could mark the United States as a leader in the global effort to respond to the water emergency.

Projects for every conceivable purpose have been designed and implemented, including waste-water treatment plants, dams, feasibility studies, training programs for regional experts, and the like. Yet there are scant resources available for some of the most compelling priorities: coordination between U.S. government bodies and other donor governments and institutions, improved data collection in the field, accelerated training programs for Middle Eastern and African water specialists, or investment in breakthrough technologies. Although there is considerable expertise and concern throughout the various agencies, the U.S. government does not currently have the will to demonstrate significant global leadership on the water issue.

In 1987, M. Peter McPherson, then administrator of the U.S. Agency for International Development (AID) and later undersecretary of the Treasury, noted that the "development of water resources is a critical foreign policy issue for the United States." Four years have passed, and McPherson's message on water has yet to catch the attention of the foreign policy establishment—both inside and outside the government.

Despite well-intentioned efforts, federal departments rarely undertake comprehensive, anticipatory planning on water challenges abroad. American experts are in the vanguard in developing conflict resolution techniques on water sharing. Yet no single agency has definitive responsibility, let alone an adequate, congressionally authorized budget to carve a foreign-policy niche for water. Thus in place of a broad strategic approach to the water dilemmas of the Middle East, the United States continues to rely on an ad hoc response. AID has spent billions of dollars on regional water projects without clearly defined, all-encompassing foreign-policy objectives.

The U.N. declared the 1980s the International Drinking Water Supply and Sanitation Decade. The World Bank and U.N. organizations—notably the U.N. Development Programme (UNDP), UNICEF, the U.N. Environment Programme, the World Health Organization, and the U.N. Center for Human Settlements—have made a resolute effort to slow the ticking clock. But neither the World Bank nor any of the major U.N. bodies has the effective political mandate or the charter to negotiate water controversies between countries unless specifically requested or to dictate appropriate water management. Instead, the most concerned international players find themselves walking a political tightwire leagues above the seas and rivers, with little expectation of a net.

The U.N.'s Decade on Water realized the provision of water installations for 700 million new users and sanitary facilities for 350 million persons. The World Bank and three multilateral regional banks—the African Development Bank, the Asian Development Bank, and the Inter-American Development Bank—provided major contributions. But the billions spent on water to date cannot keep up with exploding populations, nor have funds been linked to foreign-policy strategies for sustainable economic growth.

To respond to this emergency, the Global Water Summit Initiative was launched in January 1989 to galvanize the highest level of political leadership within donor countries and water-resource regions to face their common future. More than 40 African countries actively participated in a dialogue for action at the inaugural African Water Summit hosted by Mubarak in June 1990. The resulting Cairo Water Declaration recognized that through cooperation African water and land resources are potentially capable of sustaining several times the present population.

In an effort to respond to the escalating Middle East water crisis, a Middle East Water Summit will be hosted by Turkish President Ozal in November 1991 in Istanbul. The themes of this dialogue will parallel a major new World Bank study that includes Middle East waters, while also targeting wider regional management issues. The UNDP will play a central role in coordinating country presentations; the World Bank, agencies of the U.N., and leading donor nations will be instrumental in guiding the event.

The Summit Initiative is directed toward resource management, not political controversy. In the years ahead the survivability of the Middle East will be driven by economic sustainability as well as by politics. There is no more compelling resource challenge facing the region than water security.

The most constructive future approach by the United States and other donors would be to highlight water resource management as integral to regional security and stability. This would mean restructuring water-resource policies and institutions within Middle Eastern countries in accordance with plans for integrated economic development. Funds for the water sector must be substantially increased, but made conditional on determined efforts to institute appropriate pricing and management policies. Money for large projects alone will not ensure stable water futures for Middle Eastern nations, just as past funding for immense pet projects failed to prevent the current crisis.

The U.S. government must stop providing piecemeal aid for water projects that have little or no relationship to program planning by other donor institutions and governments. AID has maintained an informal dialogue with the World Bank over the last decade on water policy—perhaps more communication than goes on among the various agencies of the U.S. government. Yet this informal approach is ineffective, given the gravity of the situation. There must be systematic coordination among the principal players in the World Bank, U.N. agencies, the United States, and other donor governments and funds. Specifically, an office should be created within the U.S. Department of State, reporting directly to the secretary of state, that ensures coordination among U.S. agencies and with other donor institutions on water-resource projects.

The Middle East Water Summit in Istanbul is the first opportunity for decision makers to collectively address the need for a comprehensive approach to water management strategy in the Middle East. Its success, however, will be contingent on the readiness of government leaders and the international community to link water policy to larger objectives and to act decisively to carry it out. President George Bush, Secretary of State James Baker, and their colleagues in the Western alliance, the Soviet Union, and Japan must elevate the water issue to its proper strategic role in future Middle East policy planning.

A senior State Department official said recently, "Yes, water problems are very interesting. But we're dealing with global warming this year." Leading nongovernmental funding groups—reflecting the myopia of government bureaucracies—acknowledge the environmental importance of water, but explain that it is simply not on their agenda. Obliged to await a future time when it is either convenient or trendy to focus on water security. Middle Eastern countries may be beyond the point where our belated attention will stave off disaster.

Richard Armitage, former assistant secretary of defense for international security affairs, and currently the Wahda Dam mediator for the State Department, believes that American attention to this security arena is long overdue: "It is time for the United States to acknowledge that the water crisis in the Middle East is worsening and adding an extra dimension to prospective war scenarios . . . the time may be right for the administration to organize a long-term, multinational effort in this arena."

The Istanbul summit will test the willingness and resolve of the United States and its allies to finally chart a forward-looking rather than reactive policy in the Middle East. A key policy proposal to be reviewed at the summit will call for the creation of a Middle East Water Resources Policy Center with the mandate to pursue regional policy coordination, data collection, management training, and assessment of investment of needs, while also providing a forum for conflict resolution. The center should be under a multilateral umbrella of donor countries and institutions, with the leadership provided by existing U.N. organizations.

The financial requirements for such a center to be effective, and the requisite investments in water infrastructure and technology to ensure regional water security, are a mere fraction of present military expenditures in the Middle East. As Farouk El Baz, director of the Center for Remote Sensing at Boston University, has noted, the proposed center would strengthen the work of existing institutions.

Even before the Gulf crisis subsides, the United States, its allied partners, and the Soviet Union should actively encourage regional dialogue over contentious resource issues. To the oft-repeated question, "Can interstate water problems be seriously addressed before the larger political questions in the region are resolved?" there is only one response: A passive governmental approach to Middle East water scarcity will doom any future peace initiative. Middle East hatred is bountiful but Middle East water is at the point of no return. It is vital to the economic and political survivability of the region to sit down at the negotiating table. Indeed, a creative response to water cooperation could forge a new path to peace.

6

Water and Conflict in Asia?

Paul J. Smith and Charles H. Gross

Asia is another region characterized by both a tradition of conflict and se-vere freshwater supply and allocation problems. The Asia-Pacific Center for Security Studies monitors the role of water in potential dispute in Asia. In the present selection, the authors contend that water shortages are emerging as a major social and economic threat, especially in China and India. They describe how this threat has implications for human security as well as for national and international security in India, Bangladesh, and the Mekong Delta region.

Paul J. Smith has served as Research Fellow and Lt. Col. Charles H. Gross as Military Instructor at the Asia-Pacific Center for Security Studies. The Center was created to build on the strong bilateral relationships between the United States Pacific Command and the armed forces of the nations in the Asia-Pacific region by focusing on the broader multilateral approach to addressing regional security issues and concerns.

Water security is emerging as an increasingly important and vital issue for the Asia-Pacific region. Perhaps no other resource—other than oxygen—is so intricately linked to human health and survival. However, as the region's population growth continues to surge, the demand for water is increasing substantially, without a concomitant increase in water resources. Many Asian countries are beginning to experience moderate to severe water shortages, brought on by the simultaneous effects of agricultural growth, industrialization, and urbanization. In recent years, moreover, evidence indicates that water security is becoming increasingly affected by erratic weather patterns, most notably the *El Nino* and *La Nina* weather phenomena. Several countries in the region, including Indonesia and Papua New Guinea, have experienced droughts of such severity that they have caused food shortages and have

From Paul J. Smith and Charles H. Gross, "Water and Conflict in Asia?" presented at a conference of the Asia-Pacific Center for Security Studies, September 17, 1999.

threatened the long-term food supply. In the future, climate change may produce even more erratic weather and result in similar crises. Another concern in the region is growing competition over shared water resources. Singapore, for example, is highly dependent on (and vulnerable to) Malaysia for its water supplies. Many nations, such as those in the Mekong Delta region, share water resources and depend on mutual cooperation. In South Asia, conflict over freshwater has strained relations between India and Bangladesh, as well as India and Pakistan. In the future, diminishing and degraded freshwater resources could lead to internal instability in many nations, and possibly even spark interstate conflict.

To explore this complex issue, the Asia-Pacific Center for Security Studies (APCSS) held a one-day seminar on September 17, 1999, entitled "Water and Conflict in Asia?" The purpose of the seminar was to assess the current and future water security situation in the Asia-Pacific region and to identify factors that would likely influence water security in the future. In particular, the panel focused on two case studies: India-Bangladesh and the Mekong Region. The seminar also explored linkages between water security and traditional national security and national sovereignty. The seminar was divided into four sessions: (1) Current Global Outlook for Water Security; (2) Analyzing the Factors that Contribute to Water Security; (3) Analyzing Water Security Case Studies (from an interstate perspective): India-Bangladesh and the Mekong Region; (4) Policy Solutions. This report serves simultaneously as a seminar report and a research survey to explore the current and potential reality of water security problems in the Asia-Pacific region.

Water Security: Access vs. Availability

The world's freshwater supply is finite. Most of the world's water—about 97.5 percent—exists as salt water in the oceans and seas. Of the world's 2.5 percent of freshwater, roughly 99 percent is either trapped in glaciers and ice caps, held as soil moisture, or located in water tables too deep to access. Thus, only about one percent of the world's total freshwater supply is readily available for consumption by humans, animals, and for irrigation. With regard to water supplies, experts currently distinguish between the problems of "water stress" vs. "water scarcity." Water stress occurs when a country's annual water supplies drop below 1,700 cubic meters per person. When these levels reach between 1,700 and 1,000 cubic meters per person, occasional water shortages are likely to occur. However, when water supplies drop below 1,000 cubic meters per person, the country faces water scarcity which can threaten food production, undermine economic development, and harm ecosystems.[1] Today, more than 31 countries around the world, representing about 8 percent of the world population, are facing chronic freshwater shortages (thus reaching the scarcity stage), and this number will likely grow to 45 countries by the year 2025.

When analyzing freshwater and its relationship to human consumption, it is useful to delineate two concepts: availability vs. access. Availability refers to the physical presence of adequate water supplies, whereas access refers to the ability of people within a particular country or region to actually receive or gain access to clean freshwater. Obviously, these are two distinct types of problems, although they can both be present in a region experiencing water stress or water scarcity. Availability may be more dependent on physical or environmental factors (i.e., the geography of a particular country or climate change, etc.), whereas access may be more dependent on social or political factors (i.e., how much of a country's agricultural sector is dependent on irrigation, or how effective a country's municipal water supply is, etc.). Thus, when we ask the question—are we facing a water crisis?—we should actually be framing the question to reflect the problem of availability vs. the problem of access.

The Availability Issue: Is Asia Running Out of Freshwater?

In Asia, water shortages—both in the form of stress and scarcity—are emerging as a major social and economic threat, especially in China and India. In China, although freshwater resources are abundant, they are distributed unevenly and hence are unavailable to many regions of the country. The amount of rainfall in China ranges from 200 mm in inland desert areas up to 2,000 mm along the southern tropical coast.[2] Water shortages in China's urban areas are especially serious. Of the country's 640 major cities, more than 300 face water shortages. Clean water is, moreover, becoming increasingly scarce because of an increase in domestic and industrial effluents. Every year in China, thousands of tons of pollutants from agricultural, industrial, and municipal sources are dumped into the nation's rivers, lakes, and reservoirs, a trend that is common throughout the region. The economic consequences of water shortages in China are significant: water shortages in cities cause a loss of an estimated 120 billion yuan (US$11.2 billion) in industrial output each year. The cost to human health of water pollution has been estimated to be as high as 41.73 billion yuan (US$3.9 billion) per year.[3]

India is experiencing similar shortages. In 1998, a government minister warned that per capita availability of freshwater was declining due to rapid population growth and industrialization. The minister told the Indian parliament that the per capita availability of freshwater in 2025 is expected to be 1,500 cubic meters per year, as compared to 2,200 cubic meters in 1997 and 5,300 cubic meters in 1955.[4] Many of the seminar participants noted that water scarcity is likely to worsen in Asia in the years ahead. This will have a huge negative impact on food security, as Asian agriculture is already heavily reliant on irrigation, with much of the anticipated increases in food production likely to be dependent on even higher levels of irrigation and irrigation efficiency.

The Access Issue: Does Asia's Population Have Access to Safe Freshwater?

Water shortages are often described in terms of a lack of availability, but, in fact, as many experts assert, the fact that people do not have safe drinking water is often an issue of access. As Sandra Postel has argued, "It's a problem of inadequate government investment, of political will, of making it a priority to meet the basic water needs of the poor. It's a solvable problem, if we decide to do it."[5] One participant argued strongly that access to clean and safe drinking water should be an entitlement for the entire population; this does not necessary mean that it must be free. But there should be an assumption in the international community that water is essential and should be available for everyone.

In general, the question of access to safe freshwater largely depends on the level of development of a particular country. Industrialized countries in the region—for example, Japan, Singapore, and Taiwan—clearly have fewer problems with providing their populations with access to safe freshwater. Less developed countries—China and India, for example—face much greater challenges in this regard. At this stage, the seminar considered the challenge for providing water to populations of less developed countries, especially the poorest segments of these populations. Several seminar participants noted that water is an essential human rights issue; without it, no other human right would be meaningful. Thus, it was argued that assurance of adequate water supplies is implied in international human rights law. In developed countries, access to water is considered an entitlement; this mentality does not necessarily prevail in developing countries where access to safe drinking water is often a luxury, sometimes available only to the affluent. The problem in many developing countries is that water systems are frequently created as a result of local political considerations, not out of any large-scale strategic vision. Thus, market forces often do not govern the pricing of water; rather, it is subject to local political pressures. In this sense, as one participant noted, water is a "political commodity."

Factors that Influence Water Security

There are many factors that influence the availability of water and access to it. This session of the seminar attempted to identify and focus on some of the key factors that determine whether a particular nation, or region, has water security. Among the questions raised were: what are the determinants of water security? Which factors are most important? How is water security related to food security? The following were noted as being critical determinants of water security in the region.

Agriculture

One issue that consistently emerged is the impact of growing food demand on global water supplies. Experts are warning that food production will likely be seriously constrained by freshwater shortages in the next century. As one expert has noted, "the need for irrigation water is likely to be greater than currently anticipated, and the available supply of it less than anticipated."[6] This is because agriculture is extremely dependent on an adequate freshwater supply. The Green Revolution resulted in increased crop yields, but achieved these yields largely through extensive irrigation and with increased reliance on freshwater. In fact, almost 70 percent of the world's freshwater supply is devoted to agriculture, and thus is unavailable for other uses. In Asia, this reliance is even more significant because an estimated 35 to 40 percent of the region's cultivated land is irrigated and this area produces over 60 percent of Asia's total agricultural output.[7]

Thus, in Asia it is clear that the growing demand for food is a significant factor determining the supply of available freshwater. In China, for instance, it is commonly accepted that, with growing population demands, food production will need to be increased dramatically. About 70 percent of the additional food supply in China during the next 25-30 years is expected to come from irrigated lands. Because irrigation is expensive—partly attributable to its inefficiency—it will be very difficult to maintain adequate water supplies in the future. About half of the water that is used for irrigation is lost to seepage and evaporation. Irrigation is also a major concern for many other Asian countries; six Asian countries (China, India, Indonesia, Korea, Pakistan, and Sri Lanka) have in excess of 30 percent of their total cropland under irrigation.[8] Irrigation can be a powerful tool for expanding crop yields, but it can also be extremely dangerous when mismanaged. For example, mismanaging water resources can result in the erosion, waterlogging, and salinization of the soil, which in turn makes the soil less able to produce crops. Poorly managed irrigation can also result in water pollution and water-borne diseases.[9]

Industrialization

Aside from agriculture, another factor that influences the state of water security in a particular country is its degree of industrialization. Industries account for roughly 25 percent of the world's water use and that number is much higher in industrial countries (as high as 50-80 percent). In developing countries, the percentage tends to hover around 10-30 percent.[10] Industrial activity requires massive amounts of freshwater for such activities as boiling, cleaning, air conditioning, cooling, processing, transportation, and energy production.[11] As developing countries industrialize, they must use ever-greater quantities of water.

The positive side of this trend is that water used in industrial processes can be recycled, since—unlike in agriculture—very little of it is actually consumed. In developed industrial countries, the primary impetus for water recycling is compliance with pollution laws. Since it is often more economical to comply with pollution laws by recycling water, less is wasted.[12] Unfortunately such trends are not as apparent in poorer developing countries where few governments provide industry with incentives to adopt more efficient water-use practices. Consequently, although the amount of water being used for industrial purposes is decreasing in the developed world, it is actually increasing in poorer, developing countries. This further strains freshwater resources in countries already facing rapid urbanization.[13]

Environmental Factors

Environmental factors (such as pollution or climate change) can also influence water security for a particular nation or region. Many countries throughout the world routinely dump human and industrial waste into their rivers and lakes. In developing countries, roughly 90-95 percent of all domestic sewage and 75 percent of all industrial waste are discharged into surface waters without any treatment.[14] In many parts of Asia, pollution is a major culprit behind the dwindling availability of freshwater. In South Korea, for example, more than 300 factories along the Naktong River illegally discharged toxic wastes directly into the river.[15] In China, nearly three-fourths of the nation's rivers are so badly polluted that they no longer support fish life.[16] Meanwhile, all of India's 14 major rivers are polluted, primarily because they transport 50 million cubic meters of untreated sewage into India's coastal waters every year. New Delhi alone is responsible for dumping more than 200 million liters of raw sewage and 20 million liters of industrial wastes into the Yamuna River as it passes through the city on its way to the Ganges.[17] The same trend can be seen in many Southeast Asian countries. In Malaysia and Thailand, pollutants in those nations' rivers—such as pathogens, heavy metals, and various poisons from industry and agriculture—regularly exceed government standards by 30 to 100 times.[18]

Another potential environmental threat to water security in Asia is global warming and climate change. Changing weather patterns could result in droughts in areas accustomed to plentiful rainfall and vice versa. In 1997, for instance, unusual weather patterns resulting from the *El Nino* weather phenomenon left many Southeast Asian countries with little rainfall. Thailand, for example, saw very little rainfall during the May-to-November rainy season.[19] In the Philippines, drought conditions sparked more than 200,000 families in Mindanao to pour into cities in search of food supplies. Indonesian officials asserted in 1998 that the drought would result in a reduction of the country's rice-planting areas by 4.13 percent.[20] Similarly, a prolonged drought in Papua New Guinea that same year resulted in widespread food shortages, which in turn prompted neighboring countries—such as Australia—to offer food aid.[21]

Land degradation is another environmental variable that can influence the availability of water. As countries experience greater urbanization or deforestation, less land is available to absorb and hold water. Degraded land usually has reduced vegetative cover and the soil is less able to hold water; consequently, rainfall likely results in flash runoff. This leads to reduced seepage and aquifer recharge.[22] In India, land degradation has resulted in reduced aquifer recharge, even in areas that receive large amounts of annual rainfall. As a result, many village authorities in high rainfall regions in India petition the central government for drought relief.[23] Similar trends can be seen in China. In Beijing, water tables beneath the city are dropping by a rate of roughly 1-2 meters a year, and a third of the city's wells have reportedly dried up. Moreover, in recent years, more than 100 Chinese cities in northern and coastal regions have experienced severe water shortages.[24]

Deforestation is yet another challenge to water security in Asia. Deforestation is rife in Asia currently—overall, Asia's forest cover is shrinking by 1 percent a year.[25] In Indonesia, forests are shrinking at a rate of between 600,000 and 1.3 million hectares per year, for a variety of reasons, including illegal logging and the conversion of forests to large-scale commercial agriculture and timber plantations.[26] In Cambodia, forests covered over 70 percent of the country in the late 1960s; now only about half are still in existence.[27] Similar trends can be seen in Thailand where between 1961 and 1988, forest cover shrank from 55 percent of the country's land area to 28 percent.[28] Deforestation is a major factor in water security because "tropical forests protect fragile soils from temperature and rainfall extremes."[29] Moreover, if trees are removed, it can create a cycle of flooding and drought that results in extreme soil erosion and, in the most extreme cases, desertification.[30]

Demographic Factors

When looking at future scenarios involving water, it is important to consider human population growth. At the beginning of the 20th century, the world's population was roughly 1.6 billion people, but by 1990 it had increased to around 5.3 billion—an increase of 330 percent.[31] Currently, the world's population is increasing by around 80 million per year and is expected to reach

8.5 billion by the year 2025. Roughly half of this population will live in Asia—although Asian countries only occupy about 16 percent of the world's total land surface. Population growth in Asia is seen as a major challenge for water security in the region.

Related to population growth is the growing trend of urbanization, a phenomenon that is especially apparent in Asia. Among other things, urbanization is expected to shift water out of agriculture to supply drinking water for growing cities.[32] In China, growing industrialization and urbanization are requiring increased amounts of water, the same water that would have gone to agriculture. Roughly half of China's cultivated land is irrigated; as demand for water rises, the country will need to deploy water-saving and waste-treatment technology.[33]

Conservation Factors

Many seminar participants agreed that a key factor in water security is the degree of wastage that occurs. If water were used more efficiently—in agricultural, industrial, and municipal settings— it could help insure water security. In many irrigation systems, as little as 37 percent of the water used is actually absorbed by crops; the remainder is lost through evaporation, seepage, or runoff.[34] According to the Food and Agriculture Organization of the United Nations (FAO), more than 10 to 20 percent of the water used for agricultural purposes could be saved if more efficient irrigation methods were utilized. In Pakistan, for instance, if the efficiency of the irrigation system could be increased by 10 percent, the water saved could irrigate another 2 million hectares.[35]

Water in urban areas is also wasted. In developed countries, experts calculate that about 10 percent of water is lost due to leaks in municipal water networks; in developing countries, this number could be as high as 60 percent.[36] One participant argued for encouraging greater water-use efficiency by privatizing urban water supply and waste management, increasing service fees, transferring government responsibilities to beneficiaries or customers, and removing all subsidies from all water-related services.[37]

Freshwater as a Security Concern

In the post Cold War era, the definition of security is being expanded to include a host of non-traditional issues such as environmental degradation and transnational crime. Food, or more specifically a shortage of food, is acknowledged as a serious security concern in many Asian nations. With burgeoning populations, poverty, and little hope of dramatically expanding agricultural activities, the sustainability of food supplies is becoming a key security concern for government officials. Similarly, in some quarters the availability of clean freshwater is increasingly being characterized as a security issue.

One could argue that perhaps water security really is not a security concern in and of itself, or that it should fall under the larger rubric of "environmental security" or "resource depletion." Nevertheless, regardless of how it is defined, it was the consensus of the seminar that freshwater scarcity poses a very serious, complex, and potentially wide-ranging threat to regional stability. This threat could manifest itself in a number of different ways, such as directly in the form of violent conflicts over freshwater resources, or indirectly by causing large-scale migration and food shortages. It was also recognized that to fully appreciate the complexity of the water security issue, it has to be viewed on three basic levels.

Human Security

Freshwater can become a security issue when it is linked to so-called "human security," which encompasses a variety of issues that have an impact on human health and well-being. From this perspective, water is a clear security problem if one considers the large number of human deaths that occur as a result of unsafe or inadequate water. Approximately 25,000 people die every day from water-related diseases. In Bangladesh, it is estimated that three-quarters of all diseases are linked to unsafe water and inadequate sanitation facilities. Experts estimate that about 60 percent of all infant mortality throughout the world is tied to infectious and parasitic diseases, most of them related to water.[38] Diarrheal diseases, moreover, are prevalent in countries with inadequate sewage treatment. An estimated 4 billion people per year contract diarrheal disease, and among that number approximately 3-4 million die annually, and most of these people are young children.[39] Unsanitary water is clearly a major health threat for millions in the developing world.

Regarding the inclusion of freshwater as a security issue under the banner of "human security," one participant noted that conflict could be divided between acute conflict and structural conflict, since "conflict is fundamentally an incompatibility of interests." Acute conflict—violence whether among individuals or among states—obviously results in human casualties; on the other hand, structural conflict also results in human carnage and can, in fact, be much larger in scale. The problem of access to water is a structural conflict problem that results in thousands of deaths every day. If security is defined, at least partly, by number of deaths, then clearly water is a security issue.

Internal Security and Governance

The specific impact of freshwater on intra-state security is far more complex and less easily ascertained. Although the potential for conflicts among countries over shared water resources receives much attention in the popular media, its impacts within nation-states are far more insidious and indirect. Water insecurity constrains economic development and contributes to a host of corrosive social behaviors that can, in turn, produce violence within societies.[40] Freshwater scarcity, often causally related with other factors such as poverty, population growth, infrastructure problems, and environmental degradation, can escalate the aforementioned "human security" problem into a national security issue. Water security can be the catalyst for large-scale migration and ethnic conflicts, which ultimately, in more dire situations, can result in a decline in effective governance, potentially leading to a "failed state."

International Security

Most of the participants tended to agree that disputes among nations solely over freshwater resources are not likely to spark violent conflict. Nevertheless, there was an understanding that water security issues can have a destabilizing effect on regional and international security. Spawned by globalization, the increasing economic and political interdependence of nations ultimately means greater potential for spillover of problems. Ethnic unrest, mass migration, and declining economic conditions, fanned by freshwater scarcity, are not likely to be confined neatly within a country's borders. Additionally, the same factors that undermine the domestic effectiveness of a government systematically erode its ability to interact on an international level. This can have an adverse effect on negotiation and implementation of a wide variety of international agreements that range from collective security to economic and global environmental issues.

Water is increasingly viewed as a strategic resource, one that is to be protected and valued. Consequently, when one or more countries share water resources, the potential for disputes or conflicts is always present. Although no nation has yet gone to war over water, this potential scenario could unfold given the right conditions. As one study has suggested, "a set of factors including demographics, rising demand resulting from improved living standards, the predominance of upstream over downstream—the first-served control the flow of rivers—may stoke smoldering conflicts."[41]

Political conflict between nation-states over access to water rights is partly the result of unsettled questions in international law. Four major approaches to water rights include: absolute sovereignty, prior appropriation (acquired and historical), riparian, and equitable utilization. The first two, absolute sovereignty and prior appropriation, tend to benefit upstream states at the expense of all other parties. For example, under principles of absolute sovereignty (also known as the "Harmon Doctrine"), a state can do what it pleases with its water resources regardless of any impact on a neighboring state. This is similar to the prior appropriation doctrine ("first in time, first in right") that was common in the western United States during the early 1800s. Under this doctrine, the upstream party has first rights to the water; only if it doesn't use them do other parties have a chance to determine usage.

Obviously the above principles appeal to upstream nations, and particularly to *strong* and *powerful* upstream nations. As one Chinese expression puts it, "upstream doesn't suffer." However, more equitable approaches to water rights are encapsulated in principles such as riparian rights and equitable utilization. Equitable utilization tends to benefit both upstream and downstream states and is especially beneficial to a weaker country that happens to be a downstream state. In fact, as one participant noted, even strong upstream countries have, in practice, tended to compromise with weaker downstream neighbors in order to promote some degree of equitable utilization of water resources.[42]

To examine the role of water in international relations, the seminar considered two case studies: India-Bangladesh and the Mekong Delta region.

India-Bangladesh

For many years, India and Bangladesh have exchanged sharp accusations over shared river resources. In 1993, tensions between India and Bangladesh boiled over when the dry-season flow of the Ganges [Ganga] River reached severely low levels, and resulted in crop losses in Bangladesh. Later in October 1995, Bangladesh Prime Minister Begum Khaleda Zia delivered an address to the United Nations in which she called India's diversion of river water near the border "a gross violation of human rights and justice."[43] India's establishment of the "Farakka Barrage" on the Ganges near the border with Bangladesh has also sparked conflict and disagreement between the two nations. India's purpose in building the barrage was to divert water to the Calcutta port, but Bangladesh contends that such diversion has resulted in falling water tables and greater water salinity downstream for Bangladesh. Dhaka has even proposed an alternative Ganges Barrage to solve the problems created by the first barrage.[44]

Water disputes between India and Bangladesh, as the presenter noted, have been subsumed under the overall difficult relations that have persisted between the two nations. As would be expected, the two nations see the dispute from different perspectives. According to the Bangladeshi view of the dispute, there was a "unilateral diversion" of the waters of the Ganga by India at the Farakka barrage which was detrimental to Bangladesh. Consequently, according to the Bangladeshi perspective, the resulting reductions in flows had severe adverse effects on Bangladesh and the policy reflected a classic case of a more powerful country disregarding the legitimate interests of a smaller and weaker neighbor. This particular view is prevalent throughout Bangladesh and has become a significant issue in the nation's electoral politics.

India, on the other hand, subscribes to a very different view of the issue. Among Indian bureaucrats, there has been a perception that Bangladesh was extremely rigid and unreasonable regarding this issue and had greatly over-stated its water needs. Another problem was rooted in India's federal struc-ture: individual Indian states tended to view the Indian central government as overly generous toward Bangladesh, at their expense. In any case, from a political perspective, the water dispute between India and Bangladesh has contributed to a deterioration of relations between the two nations. Bangladesh has pleaded with India for a "minimum guarantee" agreement (with regard to the water flow). Nevertheless, the two countries were able to reach an agree-ment in 1996 when the "Treaty on the Sharing of the Waters of the Ganga" was signed. Although some political parties on both sides were dissatisfied with the treaty, it was generally accepted by most political leaders (although in India, several states, including Bihar and Uttar Pradesh, have complained that their interests have not been properly taken into account).

Since the treaty was signed, India has been relatively satisfied with the outcome; Bangladesh, however, continues to have a number of problems with it, primarily attributable to perceptions that the quantity of water actually received does not match expectations brought about by the treaty. Tensions between Bangladesh and India may appear to be sparked by conflict over water, but as one participant noted, "it is not always a case of conflicts over water resources leading to a worsening of political relations, though that does happen on occasion; it is more often a case of a difficult political relationship rendering the water issue more intractable."[45]

Mekong Delta Region

If recent agreements between India and Bangladesh on water-sharing can be seen as a success, then the Mekong Delta region would probably reflect the *realpolitik* dimension of water conflict. The Mekong River, considered the 10th largest river in the world in terms of volume of water, runs for approxi-mately 2,600 miles from its origins in Qinghai Province, China, through Yunnan and southward through or by Myanmar, Laos, Cambodia, Thailand, and Vietnam. In China, the river is very rugged and drops a total of 5,000 meters from its source to the Lao border. At that point, the river descends at a more gentle grade as it meanders toward the South China Sea in southern Vietnam.

Many millions of people are dependent on the Mekong River (and the larger Mekong basin) for agricultural and fishing purposes. Thailand and Laos are interested in the river's potential in producing hydro-electricity. Laos, moreover, sees the river as critical for its agricultural interests. Similarly,

Cambodia and Vietnam rely on the Mekong for agriculture and, moreover, Cambodia is particularly dependent on the river for its valuable fishing industry. The Mekong also provides critical transportation corridors.

Since 1957, when the Mekong Committee was established, there have been various regional initiatives to develop the basin. However, some earlier efforts were derailed by war in Indochina. Later, an "Agreement on Cooperation for Sustainable Development of the Mekong River Basin Agreement" established the Mekong River Commission, which first met in Hanoi in 1995. A year earlier, the Quadripartite Economic Cooperation plan (QEC), which was composed of Myanmar, Thailand, China, and Laos, established guidelines for freedom of navigation of the upper reaches of the Mekong in an effort to foster transportation and tourism.

Other regional efforts to support development of the Mekong include those initiated by the Asian Development Bank (ADB) and ASEAN. In recent years, the ADB has supported the development of the Greater Mekong Subregion (GMS), composed of all six riparian states, with a particular emphasis on trade, transportation, energy, human resource development, etc. As for ASEAN, the ASEAN Mekong Basin Development Corporation was established and is being coordinated by Malaysia (with China serving in an observer status).

Despite these numerous ambitious plans, developing the Mekong Subregion has faced numerous obstacles. First, there has been a lack of adequate coordination among the various international agencies and national programs. Funding constraints have also presented a challenge; the Greater Mekong Subregion (GMS) is expected to require US$40 billion over the next 25 years. Moreover, development plans have been derailed, at least temporarily, by Southeast Asia's economic crisis. Finally, there are numerous tensions among various social and economic groups over what should be done with the water. Non-governmental organizations (NGOs), for example, have varied and often contradictory agendas for the region.

The presenter on this issue was much less sanguine about the possibility for cooperation among the major parties that border the Mekong River. China plays a major role in this region, but it still refuses to join regional organizations. China has a number of strategic interests; first, China is interested in transportation and using the Mekong River for transportation. Secondly, China is eager to have access to the Indian Ocean and badly wants an outlet. In 1995, China refused to sign the regional agreement, stating that "whatever action it takes to exploit the Mekong's potential is purely an internal matter."[46]

Conclusion

Access to clean, safe freshwater is recognized universally as one of the most basic and vital needs of humanity. Yet with the world population projected to increase to nearly 9 billion over the next few decades, bringing with it the associated need for greater food production and industry, it stands to reason that shortages of clean freshwater can potentially have broad and far-reaching security implications.

At its most fundamental level, freshwater security is a human security problem. The health of millions of people is already jeopardized by short-ages and pollution of freshwater supplies, particularly in poor developing nations. Nonetheless, in the larger context, this so-called human security is-sue has the potential to affect more traditional concepts of security, with con-sequences beyond local, provincial, and national borders. Although most agree that the possibility that sovereign nations will engage in direct conflict over freshwater resources is unlikely (in the short term), water insecurity can indi-rectly affect events that have a direct bearing on regional and international security.

Clean freshwater is not only essential for human life, but also for eco-nomic development and agriculture. Consequently, a severe reduction in wa-ter resources can damage a nation's economy and food supply. Such a scenario could potentially lead to social unrest and exacerbate existing ethnic, racial, and societal conflicts. A parallel problem is that these same economic and social problems may systematically erode a government's ability to deal with them. In extreme cases governance itself may be undermined, resulting in internal chaos and national collapse. The international "spill over" effects of such outcome—such as mass refugee outflows—would be destabilizing for neighboring countries.

As the supply of freshwater diminishes throughout the world, many ex-perts see the need for a "blue revolution" (similar to what the "green revolu-tion" was for food). Such a revolution is necessary, according to these experts, in order to arrest the continued trend of dwindling freshwater resources and its consequences. Reliance on technical solutions—such as desalination, water transport by tankers and other non-conventional solutions—are likely to pro-vide only limited solutions. The costs of these solutions are generally prohi-bitive and they do little to address the major water needs of the next 25 years.[47]

In short, there needs to be recognition that water insecurity (in the form of water stress or water scarcity) is not an isolated problem. Its effects can extend to human, national, regional, and international security. Consequently, governments in the Asia-Pacific region should encourage and promote more effective conservation efforts, greater environmental awareness, and the rec-ognition that all people have a basic need and right to clean freshwater.

Notes

1. "Solutions for a Water-Short World," *Population Reports* (vol. 26, no. 1) Sep-tember 1, 1998.

2. Bert L. Kramer, "Factors that Influence Water Security," paper prepared for the "Water and Conflict Seminar," held at the Asia-Pacific for Security Studies, Honolulu, Hawaii (September 17, 1999).

3. *World Resources 1998–99: A Guide to the Global Environment* (New York: Oxford University Press, 1998).

4. "Freshwater Availability Going Down in India," *Deutsche Press-Agentur*, July 22, 1998.

5. Jim Motavalli and Elaine Robbins, "The Coming Age of Water Scarcity," *E*, Sep/Oct 1998.

6. Sandra L. Postel, "Water for Food Production: Will There Be Enough in 2025?" *BioScience*, August 1998. See chapter 4, this volume.

7. Bert L. Kramer, "Factors that Influence Water Security," Paper presented to the Asia-Pacific Center for Security Studies Seminar on "Water and Conflict in Asia" (Honolulu, September 17, 1999).

8. Ibid.

9. William Bender and Margaret Smith, "Population, Food, and Nutrition," *Population Bulletin*, vol. 51, no. 4 (Washington, DC: Population Reference Bureau, 1997).

10. Sandra Postel, *Last Oasis: Facing Water Scarcity* (New York: W.W. Norton and Company, 1997), p. 136.

11. Kent Hughes, "The Strategic Importance of Water," *Parameters*, Spring 1997.

12. Sandra Postel, *Last Oasis: Facing Water Scarcity* (New York: W.W. Norton and Company, 1997), p. 37.

13. Ibid., p. 143.

14. "Solutions for a Water-Short World," *Population Reports* (vol. 26, no. 1) September 1, 1998.

15. Sandra Postel, *Last Oasis: Facing Water Scarcity* (New York: W. W. Norton and Company, 1997), p. 143.

16. "Solutions for a Water-Short World," *Population Reports* (vol. 26, no. 1) September 1, 1998.

17. Ibid.

18. Ibid.

19. Doungsuda Fungladda, "Water Shortage in Thailand Threatens Stability in Farm Sector," *The Nikkei Weekly*, February 15, 1999, p. 20.

20. Gary Mead, "Drought Hits Rice Crop in Indonesia," *Financial Times*, August 20, 1998, p. 26.

21. "One in Four Hit by Drought," *BBC Summary of World Broadcasts*, January 8, 1998.

22. Sandra Postel, *Last Oasis: Facing Water Scarcity* (New York: W.W. Norton and Company, 1997), p. 35.

23. Ibid.

24. Ibid.

25. *Emerging Asia: Changes and Challenges* (Manila: Asian Development Bank, 1997).

26. Charles Victor Barber, "Forest Resource Scarcity and Social Conflict in Indonesia," *Environment*, May 1998.

27. "Cambodia Trade: Disappearing Trees," *EIU ViewsWire* (Economist Intelligence Unit), February 24, 1997.

28. "Thailand: Demographic and Social Trends," *EIU Country Forecasts* (Economist Intelligence Unit), March 7, 1997.

29. Alan Dupont, *The Environment and Security in Pacific Asia* (Adelphi Paper, 1998), Chapter 5 on "Water Scarcity," p. 62.

30. Ibid.

31. Bert L. Kramer, "Factors that Influence Water Security," paper prepared for the "Water and Conflict Seminar," held at the Asia-Pacific Center for Security Studies, Honolulu, Hawaii (September 17, 1999).

32. Sandra L. Postel, "Water for Food Production: Will There Be Enough in 2025?" *BioScience*, August 1998.

33. Frederick Cook, "Grain Galore: China's Focus on Grain Production," *The China Business Review* Vol. 24, No. 5 (September 19, 1997), p. 8.

34. Kent H. Butts, "The Strategic Importance of Water," *Parameters*, Spring 1997.

35. *Emerging Asia: Changes and Challenges* (Manila: Asian Development Bank, 1997).

36. France Bequette, "Water: Will There Be Enough? Fresh or Drinking Water," UNESCO Courier, June 1998, p. 42.

37. Bert L. Kramer, "Factors that Influence Water Security," paper prepared for the "Water and Conflict Seminar," held at the Asia-Pacific Center for Security Studies, Honolulu, Hawaii (September 17, 1999).

38. "Solutions for a Water-Short World," *Population Reports* (vol. 26, no. 1) September 1, 1998.

39. Ibid.

40. Thomas F. Homer-Dixon, "Environment, Scarcity, and Violence," Princeton University Press, 1999, p. 69.

41. France Bequette, "Water: Will There Be Enough? Fresh or Drinking Water," *UNESCO Courier*, June 1998, p. 42.

42. James E. Nkkum, "Some Factors that Influence Water Security, and Some that Don't," paper prepared for the "Water and Conflict Seminar," held at the Asia-Pacific Center for Security Studies, Honolulu, Hawaii (September 17, 1999),

43. Sandra Postel, *Last Oasis: Facing Water Scarcity* (New York: W.W. Norton and Company, 1997), p. xxiii.

44. Rajendra Dahal, "Development–Nepal: South Asian Mega-Projects Spark Water Quarrels," *Inter Press Service*, June 16, 1998.

45. Ramaswamy R. Iyer, "Ganga Waters: Dispute and Resolutions," paper prepared for the "Water and Conflict Seminar," held at the Asia-Pacific Center for Security Studies, Honolulu, Hawaii (September 17, 1999).

46. Alan Dupont, *The Environment and Security in Pacific Asia* (London: International Institute for Strategic Studies, 1998).

47. Bert L. Kramer, "Factors that Influence Water Security," paper prepared for the "Water and Conflict Seminar," held at the Asia-Pacific Center for Security Studies, Honolulu, Hawaii (September 17, 1999).

7

Life—or Death—for the Salton Sea?

Robert H. Boyle

We tend to focus on the implications for humans of freshwater overexploitation and decline. But it is increasingly clear that most terrestrial ecosystems also depend on freshwater for their health. In other words, using all the available freshwater for the needs of people would have serious consequences for the health of ecosystems upon which humans and many other animals depend. In this chapter, Robert Boyle takes a look at the slow death of the Salton Sea in California, which began life as a freshwater lake. After almost a century of intense human use, the Salton Sea is increasingly polluted with agricultural runoff and hazardous materials that have made it increasingly unfit as a source for migratory waterfowl.

Robert H. Boyle's efforts on behalf of the Hudson River Fishermen's Association (which he founded in 1966) led to the first prosecutions of industrial polluters in the United States. A staff writer for thirty-four years at Sports Illustrated, *he has authored numerous articles on the environment. He is the author, co-author, or editor of more than eight books on major environmental issues.*

You half expect to hear Captain Kirk say, "Beam me down, Scotty. This is the strangest lake I've ever seen." Illuminated by a G-Class star and flanked by Martian-like mountains with ancient dry washes, the reddish brown lake covers 380 square miles of a deep desert bowl. Mud volcanoes bubble along its southeastern shore, the rotten-egg stench of hydrogen sulfide pervades its backwaters, and yet hundreds of thousands of birds, many strange to the eye, feed along the edges of the lake or bob on the open water. And there on the western shore lies the outline of a lost city.

This bizarre body of water is not on some strange planet in a distant galaxy. It is the Salton Sea in the southeastern corner of California near the

From Robert H. Boyle, "Life—or Death—for the Salton Sea?" *Smithsonian* (June 1996): 87–96. Reprinted by permission of Robert H. Boyle.

Mexican border; the lost city is Salton City, laid out for 40,000 people and never finished.

That was in the late 1950s, when the Salton Sea was supposed to become the Golden State's great new playland, a whole new concept of Southern California living, with an "alluring combination of the desert and the sea." M. Penn Phillips and other developers of Salton City bought 19,600 acres that they subdivided on paper for house lots, shops, schools, parks and churches. They spent $1 million on a freshwater distribution system with 260 miles of water lines. They put in power lines and 250 miles of paved streets in elegantly contoured patterns, with names like Sea Kist Avenue and Shore Jewel Avenue. They built a yacht club and lavished $350,000 on an 18-hole golf course. Developer Ray Ryan, a big-time gambler with reputed mob connections, bought land on the other side of the sea and sank more than $2 million into a resort he named the North Shore Beach and Yacht Club.

While real estate salesmen gave the pitch to those who came down from Palm Springs or Los Angeles to look over lots or to party, visiting celebrities—Frank Sinatra, Jerry Lewis and Linda Darnell—added to the hype. Even so, construction crawled in the desert heat, and in the late 1960s sales went nowhere. Unexpected heavy rains kept raising the level of the sea and flooding shoreline homes and buildings. A steadily growing concern set in about the water's brownish tinge, about pollution levels and the increasing salt content.

Today Ryan's North Shore Beach and Yacht Club is deserted, its breakwater submerged and its swimming pool crumbling. Across the water, although chamber of commerce brochures still welcome folks to "The Fabulous Salton Sea . . . Sea, Air and Sun for Healthy Desert Fun," visitors northbound on Route 86 to Salton City find not sailboats and bikini-clad blondes on water skis, or docks packed with pleasure boats but, instead, a scattering of houses, modest RV parks, defunct motels and empty lots on streets often shaggy with tall grass.

The Salton Sea has been described as a "mistake of man and perhaps of nature." But it is in fact a perplexing and spectacular example of a collaboration between the two with unexpected results. The surface of the sea lies 227 feet below the level of the ocean in one of the hottest, driest desert sinks in the world. It came about by accident 90 years ago. That was when the Colorado River violently broke away from its southerly course toward the Gulf of California, and flowed west, then north, from Mexico, creating the Salton Sea.

The new sea was 45 miles long, 17 miles wide and about 80 feet deep. After engineers got the Colorado under control, the sea should have dried up through evaporation. It has no outlets and lies in an area with only 2.3 inches of rain a year and temperatures that reach 120 degrees F. But year after year it has been sustained by drainwater from the 500,000 acres of heavily watered and fertilized growing fields of the Imperial Valley, one of the most fruitful desert irrigation projects in history. In the 1920s the sea was officially designated as the Imperial Valley's catch basin. Agricultural wastewater carries various nutrients, including nitrates, as well as pesticides, potentially toxic levels of the element selenium, and four million tons of salt leached from the soil every year. The sea began life as the largest freshwater lake in California, with rainbow trout originally tumbled into it by the Colorado. Today it is 25 percent saltier than the Pacific Ocean, and getting saltier.

Miles of canals lead Colorado River water through the Imperial Valley, feeding into the Salton's two major tributaries, the Alamo River and the New River. Both flow north from Mexico, receiving drainwater along the way. Considered the most polluted river in the United States, the New glugs through Mexicali, Mexico, a city of more than 750,000 people that dumps in raw sewage, inadequately treated sewage, leachate from landfills, and industrial and slaughterhouse wastes, as well as a visible assortment of trash, toilet paper, dead dogs and phosphate detergents. In fact, most of the bacteria from Mexico seems to die off before its waters reach the Salton Sea. But the appalling condition of the New River serves to stigmatize the sea.

By reputation, the Salton Sea has become a kind of *mer noire*, the marine version of a Hollywood *film noir*. Its southern approaches, in their own way, are as unsettling as the desolation on the western shore or at Ray Ryan's North Shore Beach and Yacht Club. Anyone heading north through the Imperial Valley is overpowered by the smell of fertilizers and cattle feedlots. The landscape is flat, composed of green rectangles defined by drainage ditches. Bales of alfalfa as high and long as an aircraft carrier's deck are stacked along the roads. At the sea's southern rim, geothermal energy plants bear signs, scary if common in this environmentally conscious state, that read: "Area contains chemicals known . . . to cause cancer, birth defects, or other reproductive harm."

Despite a large amount of effluence, the sea was for years one of the greatest fishing spots in California, and has long been one of America's great birding spots. It is a critical station on the Pacific Flyway, and a nesting, feeding and resting ground of international importance, with birds coming from many parts of the world. The sea is listed as a hot spot on a video game called "Gone Birding"; birders flock to its shores, listing their sightings on clipboards maintained at ornithological sites. At least 380 species have been reported, a number exceeded in North America only by the Texas coast in spring. Some are threatened or endangered.

"As many as 5,000 brown pelicans occasionally spend the summer on the sea," says biologist Bill Radke of the U.S. Fish and Wildlife Service, who, until recently, was stationed at the Salton Sea National Wildlife Refuge. "About a third of the world's population of Yuma clapper rails depend upon its wetlands, replenished by irrigation drainwater from adjacent farmlands. The sea provides the only inland nesting sites in the United States for gull-billed terns and provides three of only five nesting sites that exist in the Western U.S. for black skimmers."

In recent years, though, there have been increasing signs of trouble. Early in 1992, Radke was appalled to see a number of eared grebes stagger up on shore to die. Many were so disoriented that they stood still while gulls tore into their flesh and began eating them on the spot. This continued well into March, until the final death toll rose, by conservative estimates, to 150,000 grebes. Radke helped collect 40,000 carcasses. Necropsies ruled out infectious disease as the cause of death, but the tissues of some of the dead birds contained three times more selenium than that of grebes he had tested at the Salton Sea three years earlier.

Selenium is a mysterious, sulphur-like element, deposited by prehistoric volcanic eruptions. It is found in many dry parts of the West, and when seleniferous land is irrigated, selenium can be carried into a watercourse. Though it is an essential trace element for growth in animals and humans, there is a narrow tolerance margin between beneficial and toxic doses. As little as two parts per billion in water can render aquatic vegetation and invertebrates hazardous to birds that eat them.

At present, the selenium level in Salton water is only one part per billion—not yet dangerous. But at the sea's silted bottom, the level ranges from 200 to 2,500 times higher. Pile worms live in the silt and are eaten by fish, which in turn are preyed on by fish-eating birds such as grebes. In the winter of 1994, another 10,000 to 20,000 eared grebes died at the sea after behaving in the same strange fashion as the birds Radke had observed in 1992. The exact cause is not yet known. Stuart Hurlbert of San Diego State University believes that toxic phytoplankton is responsible, and recent studies reinforce this view. But in 1994 Joseph Skorupa, a biologist with the U.S. Fish and Wildlife Service who has been working on selenium contamination elsewhere in California, pointed out that "virtually any time birds are exposed to above background concentrations of selenium, as they clearly are at the Salton Sea, the potential for increased susceptibility to disease exists."

Until recently, almost nothing was really done to try to end problems affecting the sea. This is partly because they have evolved so slowly and partly because they involve conflicting claims to water-sharing in the desert; in a prime agricultural area, such claims will clearly be difficult and expensive to rectify. But the threat of selenium and effluents to bird life has helped draw attention to the sea's multiple troubles.

Its water level tends to rise erratically, damaging the little towns that cling to its western shore, where waterfronts are constantly eroded and trees are destroyed. In the village of Desert Shores recently, the Imperial Irrigation District had to bulldoze a dike into place but still found itself obliged to buy up a few waterfront lots rather than risk lawsuits. For years a successful saltwater fishery, the sea may soon be so salty that even ocean fish won't survive in it. Rich in nutrients from Imperial Valley drainoff, it often has a red-brown algal bloom. Even worse, on bad days—mostly in summer—when the wind is right, the stench of the sea is said to reach 50 miles, all the way up to Palm Springs.

Fortunately, this unusual sea has an unusual champion. He is Norman E. Niver, a 66-year-old musician who now and then used to play bass for his actor friends Alice Faye and the late Phil Harris. "Phil liked the sea," Niver says, "but Alice thought it was a toilet bowl." Niver, a compact, 239-pound, gray-haired bundle of energy, and his wife, Connie, a bar manager, live on the water in the failed resort center of Salton City. They bought their house in 1977. Lots were already cheap and, at as little as $2,500 per quarter-acre, are cheaper still today.

The Nivers and some 5,000 other folks, including flocks of "snowbirds" who from October to March migrate to trailer and RV parks in the three or four towns beside the scenic sea, constitute a close-knit, convivial community heavily sprinkled with retirees. They are attracted to tiny Desert Shores, Salton City and Salton Sea Beach by bargain-basement prices, an almost frontier-like camaraderie and a beakerful of the warm South. (Space for trailers and RVs ranges from $150 to $210 per month.) This is pancake breakfast country, given to pickup classes in painting and ceramics, "Golden Girls" amateur shows, Easter egg hunts, and brisk rounds on a nearly defunct golf course.

"Let's face it," says David Barrett, 73, "by golf course standards it's a wreck, but it gives a lot of people pleasure." Like a good many snowbirds, Barrett, a World War II bomber pilot from Vancouver, British Columbia, is a Canadian. He is also the leader of an over-60 group called the Rat Pack whose members regularly bang around the rugged desert nearby on motorcycles. Indeed, at the seaside, wheels rather than water seem to provide most of the excitement. The highlight of the winter season is Treasure Trails, an event in which hundreds of people blast off into the desert in dune buggies, pickups, motorcycles, jeeps and "rails" (cars with no sides) in search of 175 or so buried treasure chests artfully hidden by the event's sponsors.

Barrett, who has been coming back to the sea for 15 years, says, "There's no necessity to put foot in the water." Every year there have been rumors of plans to fix up the sea, he says, but he doubts anything will happen in his lifetime. He is philosophical about it, perhaps in part because "if the sea were clean, this place would be another Palm Springs, and goodbye to us all."

Norm Niver also defends the sea for its virtues and tries to overlook its faults. The only drawback to living by the sea Niver will admit to is his air-conditioning bill. With summer temperatures that hit 117 in the shade, it costs $300 a month to cool the house down to 80, and then he has to keep wiping the condensation off the windows. But he is a year-round resident, a birder

and a fisherman, and he does not take the condition of the sea philosophi-
cally at all. Even though health officials have warned since 1986 that no one
should eat more than eight ounces of any Salton Sea fish in a two-week period, and that women of childbearing age and children under 14 should ab-
stain completely, Niver regularly eats the orangemouth corvina he catches.
"They're delicious," he insists, adding with a grin that he also fed "tons" of
corvina to his cat Charles, who died a couple of years ago at the hoary age
of 19.

Niver's immediate fear is that increasing salinity will put an end to the
fish, with reverberating effects on some 60 species of fish-eating birds that
use the sea. In the 1960s and '70s, the Salton Sea was one of California's
most productive sport fisheries, with huge schools of corvina, some weighing up to 32 pounds. Now, Niver admits, the number of corvina has dropped
and the fish are generally on the small side, 4 to 10 pounds. Though thousands of Californians still camp out in the state recreational areas along the
eastern shore, anglers don't use the sea in anything like the numbers that they
once did. On the western shore, the few motels that once housed them are
abandoned. Experts say that if the salinity continues to increase at its present
rate of about 0.8 parts per thousand per year, in less than ten years almost all
fish will be gone.

By 1992 Niver's never-ending warnings about increasing salinity helped
goad local politicians into setting up the Salton Sea Authority to improve
water quality. "He's been a great help," says Brad Luckey, an Imperial Valley
farmer and county supervisor and one of the eight directors of the authority.
Luckey put Niver on the Imperial County Planning Commission and last year
named him the very first appointee to a brand-new Citizens Advisory Committee to the Salton Sea Authority.

Over the years, according to Niver, there has been little or no support
from any major environmental group. Gary Polakovic of the Riverside *Press-
Enterprise* reports criticism of environmental groups like the Sierra Club and
the Audubon Society for doing nothing about the plight of Salton Sea wildlife. Niver adds, "They apparently think that if they get involved here, they'll
lose on other water issues in the state."

It is clear that the sea's problems will not be solved any time soon. They
are the product not merely of greed and neglect but of geology. The sea, the
Coachella Valley to the north, and the Imperial Valley with its 500,000 acres
of irrigated fields to the south, all sit in a vast depression not unlike a serving
platter, known as the Salton Sink. Thirty million years ago the sink was part
of the Gulf of California, the terminus of the Colorado River which rises in
the Rockies. The river got its name, Rio Colorado—Red River—from the
loads of brick-colored silt it carried on its way down to the gulf. The river's
silt, as folks used to say, was "too thin to plow, too thick to drink." Until 1936,
when Boulder (now Hoover) Dam was built to regulate the Colorado's flow,

the river carried 160 million tons of suspended sediment a year past Yuma, Arizona.

As the ground leveled and the river slowed, approaching its delta at the Gulf of California, the suspended sediment—from silt to rocks—kept settling out. Periodically the buildup of sediment blocked the river's path to the delta. When this happened and the river exploded in full flood, it would flip like a loose garden hose to the west and, following gravity, pour down into the Salton Sink.

Whenever a new wall of sediment blocked the river's path into the sink, the Colorado would flip back east to its original course to the delta. Flip-flopping over the ages, the Colorado sluiced into the sink often enough to create a well-worn channel and a series of huge Salton Seas, each of which eventually evaporated when the river stopped flowing into it. In some places in the Imperial Valley, the sediments, layered like stacked pancakes, are 12,000 feet deep. Anyone who has ever wondered what happened to the earth and rock that used to be in the Grand Canyon, should wonder no more: a fair amount lies deposited in the Salton Sink.

The last of these prehistoric Salton Seas, named Lake Cahuilla after a local Indian tribe, dried up 400 years ago. A hundred miles long and as much as 35 miles wide, Lake Cahuilla left a bathtub ring of calcium carbonate and mollusk shells on the cliffs, more than 200 feet above the Salton Sea today. The bottom of the present sea lies 278 feet below sea level, only 4 feet shy of the lowest point in the United States, the bottom of Death Valley.

The idea of irrigating the valley with Colorado water and farming the salty desert had been around for years. But nothing came of it until 1900. That year, one Charles Robinson Rockwood of the California Development Company met with George Chaffey, a self-educated irrigation engineer from Canada. Chaffey and his brother William had already built irrigation settlements near Los Angeles, so Rockwood proposed that they join forces to develop the southern half of the Salton Sink for agriculture. The soil was deep and rich; because of the year-round growing season, farmers could harvest two crops and multiple cuttings of alfalfa a year. The Southern Pacific's main line passed nearby so that fresh produce could be rushed East in winter at high prices. The sink could be irrigated by a gravity-flow canal from the Colorado River, which flowed into Mexico only 50 miles to the east and at a level several hundred feet higher than the sink's floor.

Then as now, shifting Sahara-like sand dunes lay between the river and the sink in California. There were no dunes just south of the border, so Chaffey decided to run a canal through Mexico using the Colorado's old channel to the sink. The canal turned north into the United States east of Mexicali. From there the channel, now known as the Alamo River, led almost straight north. Like a true promoter, Chaffey grandly christened the southern half of the sink the "Imperial Valley," and in May of 1901, Colorado River water began flowing into it. In a few years the valley had 700 miles of irrigation ditches. Settlers piled in, homesteading federal land or buying it outright from the railroad. To get irrigation water, they had to buy stock in water companies controlled by the Imperial Land Company, a front for Chaffey and Rockwood's California Development Company. "Cost of water stock averaged $22 a share—$3,520 for a farm of 160 acres," David Lavender notes in *California, Land of New Beginnings*. "Imperial Land was most obliging about selling this stock on credit, taking as security a mortgage on the purchaser's land."

By 1904 there were 100,000 acres under irrigation. Then silt blocked up the head of the canal. Water delivery to farmers was all but cut off. Lawsuits loomed. In the fall of 1904, the California Development Company made a cut in the river to bypass the blockage. During the spring floods of 1905, the Colorado, completely out of control, rushed through the cut and surged on into the Alamo River, its old overflow channel, then plunged on into the New River. Digging into the soft soil, it created a 28-foot-high waterfall, scouring out the river's channel to a width of a quarter-mile.

For nearly two years the great river continued to pour through the Imperial Valley where impromptu dikes and levees partly protected the agriculture. Most of the water rolled on north into the deepest part of the sink. It was not until February 1907 that a work force of 2,000 laborers, recruited from six Indian tribes, and 3,000 railroad cars of rock and gravel finally succeeded in turning the Colorado back toward the gulf. This desperate engineering feat was hailed as a victory of capitalism over nature. In 1911 it inspired a book, *The Winning of Barbara Worth* by popular novelist Harold Bell Wright, and in 1926 a movie version starring Ronald Colman, which marked the film debut of Gary Cooper. But it cost the Southern Pacific $3 million.

This new Salton Sea soon attracted its first resident birds, and a flock of government scientists who came to document evaporation rates. Evaporation caused the sea to shrink. It is only 35 miles long by 15 wide. But it did not dry up as expected, because, to prevent a killing buildup of salts in the soil, drainwater was still being flushed into it from the irrigated fields of the expanding Imperial Valley. In 1928, Congress called for construction of the Hoover Dam and an irrigation canal from the Colorado to the valley, this one entirely within the United States, thus the rah-rah name "All-American Canal."

Besides salts and selenium, Imperial Valley drainage carries high levels of nitrogen and phosphorus, which promote a superabundance of phytoplankton, including the algal dinoflagellates that help turn the water reddish brown and give off an awful stench after they die and decompose. But in dealing with all this, the needs of agriculture, a politically powerful force in California, came first. The Imperial Valley is a gold mine now worth something like $1 billion a year to the state's farmers. The salts would have been deadly to farming; they didn't seem to do much harm in the sea. And for years the

California Fish and Game people found ways to accommodate to salt. By the late 1920s, increasing salinity had done in the rainbow trout and other fresh-water fish that washed in with the flood. By 1950, when the sea's salinity was already equal to that of the ocean, state biologists began netting whatever they could in the Gulf of California and dumping the catch in the sea. A few species caught on big, most notably the voracious orangemouth corvina (*Cynoscion xanthulus*), and the little gulf croaker (*Bairdiella icistia*), on which the corvina preyed, which was why, for several decades, the now-scorched sea was one of the great draws in California for poor man's fishing.

In recent years the U.S. Geological Survey and the Fish and Wildlife Service have released joint studies conducted in response to concern about drainwater contamination that could "pose a threat to human health and to the survival of fish and wildlife resources of the Salton Sea area." One study concluded that "drainwater contaminants, including selenium and DDE [which results from the slow decomposition of DDT], are accumulating in tissues of migratory and resident birds that use food sources in the Imperial Valley and Salton Sea. Selenium concentrations in fish-eating birds, shorebirds . . . could affect reproduction." Water-fowl and fish-eating birds in the Imperial Valley might be having troubles because of DDE. High concentrations "were found in birds feeding in agricultural fields on invertebrates and other food items."

Because the use of DDT was banned in the United States in 1972, it was believed that DDE should have disappeared by now, but it comes from pre-ban applications of DDT in the Imperial Valley. "The stuff is simply not break-ing down here," Radke says. "It's a different story in the East, where there's a lot of rainfall, but out here DDE seems to sit forever. Significant eggshell thinning is a problem with every fish-eating bird at the sea—all the egrets, night herons, great blue herons and black skimmers. Great blues are down by 95 percent."

Little can be done about the DDE. Whether something can be done about the amount of selenium coming in with the Colorado River irrigation water is another question, and one that will grow hotter as more and more birds are affected.

The most straightforward problem seems to be salinity. Early in 1994, the Salton Sea Authority held its first symposium on the topic. Since then two solutions have been studied. One involves switching more fresh water into the sea from the Colorado River in years of high flow, while simulta-neously siphoning off saline water from the sea and piping it 45 miles south to the Laguna Salada in Mexico, a plan that would need the agreement of the Mexican government. Estimated cost: $110 million. Another is to build a dike to seal off one end of the sea, keeping it as a saline drainoff from the Imperial Valley while maintaining a freshwater flow into the other part. Esti-mated cost: $100 million.

The authority had $10 million to spend on exploring solutions and agreeing on one. It hopes to come up with a decision by this July. Its members represent both Imperial County and Riverside County, the two counties that enclose the sea. It is understood that unless they can agree, no help will be coming from the state or from national environmental groups. "Unless we are willing to stand up and put our money where our mouth is, nobody in the local, state or federal government is going to care," says Brad Luckey. "If we don't go get rid of the salt and keep the fishery alive, then we've lost the sea."

8

Synthesis of Scientific-Technical Information Relevant to Article 2 of the UN Framework Convention

Intergovernmental Panel on Climate Change (IPCC)

Climate change, and particularly global warming, are among the hottest topics of the early twenty-first century. This selection presents one of the latest scientific assessments of the global warming phenomenon and its likely impacts. These assessments, publicly available and constantly updated on the Internet, are the result of research by hundreds of scientists selected by nations around the world. The two essential findings are very clear: global climate is becoming warmer, and humans are playing a major role in that process. The implications of these findings are less clear. Because the globe's climate is astoundingly complex, even researchers using the most recent computer modeling are unable to accurately predict the outcomes of global warming for either humans or the natural resources and ecosystems on which we depend.

Global warming provides the best current example of an area in which governments, societies, and individuals will have to come together in order to develop and implement workable solutions. At present, the one major international attempt to reverse global warming, the Kyoto Protocol, has been stalled by the actions of the United States; shortly after taking office in 2001, President Bush called the Kyoto Protocol fatally flawed. The motives of the United States are mixed. On the one hand, the protocol sets clearly unattainable targets for the near future. But on the other hand, no American president in the past two decades has wanted to risk political support by mandating even modest changes in energy consumption, automobile production, and

From Intergovernmental Panel on Climate Change (IPCC), "Synthesis of Scientific-Technical Information relevant to interpreting Article 2 of the UN Framework Convention on Climate Change," *IPCC Second Assessment Synthesis*, paragraphs 1.2–4.18 and 8.1–8.4. Figures and table omitted. Reprinted by permission of IPCC.

industrial activity that would significantly curtail the U.S. emission of green-house gases into the atmosphere. The great irony is that the world's leader in causing global warming has thus far failed to adopt a leadership role in seeking global solutions. Assuming the responsibility for this and other major environmental issues will be a great challenge for twenty-first-century officials in the United States.

The Intergovernmental Panel on Climate Change (IPCC) was established in 1988 by the World Meteorological Organization and the United Nations Environment Programme. The role of the IPCC is to assess the scientific, technical, and socio-economic information relevant for the understanding of the risk of climate change. It bases its assessment on peer-reviewed and -published scientific and technical literature.

Following a resolution of the Executive Council of the World Meteorological Organization (July 1992), the IPCC decided to include an examination of approaches to Article 2, the Objective of the UN Framework Convention on Climate Change (UNFCCC), in its work programme. It organized a workshop on the subject in October 1994 in Fortaleza, Brazil, at the invitation of the Government of Brazil. Thereafter, the IPCC Chairman assembled a team of lead authors (listed at the end of this report in the Appendix) under his chairmanship to draft the Synthesis. The team produced the draft which was submitted for expert and government review and comment. The final draft Synthesis was approved line by line by the IPCC at its eleventh session (Rome, 11–15 December 1995), where representatives of 116 governments were present as well as 13 intergovernmental and 25 non-governmental organizations. It may be noted for information that all Member States of the World Meteorological Organization and of the United Nations are Members of the IPCC and can attend its sessions and those of its Working Groups. The Synthesis presents information on the scientific and technical issues related to interpreting Article 2 of the UNFCCC, drawing on the underlying IPCC Second Assessment Report. Since the Synthesis is not simply a summary of the IPCC Second Assessment Report, the Summaries for Policymakers of the three IPCC Working Groups should also be consulted for a summary of the Second Assessment Report.

During the past few decades, two important factors regarding the relationship between humans and the Earth's climate have become apparent. First, human activities, including the burning of fossil fuels, land-use change and agriculture, are increasing the atmospheric concentrations of greenhouse gases (which tend to warm the atmosphere) and, in some regions, aerosols (microscopic airborne particles, which tend to cool the atmosphere). These changes in greenhouse gases and aerosols, taken together, are projected to change regional and global climate and climate-related parameters such as temperature, precipitation, soil moisture and sea level. Second, some human communities have become more vulnerable[1] to hazards such as storms, floods and droughts as a result of increasing population density in sensitive areas such as river basins and coastal plains. Potentially serious changes have been identified, including an increase in some regions in the incidence of extreme high-temperature events, floods and droughts, with resultant consequences for fires, pest outbreaks, and ecosystem composition, structure and functioning, including primary productivity.

Scientific and technical assessments of climate change and its impacts have been conducted by the Intergovernmental Panel on Climate Change (IPCC). The First Assessment, published in 1990, provided a scientific and technical base for the UN Framework Convention on Climate Change (UNFCCC) which was open for signature at the Earth Summit in Rio in 1992.

The ultimate objective of the UNFCCC, as expressed in Article 2 is: ". . . stabilization of greenhouse gas concentrations in the atmosphere at a level that would prevent dangerous anthropogenic interference with the climate system. Such a level should be achieved within a time-frame sufficient to allow ecosystems to adapt naturally to climate change, to ensure that food production is not threatened and to enable economic development to proceed in a sustainable manner."

The challenges presented to the policymaker by Article 2 are the determination of what concentrations of greenhouse gases might be regarded as "dangerous anthropogenic interference with the climate system" and the charting of a future which allows for economic development which is sustainable. The purpose of this synthesis report is to provide scientific, technical and socio-economic information that can be used, inter alia, in addressing these challenges. It is based on the 1994 and 1995 reports of the IPCC Working Groups.

The report follows through the various matters which are addressed in Article 2. It first briefly summarizes the degree of climate change—the "interference with the climate system"—which is projected to occur as a result of human activities. It then goes on to highlight what we know about the vulnerabilities of ecosystems and human communities to likely climate changes, especially in regard to agriculture and food production and to other factors such as water availability, health and the impact of sea-level rise which are important considerations for sustainable development. The task of the IPCC is to provide a sound scientific basis that would enable policymakers to better interpret dangerous anthropogenic interference with the climate system.

Given current trends of increasing emissions of most greenhouse gases, atmospheric concentrations of these gases will increase through the next century and beyond. With the growth in atmospheric concentrations of greenhouse gases, interference with the climate system will grow in magnitude and the likelihood of adverse impacts from climate change that could be judged dangerous will become greater. Therefore, possible pathways of future net emissions were considered which might lead to stabilization at different levels and the general constraints these imply. This consideration forms the next part of the report and is followed by a summary of the technical and policy options for reducing emissions and enhancing sinks of greenhouse gases.

The report then addresses issues related to equity and to ensuring that economic development proceeds in a sustainable manner. This involves addressing, for instance, estimates of the likely damage of climate change impacts, and the impacts, including costs and benefits, of adaptation and mitigation. Finally, a number of insights from available studies point to ways of taking initial actions (see the section on The Road Forward) even if, at present, it is difficult to decide upon a target for atmospheric concentrations, including considerations of time-frames, that would prevent "dangerous anthropogenic interference with the climate system."

Climate change presents the decision maker with a set of formidable complications: considerable remaining uncertainties inherent in the complexity of the problem, the potential for irreversible damages or costs, a very long planning horizon, long time lags between emissions and effects, wide regional variations in causes and effects, an irreducibly global problem, and a multiple of greenhouse gases and aerosols to consider. Yet another complication is that effective protection of the climate system requires international cooperation in the context of wide variations in income levels, flexibility and expectations of the future; this raises issues of efficiency and infra-national, international and intergenerational equity. Equity is an important element for legitimizing decisions and promoting cooperation.

Decisions with respect to Article 2 of the UNFCCC involve three distinct but interrelated choices: stabilization level, net emissions pathway and mitigation technologies and policies. The report presents available scientific and technical information on these three choices. It also notes where uncertainties remain regarding such information. Article 3 of the UNFCCC identifies a range of principles that shall guide, inter alia, decision-making with respect to the ultimate objective of the Convention, as found in Article 2. Article 3.3[2] provides guidance, inter alia, on decision-making where there is a lack of full scientific certainty, namely, that the Parties should:

> take precautionary measures to anticipate, prevent or minimize the causes of climate change and mitigate its adverse effects. Where there are threats of serious or irreversible damage, lack of full scientific certainty should not be used as a reason for postponing such measures, taking into account that policies and measures to deal with climate change should be cost effective so as to ensure global benefits at the lowest possible cost. To achieve this, such policies and measures should take into account different socio-economic contexts, be comprehensive, cover all relevant sources, sinks and reservoirs of greenhouse gases and adaptation and comprise all economic sectors. Efforts to address climate change may be carried out cooperatively by interested Parties.

The Second Assessment Report of the IPCC also provides information in this regard.

The long time-scales involved in the climate system (e.g., the long residence time of greenhouse gases in the atmosphere) and in the time for replacement of infrastructure, and the lag by many decades to centuries between stabilization of concentrations and stabilization of temperature and mean sea level, indicate the importance for timely decision-making.

Anthropogenic Interference with the Climate System

Interference to the Present Day

In order to understand what constitutes concentrations of greenhouse gases that would prevent dangerous interference with the climate system, it is first necessary to understand current atmospheric concentrations and trends of greenhouse gases, and their consequences (both present and projected) to the climate system.

The atmospheric concentrations of the greenhouse gases, and among them, carbon dioxide (CO_2), methane (CH_4) and nitrous oxide (N_2O), have grown significantly since pre-industrial times (about 1750 A.D.): CO_2 from about 280 to almost 360 ppmv,[3] CH_4 from 700 to 1720 ppbv and N_2O from about 275 to about 310 ppbv. These trends can be attributed largely to human activities, mostly fossil-fuel use, land-use change and agriculture. Concentrations of other anthropogenic greenhouse gases have also increased. An increase of greenhouse gas concentrations leads on average to an additional warming of the atmosphere and the Earth's surface. Many greenhouse gases remain in the atmosphere—and affect climate—for a long time.

Tropospheric aerosols resulting from combustion of fossil fuels, biomass burning and other sources have led to a negative direct forcing and possibly also to a negative indirect forcing of a similar magnitude. While the negative forcing is focused in particular regions and subcontinental areas, it can have continental to hemispheric scale effects on climate patterns. Locally, the aerosol forcing can be large enough to more than offset the positive forcing due to greenhouse gases. In contrast to the long-lived greenhouse gases, anthropogenic aerosols are very short-lived in the atmosphere and hence their radiative forcing adjusts rapidly to increases or decreases in emissions.

Global mean surface temperature has increased by between about 0.3 and 0.6°C since the late 19th century, a change that is unlikely to be entirely natural in origin. The balance of evidence, from changes in global mean surface air temperature and from changes in geographical, seasonal and vertical patterns of atmospheric temperature, suggests a discernible human influence on global climate. There are uncertainties in key factors, including the magnitude and patterns of long-term natural variability. Global sea level has risen by between 10 and 25 cm over the past 100 years and much of the rise may be related to the increase in global mean temperature.

There are inadequate data to determine whether consistent global changes in climate variability or weather extremes have occurred over the 20th century. On regional scales there is clear evidence of changes in some extremes and climate variability indicators. Some of these changes have been toward greater variability, some have been toward lower variability. However, to date it has not been possible to firmly establish a clear connection between these regional changes and human activities.

Possible Consequences of Future Interference

In the absence of mitigation policies or significant technological advances that reduce emissions and/or enhance sinks, concentrations of greenhouse gases and aerosols are expected to grow throughout the next century. The IPCC has developed a range of scenarios, IS92a-f, of future greenhouse gas and aerosol precursor emissions based on assumptions concerning population and economic growth, land-use, technological changes, energy availability and fuel mix during the period 1990 to 2100. By the year 2100, carbon dioxide emissions under these scenarios are projected to be in the range of about 6 GtC[4] per year, roughly equal to current emissions, to as much as 36 GtC per year, with the lower end of the IPCC range assuming low population and economic growth to 2100. Methane emissions are projected to be in the range 540 to 1170 Tg[5] CH_4 per year (1990 emissions were about 500 Tg CH_4); nitrous oxide emissions are projected to be in the range 14 to 19 Tg N per year (1990 emissions were about 13 Tg N). In all cases, the atmospheric concentrations of greenhouse gases and total radiative forcing continue to increase throughout the simulation period of 1990 to 2100.

For the mid-range IPCC emission scenario, IS92a, assuming the "best estimate" value of climate sensitivity[6] and including the effects of future increases in aerosol concentrations, models project an increase in global mean surface temperature relative to 1990 of about 2°C by 2100. This estimate is approximately one-third lower than the "best estimate" in 1990. This is due primarily to lower emission scenarios (particularly for CO_2 and CFCs), the inclusion of the cooling effect of sulphate aerosols, and improvements in the treatment of the carbon cycle. Combining the lowest IPCC emission scenario (IS92c) with a "low" value of climate sensitivity and including the effects of future changes in aerosol concentrations leads to a projected increase of about 1°C by 2100. The corresponding projection for the highest IPCC scenario (IS92e) combined with a "high" value of climate sensitivity gives a warming of about 3.5°C. In all cases the average rate of warming would probably be greater than any seen in the last 10,000 years, but the actual annual to decadal changes would include considerable natural variability. Regional temperature changes could differ substantially from the global mean value. Because of the thermal inertia of the oceans, only 50-90% of the eventual equilibrium temperature change would have been realized by 2100 and temperature would continue to increase beyond 2100, even if concentrations of greenhouse gases were stabilized by that time.

Average sea level is expected to rise as a result of thermal expansion of the oceans and melting of glaciers and ice-sheets. For the IS92a scenario, assuming the "best estimate" values of climate sensitivity and of ice melt sensitivity to warming, and including the effects of future changes in aerosol concentrations, models project an increase in sea level of about 50 cm from the present to 2100. This estimate is approximately 25% lower than the "best estimate" in 1990 due to the lower temperature projection, but also reflecting improvements in the climate and ice melt models. Combining the lowest emission scenario (IS92c) with the "low" climate and ice melt sensitivities and including aerosol effects gives a projected sea-level rise of about 15 cm from the present to 2100. The corresponding projection for the highest emission scenario (IS92e) combined with "high" climate and ice-melt sensitivities gives a sea-level rise of about 95 cm from the present to 2100. Sea level would continue to rise at a similar rate in future centuries beyond 2100, even if concentrations of greenhouse gases were stabilized by that time, and would continue to do so even beyond the time of stabilization of global mean temperature. Regional sea-level changes may differ from the global mean value owing to land movement and ocean current changes.

Confidence is higher in the hemispheric-to-continental scale projections of coupled atmosphere-ocean climate models than in the regional projections, where confidence remains low. There is more confidence in temperature projections than hydrological changes.

All model simulations, whether they were forced with increased concentrations of greenhouse gases and aerosols or with increased concentrations of greenhouse gases alone, show the following features: greater surface warming of the land than of the sea in winter; a maximum surface warming in high northern latitudes in winter, little surface warming over the Arctic in summer; an enhanced global mean hydrological cycle, and increased precipitation and soil moisture in high latitudes in winter. All these changes are associated with identifiable physical mechanisms.

Warmer temperatures will lead to a more vigorous hydrological cycle; this translates into prospects for more severe droughts and/or floods in some places and less severe droughts and/or floods in other places. Several models indicate an increase in precipitation intensity, suggesting a possibility for more extreme rainfall events. Knowledge is currently insufficient to say whether there will be any changes in the occurrence or geographical distribution of severe storms, e.g., tropical cyclones.

There are many uncertainties and many factors currently limit our ability to project and detect future climate change. Future unexpected, large and rapid climate system changes (as have occurred in the past) are, by their nature, difficult to predict. This implies that future climate changes may also involve "surprises." In particular, these arise from the non-linear nature of the climate system. When rapidly forced, non-linear systems are especially subject to unexpected behaviour. Progress can be made by investigating non-linear processes and sub-components of the climatic system. Examples of such non-linear behaviour include rapid circulation changes in the North Atlantic and feedbacks associated with terrestrial ecosystem changes.

Sensitivity and Adaptation of Systems to Climate Change

This section provides scientific and technical information that can be used, inter alia, in evaluating whether the projected range of plausible impacts constitutes "dangerous anthropogenic interference with the climate system" as referred to in Article 2, and in evaluating adaptation options. However, it is not yet possible to link particular impacts with specific atmospheric concentrations of greenhouse gases.

Human health, terrestrial and aquatic ecological systems, and socio-economic systems (e.g., agriculture, forestry, fisheries and water resources) are all vital to human development and well-being and are all sensitive to both the magnitude and the rate of climate change. Whereas many regions are likely to experience the adverse effects of climate change—some of which are potentially irreversible—some effects of climate change are likely to be beneficial. Hence, different segments of society can expect to confront a variety of changes and the need to adapt to them.

Human-induced climate change represents an important additional stress, particularly to the many ecological and socio-economic systems already affected by pollution, increasing resource demands, and non-sustainable management practices. The vulnerability of human health and socio-economic systems—and, to a lesser extent, ecological systems—depends upon economic circumstances and institutional infrastructure. This implies that systems typically are more vulnerable in developing countries where economic and institutional circumstances are less favourable.

Although our knowledge has increased significantly during the last decade and qualitative estimates can be developed, quantitative projections of the impacts of climate change on any particular system at any particular location are difficult because regional-scale climate change projections are uncertain; our current understanding of many critical processes is limited; systems are subject to multiple climatic and non-climatic stresses, the interactions of which are not always linear or additive; and very few studies have considered dynamic responses to steadily increasing concentrations of greenhouse gases or the consequences of increases beyond a doubling of equivalent atmospheric CO_2 concentrations.

Unambiguous detection of climate-induced changes in most ecological and social systems will prove extremely difficult in the coming decades. This is because of the complexity of these systems, their many non-linear feedbacks, and their sensitivity to a large number of climatic and non-climatic factors, all of which are expected to continue to change simultaneously. As future climate extends beyond the boundaries of empirical knowledge (i.e., the documented impacts of climate variation in the past), it becomes more likely that actual outcomes will include surprises and unanticipated rapid changes.

Sensitivity of Systems

Terrestrial and Aquatic Ecosystems

Ecosystems contain the Earth's entire reservoir of genetic and species diversity and provide many goods and services including: (i) providing food, fibre, medicines and energy; (ii) processing and storing carbon and other nutrients; (iii) assimilating wastes, purifying water, regulating water runoff, and controlling floods, soil degradation and beach erosion; and (iv) providing opportunities for recreation and tourism. The composition and geographic distribution of many ecosystems (e.g., forests, rangelands, deserts, mountain systems, lakes, wetlands and oceans) will shift as individual species respond to changes in climate; there will likely be reductions in biological diversity and in the goods and services that ecosystems provide society. Some ecological systems may not reach a new equilibrium for several centuries after the climate achieves a new balance. This section illustrates the impact of climate change on a number of selected ecological systems.

Forests: Models project that as a consequence of possible changes in temperature and water availability under doubled equivalent CO_2 equilibrium conditions, a substantial fraction (a global average of one-third, varying by region from one-seventh to two-thirds) of the existing forested area of the world will undergo major changes in broad vegetation types—with the greatest changes occurring in high latitudes and the least in the tropics. Climate change is expected to occur at a rapid rate relative to the speed at which forest species grow, reproduce and re-establish themselves. Therefore, the species composition of forests is likely to change; entire forest types may disappear, while new assemblages of species and hence new ecosystems may be established. Large amounts of carbon could be released into the atmosphere during transitions from one forest type to another because the rate at which carbon can be lost during times of high forest mortality is greater than the rate at which it can be gained through growth to maturity.

Deserts and desertification: Deserts are likely to become more extreme—in that, with few exceptions, they are projected to become hotter but not significantly wetter. Temperature increases could be a threat to organisms that exist near their heat tolerance limits. Desertification—land degradation in arid, semi-arid and dry sub-humid areas resulting from various factors, including climatic variations and human activities—is more likely to become irreversible if the environment becomes drier and the soil becomes further degraded through erosion and compaction.

Mountain ecosystems: The altitudinal distribution of vegetation is projected to shift to higher elevations; some species with climatic ranges limited to mountain tops could become extinct because of disappearance of habitat or reduced migration potential.

Aquatic and coastal ecosystems: In lakes and streams, warming would have the greatest biological effects at high latitudes, where biological productivity would increase, and at the low-latitude boundaries of cold- and cool-water species ranges, where extinctions would be greatest. The geographical distribution of wetlands is likely to shift with changes in temperature and precipitation. Coastal systems are economically and ecologically important and are expected to vary widely in their response to changes in climate and sea level. Some coastal ecosystems are particularly at risk, including saltwater marshes, mangrove ecosystems, coastal wetlands, sandy beaches, coral reefs, coral atolls and river deltas. Changes in these ecosystems would have major negative effects on tourism, freshwater supplies, fisheries and biodiversity.

Hydrology and Water Resources Management

Models project that between one-third and one-half of existing mountain glacier mass could disappear over the next hundred years. The reduced extent of glaciers and depth of snow cover also would affect the seasonal distribution of river flow and water supply for hydroelectric generation and agriculture. Anticipated hydrological changes and reductions in the areal extent and depth of permafrost could lead to large-scale damage to infrastructure, an additional flux of carbon dioxide into the atmosphere, and changes in processes that contribute to the flux of methane into the atmosphere.

Climate change will lead to an intensification of the global hydrological cycle and can have major impacts on regional water resources. Changes in the total amount of precipitation and in its frequency and intensity directly affect the magnitude and timing of runoff and the intensity of floods and droughts; however, at present, specific regional effects are uncertain. Relatively small changes in temperature and precipitation, together with the non-linear effects on evapotranspiration and soil moisture, can result in relatively large changes in runoff, especially in arid and semi-arid regions. The quantity and quality of water supplies already are serious problems today in many regions, including some low-lying coastal areas, deltas and small islands, making countries in these regions particularly vulnerable to any additional reduction in indigenous water supplies.

Agriculture and Forestry

Crop yields and changes in productivity due to climate change will vary considerably across regions and among localities, thus changing the patterns of production. Productivity is projected to increase in some areas and decrease in others, especially the tropics and subtropics. Existing studies show that on the whole, global agricultural production could be maintained relative to baseline production in the face of climate change projected under doubled equivalent CO_2 equilibrium conditions. This conclusion takes into account the beneficial effects of CO_2 fertilization but does not allow for changes in agricultural pests and the possible effects of changing climatic variability. However, focusing on global agricultural production does not address the potentially serious consequences of large differences at local and regional scales, even at mid-latitudes. There may be increased risk of hunger and famine in some locations; many of the world's poorest people—particularly those living in subtropical and tropical areas and dependent on isolated agricultural systems in semi-arid and arid regions—are most at risk of increased hunger. Global wood supplies during the next century may become increasingly inadequate to meet projected consumption due to both climatic and non-climatic factors.

Human Infrastructure

Climate change clearly will increase the vulnerability of some coastal populations to flooding and erosional land loss. Estimates put about 46 million people per year currently at risk of flooding due to storm surges. In the absence of adaptation measures, and not taking into account anticipated population growth, a 50-cm sea-level rise would increase this number to about 92 million; a 1-meter sea-level rise would raise it to about 118 million. Studies using a 1-meter projection show a particular risk for small islands and deltas. This increase is at the top range of IPCC Working Group I estimates for 2100; it should be noted, however, that sea level is actually projected to continue to rise in future centuries beyond 2100. Estimated land losses range from 0.05% in Uruguay, 1.0% for Egypt, 6% for the Netherlands and 17.5% for Bangladesh to about 80% for the Majuro Atoll in the Marshall Islands, given the present state of protection systems. Some small island nations and other countries will confront greater vulnerability because their existing sea and coastal defense systems are less well established. Countries with higher population densities would be more vulnerable. Storm surges and flooding could threaten entire cultures. For these countries, sea-level rise could force internal or international migration of populations.

Human Health

Climate change is likely to have wide-ranging and mostly adverse impacts on human health, with significant loss of life. Direct health effects include increases in (predominantly cardio-respiratory) mortality and illness due to an anticipated increase in the intensity and duration of heat waves. Temperature increases in colder regions should result in fewer cold-related deaths. Indirect effects of climate change, which are expected to predominate, include increases in the potential transmission of vector-borne infectious diseases (e.g., malaria, dengue, yellow fever and some viral encephalitis) resulting from extensions of the geographical range and season for vector organisms. Models (that entail necessary simplifying assumptions) project that temperature increases of 3-5°C (compared to the IPCC projection of 1-3.5°C by 2100) could lead to potential increases in malaria incidence (of the order of 50–80 million additional annual cases, relative to an assumed global background total of 500 million cases), primarily in tropical, subtropical and less well-protected temperate-zone populations. Some increases in non-vector-borne infectious diseases—such as salmonellosis, cholera and giardiasis—also could occur as a result of elevated temperatures and increased flooding. Limitations on freshwater supplies and on nutritious food, as well as the aggravation of air pollution, will also have human health consequences.

Quantifying the projected impacts is difficult because the extent of climate-induced health disorders depends on numerous coexistent and interacting factors that characterize the vulnerability of the particular population, including environmental and socio-economic circumstances, nutritional and immune status, population density and access to quality health care services. Hence, populations with different levels of natural, technical and social resources would differ in their vulnerability to climate-induced health impacts.

Technology and Policy Options for Adaptation

Technological advances generally have increased adaptation options for managed systems. Adaptation options for freshwater resources include more efficient management of existing supplies and infrastructure; institutional arrangements to limit future demands/promote conservation; improved monitoring and forecasting systems for floods/droughts; rehabilitation of watersheds, especially in the tropics; and construction of new reservoir capacity.

Adaptation options for agriculture—such as changes in types and varieties of crops, improved water-management and irrigation systems, and changes in planting schedules and tillage practices—will be important in limiting negative effects and taking advantage of beneficial changes in climate. Effective coastal-zone management and land-use planning can help direct population shifts away from vulnerable locations such as flood plains, steep hillsides and low-lying coastlines. Adaptive options to reduce health impacts include protective technology (e.g., housing, air conditioning, water purification and vaccination), disaster preparedness and appropriate health care.

However, many regions of the world currently have limited access to these technologies and appropriate information. For some island nations, the high cost of providing adequate protection would make it essentially infeasible, especially given the limited availability of capital for investment. The efficacy and cost-effective use of adaptation strategies will depend upon the availability of financial resources, technology transfer, and cultural, educational, managerial, institutional, legal and regulatory practices, both domestic and international in scope. Incorporating climate-change concerns into resource-use and development decisions and plans for regularly scheduled investments in infrastructure will facilitate adaptation.

Analytical Approach to Stabilization of Atmospheric Concentration of Greenhouse Gases

Article 2 of the UN Framework Convention on Climate Change refers explicitly to "stabilization of greenhouse gas concentrations." This section provides information on the relative importance of various greenhouse gases to climate forcing and discusses how greenhouse gas emissions might be varied to achieve stabilization at selected atmospheric concentration levels.

Carbon dioxide, methane and nitrous oxide have natural as well as anthropogenic origins. The anthropogenic emissions of these gases have contributed about 80% of the additional climate forcing due to greenhouse gases since pre-industrial times (i.e., since about 1750 A.D.). The contribution of CO_2 is about 60% of this forcing, about four times that from CH_4.

Other greenhouse gases include tropospheric ozone (whose chemical precursors include nitrogen oxides, non-methane hydrocarbons and carbon monoxide), halocarbons[7] (including HCFCs and HFCs) and SF_6. Tropospheric aerosols and tropospheric ozone are inhomogeneously distributed in time and space and their atmospheric lifetimes are short (days to weeks). Sulphate aerosols are amenable to abatement measures and such measures are presumed in the IPCC scenarios.

Most emission scenarios indicate that, in the absence of mitigation policies, greenhouse gas emissions will continue to rise during the next century and lead to greenhouse gas concentrations that by the year 2100 are projected to change climate more than that projected for twice the pre-industrial concentrations of carbon dioxide.

Stabilization of Greenhouse Gases

All relevant greenhouse gases need to be considered in addressing stabilization of greenhouse gas concentrations. First, carbon dioxide is considered which, because of its importance and complicated behaviour, needs more detailed consideration than the other greenhouse gases.

Carbon Dioxide

Carbon dioxide is removed from the atmosphere by a number of processes that operate on different time-scales. It has a relatively long residence time in the climate system—of the order of a century or more. If net global anthropogenic emissions[8] (i.e., anthropogenic sources minus anthropogenic sinks) were maintained at current levels (about 7 GtC/yr including emissions from fossil-fuel combustion, cement production and land-use change), they would lead to a nearly constant rate of increase in atmospheric concentrations for at least two centuries, reaching about 500 ppmv (approaching twice the pre-industrial concentration of 280 ppmv) by the end of the 21st century. Carbon cycle models show that immediate stabilization of the concentration of carbon dioxide at its present level could only be achieved through an immediate reduction in its emissions of 50-70% and further reductions thereafter.

Carbon cycle models have been used to estimate profiles of carbon dioxide emissions for stabilization at various carbon dioxide concentration levels. Such profiles have been generated for an illustrative set of levels: 450, 550, 650, 750 and 1000 ppmv. . . . The steeper the increase in the emissions (hence concentration) in these scenarios, the more quickly is the climate projected to change.

Any eventual stabilized concentration is governed more by the accumulated anthropogenic carbon dioxide emissions from now until the time of stabilization, than by the way those emissions change over the period. This means that, for a given stabilized concentration value, higher emissions in early decades require lower emissions later on. . . .

Given cumulative emissions, and IPCC IS92a population and economic scenarios for 1990–2100, global annual average carbon dioxide emissions can be derived for the stabilization scenarios on a per capita or per unit of economic activity basis. If the atmospheric concentration is to remain below 550 ppmv, the future global annual average emissions cannot, during the next century, exceed the current global average and would have to be much lower before and beyond the end of the next century. Global annual average emissions could be higher for stabilization levels of 750 to 1000 ppmv. Nevertheless, even to achieve these latter stabilization levels, the global annual average emissions would need to be less than 50% above current levels on a per capita basis or less than half of current levels per unit of economic activity.[9]

The global average annual per capita emissions of carbon dioxide due to the combustion of fossil fuels is at present about 1.1 tonnes (as carbon). In addition, a net of about 0.2 tonnes per capita are emitted from deforestation and land-use change. The average annual fossil fuel per capita emission in developed and transitional economy countries is about 2.8 tonnes and ranges from 1.5 to 5.5 tonnes. The figure for the developing countries is 0.5 tonnes ranging from 0.1 tonnes to, in some few cases, above 2.0 tonnes (all figures are for 1990).[10]

Using World Bank estimates of GDP (gross domestic product) at market exchange rates, the current global annual average emission of energy-related carbon dioxide is about 0.3 tonnes per thousand 1990 U.S. dollars output. In addition, global net emissions from land-use changes are about 0.05 tonnes per thousand U.S. dollars of output. The current average annual energy-related emissions per thousand 1990 U.S. dollars output, evaluated at market exchange rates, is about 0.27 tonnes in developed and transitional economy countries and about 0.41 tonnes in developing countries. Using World Bank estimates of GDP at purchasing power parity exchange rates, the average annual energy-related emissions per thousand 1990 U.S. dollars output is about 0.26 tonnes in developed and transitional economy countries and about 0.16 tonnes in developing countries.[11]

Methane

Atmospheric methane concentrations adjust to changes in anthropogenic emissions over a period of 9 to 15 years. If the annual methane emissions were immediately reduced by about 30 Tg CH_4 (about 8% of current anthropogenic emissions), methane concentrations would remain at today's levels. If methane emissions were to remain constant at their current levels, methane concentrations (1720 ppbv in 1994) would rise to about 1820 ppbv over the next 40 years.

Nitrous Oxide

Nitrous oxide has a long lifetime (about 120 years). In order for the concentration to be stabilized near current levels (312 ppbv in 1994), anthropogenic sources would need to be reduced immediately by more than 50%. If emissions of nitrous oxide were held constant at current levels, its concentration would rise to about 400 ppbv over several hundred years, which would increase its incremental radiative forcing by a factor of four over its current level.

Further Points on Stabilization

Stabilization of the concentrations of very long-lived gases, such as SF_6 or perfluorocarbons, can only be achieved effectively by stopping emissions.

The importance of the contribution of CO_2 to climate forcing, relative to that of the other greenhouse gases, increases with time in all of the 1S92 emission scenarios (a to f). For example, in the IS92a scenario, the CO_2 contribution increases from the present 60% to about 75% by the year 2100. During the same period, methane and nitrous oxide forcings increase in absolute terms by a factor that ranges between two and three.

The combined effect of all greenhouse gases in producing radiative forcing is often expressed in terms of the equivalent concentration of carbon dioxide which would produce the same forcing. Because of the effects of the other greenhouse gases, stabilization at some level of equivalent carbon dioxide concentration implies maintaining carbon dioxide concentration at a lower level.

The stabilization of greenhouse gas concentrations does not imply that there will be no further climate change. After stabilization is achieved, global mean surface temperature would continue to rise for some centuries and sea level for many centuries. . . .

The Road Forward

The scientific, technical, economic and social science literature does suggest ways to move forward towards the ultimate objective of the Convention. Possible actions include mitigation of climate change through reductions of emissions of greenhouse gases and enhancement of their removal by sinks, adaptation to observed and/or anticipated climate change, and research, development and demonstration to improve our knowledge of the risks of climate change and possible responses.

Uncertainties remain which are relevant to judgement of what constitutes dangerous anthropogenic interference with the climate system and what needs to be done to prevent such interference. The literature indicates, however, that significant "no regrets" opportunities are available in most countries and that the risk of aggregate net damage due to climate change, consideration of risk aversion and the precautionary approach, provide rationales for actions beyond "no regrets."[12] The challenge is not to find the best policy today for the next 100 years, but to select a prudent strategy and to adjust it over time in the light of new information.

The literature suggests that flexible, cost-effective policies relying on economic incentives and instruments as well as coordinated instruments can considerably reduce mitigation or adaptation costs, or can increase the cost-effectiveness of emission reduction measures. Appropriate long-run signals are required to allow producers and consumers to adapt cost effectively to constraints on greenhouse gas emissions and to encourage investment research, development and demonstration.

Many of the policies and decisions to reduce emissions of greenhouse gases and enhance their sinks, and eventually stabilize their atmospheric concentration, would provide opportunities and challenges for the private and public sectors. A carefully selected portfolio of national and international responses of actions aimed at mitigation, adaptation and improvement of knowledge can reduce the risks posed by climate change to ecosystems, food security, water resources, human health and other natural and socio-economic systems. There are large differences in the cost of reducing greenhouse gas emissions, and enhancing sinks, among countries due to their state of economic development, infrastructure choices and natural resource base. International cooperation in a framework of bilateral, regional or international agreements could significantly reduce the global costs of reducing emissions and lessening emission leakages. If carried out with care, these responses would help to meet the challenge of climate change and enhance the prospects for sustainable economic development for all peoples and nations.

Appendix

Drafting team for the synthesis: Bert Bolin (Chairman of the IPCC and Chairman of the Drafting Team); John T. Houghton; Gylvan Meira Filho; Robert T. Watson; M. C. Zinyowera; James Bruce; Hoesung Lee; Bruce Callander; Richard Moss; Erik Haites; Roberto Acosta Moreno; Tariq Banuri; Zhou Dadi; Bronson Gardner; José Goldemberg; Jean-Charles Hourcade; Michael Jefferson; Jerry Melillo; Irving Mintzer; Richard Odingo; Martin Parry; Martha Perdomo; Cornelia Quennet-Thielen; Pier Vellinga; Narasimhan Sundararaman (Secretary of the 1PCC).

Notes

1. Vulnerability defines the extent to which climate change may damage or harm a system. It depends not only on a system's sensitivity but also on its ability to adapt to new climatic conditions.

2. Kuwait registered its objection to quoting only subparagraph 3 of Article 3 and not the Article in its entirety.

3. ppmv stands for parts per million by volume; ppbv stands for parts per billion (thousand million) by volume. Values quoted are for 1992.

4. To convert GtC (gigatonnes of carbon or thousand million tonnes of carbon) to mass of carbon dioxide, multiply GtC by 3.67.

5. Tg: teragram is 10^{12} grams.

6. In IPCC reports, climate sensitivity usually refers to long-term (equilibrium) change in global mean surface temperature following a doubling of atmospheric equivalent CO_2 concentration. More generally, it refers to the equilibrium change in surface air temperature following a unit change in radiative forcing (°C/Wm-2).

7. Most halocarbons, but neither HFCs nor PFCs, are controlled by the Montreal Protocol and its Adjustments and Amendments.

8. For the remainder of this section, "net global anthropogenic emissions" (i.e., anthropogenic sources minus anthropogenic sinks) will be abbreviated to "emissions."

9. China registered its disagreement on the use of carbon dioxide emissions derived on the basis of a per unit economic activity.

10. The Panel agreed that this paragraph shall not prejudge the current negotiations under the UNFCCC.

11. The Panel agreed that this paragraph shall not prejudge the current negotiations under the UNFCCC.

12. "No regrets" measures are those whose benefits, such as reduced energy costs and reduced emissions of local/regional pollutants, equal or exceed their cost to society, excluding the benefits of climate change mitigation. They are sometimes known as "measures worth doing anyway."

References

1. IPCC, 1990:
    (i) Climate Change, The IPCC Scientific Assessment
    (ii) Climate Change, The IPCC Impacts Assessment
    (iii) Climate Change, The IPCC Response Strategies
    (iv) Overview and Policymakers Summary
2. IPCC, 1992:
    (i) Climate Change 1992, The Supplementary Report to the IPCC Scientific Assessment
    (ii) Climate Change 1992, The Supplementary Report to the IPCC Impacts Assessment
3. IPCC, 1994: Climate Change 1994, Radiative Forcing of Climate Change and an Evaluation of the IPCC IS92 Emission Scenarios
4. IPCC, 1995:
    (i) Climate Change 1995, The IPCC Second Assessment Synthesis of Scientific-Technical Information Relevant to Interpreting Article 2 of the UN Framework Convention on Climate Change
    (ii) Climate Change 1995, The Science of Climate Change
    (iii) Climate Change 1995, Scientific-Technical Analyses of Impacts, Adaptations and Mitigation of Climate Change
    (iv) Climate Change 1995, The Economic and Social Dimensions of Climate Change

9

Shadows of the Climate Future

Stephen H. Schneider

This piece portraying the possible effects on daily life of a warmer world was written more than ten years ago. At the time, author Stephen Schneider was criticized for being alarmist, yet some of his dire predictions appear now to be right on target. Global climate and atmospheric change are increasingly affecting the daily lives of humans and other living things. How many scenarios that Schneider predicted in 1989 do you now read about in the news or experience directly?

Schneider is Professor of Environmental Biology and Global Change at Stanford University. He has done pioneering modeling work in the fields of atmospheric science and global climatology, including the relationship of biological systems to global climate change.

No one can know the future, at least not in detail. But enough is known to allow us to fashion plausible scenarios of events that could well take place if current trends and present understanding are even partly true. This chapter, while obviously fictional, is meant to provide a feeling for what a year in the greenhouse century might have in store for us if nothing is done to deal with the growing problem of global warming.

In New York City, water restrictions had been in effect for almost a month, lawns were browning, swimming pools had been covered, and the evening news was filled with stories of stiff fines and public reprimands for scofflaw families caught violating the ordinance. But at least a million New Yorkers thought they would enjoy watching green grass on television one afternoon the league-leading New York Mets were scheduled to play the Chicago Cubs in a doubleheader at Wrigley Field.

From Stephen H. Schneider, *Global Warming: Are We Entering the Greenhouse Century?* (San Francisco: Sierra Club Books, 1989), 1–12. Reprinted by permission of Sierra Club Books.

Although New Yorkers had heard that heat waves in Chicago were even more intense than in New York that summer, the city by Lake Michigan had been able to keep the baseball field green, and the ivy outfield walls of the traditional ball park were as green as the grass. The climate may be changing, people thought, but at least Wrigley Field has been stable this century. Even the temporary experiment with lights and night games in the late 1980s had eventually been overruled by the protests of baseball purists and angry neighbors.

The Sunday doubleheader began at the traditional 1:00, but by 5:00, with the Mets comfortably ahead in the fourth inning of the second game, the sky began to darken. As the sun sank lower, its rays barely penetrated a thick layer of dark haze, the likes of which hadn't been seen in decades. It was the strangest thing to happen to sports in Chicago, one old-timer said, since the "fog bowl of '89," when the Chicago Bears football team beat the Philadelphia Eagles in a game almost totally obscured by fog. By 6:42, before the minimum regulation five and one-half innings could be played out, this baseball game had to be called.

What happened that Sunday afternoon in Chicago actually originated over a thousand miles away in Saskatchewan, where a very intense three-week heat wave had come on the heels of a dry spring. Relative humidities had been abnormally low for the previous week. Then a weak cold front came through, triggering many relatively rainless thundershowers. From the lightning, fires broke out simultaneously over several thousand square miles. Within days, an area nearly the size of New Jersey had burned, and the drifting smoke was so thick over the Midwest that the late afternoon looked more like twilight for several days,[1] including the Sunday afternoon when the second game of an important doubleheader was dimmed out of the record book.

Other climatic effects were far more serious than a called baseball game, however. For twelve of the fourteen days preceding that Sunday game, New York City had experienced temperatures above 35°C (95°F—by then the United States had finally gone metric), substantially increasing the demand for water. Torrents gushed onto city streets from illegally opened fire hydrants. The health department issued smog alerts announcing that low-level ozone had reached historic highs. The elderly and people with asthma or lung disease were cautioned to stay indoors on Monday, when normal traffic and industrial activity would once again dump pollutants into the still-hot air.

The evening news reported that already six hundred people—mostly the sick, elderly, or poor without protection of air-conditioning—had died that month of causes directly attributable to heat stress. Nevertheless, this was a substantial reduction from the heat-death numbers a few decades earlier. Beginning in the 2010s, New York had attempted to air-condition all buildings to reduce the physiological distress from ever-increasing heat waves. This city policy was not without opponents, however, for a number of critics pointed out that humans can acclimatize their bodies to hot weather, and that although air-conditioning would clearly protect the weak and vulnerable segments of the population, continuous air-conditioning on a massive scale would also reduce people's ability to acclimatize. Then, should a superhot week descend on the city, with an excessive demand for air-conditioning resulting in power failures or brownouts, even more people would be vulnerable to heat stress.

Later that week the national news media carried a story of growing conflict between New York City water authorities and those in charge of the reservoirs along the Delaware River. It seemed absurd to most New Yorkers that at this time of heat stress, Delaware River water was being sent downriver into the ocean rather than to New York simply because of an old legal requirement that mandated upstream releases of fresh water to protect Philadelphia, as well as downstream fisheries, from encroaching salinity. When the river flow was slow, as it was this drought year, ocean water backed up into the Delaware estuary, threatening fisheries and fragile ecosystems, as well as groundwater storage. The Hudson River was also having salinity problems. The increased salinity of both rivers was due not only to drought and reduced freshwater flows but also to the rising sea level—more than a centimeter (nearly half an inch) per year for the past several decades. The reservoir shortfall at upstate New York, combined with the reduced transfer from the Delaware Basin, was becoming so critical that the city looked to its emergency backup station, located nearly 150 kilometers (about 90 miles) north on the Hudson River at Hyde Park. Unfortunately, the river flow was so low this year, and sea level had crept so far, that salt water intrusion had rendered Hudson River water at Hyde Park essentially undrinkable.

One enterprising reporter dug up a quote from an old 1987 report by the mayor's Intergovernment Task Force on New York Water Supply that had warned of the likelihood of the current crisis:

> The greenhouse effect could have profound implications for the region's water supply with impacts on the salt front in the Hudson and Delaware rivers, the groundwater resources of Long Island, and rainfall patterns in the region as a whole. Planning for the city's water supply future must take these possible impacts into account, and planners should keep informed about continuing work on this important area.

Capping off the reporter's story were the now-fateful replies of city water planners to such a threat. When the prospect of the greenhouse century had gained professional attention in the late 1980s, the American Association for the Advancement of Science (AAAS) had sponsored studies on the implications of projected climatic changes on water supplies throughout the century. In a 1989 study by Clark University water engineer Harry E. Schwarz and his doctoral student Lee A. Dillard, dozens of district water planners and managers were questioned about what the then very uncertain projections of climatic change might mean to their planning efforts. New York City officials had boasted that "the system is robust" and probably could withstand considerable climatic change. They stressed that before making costly adjustments to anticipate the possibility of climatic change, superiors would need "new unanimity among scientific and professional bodies," since "prediction of change in fifty years or so would only affect thinking and not action." The officials concluded that "everyone has to start to consider change, but New York City is not going to be the first to act."[2]

Meanwhile, a decade before the baseball game was dimmed out, Long Island authorities had begun to undertake the extremely expensive project of building levees across the southern shores to protect barrier islands such as Long Beach, Atlantic Beach, and Fire Island. Already $40 billion of what had been an estimated $80-billion project had been expended, but work was only one-third completed. Numerous minor flooding incidents had occurred during unusual high tides when Nor'easters blew up the coast, but except for the $100 million cost of pumping offshore sand back onto the beaches, Long Island had come through pretty well. Most officials believed that when the levees were completed in the next decade, they would both protect the southern shore from the rising sea level and buffer the island's critical freshwater aquifers from saltwater intrusion.

That year the ocean off Florida and Cape Hatteras was unusually warm. Forecasters were becoming increasingly nervous as they anticipated the onset of the hurricane season. It had long been known that the warmer the water, the more evaporative energy is pumped into a hurricane, thereby lowering its central pressure.[3] The lower the central pressure, the greater the intensity of the winds in the interior wall and the higher the potential "storm surge" of water in front of the hurricane. For the New Jersey-New York area, serious storm surges had had a recurrence likelihood of only one in a few hundred years. But with the unusually warm offshore water in the Atlantic this year, such historically favorable odds provided much less comfort than the long-term statistics had promised.

By the second week in September, a major hurricane was coming out of the Caribbean. Hurricane George was of near-record intensity as it hit southern Florida with storm tides as high as 4 meters (12 feet), bringing devastation to Miami, the Everglades, and the Florida Keys. Advance warning and prompt evacuation kept loss of life to less than a hundred, but property damage estimates were in excess of $1 billion.

As the storm made its way out across the Gulf Stream into the anomalously warm Atlantic, it began to grow; its central pressure dropped until somewhere off Cape Hatteras it had the lowest pressure ever recorded for a storm that far north. All coastal areas from Cape Hatteras to Block Island were evacuated over the next twenty-four hours, a civil defense move that kept loss of life to a minimum. Nevertheless, several dozen thrill seekers and other unusual-weather fans lost their lives as Hurricane George passed off the eastern tip of Long Island at high tide, some ten years before the Long Island levees were to be completed.

Although George brought welcome relief from the drought as ten inches of rain substantially replenished reservoirs, restored flow to the Hudson River, and pushed the salt wedge safely to the south, devastation to the Jersey shore and Long Island was immense. Hundreds of thousands of structures were damaged or destroyed; beaches eroded; partially completed levees breached; roads, bridges, and power lines washed away; and one low-lying toxic waste disposal plant shattered.

The political aftermath of this "storm of the century" was swift and sure, even if late: the United States began a push to rapidly establish a much more vigorous "law of the atmosphere" to replace the weak and chiefly symbolic agreement grudgingly passed by the United Nations at the end of the twentieth century. The old agreement had simply called for nations to use energy more efficiently, develop renewable energy resources more vigorously, and reforest where economically feasible. It had set up a small fund to help bring these changes about and had resulted in an estimated 10% reduction in the rate of buildup of carbon dioxide, methane, and other trace greenhouse gases. Nevertheless, these gases had more than doubled from their preindustrial values.

But now the United States was calling for substantial emission limits from each nation and a crash program to power the world with hydrogen produced from electricity. The electricity would be produced at a number of desert solar collector sites as well as at a few remotely located power parks containing a large concentration of small-scale nuclear reactors with specially designed fuel cycles and cooling mechanisms to prevent meltdown even in the event of operator incompetence. It had been recognized for decades that the seriousness of fossil fuel pollution required building of more of these power plants as their costs also slowly decreased relative to coal-powered plants. But their implementation was too slow to prevent a rapid buildup of greenhouse gases, a buildup that could have been cut in half if taxes on fossil fuels hadn't been rejected by Congress in the 1990s.

It had taken the enormity of a Hurricane George for politicians finally to realize the immediacy and urgency of the problem of climate warming and to take legislative steps to control the industrial and agricultural sources of the problem. Too bad so much time had been wasted, in which much of the current problem could have been abated.

While Chicagoans were not sorry that the second game of the doubleheader with the Mets was canceled (given that the Cubs were losing badly), people were growing weary of this hot summer. In downstate Illinois, in what used to be one of the most productive agricultural areas in the country—a spot that had provided a major shot in the arm to the U.S. economy through its export of corn—frequent drought was producing an economic collapse of crisis proportions. Large corporate farms that were able to purchase water rights and implement efficient irrigation systems had bought out failing family farms at low prices and were now growing winter wheat instead of corn in the cooler, moister weather of fall and early spring. Most smaller farmers or family farmers had either gone out of the farm business or joined the steady flight of immigrants up to northern Michigan, Wisconsin, and Minnesota, which due to the 3°C (5°F) climate warming that had taken place so far in this greenhouse century were now warm enough for growing corn, yet because of their more northerly latitude were less afflicted with intense heat.

The evening news in Minneapolis was punctuated with Minnesota conservation officials' complaints about the rapid rate of deforestation of the state's northern areas accompanying the northward migration of the corn belt. At the same time as land was being cleared for new agriculture, Minnesota was experiencing a rapid rate of forest dieback brought about by the warmer winters and increasingly frequent intense heat waves of the last few decades. While forest managers were fairly certain that maples and other hardwoods would eventually move in to replace the dying firs, they were concerned that it would take a dedicated planting effort to fill the several-hundred-year gap between the death of the fir forest and the natural succession to a mature, robust hardwood forest. Officials therefore also called for new reserves to help keep the influx of farmers away from some of the shrinking forest areas. Also problematic was the extreme fire danger posed by the dead and dying trees, especially during major hot spells like this summer.

Chicagoans had become used to depressing farm news in many small towns in the former corn belt, but they were becoming increasingly alarmed as the shores of Lake Michigan kept receding, with far-reaching economic and health effects. To begin with, ten years ago a number of developers had built dock facilities and highrise condos out into the lake; with increasing drought, the lake level dropped several feet, leaving docks and condos high and dry. Then a freak wet period of five years caused lake levels to rise above the level at which the condos had been built, nearly destroying those speculative developments. Now, a series of dry years with warm summers had caused lake levels to drop well below the level of a decade ago, and politicians argued constantly about whether developers should be allowed to follow the receding lake shore. Who would insure against the loss if lake levels rose again?

Who also should pay for the rebuilding of port facilities and the dredging of channels and locks connecting the Chicago River with the receding lake? And who should fund the hundreds of millions of dollars needed to relocate water intake and outflow pipes? Should the cost be borne by local communities or by a multistate bureaucracy under consideration by the lake states of Wisconsin, Illinois, Indiana, and Michigan? Already an international agency had been set up between Michigan, Ohio, Pennsylvania, New York, and Ontario, Canada, to deal with Lake Erie problems. As Lake Erie water levels had dropped, ships had had to go with lighter loads to prevent hitting bottom, except in areas where dredging was done. After a number of decades of costly losses in shipping tonnage, the international commission had eventually undertaken massive dredging, and shipping through Lake Erie had already shown signs of rebound. Now Lake Michigan neighbors were facing the same problems.

Another serious problem facing the four Lake Michigan states was the nearly one hundred identified "hot spots" where fifty years' worth of toxic contaminants had accumulated in shore sediments. With the lower lake level a wide variety of these toxic sediments had begun to emerge and through erosion were threatening the water quality of the lake. Should the four states create a mini superfund to deal with this dramatic problem or could federal aid be brought in? Already the federal government was facing hundreds of billions of dollars of extra bills to accelerate renewable energy systems, shore up coastlines, build irrigation and water control facilities, and deal with the social problems of the outmigration from lower midwestern farms and the collapse of coal mining as coal increasingly became an internationally unacceptable fuel.

Although not every year had been as dramatic as this, the increasing frequency of droughts, severe flooding episodes, air pollution crises, heat-stress days, brownouts, and forest fires was already stretching the national treasury. Fortunately, the urgent need for environmentally sustainable development had become an international priority in recent decades, and the emergence of a politically united Europe (East and West) along with a nonexpansionist Soviet Union had allowed a halving of military budgets on both sides. Resources were finally freed from military expenditures to deal with the growing environmental pressures of the greenhouse century and the development demands of still-overpopulated, underdeveloped, and overpolluted Third World countries.

Californians had felt relatively fortunate for the past decade or so, having largely escaped the intense heat waves and damaging storm surges of the East Coast. To be sure, there were a number of intensely unpleasant days, especially in Los Angeles, with a week or so each year of temperatures above 38°C (100°F) and serious air pollution crises, but by and large Californians had come through unscathed.

The one group that had suffered from the climatic warming trends of recent decades was the Central Valley farmers, who were heavily dependent upon irrigation. Agricultural water use had been heavily subsidized in the twentieth century, thus allowing rich development of these naturally fertile but hot and dry lands. However, as urban populations in southern California and the Bay Area had increased, competition for water had tripled its price to agriculture—a price now more accurately reflecting the actual cost of water engineering projects and their operating and maintenance expenses.

Although California had not been as stricken by drought as the Midwest or the East, its water supply was being seriously threatened from out of state. That is, the upper-Colorado-River-basin states of Colorado, Utah, and Wyoming were now suing the lower-basin states of California, Nevada, and Arizona to reduce the amount of water allocated to the latter by the Colorado River Compact of 1922. The upper-basin states complained that the compact erroneously forced them to provide a fixed amount of water to the lower-basin states, an allocation naively based on a two-decade experience with Colorado River water flow rates, which then averaged more than 17 million acre-feet per year at Lee's Ferry in northern Arizona. It had seemed equitable at the time for the upper-basin states to keep 7.5 million acre-feet and for the lower-basin states to receive 7.5 million acre-feet, with the remaining 2 million acre-feet reserved for Mexico and for maintenance of the water quality. For some reason, the fixed number of 7.5 million acre-feet was set as the annual obligation of the upper-basin states to the lower-basin states, regardless of what the actual flow rates might be in the future.

Soon after 1922 came the infamous Dust Bowl years of the 1930s, and yearly Colorado River flows dropped by more than half. It also became clear from long-term analysis that the average annual flow rate for the Colorado when calculated over centuries was only something like 13 million acre-feet, and therefore the 1922 compact should have allocated only 5 or 6 million acre-feet to the lower-basin states to begin with.[4]

A law is a law, California had always argued, and that combined with the fact that throughout the twentieth century the upper-basin states had not fully developed their own allotment had kept the shaky compact temporarily free from legal challenge. However, with hotter summers and shorter snow seasons of late, annual river flows had averaged only about 10 million acre-feet, and the upper-basin states had been left with only 2.5 million acre-feet, well below their own needs. Water-threatened Californians and Arizonans were not taking the court challenge lightly.

This looked like a particularly difficult year. Projections made in the late 1980s for population increases and water demands in southern California were turning out to be underestimates, perhaps because planners had not anticipated the outmigration from the Northeast and Midwest due to the collapse of family farms and the growing intensity of summer heat waves. Furthermore, Dallas, which in the 1980s already had a one-in-three chance of five or more days of 38°C (100°F) in a row, had warmed to the point where that kind of heat wave routinely occurred three out of every four years.[5] Thousands of Texans chose to flee the heat and more frequent coastal flooding and move to southern California despite the increasing price of land, the overcrowding, the water shortages, and the air pollution. Although California had the potential for increased water storage—even the ability to cope with reduced rainfall and snowfall—through the damming of wilderness rivers and creation of lakes, only a small fraction of that potential had been tapped because of opposition from northern California conservation groups dedicated to protecting wilderness areas and those arguing it was fiscally irresponsible to spend billions to water more lawns in Los Angeles when it was already overpopulated.

What made this year particularly worrisome was the fact that the ongoing rise in sea level had begun to push salt water farther and farther into San Francisco Bay and the Sacramento Delta. In anticipation of this increasing water level, California had built a large number of levees at a cost of over $4 billion, but this year, because of the reduced river flow into the Sacramento Delta, water officials had been legally required to release more fresh water into the delta to prevent loss of habitat critical to fisheries, the shrimp industry, and many species of birds. This regulation was meeting with intense hostility from water users in the south, who saw these northern water releases as being wasted on wildlife instead of being put to "productive" use in the Southland. California had already passed an emergency rule prohibiting watering of lawns and golf courses and the filling of swimming pools, the latter being a particularly hard blow to the influential, rich, and famous in this relatively hot summer.

Northern Californians were also experiencing a decrease in water availability since the storm track didn't migrate down into their area until later in midwinter and then left earlier in the spring. Nevertheless, water was not northern California's biggest concern, but rather the frequent episodes of smoky skies that were a constant reminder of the growing intensity and scale of wildfires. Extra-heavy storms in the winter, though less frequent now, generally nurtured good winter and spring growth in forest and chaparral areas. However, the early dry seasons and hot summers of late had increased the fire potential. Moreover, pressure from homeowners, ranchers, and the timber industry had kept firefighting activities at a maximum over the past several decades, thus allowing a critically high buildup of underbrush and dead branches. This dry summer needed only a few irresponsible campers or some normal lightning activity to cover the northern half of the state—and much of the West—in smoke. That California would escape this fate for yet another year was by no means assured as the September fire-danger season began.

The scenarios just sketched for sometime in the greenhouse century are contrived, of course, but they are based upon extensive studies. In fact, they could happen today, but at a much lower probability than in a warmer world. Many national and international scientific assessments of the environmental and societal impacts of plausible climatic changes caused by greenhouse gases have been undertaken in the 1980s. From these plausible scenarios, such as those just invented, we can examine the all-important question: So what if the climate changes?

Recently, I was challenged by an undersecretary of state to justify my advocacy of active policy responses to the prospect of global warming given that "there could well be some strong buffering effect in nature that climatologists hadn't yet discovered that would negate most of the large change predictions." "I agree that such a buffer may exist," I said (and he seemed pleased with himself), "but can you tell me what the probability is that it actually exists?" He quickly changed to a blank expression. "One in ten, one in five, or perhaps I'll even make it as large as one in two?" I went on. "OK, let's say one in two," he responded. "Fine," I responded. "Then there is also a one-in-two chance that change will be as large or *larger* than we currently project. In other words, we are flipping a coin with unprecedented environmental change on one of the faces. With those kinds of odds and potentially dramatic impacts, I feel quite justified in advocating policy consideration for prudent actions that can slow down the rate of change and at the same time offer multiple additional benefits to society." "I agree that those kinds of actions may be warranted," he conceded, "but until you scientists can offer very confident, less speculative scenarios, I doubt governments will take dramatic or costly actions."

How solid a scientific case, then, can we make to back up concern over global warming?

Notes

1. Fires in Alberta in 1950 did indeed generate so much smoke that lights had to be turned on in the middle of afternoon baseball games in the U.S. Midwest. The fact that smoke from such fires was later observed high in the atmosphere over England by Royal Air Force pilots made this incident part of the controversy over "nuclear winter," the notion advanced by P. J. Crutzen and J. W. Birks, "The Atmosphere after a Nuclear War: Twilight at Noon," *Ambio* 11 (1982): 115–25. This idea postulates that smoke generated from fires in the aftermath of a nuclear war could blanket much of the globe, blocking out the sun and causing winterlike conditions in any season (as suggested by R. P. Turco, O. B. Toon, T. P. Ackerman, J. B. Pollack, and C. Sagan, "Nuclear Winter: Global Consequences of Multiple Nuclear Explosions," *Science* 222 [1983]: 1283–92). For a recent review of the nuclear winter controversy, see S. H. Schneider and S. L. Thompson, "Simulating the Climatic Effects of Nuclear War," *Nature* 333 (1988): 221–27. A description of the 1950 Alberta fires can be found in H. Wexler, "The Great Smoke Pall," *Weatherwise* 3 (September 24–30, 1950): 6–11.

2. These quotes can be found in H. Schwarz and L. Dillard, "Urban Water," Chap. 15 in *Climate Change and U.S. Water Resources,* ed. P. E. Waggoner (New York: Wiley & Sons, in press [1990]).

3. K. Emanuel, "The Dependence of Hurricane Intensity on Climate," *Nature* 326 (1987): 483–85.

4. The Colorado River Compact allotments are no fiction. Indeed, the framers of the compact actually allocated a fixed amount of water rather than a percentage of water, without knowing that the compact was drawn up after a historic high-flow period, which made those fixed water allocations highly questionable. An interesting history of the compact and this issue is given by B. G. Brown, "Climate Variability and the Colorado River Compact: Implications for Responding to Climate Change," in *Societal Responses to Regional Climatic Change: Forecasting by Analogy,* ed. M. H. Glantz (Boulder, Colo.: Westview Press, 1988), 279–305.

5. L. O. Mearns, R. W. Katz, and S. H. Schneider calculated that in July in Dallas, Texas, a 3°F rise in mean temperature could increase the probability of five or more consecutive days above 100°F (38°C) from today's value of about one day in three to a future value of two days in three ("Changes in the Probabilities of Extreme High Temperature Events with Changes in Global Mean Temperature," *Journal of Climate and Applied Meteorology* 23 [1984]: 1601–13).

10

Human Alteration of the Global Nitrogen Cycle
Causes and Consequences

Peter M. Vitousek, John Aber,
Robert W. Howarth, Gene E. Likens,
Pamela A. Matson, David W. Schindler,
William H. Schlesinger, and G. David Tilman

This selection gives a sense of the very sophisticated nature of scientific research into aspects of human-caused changes in the Earth's atmosphere. The focus is the global nitrogen cycle, an important topic because it reminds us that human-caused climate change is not restricted to greenhouse gases and global warming. It has other equally complicated and equally troubling aspects.

Vitousek is Professor of Population Biology at Stanford University. He has carried out extensive experimental and comparative studies of nutrient cycling in tropical and temperate forests.

This report presents an overview of the current scientific understanding of human-driven changes to the global nitrogen cycle and their consequences. It also addresses policy and management options that could help moderate these changes in the nitrogen cycle and their impacts.

The Nitrogen Cycle

Nitrogen is an essential component of proteins, genetic material, chlorophyll, and other key organic molecules. All organisms require nitrogen in order to

From Peter M. Vitousek et al., "Human Alteration of the Global Nitrogen Cycle: Causes and Consequences," *Issues in Ecology* (February 1997). Reprinted by permission of The Ecological Society of America.

live. It ranks fourth behind oxygen, carbon, and hydrogen as the most common chemical element in living tissues. Until human activities began to alter the natural cycle, however, nitrogen was only scantily available to much of the biological world. As a result, nitrogen served as one of the major limiting factors that controlled the dynamics, biodiversity, and functioning of many ecosystems.

The Earth's atmosphere is 78 percent nitrogen gas, but most plants and animals cannot use nitrogen gas directly from the air as they do carbon dioxide and oxygen. Instead, plants—and all organisms from the grazing animals to the predators to the decomposers that ultimately secure their nourishment from the organic materials synthesized by plants—must wait for nitrogen to be "fixed," that is, pulled from the air and bonded to hydrogen or oxygen to form inorganic compounds, mainly ammonium (NH_4) and nitrate (NO_3), that they can use.

The amount of gaseous nitrogen being fixed at any given time by natural processes represents only a small addition to the pool of previously fixed nitrogen that cycles among the living and nonliving components of the Earth's ecosystems. Most of that nitrogen, too, is unavailable, locked up in soil organic matter—partially rotted plant and animal remains—that must be decomposed by soil microbes. These microbes release nitrogen as ammonium or nitrate, allowing it to be recycled through the food web. The two major natural sources of new nitrogen entering this cycle are nitrogen-fixing organisms and lightning.

Nitrogen-fixing organisms include a relatively small number of algae and bacteria. Many of them live free in the soil, but the most important ones are bacteria that form close symbiotic relationships with higher plants. Symbiotic nitrogen-fixing bacteria such as the Rhizobia, for instance, live and work in nodules on the roots of peas, beans, alfalfa and other legumes. These bacteria manufacture an enzyme that enables them to convert gaseous nitrogen directly into plant-usable forms.

Lightning may also indirectly transform atmospheric nitrogen into nitrates, which rain onto soil.

Quantifying the rate of natural nitrogen fixation prior to human alterations of the cycle is difficult but necessary for evaluating the impacts of human-driven changes to the global cycling of nitrogen. The standard unit of measurement for analyzing the global nitrogen cycle is the teragram (abbreviated Tg), which is equal to a million metric tons of nitrogen. Worldwide, lightning, for instance, fixes less than 10 Tg of nitrogen per year—maybe even less than 5 Tg. Microbes are the major natural suppliers of new biologically available nitrogen. Before the widespread planting of legume crops, terrestrial organisms probably fixed between 90 and 140 Tg of nitrogen per year. A reasonable upper bound for the rate of natural nitrogen fixation on land is thus about 140 Tg of N per year.

Human-Driven Nitrogen Fixation

During the past century, human activities clearly have accelerated the rate of nitrogen fixation on land, effectively doubling the annual transfer of nitrogen from the vast but unavailable atmospheric pool to the biologically available forms. The major sources of this enhanced supply include industrial processes that produce nitrogen fertilizers, the combustion of fossil fuels, and the cultivation of soybeans, peas, and other crops that host symbiotic nitrogen-fixing bacteria. Furthermore, human activity is also speeding up the release of nitrogen from long-term storage in soils and organic matter.

Nitrogen Fertilizer

Industrial fixation of nitrogen for use as fertilizer currently totals approximately 80 Tg per year and represents by far the largest human contribution of new nitrogen to the global cycle. That figure does not include manures and other organic nitrogen fertilizers, which represent a transfer of already-fixed nitrogen from one place to another rather than new fixation.

The process of manufacturing fertilizer by industrial nitrogen fixation was first developed in Germany during World War I, and fertilizer production has grown exponentially since the 1940s. In recent years, the increasing pace of production and use has been truly phenomenal. The amount of industrially fixed nitrogen applied to crops during the decade from 1980 to 1990 more than equaled all industrial fertilizer applied previously in human history.

Until the late 1970s, most industrially produced fertilizer was applied in developed countries. Use in these regions has now stabilized while fertilizer applications in developing countries have risen dramatically. The momentum of human population growth and increasing urbanization ensures that industrial fertilizer production will continue at high and likely accelerating rates for decades in order to meet the escalating demand for food.

Nitrogen-Fixing Crops

Nearly one third of the Earth's land surface is devoted to agricultural and pastoral uses, and humans have replaced large areas of diverse natural vegetation with monocultures of soybeans, peas, alfalfa, and other leguminous crops and forages. Because these plants support symbiotic nitrogen-fixers, they derive much of their nitrogen directly from the atmosphere and greatly increase the rate of nitrogen fixation previously occurring on those lands. Substantial levels of nitrogen fixation also occur during cultivation of some non-legumes, notably rice. All of this represents new, human-generated stocks of biologically available nitrogen. The quantity of nitrogen fixed by crops is more difficult to analyze than industrial nitrogen production. Estimates range from 32 to 53 Tg per year. As an average, 40 Tg will be used here.

Fossil Fuel Burning

The burning of fossil fuels such as coal and oil releases previously fixed nitrogen from long-term storage in geological formations back to the atmosphere in the form of nitrogen-based trace gases such as nitric oxide. High-temperature combustion also fixes a small amount of atmospheric nitrogen directly. Altogether, the operations of automobiles, factories, power plants, and other combustion processes emit more than 20 Tg per year of fixed nitrogen to the atmosphere. All of it is treated here as newly fixed nitrogen because it has been locked up for millions of years and would remain locked up indefinitely if not released by human action.

Mobilization of Stored Nitrogen

Besides enhancing fixation and releasing nitrogen from geological reservoirs, human activities also liberate nitrogen from long-term biological storage pools such as soil organic matter and tree trunks, contributing further to the proliferation of biologically available nitrogen. These activities include the burning of forests, wood fuels, and grasslands, which emits more than 40 Tg per year of nitrogen; the draining of wetlands, which sets the stage for oxidation of soil organic matter that could mobilize 10 Tg per year or more of nitrogen; and land clearing for crops, which could mobilize 20 Tg per year from soils.

There are substantial scientific uncertainties about both the quantity and the fate of nitrogen mobilized by such activities. Taken together, however, they could contribute significantly to changes in the global nitrogen cycle.

Human versus Natural Nitrogen Fixation

Overall, fertilizer production, legume crops, and fossil fuel burning deposit approximately 140 Tg of new nitrogen into land-based ecosystems each year, a figure that equals the upper estimates for nitrogen fixed naturally by organisms in these ecosystems. Other human activities liberate and make available half again that much nitrogen. From this evidence, it is fair to conclude that human activities have at least doubled the transfer of nitrogen from the atmosphere into the land-based biological nitrogen cycle.

This extra nitrogen is spread unevenly across the Earth's surface: Some areas such as northern Europe are being altered profoundly while others such as remote regions in the Southern Hemisphere receive little direct input of human-generated nitrogen. Yet no region remains unaffected. The increase in fixed nitrogen circulating around the globe and falling to the ground as wet or dry deposition is readily detectable, even in cores drilled from the glacial ice of Greenland.

Impacts on the Atmosphere

One major consequence of human-driven alterations in the nitrogen cycle has been regional and global change in the chemistry of the atmosphere—specifically, increased emissions of nitrogen-based trace gases such as nitrous oxide, nitric oxide, and ammonia (NH_3). Although such releases have received less attention than increased emissions of carbon dioxide and various sulfur compounds, the trace nitrogen gases cause environmental effects both while airborne and after they are deposited on the ground. For instance, nitrous oxide is long-lived in the atmosphere and contributes to the human-driven enhancement of the greenhouse effect that likely warms the Earth's climate. Nitric oxide is an important precursor of acid rain and photochemical smog.

Some of the human activities discussed above affect the atmosphere directly. For instance, essentially all of the more than 20 Tg per year of fixed nitrogen released in automobile exhausts and in other emissions from fossil fuel burning is emitted to the atmosphere as nitric oxide. Other activities indirectly enhance emissions to the atmosphere. Intensive fertilization of agricultural soils can increase the rates at which nitrogen in the form of ammonia is volatilized and lost to the air. It can also speed the microbial breakdown of ammonium and nitrates in the soil, enhancing the release of nitrous oxide. Even in wild or unmanaged lands downwind of agricultural or industrial areas, rain or windborne deposition of human-generated nitrogen can spur increased emissions of nitrogen gases from the soils.

Nitrous Oxide

Nitrous oxide is a very effective heat-trapping gas in the atmosphere, in part because it absorbs outgoing radiant heat from the Earth in infrared wavelengths that are not captured by the other major greenhouse gases, water vapor and carbon dioxide. By absorbing and reradiating this heat back toward the Earth, nitrous oxide contributes a few percent to overall greenhouse warming.

Although nitrous oxide is unreactive and long-lived in the lower atmosphere, when it rises into the stratosphere it can trigger reactions that deplete and thin the stratospheric ozone layer that shields the Earth from damaging ultraviolet radiation.

The concentration of nitrous oxide in the atmosphere is currently increasing at the rate of two- to three-tenths of a percent per year. While that rise is clearly documented, the sources of the increase remain unresolved.

Both fossil fuel burning and the direct impacts of agricultural fertilization have been considered and rejected as the major source. Rather, there is a developing consensus that a wide array of human-driven sources contribute systematically to enrich the terrestrial nitrogen cycle. These "dispersed sources" include fertilizers, nitrogen-enriched groundwater, nitrogen-saturated forests, forest burning, land clearing, and even the manufacture of nylon, nitric acid, and other industrial products.

The net effect is increased global concentrations of a potent greenhouse gas that also contributes to the thinning of the stratospheric ozone layer.

Nitric Oxide and Ammonia

Unlike nitrous oxide, which is unreactive in the lower atmosphere, both nitric oxide and ammonia are highly reactive and therefore much shorter lived. Thus changes in their atmospheric concentrations can be detected only at local or regional scales.

Nitric oxide plays several critical roles in atmospheric chemistry, including catalyzing the formation of photochemical (or brown) smog. In the presence of sunlight, nitric oxide and oxygen react with hydrocarbons emitted by automobile exhausts to form ozone, the most dangerous component of smog. Ground-level ozone has serious detrimental effects on human health as well as the health and productivity of crops and forests.

Nitric oxide, along with other oxides of nitrogen and sulfur, can be transformed in the atmosphere into nitric acid and sulfuric acid, which are the major components of acid rain.

Although a number of sources contribute to nitric oxide emissions, combustion is the dominant one. Fossil fuel burning emits more than 20 Tg per year of nitric oxide. Human burning of forests and other plant material may add about 10 Tg, and global emissions of nitric oxide from soils, a substantial fraction of which are human-caused, total 5 to 20 Tg per year. Overall, 80 percent or more of nitric oxide emissions worldwide are generated by human activities, and in many regions the result is increased smog and acid rain.

In contrast to nitric oxide, ammonia acts as the primary acid-neutralizing agent in the atmosphere, having an opposite influence on the acidity of aerosols, cloudwater, and rainfall. Nearly 70 percent of global ammonia emissions are human-caused. Ammonia volatilized from fertilized fields contributes an estimated 10 Tg per year; ammonia released from domestic animal wastes about 32 Tg; and forest burning some 5 Tg.

Effects on the Carbon Cycle

Increased emissions of airborne nitrogen have led to enhanced deposition of nitrogen on land and in the oceans. Thanks to the fertilizer effects of nitrogen in stimulating plant growth, this deposition may be acting to influence the atmosphere indirectly by altering the global carbon cycle.

Over much of the Earth's surface, the lushness of plant growth and the accumulation of standing stocks of plant material historically have been limited by scanty nitrogen supplies, particularly in temperate and boreal regions. Human activity has substantially increased the deposition of nitrogen over much of this area, which raises important questions: How much extra plant growth has been caused by human-generated nitrogen additions? As a result, how much extra carbon has been stored in terrestrial ecosystems rather than contributing to the rising concentrations of carbon dioxide in the atmosphere?

Answers to these questions could help explain the imbalance in the carbon cycle that has come to be known as the "missing sink." The known emissions of carbon dioxide from human activities such as fossil fuel burning and deforestation exceed by more than 1,000 Tg the amount of carbon dioxide known to be accumulating in the atmosphere each year. Could increased growth rates in terrestrial vegetation be the "sink" that accounts for the fate of much of that missing carbon?

Experiments in Europe and America indicate that a large portion of the extra nitrogen retained by forest, wetland, and tundra ecosystems stimulates carbon uptake and storage. On the other hand, this nitrogen can also stimulate microbial decomposition and thus releases of carbon from soil organic matter. On balance, however, the carbon uptake through new plant growth appears to exceed the carbon losses, especially in forests.

A number of groups have attempted to calculate the amount of carbon that could be stored in terrestrial vegetation thanks to plant growth spurred by added nitrogen. The resulting estimates range from 100 to 1,300 Tg per year. The number has tended to increase in more recent analyses as the magnitude of human-driven changes in the nitrogen cycle has become clearer. The most recent analysis of the global carbon cycle by the Intergovernmental Panel on Climate Change concluded that nitrogen deposition could represent a major component of the missing carbon sink.

More precise estimates will become possible when we have a more complete understanding of the fraction of human-generated nitrogen that actually is retained within various land-based ecosystems.

Nitrogen Saturation and Ecosystem Functioning

There are limits to how much plant growth can be increased by nitrogen fertilization. At some point, when the natural nitrogen deficiencies in an ecosystem are fully relieved, plant growth becomes limited by sparsity of other resources such as phosphorus, calcium, or water. When the vegetation can no longer respond to further additions of nitrogen, the ecosystem reaches a state described as "nitrogen saturation." In theory, when an ecosystem is fully nitrogen-saturated and its soils, plants, and microbes cannot use or retain any more, all new nitrogen deposits will be dispersed to streams, groundwater, and the atmosphere.

Nitrogen saturation has a number of damaging consequences for the health and functioning of ecosystems. These impacts first became apparent in Europe almost two decades ago when scientists observed significant increases in nitrate concentrations in some lakes and streams and also extensive yellowing and loss of needles in spruce and other conifer forests subjected to heavy nitrogen deposition. These observations led to several field experiments in the U.S. and Europe that have revealed a complex cascade of effects set in motion by excess nitrogen in forest soils.

As ammonium builds up in the soil, it is increasingly converted to nitrate by bacterial action, a process that releases hydrogen ions and helps acidify the soil. The buildup of nitrate enhances emissions of nitrous oxides from the soil and also encourages leaching of highly water-soluble nitrate into streams or groundwater. As these negatively charged nitrates seep away, they carry with them positively charged alkaline minerals such as calcium, magnesium, and potassium. Thus human modifications to the nitrogen cycle decrease soil fertility by greatly accelerating the loss of calcium and other nutrients that are vital for plant growth. As calcium is depleted and the soil acidified, aluminum ions are mobilized, eventually reaching toxic concentrations that can damage tree roots or kill fish if the aluminum washes into streams Trees growing in soils replete with nitrogen but starved of calcium, magnesium, and potassium can develop nutrient imbalances in their roots and leaves. This may reduce their photosynthetic rate and efficiency, stunt their growth, and even increase tree deaths.

Nitrogen saturation is much further advanced over extensive areas of northern Europe than in North America because human-generated nitrogen deposition is several times greater there than in even the most extremely affected areas of North America. In the nitrogen-saturated ecosystems of Europe, a substantial fraction of atmospheric nitrate deposits move from the land into streams without ever being taken up by organisms or playing a role in the biological cycle.

In contrast, in the northeastern U.S., increased leaching of nitrates from the soil and large shifts in the nutrient ratios in tree leaves generally have been observed only in certain types of forests. These include high-elevation sites that receive large nitrogen deposits and sites with shallow soils containing few alkaline minerals to buffer acidification. Elsewhere in the U.S., the early stages of nitrogen saturation have been seen in response to elevated nitrogen deposition in the forests surrounding the Los Angeles Basin and in the Front Range of the Colorado Rockies.

Some forests have a very high capacity to retain added nitrogen, particularly regrowing forests that have been subjected to intense or repeated harvesting, an activity that usually causes severe nitrogen losses. Overall, the ability of a forest to retain nitrogen depends on its potential for further growth and the extent of its current nitrogen stocks. Thus, the impacts of nitrogen deposition are tightly linked to other rapidly changing human-driven variables such as shifts in land use, climate, and atmospheric carbon dioxide and ozone levels.

Effects on Biodiversity and the Species Mix

Limited supplies of biologically available nitrogen are a fact of life in most natural ecosystems, and many native plant species are adapted to function best under this constraint. New supplies of nitrogen showered upon these ecosystems can cause a dramatic shift in the dominant species and also a marked reduction in overall species diversity as the few plant species adapted to take full advantage of high nitrogen out compete their neighbors. In England, for example, nitrogen fertilizers applied to experimental grasslands have led to increased dominance by a few nitrogen-responsive grasses and loss of many other plant species. At the highest fertilization rate, the number of plant species declined more than five-fold. In North America, similarly dramatic reductions in biodiversity have been created by fertilization of grasslands in Minnesota and California. In formerly species-rich heathlands across Western Europe, human-driven nitrogen deposition has been blamed for great losses of biodiversity in recent decades.

In the Netherlands, high human population density, intensive livestock operations, and industries have combined to generate the highest rates of nitrogen deposition in the world. One well-documented consequence has been the conversion of species-rich heathlands to species-poor grasslands and forest. Not only the species richness of the heath but also the biological diversity of the landscape has been reduced because the modified plant communities now resemble the composition of communities occupying more fertile soils. The unique species assemblage adapted to sandy, nitrogen-poor soils is being lost from the region.

Losses of biodiversity driven by nitrogen deposition can in turn affect other ecological processes. Recent experiments in Minnesota grasslands showed that in ecosystems made species-poor by fertilization, plant productivity was much less stable in the face of a major drought. Even in non-drought years, the normal vagaries of climate produced much more year-to-year variation in the productivity of species-poor grassland plots than in more diverse plots.

Effects on Aquatic Ecosystems

Historical Changes in Water Chemistry

Not surprisingly, nitrogen concentrations in surface waters have increased as human activities have accelerated the rate of fixed nitrogen being put into circulation. A recent study of the North Atlantic Ocean Basin by scientists from a dozen nations estimates that movements of total dissolved nitrogen into most of the temperate-zone rivers in the basin may have increased by two- to 20-fold since preindustrial times. For rivers in the North Sea region, the nitrogen increase may have been six- to 20-fold. The nitrogen increases in these rivers are highly correlated with human-generated inputs of nitrogen to their watersheds, and these inputs are dominated by fertilizers and atmospheric deposition.

For decades, nitrate concentrations in many rivers and drinking water supplies have been closely monitored in developed regions of the world, and analysis of these data confirms a historic rise in nitrogen levels in the surface waters. In 1,000 lakes in Norway, for example, nitrate levels doubled in less than a decade. In the Mississippi River, nitrates have more than doubled since 1965. In major rivers of the northeastern U.S., nitrate concentrations have risen three- to ten-fold since the early 1900s, and the evidence suggests a similar trend in many European rivers.

Again not surprisingly, nitrate concentrations in the world's large rivers rise along with the density of human population in the watersheds. Amounts of total dissolved nitrogen in rivers are also correlated with human population density, but total nitrogen does not increase as rapidly as the nitrate fraction. Evidence indicates that with increasing human disturbance, a higher proportion of the nitrogen in surface waters is composed of nitrate.

Increased concentrations of nitrate have also been observed in groundwater in many agricultural regions, although the magnitude of the trend is difficult to determine in all but a few well-characterized aquifers. Overall, the additions to groundwater probably represent only a small fraction of the increased nitrate transported in surface waters. However, groundwater has a long residence time in many aquifers, meaning that groundwater quality is likely to continue to decline as long as human activities are having substantial impacts on the nitrogen cycle.

High levels of nitrates in drinking water raise significant human health concerns, especially for infants. Microbes in an infant's stomach may convert high levels of nitrate to nitrite. When nitrite is absorbed into the bloodstream, it converts oxygen-carrying hemoglobin into an ineffective form called methemoglobin. Elevated methemoglobin levels—an anemic condition known as methemoglobinemia—can cause brain damage or death. The condition is rare in the U.S., but the potential exists whenever nitrate levels exceed U.S. Public Health Service standards (10 milligrams per liter).

Nitrogen and Acidification of Lakes

Nitric acid is playing an increasing role in the acidification of lakes and streams for two major reasons. One is that most efforts to control acid deposition—which includes acid rain, snow, fog, mist, and dry deposits—have focused on cutting emissions of sulfur dioxide to limit the formation of sulfuric acid in the atmosphere. In many areas, these efforts have succeeded in reducing inputs of sulfuric acid to soils and water while emissions of nitrogen oxides, the precursors of nitric acid, have gone largely unchecked. The second reason is that many watersheds in areas of moderate to high nitrogen deposition appear to be approaching nitrogen saturation, and the increasingly acidified soils have little capacity to buffer acid rain before it enters streams.

An additional factor in many areas is that nitric acid predominates among the pollutants that accumulate in the winter snowpack. Much of this nitric acid is flushed out with the first batch of spring meltwater, often washing a sudden, concentrated "acid pulse" into vulnerable lakes.

Adding inorganic nitrogen to freshwater ecosystems that are also rich in phosphorus can eutrophy as well as acidify the waters. Both eutrophication and acidification generally lead to decreased diversity of both plant and animal species. Fish populations, in particular, have been reduced or eliminated in many acidified lakes across Scandinavia, Canada, and the northeastern United States.

Because the extent of nitrogen-saturated ecosystems continues to grow, along with human-caused nitrogen deposition, controls on sulfur dioxide emissions alone clearly will not be sufficient to decrease acid rain or prevent its detrimental effects on streams and lakes. European governments already have recognized the importance of nitrogen in acidifying soils and waters, and intergovernmental efforts are under way there to reduce emissions and deposition of nitrogen on a regional basis.

Eutrophication in Estuaries and Coastal Waters

One of the best documented and best understood consequences of human alterations of the nitrogen cycle is the eutrophication of estuaries and coastal seas. It is arguably the most serious human threat to the integrity of coastal ecosystems.

In sharp contrast to the majority of temperate-zone lakes, where phosphorus is the nutrient that most limits primary productivity by algae and other aquatic plants and controls eutrophication, these processes are controlled by nitrogen inputs in most temperate-zone estuaries and coastal waters. This is largely because the natural flow of nitrogen into these waters and the rate of nitrogen fixation by planktonic organisms are relatively low while microbes in the sea floor sediments actively release nitrogen back to the atmosphere.

When high nitrogen loading causes eutrophication in stratified waters—where a sharp temperature gradient prevents mixing of warm surface waters with colder bottom waters—the result can be anoxia (no oxygen) or hypoxia (low oxygen) in bottom waters. Both conditions appear to be becoming more prevalent in many estuaries and coastal seas. There is good evidence that since the 1950s or 1960s, anoxia has increased in the Baltic Sea, the Black Sea, and Chesapeake Bay. Periods of hypoxia have increased in Long Island Sound, the North Sea, and the Kattegat, resulting in significant losses of fish and shellfish.

Eutrophication is also linked to losses of diversity, both in the sea floor community—including seaweeds, seagrasses, and corals—and among planktonic organisms. In eutrophied waters, for example, "nuisance algae" may come to dominate the phytoplankton community. Increases in troublesome or toxic algal blooms have been observed in many estuaries and coastal seas worldwide in recent decades. During the 1980s, toxic blooms of dinoflagellates and brown-tide organisms caused extensive die-offs of fish and shellfish in many estuaries. Although the causes are not completely understood, there is compelling evidence that nutrient enrichment of coastal waters is at least partly to blame for such blooms.

Major Uncertainties

Although this report has focused on what is known about human-driven changes to the global nitrogen cycle, major uncertainties remain. Some of these have been noted in earlier sections. This section, however, focuses on important processes that remain so poorly understood that it is difficult to distinguish human-caused impacts or to predict their consequences.

Marine Nitrogen Fixation

Little is known about the unmodified nitrogen cycle in the open ocean. Credible estimates of nitrogen fixation by organisms in the sea vary more than ten-fold, ranging from less than 30 to more than 300 Tg per year. There is some evidence that human alteration of the nitrogen cycle could alter biological processes in the open ocean, but there is no adequate frame of reference against which to evaluate any potential human-driven change in marine nitrogen fixation.

Changes in Limiting Resources

One consequence of human-driven changes in the global nitrogen cycle is a shift in the resources that limit biological processes in many areas. Large amounts of nitrogen are now deposited on many ecosystems that were once nitrogen deficient. The dominant species in these systems may have evolved with nitrogen limitation, and the ways they grow and function and form symbiotic partnerships may reflect adaptations to this limit. With this limit removed, species must operate under novel constraints such as now-inadequate phosphorus or water supplies. How are the performance of organisms and the operation of larger ecological processes affected by changes in their chemical environment for which they have no evolutionary background and to which they are not adapted?

Capacity to Retain Nitrogen

Forests and wetlands vary substantially in their capacity to retain added nitrogen. Interacting factors that are known to affect this capacity include soil texture, degree of chemical weathering of soil, fire history, rate at which plant material accumulates, and past human land use. However, we still lack a fundamental understanding of how and why nitrogen-retention processes vary among ecosystems—much less how they have changed and will change with time.

Alteration of Denitrification

In large river basins, the majority of nitrogen that arrives is probably broken down by denitrifying bacteria and released to the atmosphere as nitrogen gas or nitrous oxide. Exactly where most of this activity takes place is poorly understood, although we know that streamside areas and wetlands are important. Human activities such as increased nitrate deposition, dam building, and rice cultivation have probably enhanced denitrification, while draining of wetlands and alteration of riparian ecosystems has probably decreased it. But the net effect of human influence remains uncertain.

Natural Nitrogen Cycling

Information on the rate of nitrogen deposition and loss in various regions prior to extensive human alterations of the nitrogen cycle remains patchy. In part, this reflects the fact that all of the Earth already is affected to some degree by human activity. Nevertheless, studies in remote regions of the Southern Hemisphere illustrate that there is still valuable information to be gathered on areas that have been minimally altered by humans.

Future Prospects and Management Options

Fertilizer Use

The greatest human-driven increases in global nitrogen supplies are linked to activities intended to boost food production. Modern intensive agriculture requires large quantities of nitrogen fertilizer; humanity, in turn, requires intensive agriculture to support a growing population that is projected to double by the end of the next century. Consequently, the production and application of nitrogen fertilizer has grown exponentially, and the highest rates of application are now found in some developing countries with the highest rates of population growth. One study predicts that by the year 2020, global production of nitrogen fertilizer will increase from a current level of about 80 Tg to 134 Tg per year.

Curtailing this growth in nitrogen fertilizer production will be a difficult challenge. Nevertheless, there are ways to slow the growth of fertilizer use and also to reduce the mobility—and hence the regional and global impacts— of the nitrogen that is applied to fields.

One way to reduce the amount of fertilizer used is to increase its efficiency. Often at least half of the fertilizer applied to fields is lost to the air or water. This leakage represents an expensive waste to the farmer as well as a significant driver of environmental change. A number of management practices have been identified that can reduce the amounts of fertilizer used and cut losses of nitrogen to the air and water without sacrificing yields or profits (and in some cases, increasing them). For instance, one commercial sugar cane plantation in Hawaii was able to cut nitrogen fertilizer use by one third and reduce losses of nitrous oxide and nitric oxide ten-fold by dissolving the fertilizer in irrigation water, delivering it below the soil surface, and timing multiple applications to meet the needs of the growing crop. This knowledge-intensive system also proved more profitable than broadcasting fewer, larger applications of fertilizer onto the soil surface. The widespread implementation of such practices, particularly in developing regions, should be a high priority for agronomists as well as ecologists since improved practices provide an opportunity to reduce the costs of food production while slowing the rate of global change.

There are also ways to prevent the nitrogen that leaches from fertilized farmland from reaching streams, estuaries, and coastal waters where it contributes to eutrophication. In many regions, agricultural lands have been expanded by channelizing streams, clearing riparian forests, and draining wetlands. Yet these areas serve as important natural nitrogen traps. Restoration of wetlands and riparian areas and even construction of artificial wetlands have been shown to be effective in preventing excess nitrogen from entering waters.

Fossil Fuel Burning

The second major source of human-fixed nitrogen is fossil fuel burning. It, too, will increase markedly as we enter the next century, particularly in the developing world. One study predicts that production of nitrogen oxides from fossil fuels will more than double in the next 25 years, from about 20 Tg per year to 46 Tg. Reducing these emissions will require improvements in the efficiency of fuel combustion as well as in the interception of airborne by-products of combustion. As with improvements in fertilizer efficiency, it will be particularly important to transfer efficient combustion technologies to developing countries as their economies and industries grow.

Conclusions

Human activities during the past century have doubled the natural annual rate at which fixed nitrogen enters the land-based nitrogen cycle, and the pace is likely to accelerate. Serious environmental consequences are already apparent. In the atmosphere, concentrations of the greenhouse gas nitrous oxide and of the nitrogen-precursors of smog and acid rain are increasing. Soils in many regions are being acidified and stripped of nutrients essential for continued fertility. The waters of streams and lakes in these regions are also being acidified, and excess nitrogen is being transported by rivers into estuaries and coastal waters. It is quite likely that this unprecedented nitrogen loading has already contributed to long-term declines in coastal fisheries and accelerated losses of plant and animal diversity in both aquatic and land-based ecosystems. It is urgent that national and international policies address the nitrogen issue, slow the pace of this global change, and moderate its impacts.

11

Losing Strands in the Web of Life

John Tuxill and Chris Bright

All living things depend for their survival not only on the natural resources they most frequently use but also on the diversity of life forms around them. Because the needs and activities of each individual living thing, and each species, depend on, interact with, and affect an astounding number of other living things, the loss of individuals and species can have unexpected and unpredictable consequences. While the extinction and creation of species is an ongoing process, the current rate of extinction is very high by historical standards—higher than at any other previous time since the end of the Cretaceous period 65 million years ago when the dinosaurs perished. Most current extinctions are caused by habitat disruption; and most habitat disruption is caused by humans, as we inexorably expand our cities and our economic activities.

While it is safe to say that science now grasps the fundamental importance of biodiversity, there are at least two areas where our knowledge remains very limited. First, our understanding of the extent to which we depend upon diversity for our survival is just beginning to emerge. Second, how human activities affect diversity, and particularly how they reduce it, are only now being carefully monitored, studied, and assessed. This chapter focuses on the overall picture, reviewing current understandings of biodiversity loss in the modern world. How we might reverse the changes described here by John Tuxill and Chris Bright is unclear. But the key is very likely to be preservation, restoration, and protection of undisturbed habitat in and around human settlement.

John Tuxill is a Research Fellow with the Worldwatch Institute, where he investigates and writes about biodiversity. Chris Bright is a senior researcher on the staff of the Worldwatch Institute as well as senior editor of World Watch, *the Institute's bimonthly magazine.*

From John Tuxill and Chris Bright, "Losing Strands in the Web of Life," in *State of the World 1998: A Worldwatch Institute Report on Progress toward a Sustainable Society*, ed. Lester R. Brown et al. (New York: Norton, 1998), 41–58, 199–203. Tables omitted. © 1998 Worldwatch Institute. Reprinted by permission of W. W. Norton & Company.

Ask three doctors with different medical backgrounds about the health of a patient and you will probably get three different opinions—diagnoses that agree in general but differ considerably in emphasis and detail. Ask three environmental scientists about the health of the planet and you may hear something similar. Some environmental assessments will track changes in biogeochemical cycles—rates of soil erosion, freshwater depletion, or fluctuations in the composition of Earth's atmosphere. Others might measure the harvest and regrowth of key biological resources, such as forests, fisheries, and grasslands. But arguably the single most direct measure of the planet's health is the status of its biological diversity—usually expressed as the vast complex of species that make up the living world. Measuring biodiversity is an extremely complicated and subtle task, but four basic questions usually dominate the inquiry: How many species are there? What are they? Where are they? And what is happening to them?

The biodiversity around us today is the result of more than 3 billion years of evolution. Species declines and extinctions have always been a natural part of that process, but there is something disturbingly different about the current extinction patterns. Examinations of the fossil record of marine invertebrates suggest that the natural or "background" rate of extinctions—the rate that has prevailed over millions of years of evolutionary time—claims something on the order of one to three species per year. In stark contrast, most estimates of the current situation are that at least 1,000 species are lost a year—an extinction rate 1,000 times the background rate even with the most conservative assumptions. Like the dinosaurs 65 million years ago, humanity now finds itself in the midst of a mass extinction: a global evolutionary convulsion with few parallels in the entire history of life. But unlike the dinosaurs, we are not simply the contemporaries of a mass extinction—we are the reason for it.[1]

The loss of species touches everyone, for no matter where or how we live, biodiversity is the basis for our existence. Earth's endowment of species provides humanity with food, fiber, and many other products and "natural services" for which there simply is no substitute. Biodiversity underpins our health care systems; some 25 percent of drugs prescribed in the United States include chemical compounds derived from wild organisms, and billions of people worldwide rely on plant- and animal-based traditional medicine for their primary health care. Biodiversity provides a wealth of genes essential for maintaining the vigor of our crops and livestock. It provides pollination services, mostly in the form of insects, without which we could not feed ourselves. Frogs, fish, and birds provide natural pest control; mussels and other aquatic organisms cleanse our water supplies; plants and microorganisms create our soils.[2]

But these natural goods and services—essential though they are—constitute a minor part of the picture. Most of what we are losing is still a mystery to us. As the noted Harvard University biologist Edward O. Wilson puts it, we live on an unexplored planet. We have barely begun to decipher the intricate ecological mechanisms that keep natural communities running smoothly. We do not know—even to a rough order of magnitude—how many species there are on Earth. To date, scientists have catalogued about 1.8 million species of animals, plants, fungi, bacteria, and other organisms; most estimates of the number yet to be formally described range from 4 million to 40 million. (The single most species-rich group of organisms appears to be insects; beetles, in particular, currently account for 25 percent of all described species.)[3]

This situation presents some serious problems for exploring the dimensions of the current mass extinction—and the possible responses to it. If we do not even know how many species there are, how can we be sure about the true scale of current species losses? If we do not understand most species' ecological relationships, how can we tell what their disappearance might mean for our planet's life-support systems? One way to approach these hurdles is to focus on the groups of organisms we already know the most about—birds, mammals, reptiles, amphibians, and fish. These are the vertebrate animals, distinguished from invertebrates by an internal skeleton and a spinal column—a type of anatomy that permits, among other things, complex neural development and high metabolic rates.

Vertebrates combined total about 50,000 species, and can be found in virtually all environments on Earth, from the frozen expanses of Antarctica to scorching deserts and deep ocean abysses. By virtue of the attention they receive from researchers, vertebrates can serve as ecological bellwethers for the multitude of small, obscure organisms that remain undescribed and unknown. Since vertebrates tend to be relatively large and to occupy the top rungs in food chains, habitats healthy enough to maintain a full complement of native vertebrates will have a good chance of retaining the invertebrates, plants, fungi, and other small or more obscure organisms found there. Conversely, ecological degradation can often be read most clearly in native vertebrate population trends.[4]

Perhaps the most celebrated example of this "bellwether effect" was the intense research effort set off by the publication of Rachel Carson's *Silent Spring* in 1962, which described the danger that organochlorine pesticides pose to wild vertebrates, particularly birds. The study of wildlife toxicology is now routine: ecologists often monitor vertebrate populations as a way of checking on the general health of an ecosystem. In the North American Great Lakes, for example, researchers gauge water quality partly by examining the health of the fish. Some vertebrate declines may signal trouble that we cannot clearly see in any other way, as with the mysterious amphibian declines discussed later in this chapter.[5]

Even though vertebrates are a relatively small fraction of total biodiversity, tracking their status is a huge task. The institution leading this effort is the

World Conservation Union (known as IUCN, from its original name), an international environmental coalition that since the 1960s has published the *Red Data Book,* a listing of all animal species known to be threatened with extinction around the world. The *Red Data Book* is compiled through extensive consultation with scientists who have in-depth field knowledge of the animals concerned. When combined with various other ways of diagnosing the planet's environmental illnesses, the *Red Data Book* findings on vertebrates offer a critical insight into the biodiversity crisis—and on what we must do to halt it.

Birds: The Clearest of All Indicators

With their prominent voices, vivid colors, and unparalleled mobility, birds have won a great deal of attention from scientists and laypeople alike. As a result, we know more about the ecology, distribution, and abundance of the nearly 10,000 species of birds than we do about any other class of organisms on Earth. Not surprisingly, birds were the first animals that IUCN comprehensively surveyed, in 1992, followed by full reassessments in 1994 and 1996.[6]

The latest news is not good. Estimates are that at least two out of every three bird species are in decline worldwide, although only about 11 percent of all birds are already officially threatened with extinction. Four percent—403 species—are "endangered" or "critically endangered." These include species like the crested ibis, a wading bird that has been eliminated from its former range in Japan, the Korean peninsula, and Russia, and is now down to one small population in the remote Qinling mountains of China. Another 7 percent of all birds are in slightly better condition in terms of numbers or range size, but still remain highly vulnerable to extinction.[7]

The red-cockaded woodpecker is one vulnerable species that scientists hope is on the road to recovery. This bird is found only in mature pine forests—especially longleaf pine—in the southeastern United States, a habitat leveled by logging and agricultural clearing over the past two centuries. The woodpecker's recovery depends on the success of efforts to restore longleaf pine habitat throughout this area by prescribed burning, replicating the once common low-intensity forest fires that the pines and the woodpeckers are exquisitely adapted to.[8]

Membership in this pool of threatened species is not spread evenly among different taxonomic orders or groups of birds. The most threatened major groups include rails and cranes (both specialized wading birds), parrots, terrestrial game birds (pheasants, partridges, grouse, and guans), and pelagic seabirds (albatrosses, petrels, and shearwaters). About one quarter of the species in each of these groups is currently threatened. Only 9 percent of songbirds are threatened, but they still contribute the single largest group of threatened species (542) because they are far and away the most species-rich bird order.[9]

The leading culprits in the decline of birds are a familiar set of interrelated factors all linked to human activity: habitat alteration, overhunting, exotic species invasions, and chemical pollution of the environment. Habitat loss is by far the leading factor—at least three quarters of all threatened bird species are in trouble because of the transformation and fragmentation of forests, wetlands, grasslands, and other unique habitats by human activities, including intensive agriculture, heavy livestock grazing, commercial forestry, and suburban sprawl. In some cases, habitat alteration is intensive and large-scale, as when an internationally funded development project converts large areas of native forest to plantation crops, or a large dam drowns a unique river basin. In other instances, habitat is eroded gradually over time, as when a native grassland is fragmented into smaller and smaller patches by farming communities expanding under a growing population.[10]

Whatever the pattern, any given instance of habitat loss usually results from complex interactions between different institutions, organizations, and social groups. For instance, the conversion of tropical forest in Darién province in Panama is linked to the actions and aims of commercial logging companies, small landowners (both long-time residents and recent immigrants), large landowners, government representatives, international consumers, international development agencies, and even conservationists.[11]

The birds hit hardest by habitat loss are ecological specialists with small ranges. Such species tend to reside full-time in specific, often very local habitat types, and are most abundant in the tropical and subtropical regions of Latin America, sub-Saharan Africa, and Asia. More than 70 percent of South America's rare and threatened birds do not inhabit lowland evergreen rainforests or the commonly cited hotspot of environmental concern, the Amazon Basin. Instead, they hail from obscure but gravely disturbed habitats such as the cloud-shrouded montane forests and high-altitude wetlands of the northern and central Andes, deciduous and semiarid Pacific woodlands from western Colombia to northern Chile, and the fast-disappearing grasslands and riverine forests of southern and eastern Brazil. The long list of imperiled birds native to these little-noticed habitats signals that what is being lost in South America is not just rainforests but a far more diverse and intricate ecological mosaic, vanishing before most people have even become aware of its existence.[12]

High concentrations of gravely endangered birds are also found on oceanic islands worldwide. Birds endemic to insular habitats—that is, found nowhere else—account for almost one third of all threatened species and an astounding 84 percent of all historically known extinctions. These unfortunate numbers reflect the fact that island birds tend naturally to have smaller ranges and numbers, making them more susceptible to habitat disturbance. And since island birds are often concentrated in just a handful of popula- tions, if one such group is wiped out by a temporary catastrophe such as a drought, the birds often have few population sources from which they can recolonize the formerly occupied habitat. Equally important is that many is- land birds have evolved in isolation for thousands or even millions of years. Such species are particularly vulnerable to human hunting, as well as preda- tion and competition from nonnative, invasive species. (Invasives are highly adaptable animals and plants that spread outside their native ecological ranges—usually with intentional or inadvertent human help—and thrive in human-disturbed habitats.)[13]

It is likely that island birds have had elevated extinction rates for at least the past two millennia. Archeologists have used bird remains from Pacific islands to document a wave of extinctions as Melanesian human populations— and attendant rats, dogs, and other domestic animals—expanded across the western and central Pacific, colonizing new island chains. Disturbance of island ecosystems also was severe during the European colonial era, and ad- vanced again in our modern age of jet travel and global economic trade. As a result, island birds continue to dwindle.[14]

Among countries with more than 200 native bird species, the highest threatened share—15 percent—is found in two island archipelagos, New Zealand and the Philippines. The tiny island nation of Mauritius in the Indian Ocean has recorded 21 bird extinctions since the arrival of humans in the 1600s. Mauritian species gone forever include several species of flightless herons and the famed dodo, an aberrant flightless pigeon nearly the size of a turkey.[15]

No island birds have been more decimated than those of Hawaii, how- ever. Virtually all of Hawaii's original 90-odd bird species were found no- where else in the world. Barely one third of these species remain alive today, the rest having vanished under Polynesian and modern-day impacts, and two thirds of these continue to be threatened with extinction. The degree of eco- logical disruption in Hawaii is so great that all lowland Hawaiian songbirds are now nonnative species introduced by humans.[16]

While island species and those specific to certain habitats dominate the ranks of the world's most endangered birds, an equally disturbing trend is population declines in more widespread species, particularly those that mi- grate seasonally between breeding and wintering grounds. In the Americas, more than two thirds of the migratory bird species that breed in North America but winter in Latin America and the Caribbean declined in abundance be- tween 1980 and 1991. Some—including yellow-billed cuckoos, Tennessee warblers, and Cassin's kingbirds—declined by more than 4 percent a year. Two decades of bird surveys in Great Britain and central Europe have also revealed strong declines in long-distance migrants that winter in sub-Saharan Africa.[17]

Long-term population declines in migratory birds are tied to a host of contributing hazards. Habitat loss squeezes species on both breeding and wintering grounds, as well as at key stopping points—such as rich tidal estuaries for shorebirds—along their migratory routes. In North America, the loss of almost half of all wetlands has been a major factor behind a 30-percent drop in the populations of the continent's 10 most abundant duck species. Further south, from Mexico to Colombia, many migratory songbirds winter in coffee plantations, where coffee bushes have traditionally been grown under a shady canopy of native forest trees. Unfortunately, this habitat is disappearing as plantations intensify and replant with higher yielding, sun-tolerant coffee varieties that do not require shade. The result is that neotropical migrants must search even harder to find suitable wintering territory.[18]

Excessive hunting also remains a hazard for many migratory species. In a number of Mediterranean nations, there is an enduring tradition of pursuing all birds indiscriminately, regardless of size or status. Local species are hunted intensively for food, and migrants that breed in northern Europe must brave an annual fusillade of guns and snares as they fly south to Africa. In Italy alone, as many as 50 million songbirds are harvested every year as bite-sized delicacies.[19]

Exposure to chemical pollution is another problem that many birds face. The greatest risk of pesticide and pollution exposure occurs in developing countries, where many chemicals banned from use in industrial nations continue to be applied or discharged indiscriminately. In late 1995 and early 1996, about 5 percent of the world's population of Swainson's hawks—some 20,000 birds—died in unintentional mass poisonings on their wintering grounds in Argentina's pampas. Local farmers were applying heavy doses of an internationally manufactured organophosphate pesticide called monocrotophos to control grasshopper outbreaks on their crops. The hawks, which breed in western North America, were exposed to the chemical when they fed on the grasshoppers, one of their main winter food sources. Argentina has since banned the use of monocrotophos on grasshoppers and alfalfa, and no large hawk kills were found during the 1996–97 wintering season, but it is unclear how long it will take the Swainson's hawk population to recover from these large losses.[20]

Whether reduced by the conversion of key habitats such as wetlands, by overexploitation in the form of hunters' guns, or by chemical contamination of water and food supplies, the decline of migratory birds is sobering because it is a loss not just of individual species but of an entire ecological phenomenon. Present-day migrants must negotiate their way across thousands of kilometers of tattered and frayed ecological landscapes. The fact that many birds continue to make this journey, despite the threats and obstacles, is cause for hope and inspiration. Yet as long as bird diversity and numbers continue to spiral downward, there can be no rest in the effort to protect and restore breeding grounds, wintering areas, and key refueling sites that all birds—migratory and resident—simply cannot live without.

Mammals: A Darker Picture

When the conservation status of birds was first comprehensively assessed by IUCN, the degree of endangerment—about 11 percent—was taken as the best available estimate of endangerment for all vertebrates, invertebrates, and other life on Earth. Then in 1996, IUCN comprehensively reviewed the status of all mammal species for the first time, allowing for a full comparison with birds. Unfortunately, the news was not good—about 25 percent of all mammal species are treading a path that, if followed unchecked, is likely to end in their disappearance from Earth. This suggests that mammals are substantially more threatened than birds, and raises a larger question about which of these groups better represents the level of endangerment faced by other organisms.[21]

Out of almost 4,400 mammal species, about 11 percent are already "endangered" or "critically endangered." Another 14 percent remain vulnerable to extinction, including the Siberian musk deer, whose populations in Russia have fallen 70 percent during this decade due to increased hunting to feed the booming trade in musk, used in perfumes and traditional Asian medicine. An additional 14 percent of mammal species also come very close to qualifying as threatened under the criteria used by IUCN to assess species' status. These "near-threatened" species tend to have larger population sizes or be relatively widespread, but nonetheless face pressures that have them on the fast track to threatened status in the not-too-distant future. One near-threatened species is the African red colobus monkey. Its huge range stretches from Senegal to Kenya, but the red colobus faces hunting pressure and habitat loss everywhere it occurs, and is declining in numbers.[22]

Among major mammalian groups, primates (lemurs, monkeys, and apes) occupy the most unfortunate position, with nearly half of all primate species threatened with extinction. Also under severe pressure are hoofed mammals (deer, antelope, horses, rhinos, camels, and pigs), with 37 percent threatened; insectivores (shrews, hedgehogs, and moles), with 36 percent; and marsupials (opossums, wallabies, and wombats) and cetaceans (whales and porpoises), at 33 percent each. In slightly better shape are bats and carnivores (dogs, cats, weasels, bears, raccoons, hyenas, and mongooses), at 26 percent apiece. Rodents are the least threatened mammalian group, at 17 percent, but also the most diverse. As with songbirds, rodents still contribute the most threatened species—300—of any group.[23]

The biggest culprit in the loss of mammalian diversity in the late twentieth century is the same as that for birds—habitat loss and degradation. As humankind converts forests, grasslands, riverways, wetlands, and deserts for intensive agriculture, tree plantations, industrial development, and transportation networks, we relegate many mammals to precarious existences in fragmented, remnant habitat patches that are but ecological shadows of their former selves.

Habitat loss is a principal factor in the decline of at least three quarters of all mammal species, and is the only significant factor for many small rodents and insectivores that are not directly persecuted. The major reason primates are so threatened is their affinity for tropical forests, a habitat under siege around the globe. In regions where forest degradation and conversion have been most intense, such as South and East Asia, Madagascar, and the Atlantic forest of eastern Brazil, on average 70 percent of the endemic primate species face extinction.[24]

The loss of habitat also afflicts marine mammals, though it usually proceeds as gradual, cumulative declines in habitat quality rather than wholesale conversion of ecosystems (as when a forest is replaced by a housing development). Marine mammals, particularly those that inhabit densely populated coastal areas, now have to contend with polluted water and food, physical hazards from fishing gear, heavy competition from humans for the fish stocks on which they feed, and hazardous, noisy boat traffic. Along the coastline of Western Europe, bottlenose dolphins and harbor porpoises—the only two cetaceans that regularly use near-shore European waters—seem to be steadily declining. Seal populations in the Baltic Sea carry very high chemical pollutant loads in their tissues that appear to decrease their reproductive success.[25]

In addition to habitat loss, at least one in five threatened mammals faces direct overexploitation—excessive hunting for meat, hides, tusks, and medicinal products, and persecution as predators of and competitors with fish and livestock. Overexploitation tends to affect larger mammals disproportionately over smaller ones, and when strong market demand exists for a mammal's meat, hide, horns, tusks, or bones, species can decline on catastrophic scales.[26]

While the drastic population crashes of great whales, elephants, and rhinos are well known, the long shadow of overexploitation actually reaches much further. For instance, only the most remote or best-protected forests throughout Latin America have avoided significant loss of tapirs, white-lipped peccaries, jaguars, wooly and spider monkeys, and other large mammals that face heavy hunting pressure from rural residents. Much of this hunting is for home subsistence—wild game meat is an important source of protein in the diets of rural residents, particularly for indigenous people. One estimate pegs the annual mammal take in the Amazon Basin at more than 14 million individuals.[27]

Yet the real problem occurs when hunting is done to supply markets rather than just for home consumption. In central African forests, there is now intensive, indiscriminate hunting of wildlife for the regional trade in wild game or bushmeat. In parts of Cameroon, the Democratic Republic of the Congo (formerly Zaire), and other countries, the sale of bushmeat to traders supplying urban areas is the main income-generating activity available to rural residents. Rural and urban bushmeat consumption in Gabon has been estimated at 3,600 tons annually. The bushmeat trade is closely linked in many areas with logging operations, which is the main activity opening up roads in previously isolated areas, thereby giving hunters access to new, game-rich territory.[28]

Throughout South and East Asia, a major factor fueling excessive wildlife exploitation is the demand for animal parts in traditional medicine. Tigers—the largest of all cats—once ranged from Turkey to Bali and the Russian Far East, and have been the subject of organized conservation projects for more than two decades. At first these projects appeared to be having some success—until the mid-1980s brought a burgeoning demand in East Asia for tiger parts as aphrodisiacs and medicinal products. With the body parts of a single tiger potentially worth as much as $5 million, illegal hunting skyrocketed, particularly in the tiger's stronghold—India. Wild tigers now total barely 3,000–5,000 individuals, many in small, isolated populations that are doomed without more intensive protection.[29]

The loss of a region's top predators or dominant herbivores is particularly damaging because it can trigger a cascade of disruptions in the ecological relationships among species that maintain an ecosystem's diversity and function. Large mammals tend to exert inordinate influence within their ecological communities by consuming and dispersing seeds, creating unique microhabitats, and regulating populations of prey species. In Côte d'Ivoire, Ghana, Liberia, and Uganda, certain trees—including valuable timber species—have shown reduced regeneration after the crash of elephant populations, which the trees depend on for seed dispersal. Similarly, decades of excessive whaling reduced the number of whales that die natural deaths in the open oceans. This may have adversely affected unique deep-sea communities of worms and other invertebrates that decompose the remains of dead whales after they have sunk to the ocean floor.[30]

Mammals in most regions have been less susceptible than birds to invasive species, but there is one big exception—the unique marsupial and rodent fauna of Australia, long isolated from other continents. The introduction of nonnative rabbits, foxes, cats, rats, and other animals has combined with changing land use patterns during the past two centuries to give Australia the world's worst modern record of mammalian extinction. Nineteen mammal species have gone extinct since European settlement in the eighteenth century, and at least one quarter of the remaining native mammalian fauna remains threatened. Most declines and extinctions have occurred among small to medium-sized ground-dwelling mammals, such as bandicoots and mice, from interior Australian drylands. These habitats have been drastically altered by invasive species (particularly rabbits) in conjunction with extensive livestock grazing, land clearance for wheat cultivation, and altered fire patterns following the decline of traditional aboriginal burning of brush and grasslands.[31]

Taken together, the problems bedeviling mammals in today's world—habitat loss, overhunting, invasive species—are not all that more intensive than those faced by birds. So how can we account for the fact that one in every four mammals is in danger of extinction, compared with only one in every 10 birds? The answer, it seems, may be found in how well mammals and birds cope with the pressures placed on them by humankind. Since birds tend to be more mobile and wide-ranging, they may be able to find food and shelter more easily in the fragmented and disjointed landscapes produced by human disturbance. Birds are also smaller on average than mammals, so they require smaller ranges and fewer resources for survival—advantages when habitat and food supply become restricted. But while few other organisms have the resource demands of most mammals, few likewise are as mobile as birds, making it difficult to predict which group is a better guide for assessing the level of endangerment of other organisms.

Reptiles and Amphibians: The Hidden Fauna

Like their furred and feathered vertebrate kin, reptiles and amphibians (known collectively to scientists as herpetofauna) do not possess huge numbers of species—about 6,300 documented for reptiles and 4,000 for amphibians. Both groups share with the world's many invertebrates the fate of being less well known and relatively little studied. As a result, only a fifth of all reptile species and barely one eighth of all amphibian species have been formally assessed by scientists for their conservation status. Among reptiles, the status of turtles, crocodilians, and tuataras (an ancient lineage of two lizard-like species living on scattered islands off New Zealand) has been comprehensively surveyed. But most snakes and lizards remain unassessed, as do the two main orders of amphibians, frogs and salamanders.[32]

The herpetofauna that have been surveyed, however, reveal a level of endangerment closely in line with that of mammals. Twenty percent of surveyed reptiles currently rank as endangered or vulnerable, while 25 percent of surveyed amphibians are so designated. The country with the highest number of documented threatened herpetofauna is Australia, at 62 species, followed closely by the United States with 52 species. These are not the most species-rich countries for these creatures—Brazil, for instance, leads in amphibians and Mexico has the most reptiles—but are simply the countries where herpetofauna have been most thoroughly surveyed and monitored.[33]

Among reptiles, species are declining for reasons similar to those affect-ing birds and mammals. Habitat loss is again the leading factor, contributing to the decline of 68 percent of all threatened reptile species. In island regions, habitat degradation has combined with exotic species to fuel the decline of many unique reptiles. In Ecuador's famed Galápagos archipelago, the largest native herbivores are reptiles—long-isolated giant tortoises and land and marine iguanas found nowhere else in the world. Introduced goats are win-ning out over the native reptiles, however, and these interlopers have already eliminated unique populations of tortoises on 3 of 14 islands within the Galápagos chain. At least two other tortoise populations are in imminent danger.[34]

In addition, a surprising 31 percent of threatened reptiles are affected directly by hunting and capture by humans. This figure may be somewhat in-flated since the reptile groups most thoroughly assessed—turtles and crocodil-ians—are also among those most pursued by humans. Nevertheless, the high percentage is a clear indication of the heavy exploitation suffered by these species.[35]

The plight of sea turtles has been studied and publicized since at least the 1960s, and all seven species are judged by IUCN as endangered, with many populations continuing to dwindle. Although there has been progress on protecting sea turtles at some of their best known nesting grounds, illegal poaching of turtles for meat and eggs remains a widespread problem. Where beaches are lit at night with artificial lights, as at tourist resorts, hatchling turtles become disoriented and crawl toward the land rather than the sea. More-over, sea turtles continue to suffer inadvertent but significant mortality from nets set for fish and shrimp. In one survey of a surface driftnet some two kilometers in length set for sharks off the coast of Panama, observers counted one sea turtle accidentally entangled for every 150 meters of fishing net.[36]

Although less well known than their seagoing relatives, tortoise and river turtle species also are exploited intensively in certain regions, to the point where many populations are greatly depleted. Tortoises and river turtles throughout Southeast Asia have long been an important source of meat and eggs for local residents. There is now also a burgeoning international trade in these species to China, where they are used in traditional medicine. Accord-ing to a recent report by TRAFFIC, a group that monitors the international wildlife trade, the annual East Asian trade in tortoises and river turtles in-volves some 300,000 kilograms of live animals, with a value of at least $1 million. At least five turtle species involved in this trade are now candi-dates for the most stringent listing available under the Convention on Inter-national Trade in Endangered Species of Wild Flora and Fauna (CITES), which attempts to regulate international wildlife trade.[37]

Certain species of crocodilians still suffer from overhunting (such as black caimans in the Amazon Basin) and from pollution (such as the Indian gharial and the Chinese alligator), but this is one of the few taxonomic groups of animals whose overall fate has actually improved over the past two decades. Since 1971, seven alligator and crocodile species have been taken off IUCN's *Red Data* list, including Africa's Nile crocodile and Australia's huge estuarine crocodile. In part, these recoveries are due to the development of crocodile ranching operations, which harvest the animals for their meat and hides; when combined with effective wildlife protection efforts, this can take hunting pressure off wild populations. In Zimbabwe, crocodile ranches have been so successful that domestic crocodiles now outnumber the country's 50,000 wild crocs by three to one. In 1991, crocodile farming worldwide generated more than $1.7 million in international trade.[38]

For amphibians, direct exploitation is less of a problem. With the exception of larger frogs favored for their tasty legs, few amphibians face any substantial hunting pressure. Habitat loss remains a serious problem, however, affecting some 58 percent of threatened amphibians. Much of this is due to the drainage, conversion, and contamination of wetland habitats. In addition, the spread of road networks and vehicular traffic leads to increased amphibian mortality that can decimate local populations.[39]

In recent years, however, amphibians have captured worldwide attention due to the rapid and unexplained decline—and, in some cases, even extinction—of frog species in relatively pristine, intact ecosystems where habitat loss is not a factor. These mysterious decreases have been particularly well documented among frogs in little-disturbed mountain habitats in Central America and the western United States, as well as in 14 species of rainforest-dwelling frogs in eastern Australia.[40]

Researchers have advanced various explanations for these declines, including disease epidemics caused by invasive pathogens; increases in ultraviolet radiation, which inhibit egg development; introduced predators, particularly game fish like bass and trout; acid rain and other industrial pollutants; and unusual climatic fluctuations, such as extended drought. Most likely, it is not a single factor but rather synergistic combinations that best explain the declines. For instance, the presence of industrial pollutants may stress and weaken frogs, and make them more susceptible to infectious diseases. It may be that frogs, with their highly permeable skins and with lifecycles dependent on both aquatic and terrestrial habitats, are signaling—more clearly than any other group of organisms—the gradual but global decline of our planet's environmental health.[41]

Fish: The Darkest Picture of All

The world's fish offer the best measure of the state of biological diversity in aquatic ecosystems. Fish occur in nearly all permanent water environments, from the perpetually dark ocean abyss to isolated alpine lakes and alkaline desert springs. Fish are also unique in being far and away the most diverse vertebrate group—nearly 24,000 fish species have been formally described by scientists, about equal to all other vertebrates combined.[42]

As with reptiles and amphibians, less than 10 percent of fish species have been formally assessed for their conservation status, with marine fish (some 14,000 species) being particularly understudied. Yet even this partial assessment brings disturbing news, for the numbers suggest that one third of all fish species are already threatened with extinction. Moreover, the proportion of critically endangered species (7 percent) among fish is double that of other vertebrates.[43]

The causes of fish endangerment—habitat alteration, exotic species, and direct exploitation—are no different from those affecting other species, but they appear to be more pervasive in aquatic ecosystems. Freshwater hotspots of fish endangerment tend to be large rivers heavily disturbed by human activity (such as the Missouri, Columbia, and Yangtze rivers), and unique habitats that hold endemic fish faunas, such as tropical peat swamps, semiarid stream systems, and isolated large lakes. Saltwater hotspots include estuaries, heavily disturbed coral reefs, and other shallow, near-shore habitats.[44]

Although degradation of terrestrial habitats such as forests may be more obvious and get the most attention, freshwater aquatic habitats receive an even heavier blow from humanity. More than 40,000 large dams and hundreds of thousands of smaller barriers plug up the world's rivers—altering water temperatures, sediment loads, seasonal flow patterns, and other river characteristics to which native fish are adapted. Levees disconnect rivers from their floodplains, eliminating backwaters and wetlands that are important fish spawning grounds. The effects of river engineering works also surface in distant lakes and estuaries, whose ecologies decline when river inflows are altered. Agricultural and industrial pollution of waterways further reduces habitat for fish and other aquatic life. Agricultural runoff in the Mississippi River basin is now so extensive that when the river enters the Gulf of Mexico, the overfertilized brew of nutrients it carries sparks huge algal blooms, which deplete the water of oxygen and create a "dead zone" of some 17,600 square kilometers—nearly the size of New Jersey.[45]

As a result of all these problems, at least 60 percent of threatened freshwater fish species are in decline because of habitat alteration. This includes 26 species of darters—small, often brightly colored fish that frequented the now heavily dammed rivers of the southern United States—and 59 threatened species of fish in India recently identified by a nationwide survey by the Zoological Survey of India. Alteration of aquatic habitats has been particularly catastrophic for native fish in semiarid and arid regions, where human competition for water resources is high.[46]

In the heavily altered Colorado River system of southwestern North America, 29 of 50 native fish species are either extinct or endangered. This includes the totoaba, a marine fish that used to breed in the Colorado River delta in northwest Mexico. In most years now, the river runs dry well before it reaches the ocean. Elsewhere in semiarid areas of Mexico, river and spring systems have lost an average of 68 percent of their native and endemic fish species because of falling water tables and altered river hydrologies, both due to the water needs of a growing human population.[47]

Introductions of nonnative, often predatory fish can unravel diverse native fish assemblages in just a few years, precipitating a cascade of local extinctions. Some 34 percent of threatened freshwater fish face pressure from introduced species, but none have been more devastated than the native cichlids of East Africa's Lake Victoria, the world's second largest freshwater lake. The cichlid community was extraordinarily diverse, with more than 300 specialized species, 99 percent of which occurred only in this lake. Unfortunately the community began to collapse during the 1980s following a population explosion of the Nile perch, a nonnative predatory fish introduced to boost the lake fisheries. It did its job all too well, feeding indiscriminately on the much smaller cichlids and destroying native food webs. As many as 60 percent of the Lake Victoria cichlids may now be extinct, with only a museum specimen and a scientific name to mark their tenure on the planet.[48]

Many fish species also face a high degree of exploitation from commercial fisheries, particularly marine fish and species like salmon that migrate between salt and fresh water. About 68 percent of all threatened marine species suffer from overexploitation. The days when experts thought it impossible to deplete marine fish populations are long gone, and scientists now realize that overexploitation is a serious extinction threat for many ecologically sensitive species.[49]

Take seahorses, for example, which are captured for use in aquariums, as curios, and in traditional Chinese medicine. The global seahorse trade is very lucrative— top-quality dried seahorses have sold for up to $1,200 per kilogram in Hong Kong. Current worldwide seahorse harvests may top 20 million animals annually, and in China alone, demand is rising at almost 10 percent a year. Seahorses are unlikely to support such intensive harvesting for long because of their low reproductive rates, complex social behavior (they are monogamous, with males rearing the young), accessible habitat (shallow, inshore waters), and low mobility. Already, some 36 seahorse species are threatened by this growing, unregulated harvest.[50]

Sharks are a second group of marine fish headed for trouble. Being top ocean predators, sharks tend to be sparsely distributed, and grow and reproduce quite slowly. They are valued for their skin, meat, cartilage (reputed to have anti-cancer properties), liver oil, and especially fins, which are one of the highest-valued seafood commodities due to their popularity in East Asian cuisine. Reported worldwide shark catches have been increasing steadily since the 1940s, and topped 730,000 tons by 1994. Unreported and incidental shark

catches likely push that figure much higher, and most harvested shark species are probably already declining.[51]

Other fish have supported commercial fisheries for centuries, but now
appear unable to continue doing so in the face of additional threats from
habitat alteration and pollution. Sturgeon, one of the most ancient fish lineages, occur in Europe, northern Asia, and North America, and have long
been harvested for their eggs, famous as the world's premier caviar. Russia
and Central Asia are home to 14 sturgeon species—tops in the world—and
produce 90 percent of the world's caviar, mostly from the Black and Caspian
Sea regions. The sturgeon fishery was relatively well regulated during the
Soviet era, but massive water projects and widespread water pollution led to
sturgeon population crashes, so that all 14 species are now highly endangered. To compound the problem, sturgeon poaching is now rampant due to
minimal enforcement of fishing regulations in the post-Soviet central Asian
nations. Uncontrolled exploitation of the few stocks that remain may be the
final nail in the coffin for these magnificent fish.[52]

With the collapse of native fish faunas in many river basins and lake
systems, and with growing awareness that many marine fish are in decline,
the evidence suggests that biological diversity is faring no better underwater
than on land. As noted, one out of every three fish species now looks to be on
the path to extinction. If this percentage holds up as the conservation status
of more fish species is reviewed, it portends a grim future for other aquatic
life on Earth.

Halting the Declines

Together, the various vertebrate groups provide an unmistakable view of the
types of injuries being inflicted upon the Earth's biological systems. Habitat
alteration is the single biggest problem for most vertebrates. While we are
accustomed to thinking about forests being converted to suburbs or savannas
being ploughed into cropland, the extreme freshwater fish declines indicate
that freshwater ecosystems may be the most pervasively altered habitat of all.
Overexploitation threatens fewer species directly, but it is a major pressure
on many of the larger animals, particularly marine vertebrates. And given the
important ecological roles typical of large animals, it is reasonable to assume
that excessive hunting and fishing are now a significant ingredient in the
disruption of many ecosystems. The spread of invasive exotic species is a
third major problem, particularly in island ecosystems. Pollution and chemical contamination have been responsible for some spectacular vertebrate die-
offs, but do not yet appear to affect as many species as these other problems
do.

If the trends evident in vertebrates hold for other organisms, then extinction would appear to be a near-term possibility for about a quarter of the

world's entire complement of species. And this could well be an underestimate, since beyond the IUCN numbers looms the specter of global climate change. If the current scientific consensus on the rate and scale of climate change proves accurate, then over the next century natural communities will face a set of unprecedented pressures. A warmer climate will probably mean changes in seasonal timing, rainfall patterns, ocean currents, and various other parts of the Earth's life-support systems. In the evolutionary past, the ecological effects of abrupt climate shifts were somewhat cushioned by the possibility of movement. One part of a plant's or animal's range might dry out, for example, and become uninhabitable, but another area might grow more moist and become available for colonization. Today, with more and more species confined only to fragmented remnants of their former range, this kind of compensatory migration is less and less likely.[53]

In the face of current and expected declines, the world's governments have clear moral and practical reasons to act. One course of action should involve pursuit of the processes begun at the 1992 Earth Summit in Rio, which resulted in the Convention on Biological Diversity (CBD), now signed by 169 countries. This and other environmental treaties provide important forums for coordinating international responses to biodiversity issues. And to some degree, they can function as a sort of international mechanism for self-policing.[54]

In the struggle to preserve biodiversity, international agreements have probably made their biggest contribution in reducing the overexploitation of species, particularly those that are traded globally. But even here the record is mixed. CITES, for instance, was the mechanism through which countries agreed in 1989 to ban international trade in African elephant ivory, which for two decades had fueled heavy poaching that reduced elephant numbers from several million to 500,000 at most. Immediately following the ban, African elephant poaching appeared to drop substantially in many areas. But international demand for ivory, particularly in East Asia, has remained strong since then, while a number of elephant range countries, such as the Democratic Republic of the Congo (formerly Zaire), have experienced political instability and declines in government antipoaching efforts. As a result, poaching intensity has crept gradually back upward, and illegal elephant kills are again being reported regularly.[55]

Obviously, treaties are only as effective as the will and competence of signatory countries permit. The CBD requires all participant countries to prepare national strategies for conserving their biodiversity; because of its comprehensiveness, it represents the most thorough test to date of the international community's will to face up to the biodiversity crisis. But the primary cause of that crisis—habitat loss—is likely to escape the CBD in large measure, as it has most other treaties. Habitat loss is an issue that must be solved mainly on a national and local level.

The main approach that countries have taken to safeguard habitat has been to establish systems of national parks, wildlife refuges, forest reserves, marine sanctuaries, and other formally protected areas. Nations have steadily increased the number and extent of their protected areas during this century. At present, about 1 billion hectares of the Earth's surface is officially designated as protected, an area nearly equal in size to Canada.[56]

Protected lands safeguard some of the Earth's greatest natural treasures, and have made a big difference for some "conservation-dependent" vertebrates that would otherwise almost certainly be sliding into extinction. These include about 40 species of the famed "megafauna" of East and Southern Africa, such as giraffes, hyenas, wildebeest, and impala. The populations of these animals are presently out of danger, in large part because of an extensive reserve system in their home countries. Yet despite these notable successes, current networks of protected areas are nowhere near capable of saving most biodiversity.[57]

One reason for this failing is that protected areas do not always target sites of high biological diversity. Icy mountain peaks, for instance, are obvious and easy places for national parks due to their spectacular scenery and lack of development pressure, but they are usually not hotspots of species diversity. Although the world added more protected areas—1,431 new reserves, totalling 224 million hectares—between 1990 and 1995 than during any previous five-year period, most of the increase was due to a few huge designations in lightly populated desert and high mountain areas, such as the empty quarter of Saudi Arabia and the Qiang Tang plateau in western China. Despite these impressive numbers, many highly diverse ecosystems—from tropical dry forest to temperate river basins—continue to receive little formal protection.[58]

To help ensure that future reserve designations do the most to preserve biodiversity, conservation organizations such as the World Wide Fund for Nature and the World Conservation Union have begun mapping "ecoregions"—geographic areas defined by the unique biodiversity they contain—as a priority for deciding where to locate future protected areas. Ecoregions have recently been mapped on a continent-wide scale for North America, Latin America, and the Caribbean. Conservationists are also mapping the distribution of ecological communities against existing protected area networks in what is called a "gap analysis," looking for communities not represented in existing reserves.[59]

Another shortcoming of the reserve system is a lack of implementation. Many parks exist on paper but are completely unprotected on the ground. These "paper parks" are most common in developing countries, which hold the bulk of the world's biodiversity yet have the least in the way of money or expertise to devote to managing protected areas. As a result, many officially designated reserves are subject to agricultural development, mining, extensive poaching, and other forms of degradation.

Such scant commitment to protected areas also makes it easy to decommission them with a stroke of a pen—an all-too-frequent consequence of the rush toward some short-term bonanza in natural resource exploitation, even at the risk of appalling and permanent loss. In India, for example, politicians reduced the size of the Melghat Tiger Reserve by one third in 1992 to accommodate timber harvesting and dam construction, while more than 40 percent of the Narayan Sarovar Sanctuary was turned over by the Gujarat State Assembly in 1995 to mining companies eager to harvest the coal, bauxite, and limestone deposits found there. Narayan Sarovar was home to a rich assembly of wildlife, including wolves, desert cats, and the largest known population of the Indian gazelle.[60]

The "paper park" syndrome has deep roots; it cannot be cured simply by increased funding for protected areas management. It reflects the lack of a wider social commitment to protect biodiversity and wildlands. Without such a commitment—or a viable plan for generating it—more funding alone is unlikely to improve matters significantly. The tactics for building that commitment will vary from one society to another, but virtually everywhere the effort will require two basic strategies. Environmental education programs must be built into school curricula (preferably beginning at an early age) to help people understand the complexity and intrinsic value of natural communities. And practical, culturally sensitive development initiatives are needed that can help local people make a living from nature without permanently damaging it. Well-planned ecotourism projects can play such a role, for example, as can "biodiversity prospecting"—the search for species that might yield new chemicals, drug precursors, genes, or other beneficial products.[61]

The biggest opportunities from this dual strategy can perhaps be seen where biological diversity meets social diversity. A great deal of the natural wealth that conservationists seek to protect is actually on land and under waters long managed by local people. Long-established communities throughout Asia and Africa, as well as the indigenous cultures of the Americas, have traditionally protected many forests, mountains, and rivers as sacred sites and ceremonial centers. In some areas of Sierra Leone, for example, the best remaining native forest patches are found within sacred groves maintained by local villages. Such peoples often have a great fund of pragmatic knowledge too: they know how the local weather works; they know which organisms produce powerful chemicals; they know what grows where.[62]

Environmental education in such places must work both ways: conservationists can often learn a great deal about biodiversity from those who have lived within it for generations. Cutting such people out of the loop is not a good idea: some of the biggest mistakes in natural areas conservation have involved the forcible removal of long-term residents from newly designated parks. Relocating such individuals or denying them access to traditional plant and animal resources has generated a great deal of ill will toward protected areas worldwide. In some cases, local people have reacted by purposefully neglecting plants and animals that they had previously managed wisely for generations. Even in cases where communities have expressed a willingness to move out of a protected area voluntarily—say, to obtain better schooling for their children or improved medical care—governments have often not kept their promises to provide land and housing equal to what the relocated residents left behind.

In most of the world, therefore, conserving threatened species is as much a cultural as a biological endeavor. The various approaches developed—integrated conservation and development projects, for example, or "biosphere reserves" that use zoning schemes to integrate settlements and wildlands—are all complex undertakings. Their success will require a long-term commitment from conservationists and local residents, as well as national and international institutions.[63]

Yet even under the most optimistic scenarios, a large chunk of biodiversity will probably never receive official protection within reserves. Instead, its fate rests with how well we can create sustainable approaches to forestry, agriculture, livestock husbandry, river management, and other land uses. Developing such approaches will require a deeper understanding of how species, communities, and ecosystems interact, and how human communities traditionally and currently influence biodiversity-rich regions. It will also entail fundamental government policy reform in many areas—for instance, in eliminating subsidies for cattle ranching that clears forests (as Brazil did in the late 1980s), and strengthening land and marine tenure laws to recognize the claims of traditional communities with strong ties to land and resources.[64]

While increased funding for projects to generate sustainable natural resource use is certainly needed, this is more likely to make a difference when coupled with reductions in existing subsidies to activities that damage biodiversity. During its first three years of implementation, for example, the CBD provided $335 million in new funding for conservation through the Global Environment Facility. Yet during that same time period, global subsidies to such exploitative activities as overfishing, road building, and excessive fossil fuel burning totalled an appalling $1.8 trillion—5,373 times as much.[65]

In today's increasingly crowded and interconnected world, the most important steps we can all take to conserve biodiversity may be the least direct ones. The fate of birds, mammals, frogs, fish, and all the rest of biodiversity depends not so much on what happens in parks but what happens where we live, work, and obtain the wherewithal for our daily lives. To give biodiversity and wildlands breathing space, we must find ways to reduce the size of our own imprint on the planet. That means stabilizing and ultimately reducing the human population. It means far greater efficiency in our materials and energy use. It means intelligently planned communities. And it means educational standards that build an awareness of our responsibility in managing 3.2 billion years' worth of biological wealth. Ultimately, it means replacing our consumer culture with a less materialist and far more environmentally literate way of life.[66]

Humans, after all, are not dinosaurs. We can change. Even in the midst of this mass extinction, we still largely control our destiny, but only if we act now. The fate of untold numbers of species depends on it. And so does the fate of our children, in ways we can barely begin to conceive.

Notes

1. Calculations of background extinction rates from David M. Raup, "A Kill Curve for Phanerozoic Marine Species," *Paleobiology,* vol. 17, no. 1 (1991). Raup's exact estimate is one species extinct every four years, based on a pool of 1 million species; we list a range of one to three species per year based on current conservative estimates of total species worldwide reviewed by Nigel Stork, "Measuring Global Biodiversity and Its Decline," in Marjorie L. Reaka-Kudla, Don E. Wilson, and Edward O. Wilson, eds., *Biodiversity II: Understanding and Protecting Our Biological Resources* (Washington, DC: Joseph Henry Press, 1997). To translate rates from percentages, we have assumed a total pool of 10 million species. For previous mass extinctions, see Michael L. Rosenzweig, *Species Diversity in Space and Time* (Cambridge, U.K.: Cambridge University Press, 1995).

2. Importance of wild organisms in pharmaceutical and health care systems from Norman R. Farnsworth, "Screening Plants for New Medicines," in E.O. Wilson, ed., *Biodiversity* (Washington, DC: National Academy Press, 1988); Janet N. Abramovitz, "Valuing Nature's Services," in Lester R. Brown et al., *State of the World 1997* (New York: W.W. Norton & Company, 1997).

3. Edward O. Wilson, *The Diversity of Life* (Cambridge, MA: Belknap Press, 1992); estimates for total species on Earth are reviewed by Stork, op. cit. note 1; the high percentage of beetles among currently described species is from Terry L. Erwin, "Biodiversity at Its Utmost: Tropical Forest Beetles," in Reaka-Kudla, Wilson, and Wilson, op. cit. note 1.

4. Jonathan Baillie and Brian Groombridge, eds., *1996 IUCN Red List of Threatened Animals* (Gland, Switzerland: World Conservation Union [IUCN], 1996).

5. Rachel Carson, *Silent Spring* (Boston: Houghton Mifflin, 1962); Robert J. Hesselberg and John E. Gannon, "Contaminant Trends in Great Lakes Fish," in Edward T. LaRoe et al., eds., *Our Living Resources: A Report to the Nation on the Distribution, Abundance, and Health of U.S. Plants, Animals, and Ecosystems* (Washington, DC: National Biological Service, 1995).

6. Dates for bird conservation assessment from Baillie and Groombridge, op. cit. note 4; bird species total rounded off from ibid., and from Howard Youth, "Flying into Trouble," *World Watch,* January/February 1994.

7. Threatened species statistics from Baillie and Groombridge, op. cit. note 4; information on crested ibis from James A. Hancock, James A. Kushlan, and M. Philip Kahl, *Storks, Ibises and Spoonbills of the World* (London: Academic Press, 1992).

8. Ralph Costa and Joan Walker, "Red-Cockaded Woodpeckers," in LaRoe et al., op. cit. note 5.

9. Baillie and Groombridge, op. cit. note 4.

10. Percentage of threatened birds facing habitat loss from Baillie and Groombridge, op. cit. note 4.

11. The situation in Darién province, Panama, from personal observations of author (Tuxill).

12. Numbers calculated by Worldwatch from N.J. Collar et al., *Threatened Birds of the Americas* (Cambridge, U.K.: International Council for Bird Preservation, 1992).

13. Baillie and Groombridge, op. cit. note 4; figure of one third calculated by Worldwatch from IUCN data. Note that certain large islands relatively near mainland areas have bird fauna that are more continental than insular in composition. Thus this estimate excludes the larger islands of Japan, Sumatra, Borneo, New Guinea, and Cuba.

14. Archeological evidence for prehistoric Polynesian bird extinction wave from Richard Cassels, "Faunal Extinction and Prehistoric Man in New Zealand and the Pacific Islands," and Storrs Olson and Helen James, "The Role of Polynesians in the Extinction of the Avifauna of the Hawaiian Islands," both in Paul Martin and Richard Klein, eds., *Quaternary Extinctions: A Prehistoric Revolution* (Tucson, AZ: Academic Press, 1984).

15. Numbers for New Zealand, Philippines, and Mauritius from Baillie and Groombridge, op. cit. note 4.

16. Current bird endangerment rate from Baillie and Groombridge, op. cit. note 4; other numbers on Hawaiian birds from Olson and James, op. cit. note 14, and from Leonard Freed, Sheila Conant, and Robert Fleischer, "Evolutionary Ecology and Radiation of Hawaiian Passerine Birds," *Trends in Ecology and Evolution,* July 1987.

17. North American neotropical migrant figures from Bruce J. Peterjohn, John R. Sauer, and Chandler S. Robbins, "Population Trends from the North American Breeding Bird Survey," in Thomas E. Martin and Deborah M. Finch, eds., *Ecology and Management of Neotropical Migratory Birds* (Oxford, U.K.: Oxford University Press, 1995); European information from Katrin Bohning-Gaese and Hans-Gunther Bauer, "Changes in Species Abundance, Distribution, and Diversity in a Central European Bird Community," *Conservation Biology,* February 1996.

18. Wetlands loss and duck population declines from Youth, op. cit. note 6; coffee plantation information from Ivette Perfecto et al., "Shade Coffee: A Disappearing Refuge for Biodiversity," *Bioscience,* September 1996.

19. Mediterranean hunting figures from Youth, op. cit. note 6.

20. Information on 1995–96 hawk kills from Les Line, "Lethal Migration," *Audubon,* September–October 1996; update on 1996–97 Swainson's hawk situation from Catherine Baden-Daintree, "Pesticide Withdrawn to Save Hawk," *Oryx,* July 1997.

21. Baillie and Groombridge, op. cit. note 4.

22. Musk deer figure from "Musk Deer Declining Further," *Oryx,* January 1995; other figures from Baillie and Groombridge, op. cit. note 4; red colobus example from John F. Oates, *African Primates* (Gland, Switzerland: IUCN, 1996).

23. All figures from Baillie and Groombridge, op. cit. note 4.

24. Figure for habitat loss as endangerment cause from Baillie and Groombridge, op. cit. note 4; figure for 70 percent endemic primate endangerment calculated from species totals for Asia from A.A. Eudey, *Action Plan for Asian Primate Conservation 1987–1991* (Gland, Switzerland: IUCN, 1987), for Madagascar from Russell A. Mittermeier et al., *Lemurs of Madagascar: An Action Plan for Their Conservation 1993–1999* (Gland, Switzerland: IUCN, 1993), for Atlantic forest from Anthony B.

Rylands, Russell A. Mittermeier, and Ernesto Rodriguez Luna, "A Species List for the New World Primates (Platyrrhini): Distribution by Country, Endemism, and Conservation Status According to the Mace-Land System," *Neotropical Primates,* September 1995, and for threatened primates as per Baillie and Groombridge, op. cit. note 4.

25. European cetacean status from Mark Simmonds, "Saving Europe's Dolphins," *Oryx,* October 1994; Baltic seal information from M. Olsson and A. Bergman, "A New Persistent Contaminant Detected in Baltic Wildlife: Bis(4-Chlorophenyl) Sulfate," *Ambio,* vol. 24, no. 2 (1995); general information from Thomas Jefferson, Stephen Leatherwood, and Marc Webber, *Marine Mammals of the World* (Rome: U.N. Environment Programme/U.N. Food and Agriculture Organization, 1995).

26. Hunting as endangerment figure calculated by Worldwatch from Baillie and Groombridge, op. cit. note 4.

27. Annual Amazon Basin hunting estimate and Latin American fauna loss from Kent H. Redford. "The Empty Forest," *Bioscience,* vol. 42, no. 6 (1992); fauna loss also discussed in E.F. Raez-Luna, "Hunting Large Primates and Conservation of the Neotropical Rain Forests," *Oryx,* January 1995.

28. Bushmeat as main rural income source from David S. Wilkie, John G. Sidle, and Georges C. Boundzanga, "Mechanized Logging, Market Hunting, and a Bank Loan in Congo," *Conservation Biology,* December 1992; figure on Gabonese bushmeat consumption from Michael McRae, "Road Kill in Cameroon," *Natural History,* February 1997.

29. Peter Matthiessen, "The Last Wild Tigers," *Audubon,* March–April 1997.

30. Ecological role of large mammals from John W. Terborgh, "The Big Things That Run the World—A Sequel to E.O. Wilson," *Conservation Biology,* December 1988; elephant-dispersed trees from R.F.W. Barnes, "The Conflict between Humans and Elephants in the Central African Forests," *Mammal Review,* vol. 26, no. 2/3 (1996); whales and deep-sea biodiversity from Cheryl Butman, James T. Carlton, and Stephen Palumbi, "Whaling Effects on Deep-Sea Biodiversity," *Conservation Biology,* April 1995.

31. Figure for total Australian mammal extinctions from Ross McPhee and Clare Flemming. "Brown-eyed, Milk-giving . . . and Extinct," *Natural History,* April 1997; percentage of current fauna threatened and other details of Australian mammal declines from Jeff Short and Andrew Smith, "Mammal Decline and Recovery in Australia," *Journal of Mammalogy,* vol. 75, no. 2 (1994); and from Michael Common and Tony Norton, "Biodiversity: Its Conservation in Australia," *Ambio,* May 1992.

32. Reptile species total from Harold G. Cogger, *Reptiles and Amphibians of Australia* (Ithaca, NY: Reed Books/Cornell University Press, 1992); amphibian species total from Darrel R. Frost, ed., *Amphibian Species of the World: A Taxonomic and Geographic Reference* (Lawrence, KS: Allen Press/Association of Systematics Collections, 1985); assessment percentages and assessment status of reptile groups from Baillie and Groombridge, op. cit. note 4.

33. Baillie and Groombridge, op. cit. note 4.

34. Habitat loss percentage calculated from Baillie and Groombridge, op. cit. note 4; Galápagos Islands information from Stephen Herrero, "Galapagos Tortoises Threatened," *Conservation Biology,* April 1997.

35. Baillie and Groombridge, op. cit. note 4.

36. Status of all seven turtle species as endangered from Baillie and Groombridge, op. cit. note 4; general information on sea turtles' problems from Howard Youth, "Neglected Elders," *World Watch,* September/ October 1997; data from Panamanian waters is from field notes by the author (Tuxill), March 1997.

37. TRAFFIC report on Southeast Asia tortoise and river turtle trade cited in Catherine Baden-Daintree, "Threats to Tortoises and Freshwater Turtles," *Oryx,* April 1996.

38. Information on Amazonian crocodilians from P. Brazaitis et al., "Threats to Brazilian Crocodilian Populations," *Oryx,* October 1996; other information on crocodilians' status from Youth, op. cit. note 36.

39. Habitat loss figure for amphibians from Baillie and Groombridge, op. cit. note 4; loss of wetlands as a problem for amphibians from Andrew R. Blaustein and David B. Wake, "The Puzzle of Declining Amphibian Populations," *Scientific American,* April 1995; impacts of roads and traffic from "Frogs and Toads Take the Road Less Traveled," *Delta* (Journal of the Canadian Global Change Program), Fall 1994.

40. Western U.S. frog declines from Charles A. Drost and Gary M. Fellers, "Collapse of a Regional Frog Fauna in the Yosemite Area of the California Sierra Nevada, USA," *Conservation Biology,* April 1996; Australian frog declines from William F. Laurance, Keith R. McDonald, and Richard Speare, "Epidemic Disease and the Catastrophic Decline of Australian Rain Forest Frogs," *Conservation Biology,* April 1996.

41. Invasive pathogens as cause from Laurance, McDonald, and Speare, op. cit. note 40; UV radiation or acid rain as causes, and synergistic combinations, from Blaustein and Wake, op. cit. note 39; introduced predators as cause from Robert N. Fisher and H. Bradley Shaffer, "The Decline of Amphibians in California's Great Central Valley," *Conservation Biology,* October 1996; drought as problem from J. Alan Pounds and Martha L. Crump, "Amphibian Declines and Climatic Disturbance: The Case of the Golden Toad and the Harlequin Frog," *Conservation Biology,* March 1994.

42. Baillie and Groombridge, op. cit. note 4.

43. Ibid.

44. Large rivers as hotspots for endangered fish and saltwater hotspots from Peter B. Moyle and Robert A. Leidy, "Loss of Biodiversity in Aquatic Ecosystems: Evidence from Fish Faunas," in P.L. Fiedler and S.K. Jain, eds., *Conservation Biology: The Theory and Practice of Nature Conservation, Preservation, and Management* (New York: Chapman and Hall, 1992); tropical peat swamps as fish diversity hotspots from Peter K.L. Ng, "Peat Swamp Fishes of Southeast Asia: Diversity under Threat," *Wallaceana,* vol. 73 (1994).

45. Figure for dams worldwide from Sandra Postel, *Last Oasis,* rev. ed. (New York: W.W. Norton & Company, 1997); Mississippi dead zone from Joby Warrick, " 'Dead Zone' Plagues Gulf Fishermen," *Washington Post,* 24 August 1997.

46. Habitat endangerment percentage and darter total from Baillie and Groombridge, op. cit. note 4; Sanjay Kumar, "Indian Dams Will Drive Out Rare Animals . . . While Fish Fall Prey to Progress," *New Scientist,* 4 February 1995.

47. Wayne C. Starnes, "Colorado River Basin Fishes," in National Biological Service, U.S. Department of the Interior, *Our Living Resources 1994* (Washington, DC: 1995); Salvador Contreras and M. Lourdes Lozano, "Water, Endangered Fishes, and Development Perspectives in Arid Lands of Mexico," *Conservation Biology,* June 1994.

48. Percentage of fish threatened by invasives from Baillie and Groombridge, op. cit. note 4; Richard Ogutu-Ohwayo, "Nile Perch in Lake Victoria: Effects on Fish Species Diversity, Ecosystem Functions and Fisheries," in O.T. Sandlund, P.J. Schei, and A. Viken, eds., *Proceedings of the Norway/U.N. Conference on Alien Species* (Trondheim, Norway: Directorate for Nature Management and Norwegian Institute for Native Research, 1996); Les Kaufman and Peter Ochumba, "Evolutionary and

Conservation Biology of Cichlid Fishes as Revealed by Faunal Remnants in Northern Lake Victoria," *Conservation Biology,* September 1993.

49. Baillie and Groombridge, op. cit. note 4.

50. Ibid.; Amanda C.J. Vincent, *The International Trade in Seahorses* (Cambridge, U.K.: TRAFFIC International, July 1996).

51. Debra A. Rose, *An Overview of World Trade in Sharks and Other Cartilaginous Fishes* (Cambridge, U.K.: TRAFFIC International, 1996).

52. Vadim Birstein, "Sturgeons and Paddlefishes: Threatened Fishes in Need of Conservation," *Conservation Biology,* December 1993; Alexander Amstislavskii, "Sturgeon and Salmon on the Verge of Extinction," *Environmental Policy Review,* vol. 5, no. 1 (1991); Baillie and Groombridge, op. cit. note 4.

53. Chris Bright, "Tracking the Ecology of Climate Change," in Brown et al., op. cit. note 2.

54. Biodiversity convention requirements from Anatole F. Krattiger et al., eds., *Widening Perspectives on Biodiversity* (Gland, Switzerland: IUCN and International Academy of the Environment, 1994); ratification status from CBD Subsidiary Body for Scientific, Technical, and Technological Advice, <http://www.biodiv.org/sbstta.html>, viewed 20 October 1997.

55. Robin Sharp, "The African Elephant: Conservation and CITES," *Oryx,* April 1997; Susan L. Crowley, "Saving Africa's Elephants: No Easy Answers," *African Wildlife News,* May–June 1997.

56. Global protected area total from Catherine Baden-Daintree, "Protected Area Boom," *Oryx,* April 1997.

57. Total for conservation-dependent East African megafauna from Baillie and Groombridge, op. cit. note 4.

58. Increase in protected areas coverage in 1990–95 from Baden-Daintree, op. cit. note 56; the lack of protection given to tropical wetlands and other freshwater habitats is commented on by Norman Myers, "The Rich Diversity of Biodiversity Issues," in Reaka-Kudla, Wilson, and Wilson, op. cit. note 1.

59. Ecoregion mapping from Eric Dinerstein et al., *Una Evaluación del Estado de Conservación de las Ecoregiones Terrestres de América Latina y El Caribe* (Washington, DC: World Bank, 1995).

60. Degazetting of Indian nature reserves from Sanjay Kumar, "Mining Digs Deep into India's Wildlife Refuges," *New Scientist,* 26 August 1995.

61. The need to view protected areas as natural resources themselves has been eloquently argued by Daniel H. Janzen, "Wildland Biodiversity Management in the Tropics," in Reaka-Kudla, Wilson, and Wilson, op. cit. note 1.

62. The extent to which protected areas have been overlain on traditionally managed lands is detailed by Marcus Colchester, *Salvaging Nature: Indigenous Peoples, Protected Areas and Biodiversity Conservation* (Geneva, Switzerland: United Nations Research Institute for Social Development, 1994); and Aiah R. Lebbie and Raymond P. Guries, "Ethnobotanical Value and Conservation of Sacred Groves of the Kpaa Mende in Sierra Leone," *Economic Botany,* vol. 49, no. 3 (1995).

63. Michel P. Pimbert and Jules N. Pretty, *Parks, People and Professionals: Putting "Participation" Into Protected Area Management* (Geneva, Switzerland: United Nations Research Institute for Social Development, 1995).

64. Ronald A. Foresta, *Amazonian Conservation in the Age of Development* (Gainesville, FL: University of Florida Press, 1991).

65. Totals for Global Environment Facility funding and biodiversity-damaging subsidies from Myers, op. cit. note 58; subsidy total from David Malin Roodman,

Paying the Piper: Subsidies, Politics, and the Environment, Worldwatch Paper 133 (Washington, DC: Worldwatch Institute, December 1996).

66. Niles Eldredge, *The Miner's Canary: Unraveling the Mysteries of Extinction* (New York: Prentice Hall Press, 1991).

12

Riches from the Rainforest

Chris Wille

In this selection, Chris Wille describes the importance of biodiversity to humans in places where few people have until recently set foot: tropical moist forests. His focus is on recent efforts to enlist local experts in the development of data about biological diversity and in the local impacts of global changes such as those described in previous chapters. Costa Rica, which has led the world in developing sustainable eco-tourism, still faces major challenges in protecting its vast biodiversity.

Chris Wille is the director of the Rainforest Alliance's Sustainable Agriculture Program. The Alliance, a nonprofit, New York-based citizens' group, is the international secretariat of the Sustainable Agriculture Network, a coalition of leading Latin American conservation groups.

Gilberto Fonseca runs an insect trapline in Costa Rica's Corcovado National Park—on a forested peninsula that juts into the Pacific Ocean near the border with Panama. He lives in a rustic park guard station accessible only by bush plane or a seven-hour walk.

Wiry and tireless, Fonseca hikes for miles in the dripping forest. He is unbothered by biting insects (some go right into a collecting jar), the sudden rainstorms or the ensuing blanket of damp heat. He wears cheap rubber boots and carries no provisions, saving pack space for traps and specimen bottles.

At night, he works his light traps. By day, Fonseca moves quickly through the forest's shadows, barely pausing to snatch camouflaged insects from leaves and to turn over rocks and logs. Some insects fall to Fonseca's sweep net; others wander into his traps baited with light, meat, fruit or feces. At the end of a day he has to preserve, label and mount his haul, all to exacting specifications.

From Chris Wille, "Riches from the Rainforest," *Nature Conservancy* (January–February 1993), 12, 14–17. © 1993 The Nature Conservancy. All rights reserved. Reprinted by permission of Chris Wille and The Nature Conservancy.

Although he grew up in Costa Rica's densely populated Central Valley, Fonseca had a natural affinity for the shrinking wild spaces. He became a biologist's assistant and then a park guard. These jobs employed his skills as a woodsman, but did not satisfy his leaping curiosity about the steaming green rain forest.

So, in 1989, when he heard that Costa Rica's nascent national biodiversity institute had openings for a new breed of wilderness scout—one whose knowledge of the forest came from instinct and experience, not from textbooks—Fonseca applied. Now he is on the front lines of a bold new experiment in conservation and development: collecting plants and animals to help save them.

Even in ecologically avant-garde Costa Rica, the rain forest is under siege. A few years ago, some of the country's most progressive environmentalists began to realize that the only way to save tropical habitats was to make their value clear to everyone, from campesinos to politicians. One of the most valuable assets of a rain forest is the sheer number of living things that thrive there. So the Costa Ricans set out to prove the worth of their natural diversity.

To promote biodiversity, the conservationists realized, they needed a catalogue—an inventory of living things—so that became their top priority. And they needed a place to house the specimens, so they created the Costa Rican National Biodiversity Institute, or INBio. INBio joined forces with Costa Rica's Conservation Data Center, a team of specialists trained by The Nature Conservancy who were already busy cataloguing the country's rare plants and animals.

INBio set its sights on those creatures that had been largely ignored—the insects and microorganisms. And it created a new profession for those like Fonseca who were eager to help with the biological inventory but lacked the academic credentials: the "paratoxonomist."

Acre for acre, Costa Rica is one of the most diverse countries in the world, containing an estimated 500,000 species in an area smaller than West Virginia. For example, Costa Rica has more species of birds and trees than all of North America. And like most countries with tropical forests, Costa Rica is buzzing with insects, most of which have never been studied.

No tropical country has completed an inventory of its biodiversity—few have even started. The Costa Ricans think they can assay their prodigious biodiversity despite an impoverished university system, a burdensome foreign debt and only a handful of professional taxonomists.

"If this project were attempted in the United States or Europe, it would require an army of Ph.D.s, five to ten years of start-up training and big money," says Dr. Rodrigo Gamez, who, as an advisor to former President Oscar Arias, was one of those behind the biodiversity strategy.

"We don't have the Ph.D.s or the money, and we're almost out of time," he says. Gamez, a plant virologist and former professor of molecular biology, knows that the biodiversity clock is ticking. Rain forests are disappearing worldwide at the rate of nearly 80 acres a minute, according to the most recent satellite surveys sponsored by the United Nations. And Costa Rica, despite its green reputation and renowned park system, has done its part to keep the average up. This Central American country has lost three-quarters of its original forest cover; nobody knows how many species vanished along with it.

To give biologists a fighting chance against the chainsaws, INBio (with help from the U.S. Agency for International Development) started the parataxonomist program in 1989. It recruited Gilberto Fonseca and 14 other people from the backcountry of Costa Rica and pushed them through a five-month boot camp. The training included crash courses in everything from accounting to zoology, and lots of hands-on practice collecting and mounting specimens. Upon graduation, they were turned loose in national protected areas with orders to collect everything.

The results electrified taxonomists, that breed of scientists that wants to know the pedigree of everything. Frank Hovore, for example, is a California-based expert in long-horned woodboring beetles who has done research in Costa Rica. In a recent entomological journal, he described his amazement upon opening the beetle cabinet stocked by INBio's parataxonomists: "In this one drawer were series after series of specimens representing species never before recorded from Costa Rica, or from Central America, or, in several cases, from anywhere else. More new records and new species than I had encountered in any other single collection in a decade!"

A second group of parataxonomists was trained in 1990. In January 1992, the third class strapped on snakeboots and plunged into the field courses. Like their predecessors, these 21 recruits were highly motivated, curious and brimming with the kind of intelligence that comes from the heart, not the classroom. Unlike the first two groups, the majority of these collectors were women.

Maria Marta Chavarria, INBio's parataxonomy program coordinator, says that the course gave most of the women their first opportunity to use a microscope or a computer, mouth words like "Arthropoda," sit behind the wheel of a car or even visit the capital city of San Jose.

"It's wonderful to see them realize their capabilities," she says. "They are taking charge of their lives." Women do not have many opportunities in rural Central America, Chavarria says, and these high-energy workers are not going to let their chance slip away.

At 15, Katia Flores is the youngest of the recent graduates. She comes from an extended family with 21 members and says that being away from home for the first time was the most difficult change. She remembers the loneliness of the first days at boot camp, struggling to keep up on hikes, falling in the mud, the heat, the avalanche of strange new information to absorb, the specter of failure. Then she told herself, "I'm a *tica* [Costa Rican female], I can handle this." And she did. Now, she speaks with the quiet confidence of one who has proved herself.

"We helped each other in training," she says. "Now we have a chance to do something for ourselves, for Costa Rica."

The parataxonomists range in age from 15 to 40-something. Many have a high school education, a few have been to the university. In addition to the former park guards, farmers, hunters and housewives, a teacher, a preacher and a bartender have joined the corps. They are all natural-born naturalists with a penchant for their home forest. While plying their inherent knowledge and new skills, the parataxonomists also become outspoken defenders of Costa Rica's designated conservation areas.

The biodiversity institute is a nonprofit, nongovernment institution. It is not a museum where collections and research results are locked in archives as what Gamez calls "frozen information." The agency is a proactive promoter of biodiversity, not only willing to share information but flaunting it.

"We understand only a minute fraction of our biological wealth," Gamez says. "All those species—what do they eat? What do they make? How do they survive? How can they fit into the agro-ecosystem that Costa Rica must sustain? All these things are unopened books, written in strange languages. For Costa Rica's socioeconomic survival, and for our mutualism with the world, these books need to be opened and the languages learned."

As INBio struggles to catalogue and house the flood of specimens, professional systematists have begun to narrow the sights of the parataxonomists, focusing their efforts on groups of organisms under-represented in the collections. Now, each parataxonomist brings in 20 to 50 select plant specimens and 2,000 to 5,000 carefully mounted insects a month.

The parataxonomists are concentrating on certain groups of organisms such as the taxonomically tangled moths, certain beetles, parasitic flies and wasps, caddisflies, dragonflies and plants. One rationale for this focus is that these groups may quickly yield something beneficial to society. The beetles and plants are sources of novel chemicals. Parasitic flies and wasps are of interest because they prey on insects that may be pests.

INBio is seeking to turn this native bounty into profits for Costa Rica's conservation programs by courting agro-industry and other businesses with offerings of promising seeds, germ plasm and the possibility of new drugs.

Meanwhile, the rest of the conservation community anxiously looks on. "We have to be high on it," says Randall Curtis, the Conservancy's Costa

Rica representative. "There are so few examples out there where a country has decided to ambitiously take on an inventory of their biodiversity."

Every couple of months, the parataxonomists make the long trip to INBio in the capital city of San Jose, carrying a tall stack of specimen cases like over-due library books. There, they meet with entomologists and other scientists to review their catch. Some of the scientists are eager to see if the parataxonomists have brought in the key to their own taxonomic riddle: an undescribed species, a missing link.

This carefully selected stream of raw nature flowing from field and for-est into the laps of tropical scientists has caught the attention of museum curators and taxonomists the world over. At INBio, local and foreign taxono-mists can often be seen bent over the same trayful of dried bugs. Dr. Michael Ivie, an entomologist at Montana State University on loan to the National Science Foundation, is one of the foreign scientists taking advantage of the vast numbers of specimens the parataxonomists are collecting. He believes that the best place to look for new chemical compounds is within his spe-cialty, beetles.

"Beetles can eat everything and can detoxify everything," he says, em-phasizing the untapped potential of the five million or more beetle species that have not yet even been identified, let alone examined for their practical value as exotic chemical makers.

The parataxonomists are making the practical, commercial and scien-tific rewards of biodiversity more apparent and accessible, and this makes it easier to promote conservation. "There are three steps to conservation: Save it, figure out what you have saved, and then put it to work for humanity," says Gamez.

Costa Rica already has a good record of setting aside natural areas; nearly 25 percent of the country has reserve or park status. Now, Gamez says, they are taking steps two and three.

"People have to know something in order to value it," Gamez points out. "For example, people know wood, so they value the timber in a forest. But, in reality, the wood may be much less valuable than other parts of the forest that we have not even identified."

Gamez is the supercharged battery of the parataxonomy program. Addi-tional wattage comes from Dr. Daniel Janzen, one of the founders of the biodiversity institute and the designer of the parataxonomy training program. Janzen, who is often called the "dean of tropical ecology," divides his time between the classrooms of the University of Pennsylvania and Guanacaste, a conservation area on Costa Rica's Pacific shore.

He is best known for his efforts to restore cattle pasture in the Guanacaste area to its original state—dry tropical forest, the rarest of all endangered habitats in Central America. The remnants of dry tropical forest are threatened by fires set by ranchers and farmers, a destructive annual tradition. With the zeal of a scientist who has seen his laboratory in flames, Janzen has helped Costa Rican conservationists raise millions of dollars to save this deciduous forest. Much of the money for INBio and the Guanacaste restoration has come through The Nature Conservancy, which "is like an old-fashioned banker—friendly and trustworthy," says Janzen.

Janzen has employed local farmers and hunters as field assistants since 1974, and says they are often "smarter, tougher and more enthusiastic about the work than university graduates."

This belief and his widely varied background made Janzen the ideal choice as teacher and drill sergeant for the parataxonomists as the Costa Ricans began their audacious plan to inventory their fat slice of Creation.

Using the traditional system of annual field trips to the forest, Janzen says, "the international taxonomist has had centuries to get the world's biodiversity in order, and while he has done much, there are still centuries' worth of work left to do at that pace."

Janzen argues that tropical habitats cannot wait. "If the wildlands of Costa Rica are not quickly recognized as productive sectors of the economy, they will have no chance of surviving the coming environmental onslaught."

After a day of bug hunting and an evening trip to the light trap. Gilberto Fonseca has returned to the park station and is unloading his catch in front of a small audience of park guards and backpack campers. As he reveals cryptically colored moths, jewel-like beetles and other night creatures that blundered into his light trap, he reels off their Latin family names and tells quick ecological anecdotes about each.

When the generator shuts down and everyone else retires, Fonseca begins preparing museum-quality specimens by the light of a battery lamp. His favorites are the micro-beetles, so small that he collects them with a pipette. He pours the contents of a collecting jar into his palm—beetles, glittering like BBs.

One of the unexpected benefits of the parataxonomy program is the growth of warm, symbiotic relationships between these tough, woods-wise collectors and academicians—bonds that bridge the traditional gap between the rural users of the tropical forest and those lab-bound Ph.D.s studying it. The friendships include a spirit of healthy competition, and Fonseca chuckles as he begins to mount the minute beetles.

This batch, he says in Spanish, will confuse the hell out of them.

13

Dying Seas

Anne Platt McGinn

One of the most overlooked and misunderstood wellsprings of biodiversity is the planet's oceans and seas. Centuries of human activity along coastlines and in the open oceans have had a disastrous impact on life forms in the salt water that covers two-thirds of Earth's surface. Anne McGinn surveys the problems that human settlement and economic activity have brought to seven seas—the Black, Baltic, Caspian, Bering, Yellow, South China, and Mediterranean. She concludes by suggesting three ways that nations can act in concert to reverse the ongoing and calamitous destruction.

Anne Platt McGinn is a senior researcher at the Worldwatch Institute, where she addresses human and environmental health issues. Her current work focuses on toxic chemicals and health.

During the last four thousand years, the part of our past that we think of as the history of civilization, human settlements have tended to cluster around land-enclosed seas, rivers, and lakes. People in these settlements have been able to supply themselves with food, security, and community to a degree that would have been far more difficult in the vast inland territories—drylands, mountains, scrub forests, deserts, and steppes—that make up the bulk of the terrestrial world.

Whether it was the ancient Aegeans on the Mediterranean, the Persians on the Caspian, or the Chinese on the Yellow Sea, civilizations rose in places where small boats could exchange knowledge and goods, trade was easily conducted, fish were abundant, and the land was rich with the topsoil carried downstream by rivers.

For these reasons, the basins of the great seas were also more highly valued than other landforms, and controlling them became central to human notions of security. Security meant military control of homelands and trade

From Anne Platt McGinn, "Dying Seas," in *The Worldwatch Reader on Global Environmental Issues*, ed. Lester R. Brown (New York: Norton, 1998), 93–112. © 1998 Worldwatch Institute. Reprinted by permission of W. W. Norton & Company.

routes. It has also meant, increasingly in the past few centuries, control of the water itself—by damming tributaries, digging irrigation ditches, dredging shipping channels and harbors, and constructing breakwaters.

In just the last few decades, however, a new kind of stress has crept into the historic relationship between humans and the seas. While civilizations have continued to develop most rapidly around the coasts and rivers that feed the seas, that growth has accelerated to a point that is now dangerously unstable. Various side effects of human activity that passed unnoticed until this century have begun to ravage the very qualities that make the seas valuable— depleting both sea-based and land-based food production, fouling the human nest, and evidently even beginning to alter weather patterns for the worse.

Today, most of the world's seas are suffering from a wide range of human-caused assaults, in various lethal combinations: their ecological links to the land blocked by dams; their bottoms punctured and contaminated by oil drilling; their wildlife habitats wiped out by coastal development; and their water contaminated—or turned anoxic—by farm and factory waste. And what fish remain after these assaults are being decimated by overfishing. In the world's most biologically productive and diverse bodies of water, ecosystems are on the verge of collapse—and in some cases have already collapsed. The levels of damage and progress toward protection vary from sea to sea. But in general, compared to the open oceans, semi-enclosed seas tend to be damaged more severely and quickly because water circulation is limited and there is less dilution of pollutants.

Today, the seas are as strategically important as they ever were in the days of Kublai Khan's armada or the Greek trading ships, but for new reasons. The old preoccupation with controlling key military positions, ports, and trade routes is now rivaled by a more urgent priority: to rescue and protect the more fundamental assets that made the seas worth living near in the first place, but which are now being dangerously damaged.

To set up this protection means establishing a new paradigm for security, in which shared responsibility for sustaining the vitality of these seas becomes the basis for a mutual, rather than competitive, effort. This is something that national governments may find difficult, since it necessarily overrides traditional concepts of sovereignty and control. But most of the great seas are shared in too many ways for anything but a mutual vigilance— and coordinated defense against our own human excesses—to work. Cooperative solutions have begun to emerge in a few regions, such as the Mediterranean and the Baltic. But on other seas, conflicts are escalating— suggesting that cooperation is not likely to prevail without a fuller understanding of just what is at stake.

There are about 35 major seas in the world, some coastal and some enclosed by land. Of these, seven—the Baltic, Mediterranean, Black, Caspian, Bering, Yellow, and South China Seas—illustrate the panoply of ills that now afflict, in varying degrees, all 35. Each of these seven carries different wounds. One, the Black, is a microcosm of them all.

Black Sea: A Sea of Troubles

In ancient times it was valued for its abundance of fish, its relatively temperate climate, and its strategic location: the city of Constantinople was the gateway between East and West, capital of the Byzantine Empire, and one of the great hubs of human civilization. During the past century, the Black Sea became famous for its beach resorts where wealthy Russians and Ukrainians built their *dachas.* But in recent decades, this beautiful place has been ravaged. First, and most tragically, there has been the onset of a disease that is now endemic to enclosed or semi-enclosed bodies of water worldwide: an immense excess of marine nutrients. Like a compulsive eater who becomes increasingly obese, immobile, and finally moribund, the Black Sea has been overloaded with nutrients—fertilizer washing downstream from farms, human waste from the cities. The result has been massive eutrophication—a burgeoning growth of algae and bacteria, creating thick floating mats so dense that they block sunlight and destroy the natural ecological balance.

To this cancer-like process, other complications have been added. While the Black Sea was serving as a playground for elite Soviets during the Cold War, it was also being used as a convenient sink for all sorts of industrial activity—in an era when Soviet industries were driven by production quotas with little concern for their environmental impact. Toxic pollutants from plants ran uncontrolled down the three main tributary rivers, and growing quantities of municipal waste mingled with industrial and agricultural waste. The contaminated waters weakened the fish populations, which were further destroyed by heavy overfishing.

In this morass of biological decline, the most visible blight is the vast greenish mass that now lies over much of the water. What was once a rich, diverse ecosystem has been replaced by a monoculture of opportunistic weeds and algae. Gradually, as the dissolved oxygen supply is depleted by the algae and bacteria, the water becomes anoxic—incapable of supporting oxygen-dependent plants or animals. When the algae dies, it settles to the sea bottom, releasing hydrogen sulfide, which is poisonous to aquatic species.

A key source of the trouble can be found along a 350-kilometer stretch of northwestern shoreline where three major rivers, the Danube, the Dniester and the Dnieper, drain into the sea. The Danube delivers much of the fertilizer runoff, detergent waste, and human sewage produced by the 81 million people in the Central and Eastern European drainage basin. Each year, it dumps an estimated 60,000 tons of phosphorus and 340,000 tons of inorganic nitrogen on the shallow waters of the Black Sea shelf, which is approximately one-fourth of the sea's entire area.

In the past 25 years, the Danube's concentrations of nitrate and phosphate (stable compounds that form when nitrogen and phosphorus react with oxygen) have increased six-fold and four-fold respectively. Concentrations from the Dniester, which flows across the Ukrainian breadbasket region, have increased three-fold for nitrate and seven-fold for phosphate since the 1950s. The Dniester has also brought heavy loads of pesticides, after flowing through the fields of Ukrainian and Moldovan farmers. On the southern end of the Kremenchug reservoir, about 250 kilometers south of Kiev, the algae covering the Dnieper River is so thick that Landsat images reveal boat tracks across the river. Heavy industry also contributes to the stresses: an estimated one billion tons of mine tailings, coal ash, slag heaps, and other mineral wastes are dumped each year in the Dnieper River watershed area. And the Dnieper still suffers from the radioactive fallout of the Chernobyl nuclear disaster in 1986.

Today, 90 percent of the volume of the Black Sea is anoxic. All of the deep layers of water in the central and southern parts of the basin are anoxic, and the dead water is expanding steadily upward from the bottom. The upper tenth, while still biologically productive, is deteriorating. "I know of no other inland sea under such pressure," said Stanislav Konovalov, director of the Soviet Institute for Biology of the Southern Seas at Sevastopol, Ukraine, in 1992. Since then, conditions have worsened.

Extreme eutrophication has repercussions through the food web, causing a decline in the number of species and economic losses in both fisheries and seaside tourism. Populations of the jelly fish-like ctenophore *Mnemiopis leidyi,* first noticed in 1982, have erupted—consuming zooplankton, shellfish, and eggs and larvae of fish. At times, up to 95 percent of the Black Sea biomass consists of these gelatinous pests.

The problem is exacerbated by the long time needed for biological recovery in inland seas even under the best of conditions. It takes 167 years for water to flow from the Danube River delta southward through the sea's basin and out through the Bosporus Strait to the Mediterranean—and far longer, of course, to reach the Atlantic Ocean. Anoxic conditions in the deep bottom waters were recorded as early as 1912; today, much of the sea is oxygen-deprived. With limited freshwater supplies and virtually no flushing, the Black Sea is essentially choking to death. Some scientists say it has 10 to 15 years to live; others give it 40 years. Most fishermen and tourists say it is already dead.

To effectively reduce nutrient loads will require major changes in industrial and agricultural practices, updating of sewage treatment facilities, and reduced detergent use. Unfortunately, the needed changes seem to be neither economically nor politically realistic, given the desperate economic situations in the former Soviet and Eastern European countries. Yet, the dilemma for these countries is that if they do not invest in such changes, their resources and economics will only decline further.

Moreover, the pall of eutrophication is not the only problem confronting the Black Sea community of nations. Toxic pollution from industries in the Black Sea drainage basin, oil spills from intensive shipping, direct dumping of waste, and the disruptions of marine or coastal habitats by mineral exploration and river alteration have all added to the blight.

Between 1986 and 1992, the Black Sea's total fish catch dropped from 900,000 to 100,000 metric tons per year. Dolphin, caviar, sturgeon, anchovy, and mackerel populations have all plummeted. Altogether, the cumulative effects of dead water, poisoned water, and overfishing have already cost more than 150,000 fishing jobs. Another 2 million people who make their living from fishing and fishery-related industries are at risk. Direct economic losses have mounted to more than $250 million per year in the fishing industry, and the costs to related industries could push the figure over $1 billion. At the same time, the tourism industry has lost $300 million each year because of beach closings, unsanitary conditions, algae-clogged swimming areas, and outbreaks of cholera on both the Romanian and Ukrainian sides of the Danube delta. "The Black Sea is on the brink of extinction," the Russian newspaper *Tass* reported in 1994.

Yellow Sea: Heavy Metals

Six thousand kilometers east-southeast, between northern China and Korea, the Yellow Sea suffers its own version of the Black Sea's dysfunctional relationship with its tributary rivers. And here, too, the result has been a disaster for fisheries. But whereas the Black Sea region is moderately populated, the Yellow Sea coastal region is densely populated and growing rapidly. Here, as a result, the decline of fisheries has gone beyond the economic sphere, into overt military confrontation. And here, perhaps more than anywhere else, the fundamental dilemma—and irony—of the human relationship with the seas is illustrated in its simplest form: the more people there are to depend on the seas for food and jobs, the more pollution there is to make those assets scarcer. In China, pollution takes on a broader meaning as well—it includes huge quantities of silt from the intensive farming that takes place on every available hectare of the drainage basin.

In fact, the Yellow Sea gets its name from the ochre-colored soil that washes down the Yellow River (Huang He) out to the Bohai Sea (the large bay linking Beijing and the Yellow Sea) at a rate of 2.4 billion tons per year. Today, a more accurate name for the Yellow Sea might be the *Brownish-Red* Sea. And the problem with this silt is that it is no longer just topsoil, but is now laced with heavy metals. Just as the sea has absorbed silt for thousands of years, it now absorbs the pollution and wastes from China's rapidly industrializing coastal areas.

Currently, there are more than 670 million Chinese living on or near the coast. With an estimated 40 percent of the industrial plants located along the coast, more workers and their families are tempted to move to coastal areas every year in search of jobs. In fact, of all the migratory movements in the world today, this internal movement of rural Chinese to the coast may be the largest. Population densities along China's 13 coastal provinces average more than 600 people per square kilometer. And in the rapidly growing city of Shanghai, more than 2,000 people crowd into each square kilometer of land along the sea. These pressures are only going to get worse: most Chinese coastal cities are growing at rates fast enough to more than double their populations in just 14 years.

To keep up with demand for housing and buildings, coastal land that used to be cultivated is now developed at a rate of 3,400 square kilometers per year. This leaves aquatic and terrestrial habitat areas at an even greater disadvantage; not only are they losing ground, but they are being forced to absorb increasing volumes of runoff from more industries and more people. Not surprisingly, the coasts of China and Korea are showing signs of extraordinary stress.

Pollution from heavy metals "may be among the highest in the world" in China's coastal areas (including the Yellow Sea, East China Sea, and South China Sea), according to Fan Zhijie of the State Oceanic Administration in Dalian, China, and R. P. Côté of the Dalhousie University School for Resource and Environmental Studies in Halifax, Nova Scotia. One reason is that rapid industrialization in the region has occurred with few or no pollution control measures.

According to the Chinese *Annual of Environment Quality in Offshore of China, 1989,* the Yellow River dumped 751 tons of cadmium, mercury, lead, zinc, arsenic, and chromium, along with 21,000 tons of oil, into the Bohai Sea in 1989. The Yellow Sea itself received more than twice that quantity of heavy metals. This study also found that the greatest concentrations of toxic metals occurred in the top layer of sediment—in some cases more than 1,000 times greater than those in the water.

The contamination is thus heavily concentrated in the seabed where many species live and feed. And indeed, monitoring between 1981 and 1984 showed that the concentrations of cadmium in crustaceans (such as crabs) increased three-fold, while lead and copper in fish and mollusks (such as mussels) increased two- to four-fold. Data from 1989 found that mercury in bivalves (clams and oysters) was over 10 times the acceptable levels.

In addition to the contamination flowing in from rivers, the Yellow Sea is being contaminated by atmospheric pollution, particularly from coalburning plants and smogbound cities, and by direct dumping from coastal industries.

The Qingdao Soda Plant on Kiaochow Bay, for example, has dramatically altered the condition of sediments. Chromium levels in sediments near the plant have been recorded at levels as high as 430 mg per kilogram—enough to dramatically discolor a beach near the discharge point. In 1963, 141 types of marine animals—mollusks, crustaceans, echinoderms, and the like—were living in these sediments; by 1988, only 24 remained.

In addition to excess numbers of vessels and fishers, most of the estuaries, bays, and wetlands bordering the Yellow Sea have been polluted enough to have serious effects on fisheries—the decline of which has been drastic enough to make them targets for military intervention. North Korea declared a 50-nautical-mile military warning zone to protect its remaining fisheries from pirates and foreign fleets. Chinese fishers in the Yellow Sea have been attacked and fired at by North Korean vessels, while South Korea has arrested fishers who stray too close to its depleted grounds. In the East China Sea and South Yellow Sea, Chinese patrol boats' attacks on Russian fishing vessels have slowed only because Russia deployed a navy flotilla there and threatened to "blow pirates out of the water."

Baltic Sea: Organochlorines

In Scandinavia, the numerous rivers and fjords coming out of Sweden and Norway into the Baltic Sea have a very different look; instead of wending across wide, intensively cultivated and heavily populated valleys like so many of the world's sea-feeding tributaries, they wind through quiet, seemingly pristine forests. But these forests are also the sites—and resources for—another kind of sea-endangering industry: pulp and paper mills. In the 1940s, most of these mills began using elemental chlorine or chlorine compounds to bleach the paper—to make it white enough to satisfy consumers, publishers, and especially advertisers.

The bleaching processes release substantial amounts of organochlorine compounds into the environment. These compounds do not dissolve in water, but are lipid-soluble and accumulate readily in the fatty tissues of animals and fish. With the pulp and paper industries of Sweden and Finland now accounting for 10 percent of the world's total output, some 300,000 to 400,000 tons of chlorinated compounds are released each year—much ending up in the Baltic Sea.

What happens when these compounds find their way up the food chain into humans and other higher animals has become a subject of intense scientific scrutiny in the past decade—with the weight of evidence linking them not only to cancer but to reproductive and endocrine diseases.

Among the early inklings of these effects were reports of die-offs in sea eagles, seals, and minks, first observed on the shores of the Swedish coast in the late 1950s. Since then, these species have suffered severe declines and are now almost extinct. Studies of other species in decline—including both marine mammals and such fish as herring, cod, sprat, and salmon—show that they too contain high levels of organochlorines. Compared to fish in the neighboring North Sea, fish in the Baltic have been found to contain concentrations of these chemicals three to ten times greater.

In addition to the population declines or collapses, marine biologists report a disturbing increase in birth defects in populations with high organochlorine levels. Among Baltic gray seals, half the females observed in one study were incapable of breeding because of deformed uteri horns. Among baby seals, eggshell-fragile skulls and skull bone lesions were believed to be caused by the immune suppression effects of exposure to PCBs. Unfortunately, these trends were not well documented until the late 1980s. Now the effects are so far along and pollution is so great that it is "almost too late to do anything about it," according to Susan Shaw, Executive Director of the Marine Environmental Research Institute in New York City, who works with marine biologists in Sweden.

For epidemiologists, the witches' brew of organochlorines (11,000 have been identified) is trouble enough. But in the Baltic, other ingredients are being added to the mix as well. For years, this sea served as a receptacle for the untreated sewage and industrial wastewater generated by areas under Communist rule, such as Upper Silesia in Poland and Ostrava in the Czech Republic. A 1991 *Ambio* article, for example, indicates that atmospheric metal input is the most important source of metal contamination in the Baltic area. Metal concentrations in the region have increased five-fold over the last 50 years, largely as a result of burning fossil fuels. Fish from many coastal areas are now blacklisted, because they contain too much mercury. But with the sources of Baltic pollution so diffused, it is difficult—with one major exception—to detect and monitor the polluters.

The exception is the pulp and paper mills. In the last few years, the European community has moved to impose new restrictions on chlorine bleaching. How well they succeed may go a long way toward determining the health of the Baltic for future generations—both of marine life and of the people who depend on it.

Caspian Sea: The Control of Rivers and Resources

A majority of the major seas are only partially enclosed, which gives them at least some—albeit very limited—opportunity to recover. With the Black Sea, there is at least a narrow channel to the Mediterranean. But about 500 kilometers east of the Black, the smaller Caspian Sea is entirely enclosed and its riverine lifelines have been more manipulated—and strangled. As a consequence, it has even less absorptive capacity. Yet, it too has had to serve as a receptacle for massive amounts of waste. And that collision of interests has produced an outcome of ironic and tragic simplicity: the Caspian's most valued product—its caviar—has been virtually wiped out.

Perhaps nowhere else is the human bent for controlling and manipulating—and its effects on nature—so pronounced as in the Caspian. Over the centuries, powerful rivals have fought to control this sea's strategic rivers and ports. In the late nineteenth century, an oil boom in Azerbaijan gave birth to a major industrial center on the Caspian's western shore, in the area around Baku; during World War II, the Soviet war effort was powered almost entirely by Baku's oil. And since the breakup of the Soviet Union, there have been ongoing discussions among Azerbaijan, Russia, Kazakhstan, Turkmenistan and Iran, as well as Western oil companies, about access to oil supplies.

If the southern part of the Caspian drainage area is strategically important for oil, the north is strategic for its agricultural resources and hydroelectric power. It produces one-fifth of the former Soviet countries' total crop yield, and one-third of their industrial output. In the last forty years, a string of dams and hydropower plants has been built along the Volga River, to supply electric power to the industries and to irrigate the crops. These uses have lowered water levels enough to severely impair the Volga's capacity to dilute waste and runoff, upsetting the natural balances of salinity, temperature, and oxygen in water stream.

The Volga is the Caspian's major source of contamination. Draining the area from north of Leningrad to south of Tehran, it was forced to accept more than one-fourth of all the wastewater disgorged by Russia. From petrochemical factories alone, some 67,000 tons of wastes flush into the sea each year. Further south, Azerbaijan cities and industries dump an estimated 250 and 300 million cubic meters of sewage and waste into the sea each year.

As a result, here too, fisheries have collapsed. The catches of pike and perch, for example, have dropped by 96 percent in the past three decades. But the biggest shock to this region has been the fate of its caviar—or sturgeon's eggs. The Caspian Sea used to produce 90 percent of the world's supply of this prized delicacy, still known as the "black pearls of the Caspian." But the number of sturgeon returning to the Caspian from the Volga River has declined drastically, primarily because of obstructed migratory paths, overfishing, and pollution.

In the 1970s, it was not uncommon to find a specimen that was 60 years old and weighed 900 pounds. Today, an estimated 90 percent of the sea's sturgeon are killed before they are mature enough to reproduce—and the typical adult is just 18 years old and weights 77 pounds. In the Iranian Sefid Rud River delta in the southern Caspian, the commercial catch of sturgeon dropped from 6,700 tons in 1961 to less than one-half ton in 1993. The World Conservation Union (IUCN) listed Caspian Sea sturgeon as endangered in its 1996 Red List of threatened and endangered species.

This pattern of accelerating decline is being played out in virtually every fishery of every sea in the world. As supplies dwindle, fish are captured at earlier stages of their life cycle. With fewer fish available, fishers turn to more desperate measures to capture them. A vicious circle, already hastened by contamination from human and industrial waste, river diversion projects, and sheer growth in human population, accelerates still further. One result is to drive the search for food farther afield, to parts of the planet where supplies have not yet been exhausted.

Bering Sea: To the Ends of the Earth

In the far northern reaches of the Pacific Ocean, enclosed by the Aleutian island chain and the Russian Kamchatka peninsula, the Bering Sea receives nutrient-rich ocean currents and replenishing water from the south to support its abundant marine mammals, plants, and fish. In gulfs, bays, and ocean waters that are relatively free of pollution and habitat destruction, marine life thrives. One might suppose that this sea, at least, is safe. But it is not.

Unlike the other seas discussed here, the Bering Sea has not supported a large human population. But as demand for food has risen, and with it the technology of extraction, the Bering is proving an asset of central importance to the food security of the human world at large.

The Bering Sea is "perhaps the richest marine region in the world ocean, as evidenced by the number of species and their biomass," according to economist Natalia Mirovitskaya of Russia's Institute of World Economy and International Relations and marine scientist J. Christopher Haney of the Woods Hole Oceanographic Institution in Massachusetts. The Northwestern Pacific as a whole (including the Sea of Okhotsk, Sea of Japan, Yellow Sea and East China Sea) has an exceptionally high marine productivity—yielding up to 917 kilograms per square kilometer each year, compared to an average world ocean productivity of less than 189 kilograms.

Yet, despite its geographic remoteness, some species in the the Bering Sea are already being ravaged by overfishing and mismanagement. Wasteful fishing practices in the groundfish industry, for example, have contributed to annual losses of $250 million in the Bering Sea and Gulf of Alaska crab fisheries. The Alaskan pollack industry took off in the 1960s, with dramatic increases in catch attracting new investment in the industry. Between the early 1970s and the late 1980s, the United States and Canada increased their catches in this region four-fold—and were joined by an influx of fishers from Russia, Korea, China, and Japan.

Alaska or walleye pollack is now one of the world's biggest catches. In 1994, 4.3 million metric tons of it were taken, worldwide. But in the central Bering Sea, catches of pollack crashed from a peak of nearly 1.5 million metric tons in 1989 to 11,000 in 1992—a 99 percent decline in just three years primarily because of overfishing in the "Donut Hole," an area of international water outside the bounds of the Russian and American Exclusive Economic Zone (EEZ) jurisdictions, where Russian, American, Japanese, Korean, Chinese, and even Polish fishing vessels all compete in the search for pollack.

South China Sea: "A Disaster Waiting to Happen"

Some 6,000 kilometers down the Pacific Rim from the Bering Sea, the South China Sea serves a region as heavily populated as the Bering is sparse—yet some of its troubles are uncannily similar. It's a region where virtually all of the problems afflicting seas worldwide are being further exacerbated by political conflict—over fisheries, oil fields, military control, and the competing interests of commercial and local economies. But what in the Bering Sea is described as a "donut hole" might be better compared in the South China Sea to a Charybdis—the treacherous whirlpool of Greek mythology.

China, the largest of the South China's many antagonists, has claimed exclusive domain over a large part of this sea, including the Spratley Islands, ever since Chinese merchants first took to its waves in the 15th century. The claim is rejected by other countries because it limits access to fisheries, seabed oil and minerals, shipping lanes, and navigational rights. The disagreement is particularly contentious between China and Vietnam, and in areas around Taiwan, Brunei, Malaysia, and the Philippines where EEZ boundaries overlap.

China is now expanding its claims to include coveted oil fields—further escalating the disputes. Oil was first discovered in the area in 1976, and there are now an estimated 80 to 100 oil wells in the South China Sea. The Philippines, Vietnam, Taiwan, and the United States all have interests there, and tensions have been rising over who owns what. The United States began funding Indonesia's war in East Timor around the time of that discovery, partly to protect its oil interests in the region. And in the 1980s, China tripled the size of its South China naval fleet—suggesting that it, too, may be willing to wage war over these resources.

A 1991 newspaper article from Bandung, Indonesia, describes the South China Sea as "a disaster waiting to happen." It warns of the potential for ecological disaster caused by uncontrolled commercial activity, but its message is no less applicable to the burden of environmental degradation the sea is already carrying. And the fact that the South China Sea serves as a strategic military zone complicates the picture—and raises tensions—even further. Military bases are located throughout the region, navy ships patrol the waters, and spent nuclear fuel is shipped through the area.

Mediterranean: Tankers and Tourists

Few seas have played more vital roles in the rise of human civilizations—and the support of their rapidly growing populations over the past four millennia—than the Mediterranean. Providing access to three continents, it played key roles in the rise of Aegean, Egyptian, Phoenician, Greek, and Roman empires, and to the development of historic exchanges of information and culture between places as far-flung as China, Britain, and Ethiopia. Today, it is bordered by 18 countries, all of which are as dependent on the sea as their predecessors were. Yet, the Mediterranean, like the other seas, is being subjected to heavy degradation—with the prospect of irreversible losses to its dependent human communities.

Concern about this degradation began to emerge in the 1960s and 1970s, with a series of tanker spills and severe chemical leaks. The heart of the Mediterranean, the Lake of Santa Gida near Cagliari, Sardinia, was a fertile breeding area for 10,000 water birds. But it was also a repository for mercury effluent from petrochemical factories. Mercury contamination was so severe in the fall of 1976 that the regional government had to block off the entrance to the lake, remove all the shellfish, and dredge the bottom to remove any traces of the metal.

While marine scientists had warned for many years of marine degradation, it was not until fishers were banned from contaminated waters, beachgoers were forced to go home early, and oil-covered seals and dolphins made the nightly news, that—with tourist revenue at stake—the first actions were taken. Tourism is critical to the Mediterranean economy; each summer, the seasonal population on the sea's coasts almost doubles, adding 100 million visitors each year to the region's more than 160 million residents.

The Mediterranean is especially vulnerable to pollution because it is a major shipping and transport route between the Middle East and Europe—meaning that there is heavy traffic of oil tankers. It also has naturally low levels of rainfall, nutrients, and species diversity, which, combined with increasing levels of urban and coastal pollution, leave the sea with little leeway. Luckily, in the 1970s, developing and industrialized countries around the region realized that the sea was sick, and for environmental reasons and self-interest they joined together to try to prevent it from getting worse.

In 1975, Mediterranean countries were the first to approve a UNEP sponsored regional sea program—and today, arguably, the condition of the Mediterranean is not as bad as it would have been without the Mediterranean Action Plan (MEDAP). The first issue MEDAP tackled was marine dumping, in the Barcelona Convention. A Regional Oil Center was established on Malta in 1976 to provide training, information, emergency management programs, and waste retention facilities in ports. But the problems did not stop: in the 1980s, one fifth of the world's oil spills occurred in the Mediterranean Sea.

With growing concern for regional environmental issues, the debate and discussions moved beyond the issues of oil pollution and dumping, to a more comprehensive definition and understanding of marine pollution. Likewise, the action plan itself evolved from a general framework to specific substance- and media-based limits and controls. The Land-Based Protocol, signed and finalized in 1980, was a significant achievement because it set limits on industrial, agricultural, and municipal emissions into the Mediterranean in addition to controlling wastes in rivers and air—thus establishing clear links between land pollution and marine pollution. In November 1995, member states of MEDAP agreed, in principle, to turn the Mediterranean basin into a trade-free zone by 2010. In response, the European Union pledged $6 billion in aid to help its less developed coastal neighbors clean up pollution, combat poverty, and improve environmental protection and enforcement.

Re-Setting the Compass

The world's seas, crucial to both human economies and the planet's life systems, have been gravely injured. Human actions have done most of the damage, some of it now irreversible. Even so, few agreements have been reached on how joint efforts can be made to save these shared resources.

Existing agreements are staked on archaic claims of rights to extraction and control. When no claims exist, as in the Bering Sea "Donut Hole," or when claims overlap, as in the South China Sea, a gold rush mentality has brought growing tensions.

Among the Earth's sea-dependent populations, there appears to be little or no money for marine protection, or in many cases even for basic sanitation services and sewage treatment. Subsistence fishers, seasonal dockworkers, small-scale farmers, and migrant workers are encountering growing hardship. As resources become scarce and tensions rise, the fishing industry, tourist resorts, oil and gas developers, and shipping facilities are all taking losses.

To reverse these losses will require at least three politically difficult but ecologically essential steps. The first is to reduce and restrict the use of damaging chemicals: chlorine in paper bleaching, and phosphates, nitrates, and chlorine in detergents and pesticides. These are chemicals that persist in the environment, bioaccumulate in animal tissues, cause direct damage to individual species and entire aquatic ecosystems, exacerbate anoxia, and disrupt the Earth's carbon cycle. Banning or limiting their use will allow ecosystems to slowly re-establish their natural equilibrium.

The second step is to secure financial commitments from industrial countries and private companies, to invest in basic infrastructure to handle the sewage and waste from cities. This is already being done in the Baltic where Finland, Sweden, Denmark, and Germany are helping eastern Baltic countries to pay for sewage treatment plants. Recently, the European Bank for

Reconstruction and Development committed $67 million to construct a sewage treatment plant in Tallinn, the capital of Estonia.

The third, and most critical, step is to secure cooperation—commitment to joint management in lieu of preoccupation with extraction and control—at all levels of community and government. On the international level, an instructive model is the Ronneby Declaration, signed in 1990 by all of the Baltic Sea countries, members of the European Union, and four multilateral banks. This agreement identifies 132 pollution hot spots in the Baltic region, most of them in the former Eastern bloc countries. To clean up the hot spots, a 20-year, $25.6 billion Joint Comprehensive Environmental Action Program underwrites investments in sewage treatment, the refitting of pulp and paper plants, and other pollution control efforts. Similarly, environment ministers from Bulgaria, Georgia, Romania, Russia, Turkey, and Ukraine signed the Black Sea Strategic Action Plan in October 1996. The agreement calls upon Black Sea states to reinforce regulations and fines for polluters, introduce a regional fisheries licensing and quota system, ban disposal of all municipal solid waste, install waste reduction plans in 10 designated "hot spots," improve wetlands management, and expand conservation areas in estuaries and coastal zones. At the community level, a successful example can be found in the Gulf of Thailand, where several Buddhist and Muslim fishing villages are working with local activists and the U.S.-based Earth Island Institute to close the inner reaches of Kuntulee Bay to pushnets and trawlers. Each of these cases shows how action and change can happen even in the absence of political agreement.

Finally, we need a philosophical change of heart to reconnect ourselves with the seas that have supported our civilizations since the dawn of history. We may not need to restore the seas to their original pristine conditions—that may no longer be possible. But we urgently need to rehabilitate and protect whatever ecological and economic value can still be salvaged.

14

Easter Island's End

Jared Diamond

Sustainable solutions are not easily come by. In presenting a set of readings on this topic in the final section of this book, I do not mean to imply that sustainable solutions are easily developed or implemented. Sustainability truly represents the final frontier in our understanding of human interaction with the environment. But it seems clear that sustainable practices can be defined and widely adopted by individuals as well as by governments and the private sector, and they can have a major effect on future outcomes.

The first selection in this section strikes a cautionary note. The civilization of Easter Island reached very high levels of development and sophistication before succumbing to pressures caused by unsustainable use of the small island's fragile resource base. Jared Diamond charts the growing overreliance on resources, particularly trees, which supplied the material needed to make canoes sturdy enough to fish beyond the island's coastal zone. The great stone heads of Easter Island serve as mute testimony to the reality of unsustainable development.

Jared Diamond is a medical researcher and professor of physiology at the UCLA School of Medicine. His book Guns, Germs, and Steel: The Fates of Human Societies *won a Pulitzer Prize in 1998. A MacArthur Fellow, Diamond has published over 200 articles in* Discover, Natural History, Nature, *and* Geo *magazines.*

In just a few centuries, the people of Easter Island wiped out their forest, drove their plants and animals to extinction, and saw their complex society spiral into chaos and cannibalism. Are we about to follow their lead?

Among the most riveting mysteries of human history are those posed by vanished civilizations. Everyone who has seen the abandoned buildings of the Khmer, the Maya, or the Anasazi is immediately moved to ask the same question: Why did the societies that erected those structures disappear?

From Jared Diamond, "Easter's End," *Discover* (August 1, 1995). Reprinted by permission of Jared Diamond.

Their vanishing touches us as the disappearance of other animals, even the dinosaurs, never can. No matter how exotic those lost civilizations seem, their framers were humans like us. Who is to say we won't succumb to the same fate? Perhaps someday New York's skyscrapers will stand derelict and overgrown with vegetation, like the temples at Angkor Wat and Tikal.

Among all such vanished civilizations, that of the former Polynesian society on Easter Island remains unsurpassed in mystery and isolation. The mystery stems especially from the island's gigantic stone statues and its impoverished landscape, but it is enhanced by our associations with the specific people involved: Polynesians represent for us the ultimate in exotic romance, the background for many a child's, and an adult's, vision of paradise. My own interest in Easter was kindled over 30 years ago when I read Thor Heyerdahl's fabulous accounts of his Kon-Tiki voyage.

But my interest has been revived recently by a much more exciting account, one not of heroic voyages but of painstaking research and analysis. My friend David Steadman, a paleontologist, has been working with a number of other researchers who are carrying out the first systematic excavations on Easter intended to identify the animals and plants that once lived there. Their work is contributing to a new interpretation of the island's history that makes it a tale not only of wonder but of warning as well.

Easter Island, with an area of only 64 square miles, is the world's most isolated scrap of habitable land. It lies in the Pacific Ocean more than 2,000 miles west of the nearest continent (South America), 1,400 miles from even the nearest habitable island (Pitcairn). Its subtropical location and latitude—at 27 degrees south, it is approximately as far below the equator as Houston is north of it—help give it a rather mild climate, while its volcanic origins make its soil fertile. In theory, this combination of blessings should have made Easter a miniature paradise, remote from problems that beset the rest of the world.

The island derives its name from its "discovery" by the Dutch explorer Jacob Roggeveen, on Easter (April 5) in 1722. Roggeveen's first impression was not of a paradise but of a wasteland: "We originally, from a further distance, have considered the said Easter Island as sandy; the reason for that is this, that we counted as sand the withered grass, hay, or other scorched and burnt vegetation, because its wasted appearance could give no other impression than of a singular poverty and barrenness."

The island Roggeveen saw was a grassland without a single tree or bush over ten feet high. Modern botanists have identified only 47 species of higher plants native to Easter, most of them grasses, sedges, and ferns. The list includes just two species of small trees and two of woody shrubs. With such flora, the islanders Roggeveen encountered had no source of real firewood to warm themselves during Easter's cool, wet, windy winters. Their native animals included nothing larger than insects, not even a single species of native bat, land bird, land snail, or lizard. For domestic animals, they had only chickens.

European visitors throughout the eighteenth and early nineteenth centuries estimated Easter's human population at about 2,000, a modest number considering the island's fertility. As Captain James Cook recognized during his brief visit in 1774, the islanders were Polynesians (a Tahitian man accompanying Cook was able to converse with them). Yet despite the Polynesians' well-deserved fame as a great seafaring people, the Easter Islanders who came out to Roggeveen's and Cook's ships did so by swimming or paddling canoes that Roggeveen described as "bad and frail." Their craft, he wrote, were "put together with manifold small planks and light inner timbers, which they cleverly stitched together with very fine twisted threads. . . . But as they lack the knowledge and particularly the materials for caulking and making tight the great number of seams of the canoes, these are accordingly very leaky, for which reason they are compelled to spend half the time in bailing." The canoes, only ten feet long, held at most two people, and only three or four canoes were observed on the entire island.

With such flimsy craft, Polynesians could never have colonized Easter from even the nearest island, nor could they have traveled far offshore to fish. The islanders Roggeveen met were totally isolated, unaware that other people existed. Investigators in all the years since his visit have discovered no trace of the islanders' having any outside contacts: not a single Easter Island rock or product has turned up elsewhere, nor has anything been found on the island that could have been brought by anyone other than the original settlers or the Europeans. Yet the people living on Easter claimed memories of visiting the uninhabited Sala y Gomez reef 260 miles away, far beyond the range of the leaky canoes seen by Roggeveen. How did the islanders' ancestors reach that reef from Easter, or reach Easter from anywhere else?

Easter Island's most famous feature is its huge stone statues, more than 200 of which once stood on massive stone platforms lining the coast. At least 700 more, in all stages of completion, were abandoned in quarries or on ancient roads between the quarries and the coast, as if the carvers and moving crews had thrown down their tools and walked off the job. Most of the erected statues were carved in a single quarry and then somehow transported as far as six miles—despite heights as great as 33 feet and weights up to 82 tons. The abandoned statues, meanwhile, were as much as 65 feet tall and weighed up to 270 tons. The stone platforms were equally gigantic: up to 500 feet long and 10 feet high, with facing slabs weighing up to 10 tons.

Roggeveen himself quickly recognized the problem the statues posed. "The stone images at first caused us to be struck with astonishment," he wrote, "because we could not comprehend how it was possible that these people, who are devoid of heavy thick timber for making any machines, as well as strong ropes, nevertheless had been able to erect such images."

Roggeveen might have added that the islanders had no wheels, no draft animals, and no source of power except their own muscles. How did they transport the giant statues for miles, even before erecting them? To deepen the mystery, the statues were still standing in 1770, but by 1864 all of them had been pulled down, by the islanders themselves. Why then did they carve them in the first place? And why did they stop?

The statues imply a society very different from the one Roggeveen saw in 1722. Their sheer number and size suggest a population much larger than 2,000 people. What became of everyone? Furthermore, that society must have been highly organized. Easter's resources were scattered across the island: the best stone for the statues was quarried at Rano Raraku near Easter's northeast end; red stone, used for large crowns adorning some of the statues, was quarried at Puna Pau, inland in the southwest; stone carving tools came mostly from Aroi in the northwest. Meanwhile, the best farmland lay in the south and east, and the best fishing grounds on the north and west coasts. Extracting and redistributing all those goods required complex political organization. What happened to that organization, and how could it ever have arisen in such a barren landscape?

Easter Island's mysteries have spawned volumes of speculation for more than two and a half centuries. Many Europeans were incredulous that Polynesians—commonly characterized as "mere savages"—could have created the statues or the beautifully constructed stone platforms. In the 1950s, Heyerdahl argued that Polynesia must have been settled by advanced societies of American Indians, who in turn must have received civilization across the Atlantic from more advanced societies of the Old World. Heyerdahl's raft voyages aimed to prove the feasibility of such prehistoric transoceanic contacts. In the 1960s the Swiss writer Erich von Däniken, an ardent believer in Earth visits by extraterrestrial astronauts, went further, claiming that Easter's statues were the work of intelligent beings who owned ultramodern tools, became stranded on Easter, and were finally rescued.

Heyerdahl and Von Däniken both brushed aside overwhelming evidence that the Easter Islanders were typical Polynesians derived from Asia rather than from the Americas and that their culture (including their statues) grew out of Polynesian culture. Their language was Polynesian, as Cook had already concluded. Specifically, they spoke an eastern Polynesian dialect related to Hawaiian and Marquesan, a dialect isolated since about A.D. 400, as estimated from slight differences in vocabulary. Their fishhooks and stone adzes resembled early Marquesan models. Last year DNA extracted from 12 Easter Island skeletons was also shown to be Polynesian. The islanders grew bananas, taro, sweet potatoes, sugarcane, and paper mulberry—typical Polynesian crops, mostly of Southeast Asian origin. Their sole domestic animal, the chicken, was also typically Polynesian and ultimately Asian, as were the rats that arrived as stowaways in the canoes of the first settlers.

What happened to those settlers? The fanciful theories of the past must give way to evidence gathered by hardworking practitioners in three fields: archeology, pollen analysis, and paleontology.

Modern archeological excavations on Easter have continued since Heyerdahl's 1955 expedition. The earliest radiocarbon dates associated with human activities are around A.D. 400 to 700, in reasonable agreement with the approximate settlement date of 400 estimated by linguists. The period of statue construction peaked around 1200 to 1500, with few if any statues erected thereafter. Densities of archeological sites suggest a large population; an estimate of 7,000 people is widely quoted by archeologists, but other estimates range up to 20,000, which does not seem implausible for an island of Easter's area and fertility.

Archeologists have also enlisted surviving islanders in experiments aimed at figuring out how the statues might have been carved and erected. Twenty people, using only stone chisels, could have carved even the largest completed statue within a year. Given enough timber and fiber for making ropes, teams of at most a few hundred people could have loaded the statues onto wooden sleds, dragged them over lubricated wooden tracks or rollers, and used logs as levers to maneuver them into a standing position. Rope could have been made from the fiber of a small native tree, related to the linden, called the hauhau. However, that tree is now extremely scarce on Easter, and hauling one statue would have required hundreds of yards of rope. Did Easter's now barren landscape once support the necessary trees?

That question can be answered by the technique of pollen analysis, which involves boring out a column of sediment from a swamp or pond, with the most recent deposits at the top and relatively more ancient deposits at the bottom. The absolute age of each layer can be dated by radiocarbon methods. Then begins the hard work: examining tens of thousands of pollen grains under a microscope, counting them, and identifying the plant species that produced each one by comparing the grains with modern pollen from known plant species. For Easter Island, the bleary-eyed scientists who performed that task were John Flenley, now at Massey University in New Zealand, and Sarah King of the University of Hull in England.

Flenley and King's heroic efforts were rewarded by the striking new picture that emerged of Easter's prehistoric landscape. For at least 30,000 years before human arrival and during the early years of Polynesian settlement, Easter was not a wasteland at all. Instead, a subtropical forest of trees and woody bushes towered over a ground layer of shrubs, herbs, ferns, and grasses. In the forest grew tree daisies, the rope-yielding hauhau tree, and the toromiro tree, which furnishes a dense, mesquite-like firewood. The most common tree in the forest was a species of palm now absent on Easter but formerly so abundant that the bottom strata of the sediment column were packed with its pollen. The Easter Island palm was closely related to the still-surviving

Chilean wine palm, which grows up to 82 feet tall and 6 feet in diameter. The tall, unbranched trunks of the Easter Island palm would have been ideal for transporting and erecting statues and constructing large canoes. The palm would also have been a valuable food source, since its Chilean relative yields edible nuts as well as sap from which Chileans make sugar, syrup, honey, and wine.

What did the first settlers of Easter Island eat when they were not glutting themselves on the local equivalent of maple syrup? Recent excavations by David Steadman, of the New York State Museum at Albany, have yielded a picture of Easter's original animal world as surprising as Flenley and King's picture of its plant world. Steadman's expectations for Easter were conditioned by his experiences elsewhere in Polynesia, where fish are overwhelmingly the main food at archeological sites, typically accounting for more than 90 percent of the bones in ancient Polynesian garbage heaps. Easter, though, is too cool for the coral reefs beloved by fish, and its cliff-girded coastline permits shallow-water fishing in only a few places. Less than a quarter of the bones in its early garbage heaps (from the period 900 to 1300) belonged to fish; instead, nearly one-third of all bones came from porpoises.

Nowhere else in Polynesia do porpoises account for even 1 percent of discarded food bones. But most other Polynesian islands offered animal food in the form of birds and mammals, such as New Zealand's now extinct giant moas and Hawaii's now extinct flightless geese. Most other islanders also had domestic pigs and dogs. On Easter, porpoises would have been the largest animal available—other than humans. The porpoise species identified at Easter, the common dolphin, weighs up to 165 pounds. It generally lives out at sea, so it could not have been hunted by line fishing or spearfishing from shore. Instead, it must have been harpooned far offshore, in big seaworthy canoes built from the extinct palm tree.

In addition to porpoise meat, Steadman found, the early Polynesian settlers were feasting on seabirds. For those birds, Easter's remoteness and lack of predators made it an ideal haven as a breeding site, at least until humans arrived. Among the prodigious numbers of seabirds that bred on Easter were albatross, boobies, frigate birds, fulmars, petrels, prions, shearwaters, storm petrels, terns, and tropic birds. With at least 25 nesting species, Easter was the richest seabird breeding site in Polynesia and probably in the whole Pacific.

Land birds as well went into early Easter Island cooking pots. Steadman identified bones of at least six species, including barn owls, herons, parrots, and rail. Bird stew would have been seasoned with meat from large numbers of rats, which the Polynesian colonists inadvertently brought with them; Easter Island is the sole known Polynesian island where rat bones outnumber fish bones at archeological sites. (In case you're squeamish and consider rats inedible, I still recall recipes for creamed laboratory rat that my British biologist friends used to supplement their diet during their years of wartime food rationing.)

Porpoises, seabirds, land birds, and rats did not complete the list of meat sources formerly available on Easter A few bones hint at the possibility of breeding seal colonies as well. All these delicacies were cooked in ovens fired by wood from the island's forests.

Such evidence lets us imagine the island onto which Easter's first Polynesian colonists stepped ashore some 1,600 years ago, after a long canoe voyage from eastern Polynesia. They found themselves in a pristine paradise. What then happened to it? The pollen grains and the bones yield a grim answer.

Pollen records show that destruction of Easter's forests was well under way by the year 800, just a few centuries after the start of human settlement. Then charcoal from wood fires came to fill the sediment cores, while pollen of palms and other trees and woody shrubs decreased or disappeared, and pollen of the grasses that replaced the forest became more abundant. Not long after 1400 the palm finally became extinct, not only as a result of being chopped down but also because the now ubiquitous rats prevented its regeneration: of the dozens of preserved palm nuts discovered in caves on Easter, all had been chewed by rats and could no longer germinate. While the hauhau tree did not become extinct in Polynesian times, its numbers declined drastically until there weren't enough left to make ropes from. By the time Heyerdahl visited Easter, only a single, nearly dead toromiro tree remained on the island, and even that lone survivor has now disappeared. (Fortunately, the toromiro still grows in botanical gardens elsewhere.)

The fifteenth century marked the end not only for Easter's palm but for the forest itself. Its doom had been approaching as people cleared land to plant gardens; as they felled trees to build canoes, to transport and erect statues, and to burn; as rats devoured seeds; and probably as the native birds died out that had pollinated the trees' flowers and dispersed their fruit. The overall picture is among the most extreme examples of forest destruction anywhere in the world: the whole forest gone, and most of its tree species extinct.

The destruction of the island's animals was as extreme as that of the forest: without exception, every species of native land bird became extinct. Even shellfish were overexploited, until people had to settle for small sea snails instead of larger cowries. Porpoise bones disappeared abruptly from garbage heaps around 1500; no one could harpoon porpoises anymore, since the trees used for constructing the big seagoing canoes no longer existed. The colonies of more than half of the seabird species breeding on Easter or on its offshore islets were wiped out.

In place of these meat supplies, the Easter Islanders intensified their production of chickens, which had been only an occasional food item. They also turned to the largest remaining meat source available: humans, whose bones became common in late Easter Island garbage heaps. Oral traditions of the islanders are rife with cannibalism; the most inflammatory taunt that could be snarled at an enemy was "The flesh of your mother sticks between my teeth." With no wood available to cook these new goodies, the islanders resorted to sugarcane scraps, grass, and sedges to fuel their fires.

All these strands of evidence can be wound into a coherent narrative of a society's decline and fall. The first Polynesian colonists found themselves on an island with fertile soil, abundant food, bountiful building materials, ample lebensraum, and all the prerequisites for comfortable living. They prospered and multiplied.

After a few centuries, they began erecting stone statues on platforms, like the ones their Polynesian forebears had carved. With passing years, the statues and platforms became larger and larger, and the statues began sporting ten-ton red crowns—probably in an escalating spiral of one-upmanship, as rival clans tried to surpass each other with shows of wealth and power. (In the same way, successive Egyptian pharaohs built ever-larger pyramids. Today Hollywood movie moguls near my home in Los Angeles are displaying their wealth and power by building ever more ostentatious mansions. Tycoon Marvin Davis topped previous moguls with plans for a 50,000-square-foot house, so now Aaron Spelling has topped Davis with a 56,000-square-foot house. All that those buildings lack to make the message explicit are ten-ton red crowns.) On Easter, as in modern America, society was held together by a complex political system to redistribute locally available resources and to integrate the economies of different areas.

Eventually Easter's growing population was cutting the forest more rapidly than the forest was regenerating. The people used the land for gardens and the wood for fuel, canoes, and houses—and, of course, for lugging statues. As forest disappeared, the islanders ran out of timber and rope to transport and erect their statues. Life became more uncomfortable—springs and streams dried up, and wood was no longer available for fires.

People also found it harder to fill their stomachs, as land birds, large sea snails, and many seabirds disappeared. Because timber for building seagoing canoes vanished, fish catches declined and porpoises disappeared from the table. Crop yields also declined, since deforestation allowed the soil to be eroded by rain and wind, dried by the sun, and its nutrients to be leeched from it. Intensified chicken production and cannibalism replaced only part of all those lost foods. Preserved statuettes with sunken cheeks and visible ribs suggest that people were starving.

With the disappearance of food surpluses, Easter Island could no longer feed the chiefs, bureaucrats, and priests who had kept a complex society running. Surviving islanders described to early European visitors how local chaos replaced centralized government and a warrior class took over from the hereditary chiefs. The stone points of spears and daggers, made by the warriors during their heyday in the 1600s and 1700s, still litter the ground of Easter today. By around 1700, the population began to crash toward between one-quarter and one-tenth of its former number. People took to living in caves for protection against their enemies. Around 1770 rival clans started to topple each other's statues, breaking the heads off. By 1864 the last statue had been thrown down and desecrated.

As we try to imagine the decline of Easter's civilization, we ask ourselves, "Why didn't they look around, realize what they were doing, and stop before it was too late? What were they thinking when they cut down the last palm tree?"

I suspect, though, that the disaster happened not with a bang but with a whimper. After all, there are those hundreds of abandoned statues to consider. The forest the islanders depended on for rollers and rope didn't simply disappear one day—it vanished slowly, over decades. Perhaps war interrupted the moving teams; perhaps by the time the carvers had finished their work, the last rope snapped. In the meantime, any islander who tried to warn about the dangers of progressive deforestation would have been overridden by vested interests of carvers, bureaucrats, and chiefs, whose jobs depended on continued deforestation. Our Pacific Northwest loggers are only the latest in a long line of loggers to cry, "Jobs over trees!" The changes in forest cover from year to year would have been hard to detect: yes, this year we cleared those woods over there, but trees are starting to grow back again on this abandoned garden site here. Only older people, recollecting their childhoods decades earlier, could have recognized a difference. Their children could no more have comprehended their parents' tales than my eight-year-old sons today can comprehend my wife's and my tales of what Los Angeles was like 30 years ago.

Gradually trees became fewer, smaller, and less important. By the time the last fruit-bearing adult palm tree was cut, palms had long since ceased to be of economic significance. That left only smaller and smaller palm saplings to clear each year, along with other bushes and treelets. No one would have noticed the felling of the last small palm.

By now the meaning of Easter Island for us should be chillingly obvious. Easter Island is Earth writ small. Today, again, a rising population confronts shrinking resources. We too have no emigration valve, because all human societies are linked by international transport, and we can no more escape into space than the Easter Islanders could flee into the ocean. If we continue to follow our present course, we shall have exhausted the world's major fisheries, tropical rain forests, fossil fuels, and much of our soil by the time my sons reach my current age.

Every day newspapers report details of famished countries—Afghanistan, Liberia, Rwanda, Sierra Leone, Somalia, the former Yugoslavia, Zaire—where soldiers have appropriated the wealth or where central government is yielding to local gangs of thugs. With the risk of nuclear war receding, the threat of our ending with a bang no longer has a chance of galvanizing us to halt our course. Our risk now is of winding down, slowly, in a whimper. Corrective action is blocked by vested interests, by well-intentioned political and business leaders, and by their electorates, all of whom are perfectly correct in not noticing big changes from year to year. Instead, each year there are just somewhat more people, and somewhat fewer resources, on Earth.

It would be easy to close our eyes or to give up in despair. If mere thousands of Easter Islanders with only stone tools and their own muscle power sufficed to destroy their society, how can billions of people with metal tools and machine power fail to do worse? But there is one crucial difference. The Easter Islanders had no books and no histories of other doomed societies. Unlike the Easter Islanders, we have histories of the past—information that can save us. My main hope for my sons' generation is that we may now choose to learn from the fates of societies like Easter's.

15

Neotropical Restoration Biology

Daniel H. Janzen

In this selection, biologist Daniel Janzen focuses on restoration efforts in neotropical ecosystems. He sees great hope in our ability to successfully restore disturbed environments, if not to some pristine state, then to a state that provides for sustainable interaction with humans.

Janzen, a professor of biology at the University of Pennsylvania, is one of the foremost ecologists and tropical biologists in the world. His field research has provided much of our present understanding of co-evolution in terrestrial arthropods and plants.

The New World mainland tropics can never be fully restored to an "unaltered by humans" state. This is because the first wave of professional hunters passed through the New World tropics about 10,000 years ago and extinguished most of the herbivorous megafauna (the tapir was the largest neotropical survivor). And a diverse array of predators and scavengers subsequently starved to death while they also served as "mop-up squad" for the remnants left by human hunters. This first anthropogenic megaperturbation irreversibly altered the species composition, vegetation structure, and suite of evolutionary forces in virtually all neotropical habitats. The same occurred in Australia, New Zealand, the Hawaiian Islands, Europe and less abruptly, Africa.

Then, neotropical hunting, agrarian and urban humans spent several thousand years reducing the remaining "natural" (=wild) habitats to ecological islands in an agroscape. These islands are today irrevocably reduced to sizes, configurations and biodiversities that are less than those of the pre-human landscape. And even where such a wildland has been conserved as a national park, conservation area, or other permanent wildland, environmental forces (global warming, incoming anthrochemical assault, insularization, serendipity, biodiversity introduction, etc.) continue this reduction toward an

From Daniel H. Janzen, "Neotropical Restoration Biology," *Vida Silvestre Neotropical* 4, no. 1 (1995): 3–8. Reprinted by permission of *Vida Silvestre Neotropical*.

unknown eventual equilibrium with itself and the agroscape (surrounding and distant).

Restoration is a process that is applied to various degrees to this mosaic, ranging from attempts to restore some species or ecological process within the conserved wildland, to returning a portion of the agroscape to wildland status, or to restoring some "wild" species or process to the agroscape (usually as part of the agroscape management process, as in biological control, carbon sequestration, or erosion control and water purification). In other words, restoration is a familiar and commonplace item in the toolbox of the landscape manager.

However, it does need to be emphasized that the restoration of neotropical habitats and their biodiversity, and their management and use once restored, can never be returned to the pre-human landscape. On the one hand, it is not biologically possible and it is therefore dishonest to seek funding and social support for that purpose. On the other hand, it is not socially practical; a purist pursuit of such a goal leads to an isolationism and disregard for society that will eventually cause rejection of the project by society, with subsequent jeopardy to the conserved wildland itself. This pursuit is particularly obstructionist to efforts to conserve wildlands through their non-damaging use, a use that will interfere with the goal of keeping nature pristine but not significantly impact on biodiversity overall.

The philosophy espoused here seeks to contribute to the formation of a biologically literate and stable society that seeks to have wildland patches of various sizes, configurations and biological properties coexisting with other kinds of land use —a landscape designed to have some areas urban and healthy, some areas agroscape and healthy, and some areas as wildlands permanently conserved for their use. In such a circumstance, the act of habitat "restoration" is in fact not "restoration" in the literal sense of replicating what once was, but rather a macro- (and sometimes micro-) management regime that allows an array of species to live out their lives and interactions as best they can within a new set of environmental boundaries. These boundaries are very diverse, and range from rice fields to regional climate change, from introduced species to minimal population sizes, from ecotourists to migration barriers. They can be as sharp as the interface between a cattle pasture or rice field, and a forest, or as blurred as the interface between the array of biological control agents in a pesticide-free enrichment forest and the adjacent primary forest.

The stable and developed neotropical countryside a century hence will be a mosaic of many kinds of conventional agrohabitats with patches of wildlands interspersed. These patches will range from those that are so large and unmolested that they nearly mimic pre-European conditions (e.g., a Conservation Area of several hundred thousand hectares ranging over various ecosystems), to those that are hardly more than a municipal park containing only a tiny percent of the species present when the Spaniards arrived and have almost no interactions resembling those of the past. Each of these extremes, and all the grades between, has a highly significant place in a biologically literate society that is getting the maximum return from its real estate, so to speak. And each of these extremes, and all the grades between, find themselves repeatedly on the restorationist's menu throughout the neotropics.

Those who benefit from tropical wildland land use—whether restored or original—are extraordinarily diverse in what they expect to derive from them. The restorationist must be sensitive to these wishes, or objects are being created that contain the seeds of their own demise. While the Minister of Energy may want to reforest a watershed to protect a hydroelectric dam, in fact many different kinds of restored vegetation—from carefully micromanipulated dairy pastures to timber plantations to raw wilderness—may fulfill this function and many others, all of which have the potential to reinforce the Minister of Energy. The Minister of Education may want a patch of wildland near every grade school and high school, a living laboratory and library for biodiversity literacy. However, much can be illustrated with a restored patch of forest that contains only a few percent of the species found in a relatively intact tropical forest. The Minister of Agriculture may want big blocks of wildlands in which to search for wild genes and exotic chemicals; here the maximum number of species and interactions is terribly important, much more so than in the two previously mentioned cases. It is so important that the Minister may even argue for converting a wildland to a Noah's ark—into which are stuffed not only the species that are "naturally" there, but also all the "exotics" that might be potentially of interest. A greenhouse is a greenhouse, even if it is called a national park in some other language. Such creations of free-living greenhouses (wildland areas) must be approached with extreme caution, not only because one may be destroying the site's naturally occurring biodiversity with their point of introduction. The Minister of Finance may want roads, inns, campsites, restaurants and other user-friendly structures scattered throughout the wildland area. Anything that keeps the ecotourist one day longer boosts the national treasury. And restoration here may even involve the day-to-day or year-to-year dynamics of rotating tourists among areas that have known habitat regeneration rates, or restoring impact-resistant areas where the administration can "park" ecotourists just beginning to develop their experience with tropical biodiversity.

In short, tropical restoration biology needs to begin with an analysis of what kind of human use is expected of the wildland, and to keep asking that question as the habitat develops and society's awareness of it changes. Simultaneously there is a consideration of the different biological states possible for the site, given the environmental circumstances, and how these can match up with the costs of achieving those states. Let's not get stuck in the mudhole of trying to restore the quetzal population on an elevational gradient where society will not allow the wildland to be placed so that there can be seasonal elevational migration to follow the fruiting cycles of the quetzals' food plants. Simultaneously let's not hear anyone say that a patch of tropical wildland is too small to be worth saving because its small size cannot support jaguars and tapirs. Such a wildland may be a quite comfortable home to 10,000 species of insects and 500 species of plants, and superb as a living laboratory for the local school system.

This emphasizes that the first part of analyzing human use is to determine which humans are doing the using. The goals of the local grade school can be quite different from the goals of a hydroelectric dam. And these anticipated uses are among the very top considerations in habitat restoration. And perhaps the single largest source of conflict about restoration projects is the case where different sectors of society have different uses in mind for the restored habitat.

So what hope is there for restoration biology in the neotropics? Huge hope. And this is in large part because biological literacy has began to take root throughout the neotropics. The restorationist has daily more biodiversity information with which to work, and more other biological management projects with which to relate. In February 1992 Mexico inaugurated a new national institution for the coordination and dissemination of biodiversity information, CONABIO, and thereby reinforced the process of consolidating an enormous area of conserved wildlands through coming to understand what is in them. Guatemala has a rapidly growing conservation system. It seems like almost everyone wants to guide sustainable wildland development in Belize. El Salvador is embarking on a gigantic plan to restore wildland vegetation on its Pacific coast. Nicaragua is rich in discussion of how much rainforest should be conserved and how much put into sustained-yield logging. Costa Rica has a growing National Biodiversity Institute (INBio), founded in 1989, and a new National System of Conservation Areas (SINAC), founded in 1995. Similar stories continue to unfold to the South.

The last three decades of conservation and biodiversity discussion, building on another half century of conservation attempts sprinkled here and there in the neotropics, have alerted many neotropical societies to the raw materials of restoration biology, even as other portions of society have steadily ground them up and eaten them. Now that wild biodiversity—genes, individuals, species, habitats, ecosystems—are all beginning to find a place in the structure of a biodiversity-literate and biodiversity-opportunistic society, the social circumstances for restoration biology are highly favorable. It is not surprising that this occurs in the tropics. Restoring a piece of northern prairie is likely to impact on only a very small portion of a northern society. Restoring the equivalent piece of dry forest in El Salvador could very easily be the beginning of rational watershed management in a seasonal desert, with considerable offerings in water, erosion control, carbon sequestration, biodiversity education, biodiversity prospecting and recreation to a population living right on the edge of environmental disaster.

Now that diverse sectors of neotropical society are asking for direct restoration and for reversal of the degradation processes in a variety of wildlands to be conserved, where are some of the technical challenges and what are some of the pertinent biological concepts?

Seed Sources

What should be the origin of inocula for restoration? In the ideal world, the species are still present as population fragments, and reversal of the degradation process allows the species to expand, interact with each other, and create whatever wildland comes to naturally occupy the site, given that array of species. This process is characteristic of virtually all major wildland restoration and reconstruction projects in the neotropics. It is especially true of biosphere reserves and the portions of large national parks once occupied by colonists.

Society is only just beginning to think about true habitat restoration in landscapes where the original biodiversity was largely locally extinguished (e.g., cotton fields on the Pacific side of El Salvador or Nicaragua, or deforested Caribbean islands, or huge expanses of Costa Rican pastures). Where species are truly missing from the site, or where for other reasons species that have never occupied the site are desired, then the question of the restoration goal is paramount. If the goal is to recreate tropical dry forest, for example, then there is the immediate question of whether to work hard to get dry forest genotypes or accept genotypes from rainforest areas. The tapir has been gone so long from El Salvador that the populace believes that there never were tapirs in El Salvador. Should the inocula for a restored tapir population in El Salvador come from nearby Honduranian-Nicaraguan rainforest or more distant Costa Rican dry forest? When putting a forest enriched with mahogany back on a Costa Rican 100-year-old pasture, should wild seed be brought from a nearby Conservation Area or obtained from commercial sources?

No goal of absolutely non-anthropogenic habitats is attainable, and the restorationist must become a realist at balancing the costs of near attainment of the original circumstance against the losses of more approximate attainment. "Fidelity of inocula source" is a very central question in this discussion. Ironically, the law of diminishing returns looms large. If the site is still nearly "natural," then many anguishing questions need to be asked as to just how "pure" to attempt to be in putting back the few extinguished species (and in excluding the few species that "don't belong"). It is akin to the care put into restoring an only slightly damaged 13th Century cathedral. However, if the cathedral has been reduced to rubble, and most of the bricks long ago re-moved for paving stones, the ensuing discussion among the restorationist architects and city planners will be quite different. There might even be an electric light and loudspeaker system built into the new pulpit.

Waifs and Strays

If one inventories any large area of tropical habitat (50,000+ hectares), it is likely that 1–20% of the species in a given higher taxon will be present only as waifs. These are individuals that are living, seem to be healthy, but do not maintain a viable population. They are there because there is a population elsewhere that is dispersing (or has dispersed) propagules into the site. If this "elsewhere" is removed (say, by conversion to rice fields), these species dis-appear from the remaining wildland, not because the habitat is too small or lacks the right kind of mutualists, but because these species were only there in the first place as incoming waifs.

If the tropical restorationist attempts to restore to the site all the species known previously from that site, he will find himself attempting to maintain species that were there as waifs. Stable restoration may demand the simulta-neous restoration of the source area for the colonists. On the other hand, it may well be that the only way to know if a species was a waif is to simply try to re-establish it. And even here the complication may be that it can persist as a viable population in the simplified restored habitat but could not in the fully complex original habitat.

Tropical islands may offer an extreme case of this general problem, since many of their species may be present only as colonists (most decidedly waifs) that persist until the next local (and "natural") extinction event. Islands are also so poor in species that introduced organisms may be able to survive there under abiotic conditions that they could not tolerate in a predator-rich and competitor-rich mainland habitat. And the habitat islands generated by human occupation of the mainland landscape have many of the same dynam-ics as oceanic islands.

Migrants

Each tropical ecosystem has a large number of migrants in its inventory. In-sects, birds and mammals are the most evident, but as we learn more about individual natural histories, other organisms will be added to the list. These are species that spend part of the year in one ecosystem (for one or more generations), and part of the year elsewhere. Within-tropics migration is com-monplace on a scale ranging from a few meters to hundreds of kilometers, to say nothing of those that return to the tropics during the northern winter and after exploiting the northern breeding grounds during the northern summer.

Migrants often play a major role as mutualists (pollinators, seed dispersers, etc.), carnivores (parasitids, predators), detritus producers, herbivores, food for other organisms, etc. The restorationist who tries to restore these species to an ecosystem without restoring (or conserving) the other species, habitats, and ecosystems that are needed to complete their life cycles or maintain their population viability is likely to have very limited success. Just as a national park planner cannot afford to think of each park as a thing unto itself, neither can the tropical restorationist think of a project as a lunar capsule. Or if so conceived, then there is acceptance of the substantially lowered biodiversity carrying capacity that occurs when the migrants are eliminated from a tropical habitat.

Fire

Truly natural fires (non-anthropogenic burning in non-anthropogenic vegetation) are extremely rare in most neotropical habitats and ecosystems. However, anthropogenic fires are commonplace, and have been for at least ten thousand years. It is probably best to view fire as simply another organism, and apply the same rules to it as to other species being contemplated for introduction from other continents. I should note that even what is commonly termed "natural fire" is generally not natural, since it both starts in, and gains momentum in, a highly altered environment. Yes, a lightning-generated fire can occur in the middle of the Costa Rican rainy season—as long as the lightning hits a tree standing in an abandoned pasture that has not been burned for several years and thus is standing in a pile of anthropogenic fuel.

It is fair to say that free-running anthropogenic fires are the number one difficult challenge for the restorationist in the dry neotropics, which is at least half of the terrain potentially subject to restoration. This challenge has become of particular importance because with the recent demise of the neotropical cattle industry, enormous expanses of low-grade cattle pasture are slated for return to woody crops of one kind or another, including wildlands. This restoration is both for carbon sequestration and because if the profit is gone from the beef crop, these lands are generally not suitable for other non-woody crops. The single largest barrier to putting woody crops of any sort on these old pastures is anthropogenic free-running fire, until restoration has moved far enough that the tree shade eliminates the grass. Once the wildland has been restored to a closed-canopy state similar to that of pre-human interference, the vegetation becomes either unburnable or generally supports only a litter fire that is slow-moving and relatively easily extinguished.

Good fire-elimination programs are expensive in human resources, administrative energy and dollars. However, if there are many small population and habitat fragments present, maintaining a good fire-elimination program for a conserved wildland may be by far the cheapest, most biologically effective, and durable mechanism for tropical forest restoration of large areas. This has certainly been the case with the restoration of some 60,000 ha of dry forest in the Guanacaste Conservation Area in northwestern Costa Rica.

Genetic Engineering

Agricultural unfeasibility is the greatest friend that the neotropical conservationist has ever had. It is also a good friend of the restorationist, because it has both allowed remnant populations to persist and is leading to society deciding that the seemingly low yields of conserved wildlands can in fact be tolerated (since there appears to be no use for them in conventional agriculture). Let me put it in another way. If there was a high-yield corn plant for tropical lowland latosols, there would be no lowland rainforest for us to argue about saving today. There is no tropical national park based on fertile delta soils anywhere in the world.

Genetic engineering (so-called biotechnology) offers a serious challenge to this "status quo" but it may also offer a solution, with the restorationist (and conservationist) being the go-between. The challenge is that the genetic engineering of specialty plants and animals, transnational and transcontinental introductions, and massive infusion of new "semi-domesticates" from tropical wildlands will render virtually every square meter of the tropics "productive" in the conventional agropastoral sense. If allowed to develop fully, such agricultural genetic engineering will mean that what is viewed as a degraded habitat that is available today for restoration to wildland status may well tomorrow be viewed as a fertile field for intensive agricultural management.

However, the solution may be in that restored and conserved biodiverse tropical wildlands are in fact in-situ wild zoos and botanical gardens from which the base genes, varieties and species can be prospected for the organisms to use in this agricultural genetic engineering. Wildlands are "gene banks" in many senses of the word, and will need to be retained for their banking properties.

Part and parcel of intensive agroscape micromanagement for diverse and carefully engineered animal and plant products is a thorough removal of the things that either compete or molest the "productive" organism in which so much has been invested. Throughout the tropics today, various kinds of intensive agriculture are polishing landscapes that for centuries of administrative and economic inefficiency have housed hundreds of thousands of wild species. Yes, their population structures were grossly altered, but they were still present. These are the raw materials that are often easiest for the restorationist to work with, but they are now being exposed to a very accelerated rate of local loss (even if they still persist as species in some national park established in what was once their very large geographic range). The brushy cattle pasture, the wooded rocky slope, the failed banana plantation, the abandoned hillsides on which charcoal was processed—all these "habitats" and their many analogies are a godsend for the restorationist, and the first to disappear when real First World agricultural development is applied.

Habitat Sharpening

In a large tropical site, most habitats and ecosystems blur from one into another—despite the neat lines drawn on a map to approximately demarcate them. When does dry forest stop and rain forest begin? When is it cloud forest and when is it intermediate elevation moist forest? However, if a block of tropical vegetation is restored, its boundaries with the more conventional agroscape ecosystem are often very sharp. All that is within the restored area tends to be called one thing. All that was outside is gone. The same occurs with a block of intact vegetation that is protected from advancing society. However, with restoration the apparent monomorphism of the conserved area is substantially more acute. This is because the differences among wildland habitats appear to be less, and actually are less, the earlier the stage in the restoration process. It may take millennia for species and ecological processes to sort themselves out to where once again the north side of the slope is really as different from the south side of the slope as was originally the case.

The consequence of this process for restoration biologists is that sharp edges and edge effects, and the absence of neighboring habitats that continually input other species into the focal habitat, need to be built into the management regime and explicitly considered.

Noah's Ark?

The tropical restoration project becomes of immediate interest to those who feel that their particular species are threatened at their "own" site, so they want to send them to the restoration project to be included in the reconstituted habitat. The question returns to the more basic question of what is the goal of the specific restoration project. For many projects, the presence of introduced species—whether from 10 km, 1,000 km or across an ocean barrier—is irrelevant or even beneficial. The latter is to view a specific conserved wildland as a natural ex-situ conservation site, a zoo or botanical garden.

But there are major questions to such a simplistic view. Does a given restorationist have the right to introduce a species (for whatever reason) that may in turn merrily leave the restoration area and become widely established as a pest? I don't care how endangered it is, a species of African mongoose should not be restored into a Central American conserved wildland. A firewood-starved part of Africa should not receive Central American woody "fire-wood species" without consideration of what kind of disruption this potential woody weed will bring to the rest of the African agroscape. Pets and other wild animals once removed from wildland status will be extremely disruptive if "replaced" into habitats that still contain a natural population of their species, but may be a very useful source of inoculum in areas being restored where the introduced species has been extinguished.

If a habitat is being restored, it lacks many species of carnivores, parasites, herbivores, etc. present in an "intact" tropical wildland. When species are returned from other areas, it may be necessary to simultaneously return some of their primary interactants. In other words, the Spaniards' Pleistocene gift to the neotropics—the horse—would be best only added back to a restored neotropical wildland that contains artificial predators such as selective castration or rifles.

Evolution and Insularity

The great majority of tropical mainland species have ranges over many degrees of latitude. As such, they probably did not evolve at the given point in space where the mainland conservationist is managing them. They evolved somewhere, as an isolated population on some ecological island at a time when all of the population was subject to some intense (and probably relatively monomorphic) selection. They then got back onto the ecological mainland and spread to come to occupy their present-day pre-human distribution. In short, most of us on the mainland work mostly with immigrants, invaders, and recently introduced species. Over their broad geographic distributions, there is little or no evolution going on. What you see of a species—behavior, physiology, morphology, interactions—in a tropical habitat is by and large what the species arrived at that point with. Its demography is an outcome of the interaction between it and the various habitats in which it can survive.

Now, during the past several thousand years, humans have taken these large distributions and reduced them to constellations of small patches. We have created part of the circumstances for rapid evolutionary change. We have maximized insularity, created tens of thousands of Galapagos Islands. This in turn will increase biodiversity among lineages that survive this insularization, and it will increase it even more as we generate a massive change in climate that heats up, dries out or drowns these "islands."

At this point, the restorationist suddenly appears with a new rationale. On the one hand, the restorationist might quite literally be called in to re-establish wildlands that are 10–1,000 km distant from each other, as Noah's arks for the species that are being extirpated by major changes in local climate. On the other hand, restorationists may well be called up to restore habitat bridges or "corridors" between habitat islands. In either case, the restorationist must be ready for the debate as to whether to keep species isolated in their habitat islands (and thus promote evolutionary change) or try to keep them from differentiating by maximizing genetic flow among them. Equally, the restorationist needs to be well grounded in the question of whether organisms really do use corridors, especially if the corridor occupies a different kind of habitat than that of the island.

We Do Not Live by Bread Alone

For a biologically literate tropical society, a conserved wildland is a potential national theater, public library, civic center and university. As such, the "local" citizen is inclined to want to have some conserved wildlands close to hand. Tropical areas with high human density are characteristically severely degraded. We usually don't have the option of decreeing a large pristine national park on the margin of a 1–5 million-person urbanization or area of intense agriculture. Restoration is the only option, and in these circumstances takes on the form of actually constructing an object—the wildland whose biodiversity is conserved for a variety of users from the first day.

Ecotourism, the process by which society examines the wildland, is a kind of ranching. It is memories, knowledge, stimulation, and inspiration that are marketed. And as in other kinds of ranching, the administration needs to monitor impact, improve pastures, maintain the fences, call the vet, watch the market, pay your taxes, put different kinds of livestock in different parts of the ranch, make capital investments, and train the "cowboys." And the best fertilizer is the footsteps of the administration. In contrast to the very passive kind of ranching, a kind of absentee landlordism, that may have its time and place with very large blocks of natural habitat with no need for restoration, the tropical restoration project to be used by ecotourists—and virtually all will be—is very much like a well-run ranch. The up side is that most ecotourists can read and are not dependent on the ranch for a two-year stay. The down side is that the ecotourist only lives a snapshot of the process and the place. But the restorationist plays a very dynamic and ongoing role in a large conserved wildland that maintains overall non-damaging high human use by rotating the impact, evaluating the impact, and letting areas "rest" following high-impact use.

Playing God?

In the species-poor habitats that many of us grew up in outside of the tropics, it may seem reasonable to descend into discussions of where to put what species in a restoration effort, almost as though one is growing a garden or restoring the furniture in a French castle. For example, we are likely to find someone arguing that the restoration project cannot begin until we know what was the community structure of the site before the degradation occurred.

In the biodiverse parts of the neotropics this is nonsense. Where one site originally has hundreds of species of plants and vertebrates, and tens of thousands of species of invertebrates, restoration quite frankly consists of two basic steps. First, one stops whatever were the degradational processes—or at least those that are within one's power to stop. Second, there is anguish over whether to add back any or all of the species missing but there is reason to believe were there. And in doing these introductions, one knows that some of the species are definitely not going to persist, and that some of the species will arrive on their own accord.

And Then One Just Leaves Nature Alone and Lets It Run Its Course

However, all the users are not going to leave it alone. Micromanagement of the users becomes a major action. The gains from the users need to be balanced against the changes they cause. Shall we collect seed from fine large trees in the national park for the neighbor's plantations, and if so, from old pasture-inhabiting trees (where all the seed will die) or from forest trees (where all the seed will die)? Shall we go to war against the tilapia and the trout in the rivers in neotropical national parks, or simply accept that their introduction 0–50 years ago was a callous trashing of native aquatic habitats for the pleasure of the fish hunters or for delay of the day when it has to be recognized that the habitat was grossly over-populated? Shall we scream perturbation when the ecotourists cause the peccaries and agoutis to modify their foraging ranges, or shall we recognize that their foraging ranges were irretrievably altered when the last gomphotheres and glyptodonts were speared out of the habitat? Shall we complain about altering the altered? Yes and no, depending on. . . .

We are long overdue to recognize that all neotropical wildland habitats are already managed, already undergoing restoration and degradation, and will continue to be forever. Some are managed and restored well and most are managed and restored poorly. So if we are going to play God, then let's figure out what kind of wildland greenhouses we want and get on with site-specific, society-specific, and user-specific quality management.

16

What Are Ecosystem Services?

Gretchen C. Daily

One of the newest innovations in natural-scientific and social-scientific think-ing about the environment is to assign monetary value to the environment and to the services that it provides humans. For example, forests high on a mountain a great distance from human settlement capture, hold, and purify water that is used by both the people and the river ecosystems downstream. Because the use of the water by humans can be valued, it may be possible to fix a value for the service provided by the trees and then use it to protect the upstream resource. In the two selections that follow, the concept of ecosystem services is defined. Here, in Gretchen Daily's chapter, we find some of the promise of a new approach in thinking about our relationship to the natural environment.

Gretchen Daily is a research scientist in the Department of Biological Sciences at Stanford University. An ecologist by training, Dr. Daily is work-ing to develop a scientific basis—and political and institutional backing—for managing Earth's life-support systems. Her efforts span basic science, environmental policy analysis, teaching, and public education.

Ecosystem services are the conditions and processes through which natural ecosystems, and the species that make them up, sustain and fulfill human life. They maintain biodiversity and the production of *ecosystem goods*, such as seafood, forage, timber, biomass fuels, natural fiber, and many pharma-ceuticals, industrial products, and their precursors. The harvest and trade of these goods represent an important and familiar part of the human economy. In addition to the production of goods, ecosystem services are the actual life-support functions, such as cleansing, recycling, and renewal, and they confer many intangible aesthetic and cultural benefits as well.

From Gretchen C. Daily, "What are Ecosystem Services?" *Nature's Services: Societal Dependence on Natural Ecosystems* (Washington, DC: Island Press, 1997), 3–6, 10. Reprinted by permission of Island Press.

One way to appreciate the nature and value of ecosystem services (originally suggested by John Holdren) is to imagine trying to set up a happy, day-to-day life on the moon. Assume for the sake of argument that the moon miraculously already had some of the basic conditions for supporting human life, such as an atmosphere and climate similar to those on Earth. After inviting your best friends and packing your prized possessions, a BBQ grill, and some do-it-yourself books, the big question would be, Which of Earth's millions of species do you need to take with you?

Tackling the problem systematically, you could first choose from among all the species exploited directly for food, drink, spice, fiber and timber, pharmaceuticals, industrial products (such as waxes, lac, rubber, and oils), and so on. Even being selective, this list could amount to hundreds or even several thousand species. The spaceship would be filling up before you'd even begun adding the species crucial to *supporting* those at the top of your list. Which are these unsung heroes? No one knows which—nor even approximately how many—species are required to sustain human life. This means that rather than listing species directly, you would have to list instead the life-support functions required by your lunar colony; then you could guess at the types and numbers of species required to perform each. At a bare minimum, the spaceship would have to carry species capable of supplying a whole suite of ecosystem services that earthlings take for granted. These services include:

- purification of air and water

- mitigation of floods and droughts

- detoxification and decomposition of wastes

- generation and renewal of soil and soil fertility

- pollination of crops and natural vegetation

- control of the vast majority of potential agricultural pests

- dispersal of seeds and translocation of nutrients

- maintenance of biodiversity, from which humanity has derived key elements of its agricultural, medicinal, and industrial enterprise

- protection from the sun's harmful ultraviolet rays

- partial stabilization of climate

- moderation of temperature extremes and the force of winds and waves

- support of diverse human cultures

- providing of aesthetic beauty and intellectual stimulation that lift the human spirit.

Armed with this preliminary list of services, you could begin to determine which types and numbers of species are required to perform each. This is no simple task! Let's take the soil fertility case as an example. Soil organisms play important and often unique roles in the circulation of matter in every ecosystem on Earth; they are crucial to the chemical conversion and physical transfer of essential nutrients to higher plants, and all larger organisms, including humans, depend on them (Heywood 1995). The abundance of soil organisms is absolutely staggering: under a square yard of pasture in Denmark, for instance, the soil was found to be inhabited by roughly 50,000 small earthworms and their relatives, 50,000 insects and mites, and nearly 12 million roundworms. And that is not all. A single gram (a pinch) of soil has yielded an estimated 30,000 protozoa, 50,000 algae, 400,000 fungi, and billions of individual bacteria (Ehrlich et al. 1977; Overgaard-Nielsen 1955). Which to bring to the moon? Most of these species have never been subjected to even cursory inspection. Yet the sobering fact of the matter is, as Ed Wilson put it: they don't need us, but we need them.

Ecosystem services are generated by a complex of natural cycles, driven by solar energy, that constitute the workings of the biosphere—the thin layer near Earth's surface that contains all known life. The cycles operate on very different scales. Biogeochemical cycles, such as the movement of the element carbon through the living and physical environment, are truly global and reach from the top of the atmosphere to deep into soils and ocean-bottom sediments. Life cycles of bacteria, in contrast, may be completed in an area much smaller than the period at the end of this sentence. The cycles also operate at very different rates. The biogeochemical cycling of carbon, for instance, occurs at orders of magnitude faster than that of phosphorus, just as the life cycles of microorganisms may be orders of magnitude faster than those of trees.

All of these cycles are ancient, the product of billions of years of evolution, and have existed in forms very similar to those seen today for at least hundreds of millions of years. They are absolutely pervasive, but unnoticed by most human beings going about their daily lives. Who, for example, gives a thought to the part of the carbon cycle that connects him or her to the plants in the garden outside, to plankton in the Indian Ocean, or to Julius Caesar? Noticed or not, human beings depend utterly on the continuation of natural cycles for their very existence. If the life cycles of predators that naturally control most potential pests of crops were interrupted, it is unlikely that pesticides could satisfactorily take their place. If the life cycles of pollinators of plants of economic importance ceased, society would face serious social and economic consequences. If the carbon cycle were badly disrupted, rapid climatic change could threaten the existence of civilization. In general, human beings lack both the knowledge and the ability to substitute for the functions performed by these and other cycles (Ehrlich and Mooney 1983).

For millennia, humanity has drawn benefits from these cycles without causing global disruption. Yet, today, human influence can be discerned in the most remote reaches of the biosphere: deep below Earth's surface in ancient aquifers, far out to sea on tiny tropical islands, and up in the cold, thin air high above Antarctica. Virtually no place remains untouched—chemically, physically, or biologically—by the curious and determined hand of humanity. Although much more by accident than by design, humanity now controls conditions over the entire biosphere.

Interestingly, the nature and value of Earth's life-support systems have been illuminated primarily through their disruption and loss. Thus, for instance, deforestation has revealed the critical role of forests in the hydrological cycle—in particular, in mitigating flood, drought, and the forces of wind and rain that cause erosion. Release of toxic substances, whether accidental or deliberate, has revealed the nature and value of physical and chemical processes, governed in part by a diversity of microorganisms, that disperse and break down hazardous materials. Thinning of the stratospheric ozone layer sharpened awareness of the value of its service in screening out harmful ultraviolet radiation.

A cognizance of ecosystem services, expressed in terms of their loss, dates back at least to Plato and probably much earlier:

> What now remains of the formerly rich land is like the skeleton of a sick man with all the fat and soft earth having wasted away and only the bare framework remaining. Formerly, many of the mountains were arable. The plains that were full of rich soil are now marshes. Hills that were once covered with forests and produced abundant pasture now produce only food for bees. Once the land was enriched by yearly rains, which were not lost, as they are now, by flowing from the bare land into the sea. The soil was deep, it absorbed and kept the water . . . , and the water that soaked into the hills fed springs and running streams everywhere. Now the abandoned shrines at spots where formerly there were springs attest that our description of the land is true.
>
> —Plato (quoted in Hillel, p. 104)

Ecosystem services have also gained recognition and appreciation through efforts to substitute technology for them. The overuse of pesticides, for example, leading to the decimation of natural pest enemies and concomitant promotion of formerly benign species to pest status, has made apparent agriculture's dependence upon natural pest control services. The technical problems and cost of hydroponic systems—often prohibitive even for growing high-priced, specialty produce—underscore human dependence upon ecosystem services supplied by soil. Society is likely to value more highly the services listed above, and to discover (or rediscover) an array of services not listed, as human impacts on the environment intensify and the costs and limits of technological substitution become more apparent.

References

Ehrlich, P., A. Ehrlich, and J. Holdren. 1977. *Ecoscience: Population, Resources, Environment.* San Francisco: Freeman & Co.

Ehrlich, P., and H. Mooney. 1983. "Extinction, substitution, and ecosystem services." *BioScience* 33:248–254.

Heywood, V., ed. 1995. *Global Biodiversity Assessment.* Cambridge, England: Cambridge University Press.

Hillel, D. 1991. *Out of the Earth: Civilization and the Life of the Soil.* New York: The Free Press.

Overgaard-Nielsen, C. 1955. "Studies on enchytraeidae 2: Field studies." *Natura Futlandica* 4:5–58.

17

Marine Ecosystem Services

Charles H. Peterson and Jane Lubchenco

The authors of this chapter use the ecosystem-services framework outlined in the previous selection to consider how ocean ecosystems provide economic benefits to human society. While many analysts have noted the value of tourism and fisheries, the ecosystem-services perspective allows us to identify other important roles that the oceans play, including their role in the global recycling of materials in chemicals that sustain climate and life-support systems on land. Oceans also serve to process, transform, detoxify, and sequester many of society's waste products.

Dr. Peterson, a professor at the University of North Carolina at Chapel Hill, is known for his research in marine benthic ecology and for his development of experimental approaches to testing hypotheses concerning the community organization of soft-bottom benthic systems in estuaries and lagoons. Jane Lubchenco is Professor of Marine Biology and Zoology at Oregon State University, a Pew Scholar in Conservation and the Environment, and a MacArthur Fellow. She has recently served as president of the American Association for the Advancement of Science.

The sea and all it provides to help support human society is too often taken for granted. When human population size was low and industrialization of societies was limited, this lack of appreciation had global, if not always local, defensibility. Under the influences of the present large, industrialized, and technologically empowered human society, however, the need is urgent to recognize and acknowledge explicitly the many ways in which ocean ecosystems serve to provide present and future economic value. Without such detailed valuation, costs of various activities that degrade and threaten the continued provision of ocean ecosystem services to human societies may not

From Charles H. Peterson and Jane Lubchenco, "Marine Ecosystem Services," in *Nature's Services: Societal Dependence on Natural Ecosystems*, ed. Gretchen C. Daily (Washington, DC: Island Press, 1997), 177–94. Reprinted by permission of Island Press.

be adequately considered in formulation of public policy (Ehrlich and Ehrlich 1992) and may be borne by society as a whole rather than being more fairly paid for and benefiting from the degradation. The goal of this chapter is to identify the specific ecosystem services that oceans provide so that future work can determine their economic value. Although our focus here is on economic valuation, we do not mean to imply that economic value represents the sole or even primary justification for conservation of ocean ecosystems. Ethical arguments also have considerable force and merit (Fairweather 1993).

Scope and Working Definitions

Although economists may not normally draw a distinction between goods and services, we partition the two by separating ocean ecosystem goods for discussion by Kaufman and Dayton (1996). These authors not only detail the wealth of goods produced by the oceans, including especially provision of economically valuable fishery products worldwide, but they also explain clearly how continued provision of these goods requires that the natural functioning of the ocean ecosystems that produce them be sustained indefinitely. In other words, one important ecosystem service is the biological food-web production process that results in making goods available for exploitation. Here we first review some general flaws in present management of both fisheries and environmental quality. We then identify and discuss specific services of ocean ecosystems, including: (1) global materials cycling, (2) transformation, detoxification and sequestration of pollutants and societal wastes, (3) support of the coastal ocean-based recreation, tourism, and retirement industries, (4) coastal land development and valuation, and (5) provision of cultural and future scientific values.

We adopt a broad definition of the oceans that includes estuaries. Such a broad definition seems necessary because of the extensive use of estuarine and coastal nurseries by marine organisms. In addition, evaluating the interconnections between the land and the sea is critical to achieving an understanding of important marine ecosystem services.

Fisheries and Environmental Management

While most industrialized nations have developed management schemes designed to protect water quality and the services provided by aquatic ecosystems, intrinsic flaws exist in the management process because of failure to deal properly with the uncertainty associated with scientific advice and the problem of comparing costs and benefits on differing time scales. The management process provides an arena in which inputs from natural sciences and socioeconomic sources are examined to reach some acceptable policy or specific plan. Unfortunately, the short-term costs of establishing a regulation to protect the environment are relatively easily quantified and immediate, whereas the costs of not protecting environmental quality and not preserving natural ecosystem services are less readily quantified and possess longer time horizons (Malone et al. 1993). This same inequity in the character of the costs has led to widespread overharvest of marine fish stocks and dramatic long-term loss of income to fishermen. For example, overfishing and the resultant moratorium on fishing for northern cod off eastern Canada led to twenty-seven or twenty-eight thousand unemployed in Newfoundland and Labrador in 1992 or a rate of about 30 percent unemployment (Rose 1995) as fishermen lost the valuable fisheries production services of the ocean eco-system. Fisheries management has repeatedly mortgaged the future for short-term gain, even while espousing a devotion to maximizing sustainable yield (Ludwig et al. 1993). This has occurred in part because the absence of private property rights over most fisheries removes a potential incentive for their conservation (the tragedy of the commons: Hardin 1968).

If future costs of diminished ecosystem services are discounted in any formal benefit-cost analysis by a factor greater than the inflation rate to ac-count for the time value of money, then the questions of intergenerational equity also arise in development of policy. Some would argue that inclusion of this portion of the discount rate in comparing economic costs that accrue on different time scales has the effect of weighting future costs much less than present costs. In response, one could show that productive capital is also passed on to future generations, raising their standard of living. Whether the future costs and benefits are fairly balanced is not at all clear.

Even if economic analysis were able to construct fair and balanced esti-mates of present and future costs and benefits of alternatives, there are strong arguments for adopting a risk-averse environmental policy. For example, costs of environmental clean-up and remediation are very large in contrast to pol-lution prevention, so that if we learn in the future that we have underesti-mated the extent of some permitted degradation of ecosystem services, costs of clean-up will likely be greater than what prevention would have cost. More important, our scientific uncertainties about ecosystem processes also imply a need for a precautionary principle in environmental management (see Perrings 1991) because of the potential for an unexpected and possible irre-versible collapse of ecosystem functions on which humans rely. Some func-tions of natural ecosystems are not fully replaceable by any mitigation actions, a further argument for caution in formulation of environmental policy (Gren et al. 1994).

The Ocean's Role in Global Materials Cycling

The Earth's biosphere is affected by and dependent on the large-scale global geochemical processes that cycle the materials necessary for life itself. The terrestrial biosphere is connected to the land, the atmosphere, and the sea through fundamental processes that move and transform elements. The political and cultural subdivisions of the human populations and the short time scales of human lifetimes and political contemplation can lead to a failure of human societies to consider the relationships of life on Earth to these fundamental processes occurring on global spatial scales and on time scales longer than a few years. Yet recent scientific study has revealed how radically human society is changing processes on global scales and how rapid rates of anthropogenic change are occurring, compared to time scales of natural change (NRC 1983, 1987).

A complete review of the global geochemistry of elements essential for life on Earth lies outside the scope of this chapter, but some discussion of the most alarming current disruption of natural global geochemical processes seems appropriate. Ocean ecosystems play a major role in the global geochemical cycling of all the elements that represent the basic building blocks of living organisms, carbon, nitrogen, oxygen, phosphorus, and sulfur, as well as other less abundant but necessary elements. Of these, the anthropogenic impacts on carbon and the carbon cycle are of the most pressing concern.

Ocean ecosystems are important participants in the global carbon cycle, such that in the absence of life in the sea, the equilibrium partitioning of carbon among rock (the lithosphere), the atmosphere, and ocean waters would be dramatically altered (Sarmiento et al. 1995). Berner et al. (1983) provide a nice account of the role of ocean ecosystems in the CO_2 cycle. Carbon is sequestered in continental rocks in two major forms, sedimentary organic matter (kerogen) and solid-phase carbonates. The kerogen is derived from the sedimentary remains of soft tissues of organisms, whereas carbonates in rocks come mostly from skeletons of marine plants and animals. Through interactions with the atmosphere, these carbon compounds in rocks are weathered (chemically degraded). Kerogen is oxidized to return carbon back to the atmosphere directly as CO_2. Carbonates are weathered through exposure to rainwater, which is weakly acidic (carbonic acid) as a consequence of dissolved carbon dioxide. This weathering yields dissolved bicarbonate ions, calcium, magnesium, and other cations.

After dissolved bicarbonate is returned to the sea in rainwater runoff, biological uptake produces particulate carbonate again. This incorporation of dissolved bicarbonates into skeletal tissues of marine plants and animals provides the vehicle for transfer of (bi)carbonate dissolved in ocean waters back into the sediments. Its burial there in sedimentary strata and ultimate transformation into rocks reduces the pool of atmospheric carbon dioxide and oceanic dissolved bicarbonate by storage in a solid phase in the Earth's crust. Tectonic processes release CO_2 as a gas created from subjecting the sedimentary carbonates to high pressure and temperature. This completes the crude outline of the Earth's natural carbon cycle. The marine ecosystem provides the service in this cycle of biologically transforming dissolved bicarbonate into particulate carbonates in the form of skeletons available for burial. If the sea were devoid of biota, the transfer of CO_2 from the atmosphere to the sea floor through biological production would cease and atmospheric CO_2 concentrations would rise (Berner et al. 1983, Sarmiento et al. 1995).

This service provided by ocean ecosystems represents but one example of how the ocean biota role in geochemical cycling is vital to life on land. We develop it in some detail because the consequences of release of greenhouse gases like CO_2 through fossil fuel burning are so immediate and so serious that the importance of the biological partitioning of CO_2 into the ocean also grows. Enhanced atmospheric greenhouse gases imply dramatic variations in global temperatures, changes in rainfall and land productivity patterns, and sea level rise and coastal flooding (see NRC 1983, Fischer 1984, NRC 1987).

Transformation, Detoxification, and Sequestration of Wastes

The oceans are used by human society as a repository for unwanted materials that we create and release onto land, into streams and rivers, and even into the atmosphere. Oceans are also directly used as dumping grounds for various societal wastes. The aquatic ecosystems of rivers, estuaries, and the ocean act upon these materials in a variety of ways to transform them, in some cases to detoxify them, and in other cases merely to sequester them.

Transformation—The Case of Nutrients

A universal example of how human society uses aquatic ecosystems to treat its wastes is provided by a review of the disposal of sewage wastewater (see NRC 1993). Modern secondary sewage treatment produces tremendous loadings of inorganic nutrients (nitrogen and phosphorous) in aquatic systems. Nitrogenous nutrients originating largely from fossil fuel burning are also injected into estuarine and coastal waters through acid rain (Paerl 1993). The nutrients are processed by the aquatice system, where they are removed from the water through uptake by plants, especially phytoplankton but also riparian vegetation of wetlands.

The marginal economic value of using aquatic ecosystems to scrub nutrients from sewage wastewater could be estimated by using the standard engineering formulae for calculating costs of various additional levels of treatment. For example, assuming a population of over ten thousand people, for a flow of five million gallons per day, the costs of construction alone for a treatment plant with some nutrient removal capabilities would be $4.2 million (1996 dollars) more than the $23.9 million for constructing the analogous

Advanced Treatment I plant without nutrient removal capability (EPA 1995). Increased treatment would also imply greater operating costs not included in this sample calculation.

The allowable loading of these nutrients into the aquatic system is limited by the capacity of the aquatic ecosystem to degrade microbially the organic matter produced (Nixon 1995). This process of increasing the rate of supply of organic matter to a system is termed eutrophication (Nixon 1995). Excessive eutrophication causes reduction in ecosystem services through at least two consequences, anoxia and nuisance algal blooms. An overload of organic production induces oxygen depletion, anaerobic microbial production of toxic hydrogen sulfide, and massive mortality of estuarine and marine animals. Thus, a conversion to hypereutrophic conditions transforms the entire aquatic ecosystem into one no longer supporting normal production of valuable fishes and invertebrates and no longer oxydizing the organic wastes discharged into it and produced in it by nutrient discharge (Elmgren 1989).

Eutrophication also stimulates growth of nuisance algae, such as bluegreens and dinoflagellates (Paerl 1988, Smayda 1990). These nuisance algae are often toxic to estuarine and marine animals, and in some instances threaten human health (Cosper et al. 1989). Red tide dinoflagellates can produce and release as aerosols vertebrate neurotoxins, causing long-lasting neurological injury to people who breathe the fumes. Stomach upset and disruptions of the gastrointestinal system are common symptoms of exposure to red tides. Paralytic shellfish poisoning is caused by human ingestion of shellfish exposed to toxic algae. Nuisance algal blooms often discolor the waters with reds, yellows, or browns, and release foul odors. The economic impacts of fish kills and losses to aquaculture businesses from red tides and other nuisance algal blooms are large and growing worldwide in frequency and severity (Paerl 1993).

Bivalve molluscs within the estuary act as a filter with a potential for removing excess algal production-induced eutrophication. For example, Newell (1988) calculated crudely that at historic levels of natural abundance, the oysters of Chesapeake Bay filtered a volume of water equal to the complete volume of the bay in a three-day period. The effect of such biological filtration is clearly to improve water clarity by removal of suspended materials and to transfer production from the pelagic to the benthic realms in the system (Dame 1994). Filter feeding by benthic animals can thus be viewed as one important sort of top-down control of the estuarine system that may compensate for the bottom-up enhancement induced by excess nutrient addition. Unfortunately, mismanagement of the American oyster in Chesapeake Bay and other major estuaries of the northeast and mid-Atlantic coast has led to a decline of almost two orders of magnitude in oyster abundance, diminishing one important estuarine ecosystem service. Growing eutrophication implies that restoration of oysters and other long-lived suspension-feeding bivalves may be an appropriate form of biomanipulation (see Carpenter et al. 1995) to enhance this particular ecosystem service of estuaries, now so much more in demand (Lenihan and Peterson 1996).

Detoxification

Some of society's wastes are detoxified by naturally functioning marine ecosystems, thereby representing yet another service provided free of charge to society. For example, petroleum hydrocarbons are spilled and released into the environment with great frequency. Many of the component compounds of petroleum carry important health risks to humans who are exposed to them. When in association with sediment particles, components of petroleum hydrocarbons are deposited on the floor of the estuary and ocean, where naturally occurring microbes detoxify these compounds and ultimately degrade them into carbon dioxide and water (Cerniglia and Heitcamp 1989). This is a service rendered by the microbial community of marine ecosystems. It results from aerobic processes because oxygen is the source of electrons for the degradation process catalyzed by the microbes. By inducing anoxia, eutrophication of our estuarine and marine waters endangers the valuable ecosystem service of microbial detoxification of petroleum hydrocarbons released into the environment.

Sequestration

Other important classes of toxic materials produced by industrialized human societies are not so readily degraded and transformed by ocean ecosystem processes. These include many artificial organic pollutants, such as DDT, PCB, and dioxins. Since these materials are not naturally produced, it is less likely that the microbial community has the capacity to utilize them as organic substrates, and indeed they are extremely persistent in the environment. Heavy metals, such as mercury, lead, copper, tin, zinc, and arsenic, represent another important class of pollutant released into the marine environment by industrialized societies. To some degree, the estuarine and marine ecosystems serve to transform heavy metals by binding them with sediments in a fashion that renders them biologically unavailable (Cross and Sunda 1978). However, often these pollutants are not transformed into harmless compounds by marine ecosystem processes but instead present biological hazards, placing wildlife and humans at risk (Long and Morgan 1990).

The oceans are intentionally used by many human societies as dumping grounds for various wastes, including especially toxic and harmful byproducts of industrial society, such as nuclear wastes deposited in the Arctic Ocean from the former Soviet Union. In many instances, the motivation for ocean dumping is to allow these materials to be sequestered by the ocean environment in a place that will retain them far from any possible contact with humans. This sequestering function of ocean ecosystems could conceivably be performed by a sea devoid of life; however, organically mediated sedimentation onto the sea floor helps bury and isolate much of this waste and thereby performs the intended ecosystem service. Unfortunately, complete isolation and sequestration of these materials in bottom sediments in a form that is biologically unavailable may not always be achieved (Long and Morgan 1990).

Value of Ocean Ecosystems to Tourism, Recreation, and Retirement

Naturally functioning ocean ecosystems provide direct economic value to several coastal industries in developed nations worldwide. Rarely is the dependence of those industries upon the ecosystem services clearly defined. Some limited information is available from damage assessments following large-scale pollution events, such as the *Exxon Valdez* oil spill. Otherwise, the economic work linking ecosystem function and structure to human enterprises and their valuation remains to be done.

Ecotourism

Excluding commercial fishing, the coastal industry most obviously tied to a naturally functioning ocean ecosystem is probably the tourism industry. Tourism is said to be the world's largest business (Miller and Auyong 1991). Ocean ecosystems of several sorts make huge contributions to the tourism economies of coastal regions. The three most important sets of examples of ocean ecosystem services feeding economically vital ecotourism industries and economies involve coral reef systems, polar ocean systems, and coastal estuaries and wetlands.

Coral Reef Contributions

The economic welfare of many coastal nations in the tropics is dependent on the ability to offer tourists various ocean ecosystem amenities, prominent among them opportunity for sealife viewing. This exemplifies a nonconsumptive use value of natural ocean ecosystems. For example, the majority of Caribbean islands have economies based on ecotourism, in which viewing reef fishes as well as the corals and associated invertebrates by snorkeling, diving, and glass-bottomed boats plays a major role. Even before the explosive growth of the industry and tourism more generally in the past two decades, spending by visitors accounted for 55 percent of the total GNP of the Bahamas and averaged 17 percent of GNP for the eastern and southern

Caribbean nations in 1977 (Beekhuis 1981). Such regions have a vital economic interest in preserving the functioning of the ocean ecosystems that produce these diverse, colorful marine animals.

While certain components of the coral reef ecosystem are valued directly because of their visual aesthetic appeal, namely the reef fishes, corals, and colorful benthic invertebrates, they in turn are supported by a nexus of ecosystem interactions required to sustain them. Most ecologists agree that the complexity of interactions and degree of interrelatedness among component species is higher on coral reefs than in any other marine environment (Hughes et al. 1992). This implies that the ecosystem functioning that produces the most highly valued components is also complex and that many otherwise insignificant species have strong effects on sustaining the rest of the reef system.

Coral reef ecosystems and the tourism that they generate are now seriously endangered by degradation of the corals, which form the structural habitat of this system. Although the causes of loss of coral reef habitat are numerous and not always known, many anthropogenic factors contribute (d'Elia et al. 1991). Coral bleaching has been linked to global atmospheric changes, both to global warming and to enhanced UV exposure as the ozone layer has been depleted and as enhanced tropical douldrums have smoothed the sea surface and promoted deeper penetration of damaging UV (Glynn 1991, Gleason and Wellington 1993). Exploitation of reef fishes, many of which are important herbivores, and eutrophication through discharge of sewage have led to a profusion of algae overgrowing and killing corals (Hughes 1994). Sediment erosion from improper development on coastal lands has led to coral mortality from turbidity and burial (Roberts 1993). Outbreaks of corallivorous consumers that have denuded vast reef areas may be linked to human disruptions of the ocean ecosystem. Countries such as Australia and perhaps Belize that recognize the economic importance of sustaining the coastal reef ecosystem and act effectively to protect it will prosper, while others may suffer dramatic losses of income from assuming that this ecosystem service will be provided indefinitely without management to protect it. The science-based management plans created and enforced by the Great Barrier Reef Park Authority in Australia will return huge economic rewards for sustaining the ecosystem structure, composition, and function on which such a valuable tourism industry is based (Kelleher and Kenchington 1992).

Polar Ocean Ecosystems

The economic value of ecotourism in the coastal marine environment is not limited to tropical countries with coral reefs. Coastal marine environments in high latitudes are characterized by ecosystems in which the top carnivores, charismatic seabirds and marine mammals, are abundant. The economic value of tourism to regions like Alaska is immense. Some of this is a reflection of the geological vistas, including glaciers and other inanimate components of the coastal ecosystem. However, much is related to the provision of ready opportunity to view puffins, auklets, murres, seals, otters, sea lions, killer whales, and other beloved marine wildlife. The significance of abundant wildlife and a relatively pristine ecosystem to the ecotourism of such polar regions as Alaska is reflected in economic studies of the impacts of the *Exxon Valdez* oil spill: in 1989, the revenues from visitors coming to Alaska fell 8 percent in south-central and 35 percent in southwest Alaska below the previous summer (McDowell Group 1990), which represented a $19 million loss in visitor spending. (This is an underestimate because it ignores expected increases in tourism.) Ecotourism organized to exhibit polar wildlife and coastal ecosystems is also a rapidly growing economic enterprise in New Zealand, where tours progress southward to Antarctica.

Estuarine Ecosystems

A third type of coastal marine environment that deserves special mention for its value in supporting ecotourism is the estuary, with its tidal flats, wetlands, marshes, and mangroves. Estimates of the value of the local economy of coastal wetlands through aggregate provision of recreational opportunities, fish production, storm protection, and water treatment range from $800 to $9,000 per acre (Anderson and Rockel 1991, Kirby 1993). This habitat with its high primary productivity sustains large populations of attractive and readily viewed shorebirds and waterbirds. When they can be viewed in a natural setting of lush coastal vegetation, the probing shorebirds, ducks, flamingoes, herons, egrets, gulls, and terns of this coastal marine ecosystem represent an important natural asset underlying substantial coastal tourism industries worldwide. Some specific estuarine systems come immediately to mind as the most important examples, including Kakadu in the Northern Territory of Australia, the coast of Namibia, the Everglades in Florida, and the Copper River Delta in Alaska. While these may be the most spectacular illustrations of the value of coastal estuarine ecosystem services to the tourism industry, similar economic contributions also exist in other regions with more diversified economies. Because of competing demands within the coastal region, where human population is most concentrated, and because most of those competing uses are incompatible with sustaining populations of the birds and wildlife of the estuary, proper planning in this environment needs to evaluate and consider the value of services derived from the naturally functioning ecosystem. Economically valuable tourism industries could be lost if newly permitted uses disrupted the ecosystem services on which the tourism depends.

Local Tourism, Recreation, and Retirement

Our discussion of the value of marine ecosystem services to tourism has been focused until now on ecotourism. Ecotourism represents just one part of the total contribution of naturally functioning coastal ecosystems to coastal tourism industries. Local tourism is a mainstay of many coastal economies in developed countries worldwide, and one of the important amenities that helps value one tourist destination more highly than another is the availability of various, usually nonconsumptive, uses of natural coastal marine ecosystems. Many coastal tourists look for opportunities to go sport-fishing, bird watching, or whale watching, to practice nature photography, or simply to enjoy immersion in an undegraded coastal setting. Each of these opportunities depends on sustaining function of the coastal marine ecosystem and provision of its services.

The ocean ecosystems offer other important recreational activities to tourists and residents beyond those associated with observing and enjoying local plants and animals. People extract satisfaction from water sports and activities, such as sailing, surfing, boating, and swimming in the sea. These recreational activities are also services provided by marine ecosystems from which people derive satisfaction, and they therefore have utilitarian value to tourists and residents that could be quantified. This class of ecosystem services depends largely on the abiotic components of the marine ecosystem, namely presence of a fluid surface. One could reasonably ask whether an ocean devoid of life might not continue to provide this class of services to human society. The answer is that the satisfaction derived by the majority of participants in these recreational activities is dependent on the total quality of the experience and would be diminished in the absence of graceful pelicans and dolphins or in the presence of waters characterized by foul odor, obvious discoloration, or noxious organisms like stinging jellyfish. Thus there is a biotic contribution even to this class of recreational services offered by marine ecosystems, such that policy that affects the structure and function of ocean ecosystems has potential impact on the value of those services that take advantage of the physics of the ocean service.

Ocean Ecosystem Services

The nonconsumptive (or passive use) value of a naturally functioning ecosystem can be translated in monetary value by contingent valuation analysis. When applied to valuation of natural resource damages, this approach utilizes a random survey approach to sample people's willingness to pay to prevent ecological harm of a certain sort or alternatively willingness to accept compensation for that injury to the natural ecosystem. This approach was used to construct a conservative estimate of the passive non-use value of the damages done to the marine ecosystem by the *Exxon Valdez* oil spill (Carson et al. 1994). The estimate is extremely conservative because each time a choice had to be made, the more conservative option was selected. For example, the degree of ecological damage was intentionally understated in the survey document. Survey respondents were told that ecological damages were restricted to a loss of 75–150,000 out of 1.5 million seabirds and 580 sea otters and 100 harbor seals. They were also told that these populations would return to normal within three to five years at most and that no other long-term damage would occur to the ecosystem. Furthermore, willingness to pay was used as the measure, which is typically lower than willingness to accept estimates (Hanemann 1991). The survey included only people who resided outside of Alaska, thereby involving negligible contributions from those who included any consumptive or nonconsumptive uses in their responses. Under these conditions, the median household willingness to pay to avoid another similar injury to the marine ecosystem of the Prince William Sound region of central Alaska was $31, which expands to a value of $2.8 billion summing over all households in the United States (Carson et al. 1994). This analysis does not represent valuation of the entirety of the passive non-use value of this one ecosystem, but rather just the loss of marginal value associated with the oil spill, yet the number is large. In addition, this reflects only one type of economic importance placed by the public on naturally functioning marine ecosystems, namely the existence value, ignoring all the provision of goods and other use values of the ecosystem.

The specific economic enterprises relying on tourism in the coastal regions are extensive. The tour operators represent only the tip of the iceberg of the financial value of tourism. Indeed, one method to placing a value on the economic contribution of tourism from ecosystem services is to sum the multitude of travel costs incurred by people to participate in these tourism opportunities. Tourism contributes to the transportation industry, including airlines, rails, buses, boat transport, and automobile support services. The lodging industry benefits directly and massively from tourism on the coast. This includes not only hotels and motels, but also condominiums and private rental housing. Tourists spend money on meals, supplies, and recreational equipment while visiting. The infusion of new money into a local coastal economy from tourists has cascading indirect economic benefits as those funds support jobs, investment, and other services in the local region.

Coastal Real Estate Development and Land Valuation

The quantity and quality of amenities provided by the coastal marine ecosystem also has impacts on coastal property values. Localities in demand as tourist destinations and residential areas providing attractive recreational opportunities experience heightened demand for and thus valuation of real estate. For example, comparisons of land values before and after implementation of Maryland's Chesapeake Bay Critical Area and New Jersey's Pinelands regulations revealed increases of 5–17 percent for developed and 5–25 percent for undeveloped land within the protected area (Beaton 1988). In developed and some developing countries, appeal to a highly mobile and discriminating population of retirees has great potential for dictating coastal property values. Such demographic movements have transformed South Florida and contributed immensely to its economy. For example, total economic activity in the marine recreational boating industry in Florida increased by 80 percent between 1980 and 1985 (Milton and Adams 1987). To the degree that demand for such coastal real estate is based upon amenities made available by the local marine ecosystem, this process contains intrinsic contradictions. Too many people in a coastal region can degrade the local environment and prevent the local marine ecosystem from continuing to provide the services that helped attract people initially. Consequently, recognition of the dependence of the existing local economy of a region on provision of ecosystem services is vitally important so that growth management can be used to prevent loss of the supporting ecosystem services in the future.

Cultural Value and Future Scientific Values

While difficult to quantify except perhaps by some form of contingent valuation procedures, marine ecosystems have cultural value in the present and potential for realization of scientific value to society in the future. For many groups of native peoples in industrialized countries, there is explicit legal acknowledgment of their rights to a healthy and productive natural ecosystem. For example, the various Native American cultures in Alaska, including Aleutic, Eskimo, and other native peoples, possess a traditional culture that is intrinsically dependent upon the natural ecosystem, including the marine realm. A long tradition of subsistence is based on the use of goods derived from the marine ecosystem that are extracted by the taking of plants and animals for food, clothing, shelter, fuel, medicines, and other purposes. But in addition to the provision of material goods, the natural ecosystem provides the basis of culture in these societies. The transmission of cultural information about the habits of marine animals and about the ecosystem processes that organize nature forms a centerpiece of traditional society and culture for these and many other native peoples. The natural world and the integrity of natural ecosystems also form an explicit or implicit part of the religious beliefs and cultural heritage of essentially all human religions and cultures. Such values need recognition.

One component of the wealth of society is the body of scientific knowledge that society has accumulated and that supports numerous advances in the human condition. These achievements include, of course, medical discoveries, but also improved basic understanding of the functioning of the natural ecosystems that enable technological progress to occur. Such scientific advances are achievable through exploitation of opportunity that resides in the undiscovered information contained in natural ecosystems. In a real sense, the natural ecosystem is a repository of information, a capital resource that when tapped in the future will create economic wealth and improve the welfare of human society. Although the scope and application of future scientific discoveries are impossible to predict, it is clear that failure to preserve this information bank that is the natural ecosystem represents irretrievable loss of natural capital that would generate tangible future economic value.

Lest we become transfixed by the task of placing economic value on natural ecosystems, we must recognize that the most compelling basis for the preservation of our natural heritage is still probably ethical. Preservation of species, maintenance of biodiversity, and sustaining of natural processes feels morally right. Passing on the legacy of nature to future generations should motivate most conservative actions. In this chapter, however, we have illustrated ways in which natural ocean ecosystems also contribute directly and indirectly to aspects of human enterprise that have economic value. We hope that by explicitly identifying some of the most economically important of these ocean ecosystem services, we can stimulate inclusion of their contributions to human enterprise in future benefit-cost analyses. Such economic analyses represent but one of several inputs to development of environmental policy.

Conclusions

Consideration of how ocean ecosystems provide economic benefit to human society always includes the value of fisheries production but rarely reflects complete analysis of other important services provided by ocean ecosystems. The oceans play a critical role in the global materials cycling that sustains climate and life support systems on land. In the absence of ocean biota, for example, the biological pump that injects carbonates into sediments would cease and atmospheric carbon would increase in the form of greenhouse gas CO_2, with dramatic disruptions to human society from resultant climate change and sea level rise. In combination with rivers and estuaries, ocean ecosystems serve to process, transform, detoxify, and sequester many of society's waste products. For example, if the nutrient removal from sewage wastewater now conducted by aquatic ecosystems and wetland processes were to be achieved through engineering, costs of treatment would increase tremendously. Abuse of the nutrient scrubbing service of aquatic ecosystems has a cost, however, in that nutrient overloading creates eutrophication and disrupts provision of natural ecosystem services by removing oxygen, causing fish kills, and inducing toxic algal blooms.

In addition to these geochemical functions of oceans, ocean ecosystems act to sustain valuable human business enterprises. Tourism has been identified as the world's largest business, and in coastal regions much of that tourism depends on amenities and values provided by ocean ecosystems. The beauty of the diverse and colorful coral reef animals in the tropics; the majesty of the killer whales, the penguins and puffins, and other abundant marine mammals and seabirds in polar oceans; and the profusion of wonderful waterbirds nested within a backdrop of greenery in coastal wetlands worldwide support exceptionally valuable ecotourism industries. Provision of opportunities to use and enjoy the coastal marine ecosystems contributes substantially to the value of local tourism, recreation, and retirement industries. Coastal land valuation is enhanced by preservation of natural functions of ocean ecosystems.

Traditional economic analysis does not readily quantify many of the more important human societal values vested in naturally functioning marine ecosystems. The natural ocean ecosystem forms the cultural core of several indigenous human societies and is important to the religious beliefs of many. The ocean ecosystem can also be viewed as a capital resource containing opportunity for future scientific discovery that will enhance the wealth and welfare of human society. Successful resolution of policy questions involving intergenerational equity and avoiding the trap of sacrificing long-term sustainability to avoid short-term costs is needed to ensure perpetual transmission of the legacy of value in nature. Despite a focus on economic valuation, the ethical arguments for conservation of ocean ecosystems should not be overlooked: for most people, conservation represents the right thing to do, and satisfying that moral imperative has value too.

References

Anderson, R., and M. Rockel. 1991. "Economic valuation of wetlands." Discussion paper #065. American Petroleum Institute, Washington, D.C.

Beaton, W. 1988. *The Cost of Government Regulations*, vol. 2. *A Baseline Study of the Chesapeake Bay Critical Area.* Chesapeake Bay Critical Area Commission, Annapolis, Md.

Beekhuis, J. V. 1981. "Tourism in the Caribbean: Impacts on the economic, social, and natural environments." *Ambio* 10: 325–331.

Berner, R. A., A. C. Lasaga, and R. M. Garrels. 1983. "The carbonate-silicate geochemical cycle and its effect on atmospheric carbon dioxide over the past 100 million years." *American Journal of Science* 283: 641–683.

Carpenter, S. R., S. W. Chisholm, C. J. Krebs, D. W. Schindler, and R. F. Wright. 1995. "Ecosystem experiments." *Science* 269: 324–327.

Carson, R. T., R. C. Mitchell, W. M. Hanemann, R. J. Kopp, S. Presser, and P. A. Raud. 1994. "Contingent valuation study of lost passive use:

Damages from the *Exxon Valdez* oil spill." Discussion paper 94–18. Resources for the Future, Washington, D.C.

Cerniglia, C. E., and M. A. Heitcamp. 1989. "Microbial degradation of PAH in the aquatic environment." In U. Varanasi, ed., *Metabolism of Polycyclic Aromatic Hydrocarbons in the Aquatic Environment.* CRC Press, Boca Raton, Fla.

Colborn, T. 1995. "Environmental estrogens: Health implications for humans and wildlife." *Environmental Health Perspectives* 103 (Supplement 7): 135–136.

Cosper, E. M., V. M. Bricelj, and E. J. Carpenter, eds. 1989. *Novel Phytoplankton Blooms: Coastal Marine Studies.* Springer-Verlag, Berlin.

Cross, F. A., and W. G. Sunda. 1978. "Relationship between bioavailability of trace metals and geochemical processes in estuaries." In M. L. Wiley, ed., *Estuarine Interactions.* New York: Academic Press, 1978.

Dame, R. F. 1994. "The role of bivalve filter feeder material fluxes in estuarine ecosystems." In *Bivalve Filter Feeders in Estuarine Processes,* pp. 245–269. NATO ASI Series V.G33. Springer-Verlag, Heidelberg.

D'Elia, C. F., R. W. Buddemeier, and S. V. Smith, eds. 1991. Workshop on Coral Bleaching, Coral Reef Ecosystems and Global Change: *Report of Proceedings.* Maryland Sea Grant College.

Ehrlich, P. R., and Ehrlich, A. H. 1992. "The value of biodiversity." *Ambio* 21: 219–226.

Elmgren, R. 1989. "Man's impact on the ecosystem of the Baltic Sea: Energy flows today and at the turn of the century." *Environmental Science and Technology* 9: 635–638.

EPA (Environmental Protection Agency). 1995. *1996 Clean Water Needs Survey Manual.* U.S. Environmental Protection Agency, Washington, D.C.

Fairweather, P. 1993. "Links between ecology and ecophysiology, ethics and the requirements of environmental management." *Australian Journal of Ecology* 18: 3–20.

Fischer, A. G. 1984. "The two phanerozoic supercycles." In W. A. Berggren and J. A. Van Couvering, eds., *Catastrophes and Earth History.* Princeton University Press, Princeton, N.J.

Gleason, D. F., and G. M. Wellington. 1993. "Ultraviolet radiation and coral bleaching." *Nature* 365: 836–838.

Glynn, P.W. 1991. "Coral reef bleaching in the 1980s and possible connections with global warming." *TREE* 6: 175–178.

Gren, I.M., C. Folke, K. Turner, and I. Bateman. 1994. "Primary and secondary values of wetland ecosystems." *Environmental and Resource Economics* 4: 55–74.

Hanemann, W. M. 1991. "Willingness to pay and willingness to accept: How much can they differ?" *American Economic Review* 81: 635–647.

Hardin, G. 1968. "The tragedy of the commons." *Science* 162: 1243–1248.

Hughes, T. P. 1994. "Catastrophes, phase shifts, and large-scale degradation of a Caribbean coral reef." *Science* 1547–1551.

Hughes, T. P., D. Ayer, and J. H. Connell. 1992. "The evolutionary ecology of corals." *TREE* 7: 292–295.

Kelleher, G., and R. Kenchington. 1992. *Guidelines for Establishing Marine Protected Areas.* IUCN, The World Conservation Union, Gland, Switzerland.

Kirby, K. 1993. "Wetlands not wastelands." *Scenic America Technical Information Series* 1(5): 1–8.

Lenihan, H.S., and C.H. Peterson. 1996. "How the interaction between reef habitat degradation and water quality decline induces oyster loss." *Ecology.* In review.

Long, E. R., and L. G. Morgan. 1990. *The Potential for Biological Effects of Sediment-Sorbed Contaminants Tested in the National Status and Trends Program.* National Oceanographic and Atmospheric Administration Technical Memo NOS OMA 52, NOAA, Seattle, Washington.

Ludwig, D., R. Hilborn, and C. Walters. 1993. "Uncertainty, resource exploitation, and conservation: Lessons from history." *Science* 260: 17, 36.

Malone, T.C., W. Boynton, T. Horton, and C. Stevenson. 1993. "Nutrient loadings to surface waters: Chesapeake Bay case study." In *Keeping Pace with Science and Engineering. Case Studies in Environmental Regulation,* M. R. Uman, ed., pp. 8–38. National Academy Press, Washington, D.C.

McDowell Group. 1990. *An Assessment of the Impact of the Exxon Valdez Oil Spill on the Alaskan Tourism Industry. Phase I: Initial Assessment.* Exxon Valdez Oil Spill Trustees, Anchorage, Alaska.

Miller, M. L., and J. Auyong. 1991. "Coastal zone tourism. A potent force affecting environment and society." *Marine Policy* 15: 75–99.

Milton, J. W., and C. M. Adams. 1987. "The economic impact of Florida's recreational boating industry in 1985." Technical paper no. 50. Florida Seagrant Program, Gainesville, Fla.

Newell, R. I. E. 1988. Ecological changes in Chesapeake Bay: Are they the result of overharvesting the American oyster, *Crassostrea virginica?* In *Understanding the Estuary: Advances in Chesapeake Bay Research,* pp. 536–566. Chesapeake Bay Research Consortium, Baltimore, Md.

Nixon, S. W. 1995. "Coastal marine eutrophication: A definition, social causes, and future concerns." *Ophelia* 41: 199–219.

NRC (National Research Council). 1983. *Changing Climate, Report of the Carbon Dioxide Assessment Committee.* National Academy Press, Washington, D.C.

NRC. 1987. *Responding to Changes in Sealevel: Engineering Implications.* National Academy Press, Washington, D.C.

NRC. 1993. *Managing Wastewater in Coastal Urban Areas.* National Academy Press, Washington, D.C.

Paerl, H.W. 1988. "Nuisance phytoplankton blooms in coastal, estuarine and inland waters." *Limnology and Oceanography* 33: 823–847.

Paerl, H.W. 1993. "Emerging role of atmospheric nitrogen deposition in coastal eutrophication: Biogeochemical and trophic perspectives." *Canadian Journal of Fisheries and Aquatic Science* 50: 2254–2269.

Perrings, C. 1991. "Reserved rationality and the precautionary principle: Technical change, time, and uncertainty in environmental decision making." In

Ecological Economics: The Science and Management of Sustainability, R. Costanza, ed. Columbia University Press, New York.

Roberts, C. M. 1993. "Coral reefs: Health, hazards, and history." *TREE* 8: 425–427.

Rothschild, B. J., J. S. Ault, P. Golletquer, and M. Heral. 1994. "Decline in Chesapeake Bay oyster populations: A century of habitat destruction and overfishing." *Marine Ecology Progress Series* 111: 29–39.

Sarmiento, J. L., R. Murnane, and C. LeQuere. 1995. "Air-sea CO_2 transfer and the carbon budget of the North Atlantic." *Phil. Trans. R. Soc. Lond. B.* 348: 211–219.

Smayda, T.J. 1990. "Novel and nuisance phytoplankton blooms in the sea: Evidence for a global epidemic." In E. Graneli, B. Sundstrum, L. Edler, and D. M. Anderson, eds., *Toxic Marine Phytoplankton,* pp. 29–40. Elsevier, Amsterdam.

18

Environmentally Sustainable Business Practices

Business for Social Responsibility (BSR)

An essential ingredient in seeking, developing, and applying environmentally sustainable solutions is the private sector. From small family firms to multinational corporations, businesses have a major role to play in setting development on a sustainable path. Numerous ones, in fact, have already begun to assume this responsibility. These businesses have decided that the role of the private sector in society is not simply to create value and profits, but also to perform as model citizens in the local and global community. The results of early research indicate that sustainable business practices have a significantly positive effect on the bottom line and that in most cases environmentally responsible corporate policy enhances a firm's operations in many ways.

One of the leaders in the corporate social responsibility movement is Business for Social Responsibility (BSR), an association of private firms that are serious about environmental sustainability and about providing assistance to corporate peers who likewise seek a new environmental role for their companies. We reproduce here material that is available on the BSR Website and that defines and describes various aspects of corporate social responsibility, giving examples of firms that have seen new practices influence their operations in positive ways.

Business for Social Responsibility is a global partner for responsible business leaders. Since 1992, BSR has helped companies of all sizes and sectors to achieve their objectives and efficiencies in ways that demonstrate respect for ethical values, people, communities, and the environment.

As global awareness and concern about the long-term health of the world's environment increase, some stakeholders and business leaders have begun to call on the business community to play a major role in moving the global

From Business for Social Responsibility (BSR), "Environmentally Sustainable Business Practices," BSR Website (www.bsr.org). Reprinted by permission of Business for Social Responsibility.

economy toward "sustainability." The most widely recognized definition of sustainability comes out of the 1987 Brundtland Report of the UN World Commission on Environment and Development, which defines sustainability as "meeting the needs of the present without compromising the ability of future generations to meet their needs."

Sustainability in the business context represents a progression beyond environmental regulatory compliance, eco-efficiency efforts such as energy efficiency and pollution prevention, and environmental risk management to a business model that gauges performance by a "triple bottom line" of environment, economy and equity. This new model, also known as the "three E's" of sustainability, measures the performance of businesses as they seek to improve economic efficiency, protect and restore ecological systems and enhance the well-being of people. If sustainability is to be achieved, business as usual will no longer be an option for government, private enterprises, communities or individuals. Becoming a sustainable business requires fundamental changes not only in product design, production and distribution, but also in corporate philosophy and marketing strategies. Few, if any, companies are currently considered sustainable. However, some companies are taking a leadership role in adopting more sustainable business practices.

Awareness of the business value of sustainability practices is growing. Whereas specific components of sustainability—eco-efficiency (doing more with less), pollution prevention, energy efficiency, and waste reduction—are seen by companies as providing "bottom line" cost savings, sustainability is also viewed as having the potential to expand the "top line," through the creation of new products, enhanced market share, asset retention, and other means of value-creation.

The following are examples of how sustainability initiatives create value for companies:

Access to Capital: Sustainability is increasingly viewed as proactive risk management, making companies with sustainability policies more attractive to investors and financiers. A study by a consortium of seven companies—Imperial Chemical Industries, Volvo, Unilever, Monsanto, Deutsche Bank, Electrolux, and Gerling—showed that sustainability strategies such as improving environmental compliance and developing environmentally responsible products can improve profitability and earnings per share, and help win contracts and investment approval.

Asset Retention: Extending the productivity of resources is becoming a strategic business practice across diverse industry sectors. Companies such as Xerox, Dell Computer and Interface Flooring have developed products that are leased rather than sold to customers, enabling the companies to retain much of the products' value.

Brand Image: The marketplace is becoming more environmentally sophisticated. Appealing to the ecological and social as well as economic sensibility of consumers can increase customer loyalty. Since 1990, McDonald's has enhanced its brand image by buying recycled products worth $3 billion without paying a price premium or otherwise increasing costs.

Competitive Advantage: Establishing policies to improve environmental performance beyond compliance with current regulations can help companies gain advantage over the competition. In Connecticut, a new state law rewards companies for having ISO 14001 environmental management certification and for adopting sustainability standards such as the CERES Principles or The Natural Step. The state's program includes incentives such as an expedited review of permit applications and public recognition of participating businesses through the use of an exclusive symbol or seal. Internationally, some companies in developing countries are recognizing that sustainability may give them a competitive advantage in the global economy. Bangladesh's leading industrial company, Beximco, has integrated high environmental standards into its operations and perceives social and environmental sustainability as the key to dominating the global market in yarns, fabrics and apparel.

Employee Relations: Employees appreciate a work environment that reflects their own values. Because of this, some companies have found that sustainability initiatives have helped attract and retain talented and committed employees.

Innovation: Applying sustainability principles to the design and manufacture of products has helped several leadership companies bring entirely new product lines to market. DuPont, Herman Miller and Patagonia are among those that have spurred innovation both inside their own companies and with their suppliers by applying environmental principles to product design and development.

Market Share and Profit Margins: Promoting the environmental superiority of products can be an excellent marketing strategy. Collins & Aikman Floorcoverings has experienced increased demand after offering a closed-loop recycled carpet (the company reclaims carpet for recycling back into new carpet) that, at no additional cost, meets or exceeds the performance criteria of its non-recycled counterparts. Electrolux reported that its most environmentally sound product lines accounted for 21 percent of its total European sales and 31 percent of its profits in 1999.

Productivity: Sustainable buildings—designed to minimize environmental impacts, be cost-effective to build and operate, and provide a comfortable working environment—can mean a healthier, happier and more productive work force. Boeing is among several companies that have documented significant increases in productivity, ranging from one percent to 15 percent, from the use of "green building" design elements.

Return on Investment (ROI): Taking a longer (5–10 year) rather than shorter approach to the financial assessment of capital investments can result in decisions that yield greater returns-on-investment over the life cycle of the venture. Dow Chemical's environmental initiatives are expected to yield a 30 percent to 40 percent ROI by the year 2005 and contribute to one percent of the company's revenues over 10 years.

Quality: Incorporating environmental considerations can lead to superior products. 3M's Scotchtint window film, designed to increase the energy efficiency of buildings, not only reduces overall electricity costs but also is a higher quality product than other window films. Its abrasion-resistant composition allows windows to better withstand washing and day-to-day abuse. Because the windows are more durable, replacement costs over the life-cycle of a building are minimized. Additionally, Scotchtint films block a high percentage of the sun's harmful ultraviolet (UV) radiation, thus improving protection for carpets, curtains and other furnishings, and extending their life spans.

The growth of corporate environmental initiatives stems from a wide range of internal and external forces confronting companies. They include:

Increased Visibility of Environmental Issues: Some high-profile environmental issues have propelled companies to act more swiftly. For example: Public concern about potential environmental or health impacts related to genetically modified crops has led to global negotiations to regulate trade and labeling of these products, and is propelling food and agricultural companies to reexamine their business strategies. Climate change, or global warming, which variously has been experienced in many parts of the world in the form of hotter, colder, dryer or wetter weather, has increased pressure on companies to dramatically increase energy efficiency. Media and consumer attention on controversial chemicals in consumer goods has contributed to the redesign of some products. For example, concern about phthalates, a common plastic additive used in some children's toys and other products, prompted Mattel to contract with materials developers to develop organic alternatives, which it hopes to introduce in its product line by 2001. Pressure from environmentalists and increased awareness about the environmental impacts are encouraging corporate buyers to scrutinize their wood and paper suppliers. Home Depot, for example, plans to eliminate the sale of wood products from old-growth forests by the end of 2002 and to give preference to wood that is certified to come from sustainably managed forests.

Increased Calls for Disclosure: Companies are experiencing growing demands from a variety of fronts to disclose their environmental performance. In the United States, a series of "right-to-know" laws has made a vast amount of information available to the public. Increasingly, such information is being published on the Internet, allowing customers, competitors, communities and others to know about the toxic emissions of thousands of companies on a facility-by-facility basis. Investors, too, are seeking greater disclosure. Many large, institutional investors are using environmental "screens" to target companies with the most proactive environmental records. Many companies are responding to these calls for disclosure by issuing reports that provide details of their environmental performance and by hiring outside auditors to verify the data in the reports.

Socially Responsible Investing and Shareholder Activism: Assets managed by socially responsible investment funds now exceed $2 trillion, according to the *Green Money Journal*, linking almost one in eight dollars under management in the U.S. with screened portfolios, shareholder advocacy and community investing. In 1999, the Dow Jones Indexes and Switzerland's SAM Sustainability Group launched the Dow Jones Sustainability Group Index, a new set of indices that targets increasing investor interest in companies committed to corporate sustainability. The index includes more than 200 of the world's leading companies with positive environmental records. In addition to socially responsible investing, increasing shareholder activism is leading to dialogues with corporate management about environmental responsibilities and to proxy resolutions on corporate behavior. Recently, shareholder activism has pressured companies to eliminate the use of wood products from endangered forests, to include proxy proposals on genetically modified food, and to invest in renewable energy sources.

Increased Standards and Incentives: In recent years, a number of nonregulatory standards and initiatives have helped companies to expand their environmental efforts. National and local government agencies, seeking to reduce the costs and burdens associated with keeping companies in compliance, have launched a variety of programs to encourage companies to go beyond compliance, sometimes in exchange for less regulatory oversight. Some industry standards now transcend national boundaries, affecting companies wherever they do business. Multinational treaties—such as those resulting from the 1997 Kyoto summit on global warming and the 2000 Cartagena Protocol on Biosafety—also have encouraged companies to look beyond the environmental standards their governments currently require.

Extended Product Responsibility: Companies in Europe and, increasingly, elsewhere are being required to take life-cycle responsibility for their products. Known as "extended product responsibility" or "extended producer responsibility," such mandates have required companies to create product take-back initiatives. This has led to companies redesigning their products, or their products' delivery mechanisms, to make it easier to take back products and, having done that, capture these used products' value through recycling, refurbishing, reuse or other means. In Australia, a mobile telephone recycling program sponsored by the Australian Mobile Telecommunications Association is setting up collection points in 600 retail stores to take back phone batteries, handsets and accessories. The program costs will be funded by a voluntary levy on manufacturers based on phone sales.

Dematerialization: Companies are beginning to recognize the financial benefits of reducing the raw materials and energy that go into the manufacture, delivery and use of their products and the construction and operation of their facilities. In some cases, this simply means using fewer materials to make the same products. In others it means redesigning products so that components can be recaptured for reuse or recycling at the end of their useful lives, thereby reducing the virgin materials needed for the next generation of products.

Changing Supplier Relations: Many companies have come to understand that their environmental performance is directly linked to the performance of their suppliers. As a result, leadership companies have begun to look "upstream," to the nature of the products and services they buy. Some companies have imposed supplier codes of conduct and given hands-on support and other resources to help suppliers improve their performance. Many large companies are leveraging their buying clout to persuade suppliers to reduce or eliminate toxic chemicals that are contained in their products, or to include recycled content in their goods. DaimlerChrysler, for instance, is requiring that its suppliers include 30 percent recycled content in plastic parts and 35 percent recycled content in steel and iron parts by 2002. Companies also are asking suppliers to reduce or eliminate packaging or use packaging that can be re-used or returned. In some cases, companies are providing educational or training services to help suppliers learn about new products, technologies or management strategies that will directly lead to greater environmental improvement.

Greening of the Service Sector: Traditionally, most environmental scrutiny of companies has focused on the manufacturing sector, which includes companies with the greatest resource use and emissions. Increasingly, however, scrutiny is being leveled on the service sector, a wide swath of the economy that encompasses finance, insurance and real estate; wholesalers and retailers; transportation, utilities and communications. While these sectors typically lack the smokestacks and drainpipes of other industries, they can be significant consumers of resources and energy and can generate significant toxic waste and climate-change gases. Only a relative handful of service-sector companies have environmental policies and programs, though that is expected to increase rapidly due to increased scrutiny of this sector. Although evidence is still anecdotal, the Internet may help improve the environmental performance of the service sector. The Center for Energy and Climate Solutions reported that while the U.S. economy grew by about 4 percent a year in 1997 and 1998, energy consumption barely increased, in part due to the influence of the emerging digital economy. Retail store space and transportation, for example, have declined as on-line shopping becomes more popular.

Greening of Small Business: Another significant part of the economy being scrutinized is that of small and mid-sized enterprises (SMEs). In the United States, 98 percent of all companies have fewer than 100 employees. While many of these companies don't have significant environmental impacts, many others do, such as: machine shops, metal-finishing plants, chemical refiners, printers and auto repair facilities. Regulators, too, are looking at SMEs with increased interest, viewing them as small, but cumulatively large, sources of air and water emissions. As a result, a growing number of government and private-sector programs are targeting these companies, helping them reduce waste and emissions while improving their financial performance.

A growing number of companies, government agencies, academic institutions, nongovernmental organizations [NGOs] and advocacy groups are exploring what sustainability means in terms of business practices, global issues and societal values. As an emerging area of study and practice, sustainability is attracting increasing attention on a number of fronts. Many companies are publishing sustainability reports in addition to the traditional annual and environmental performance reports. These reports not only present companies' efforts to integrate the environmental and social equity aspects of sustainability in their business practices, but also demonstrate the increased business value linked to these efforts. In increasing numbers, businesses are forming partnerships with nongovernmental organizations in order to understand and create business opportunities from emerging sustainability issues. Environmental Defense, Rainforest Action Network and the World Wildlife Fund are three examples of organizations working with multinational companies on a variety of issues. Recent partnerships have focused on green product design, innovative carbon offset programs and sustainable harvests of forest and marine products. Some leadership companies are holding seminars and workshops on sustainability in order to educate employees and launch company-wide initiatives. More and more, business leaders recognize the importance of cross-sector education as a tool for creating a cohesive sustainability business plan.

Some business and policy leaders have begun to consider the impact of the digital revolution on the emerging trend toward sustainable business practices. In the U.K., a consortium of government agencies, companies and think tanks coordinated by Forum for the Future recently launched a new initiative to explore the social and environmental impacts of e-commerce. The consortium's goal is to create "an agenda for a sustainable digital economy," including recommendations for action. The project will look ahead to 2010 to predict the effects of e-commerce on key areas including energy use, transportation, planning and social equity. The Dow Jones Company and Switzerland-based SAM Sustainability Group have partnered to create a methodology for tracking the financial performance of leading companies committed to corporate sustainability principles. Nearly 230 companies are included in the Dow Jones Sustainability Group Indexes. Findings reveal that the sustainability-driven companies outperformed their conventional counterparts in the last half of the 1990s by approximately 5 percent, with an added risk factor of one percent. Companies are identified and ranked according to five corporate sustainability criteria: technology, governance, shareholder demands, and industrial and social considerations. In a related development, stock market analysts at Innovest Strategic Advisors studied twenty-six S&P 500 electric utility companies and found that companies with the highest environmental ratings achieved significantly better financial performance than companies with the lowest ratings. One key reason cited for such findings is that strong environmental performance is a reliable indicator of quality corporate management overall, which in turn is a major determinant of relative financial performance. The U.S. Environmental Protection Agency's (EPA) Office of Solid Waste has launched a new Website on Extended Product Responsibility (EPR)—a product-oriented approach to environmental protection. EPR is one of many strategies businesses are adopting for moving toward sustainable development. EPR, as defined by the EPA, places shared responsibility on government, consumers and all industry players in the product chain for all the environmental impacts of a product over its life cycle. Although there are currently no federal mandates for product responsibility comparable to existing or proposed European programs, the EPA is encouraging a range of voluntary EPR efforts that companies can undertake such as: corporate or industry-wide stewardship programs; leasing and "servicizing" programs (meeting customers' needs by providing a service rather than selling a product); life-cycle design and management; partnerships for recycling and waste management; and take-back or buy-back programs or initiatives.

Around the world, government agencies, nongovernmental organizations and businesses are collaborating on facilitating sustainable development. One of the goals of Expo 2000, the World's Fair located in Hannover, Germany, was to show how technology could be balanced with nature. The Expo's pavilions demonstrate sustainability strategies such as constructing buildings with recycled materials or powering them with wind turbines. In India, the United Nations Development Programme, the International Development Research Centre of Canada and the Indian Ministry of Environment and Forests have partnered to develop a Website that aims to advance sustainable development, promote good practices and strengthen the democratic process through a mechanism of information exchange between the government and research organizations, NGOs, businesses and the public.

Many prominent American publications are featuring articles on top environmental business leaders, the "greening" of the bottom line, and other components of sustainability. Publications such as *Business Week* and the *New York Times* have featured stories on the business value of beyond-compliance environmental initiatives such as re-manufacturing and product take-back programs. An in-depth article on "natural capitalism" appeared in a 1999 edition of the *Harvard Business Review*, written by sustainability and business experts Amory Lovins, L. Hunter Lovins and Paul Hawken. The

Atlantic Monthly published a piece by environmental architect William McDonough and scientist Michael Braungart on "eco-effectiveness" and the next industrial revolution.

A small but growing number of universities are offering MBA programs that incorporate environmental management and sustainability in their curricula and activities. And a few NGOs are working with universities to encourage and support these efforts. For example, the Business Environment Learning and Leadership (BELL) project of the World Resources Institute has been working with business schools since 1990 to introduce environmental issues in management into curricula and research. And the Initiative for Social Innovation through Business (ISIB), launched in 1998 as a policy program of the Aspen Institute, works with business educators and business schools to test new concepts about the role of business in society.

Laws and regulations from global, national, regional or local entities are the most obvious environmental standards. Many national and local governments also have set voluntary standards beyond their legal requirements. In some cases, companies that meet or exceed these standards are given less oversight by regulatory bodies. Additionally, some standards may apply to specific products or product categories through one of the many eco-labeling programs. And there are a wide range of environmental standards promulgated by trade associations, environmental organizations, international standard-setting groups and coalitions representing a variety of interests.

International Chamber of Commerce, Business Charter for Sustainable Development contains 16 principles of environmental responsibility, providing a structure for environmental management appropriate for enterprises of all sizes. The charter's message encourages continual improvement in environmental management and practice, measurement of progress, and reporting of this progress internally and externally. The principles encourage integration of environmental management from the highest level of companies to employees, suppliers, and other stakeholders.

International Organization for Standardization (ISO) 14000 is a series of voluntary guidelines designed to create uniform environmental standards among products, companies, industries and nations. Its purpose is to avoid trade barriers from conflicting national or regional environmental standards, as well as to provide an alternative to command-and-control regulation. ISO 14001 and 14004 govern the policies, procedures and organizational structure for a company's environmental management system. Additional standards address auditing (ISO 14010, 14011 and 14012) and environmental labeling (ISO 14024), while as of 2000, standards for life-cycle assessment (ISO 14040) and environmental performance evaluations (ISO 14031) remain under development.

European Community's Eco-Management and Audit Scheme (EMAS) is a site-based registration system designed for use throughout the European

Community. It requires an environmental policy to be in existence within a company, and that it be fully supported by senior management. Among its many provisions, the standard requires that a company's environmental policy be publicized in nontechnical language and that it provide a detailed overview of the company's activities on a given site. Other required disclosure includes quantifiable data on current emissions and environmental impacts from that site, including waste generation and energy and water usage.

The CERES Principles were created by a coalition of environmental groups, socially responsible investors and public pension administrators. The coalition uses shareholder resolutions to initiate discussions of environmental responsibility with companies with the goal of getting companies to endorse the CERES Principles. The ten principles cover protection of the biosphere, sustainable use of natural resources, reduction and disposal of wastes, energy conservation, risk reduction, safe products and services, environmental restoration, informing the public, management commitment, and audits and reports. CERES signatories are expected to publish publicly available annual statements disclosing their progress on meeting these 10 principles.

The Global Reporting Initiative (GRI) promotes international harmonization in the reporting of corporate environmental, social and economic performance information to enhance responsible decision-making. The GRI is convened by CERES and incorporates the active participation of corporations, nongovernmental organizations, international organizations, business associations, universities, and other stakeholders from around the world. GRI released its Sustainability Reporting Guidelines for comment and pilot testing in 1999, and expects to release the final version in 2000. The Guidelines are designed to create a globally accepted common framework for corporate sustainability reporting.

The Natural Step , a nonprofit environmental education organization with branches in several countries, established four scientifically based "systems conditions" that form a set of operating principles for companies and institutions. The systems conditions state that (1) nature cannot withstand a systematic build-up of dispersed material mined from the Earth's crust (e.g., minerals, oil, etc.); (2) nature cannot withstand a systematic build-up of persistent compounds made by humans; (3) nature cannot take a systematic deterioration of its capacity for renewal (e.g., harvesting fish faster than they can replenish); and (4) we must consider human enterprise as a whole by being efficient with regard to resource use and waste generation. Participating companies aren't expected to endorse the systems conditions so much as to engage in training programs that incorporate the principles. The principles can help companies comply with environmental management systems such as ISO 14001 and EMAS.

The Social Venture Network's Standards of Corporate Social Responsibility contains nine principles, addressing areas including ethics, financial returns and environmental protection. SVN is a network of business and social entrepreneurs dedicated to the proposition that business can be a potent force for solving social problems. SVN's Standards include an environmental protection principle that encourages businesses to promote sustainable development with products, processes, services, and other activities; to commit to minimizing the use of energy and natural resources and decreasing waste and harmful emissions; and to integrate these considerations into day-to-day management decisions.

Implementing environmental initiatives differs for each company, depending on a number of factors, including a company's sector, size and culture. Manufacturing-based companies confront a wide range of environmental challenges, while retail or service-sector companies face a smaller range. Larger companies typically have more resources to devote to environmental initiatives, and often have dedicated staff committed to this arena. Smaller firms may not have full-time environmental professionals. Although some companies address environmental issues one facility or department at a time, increasingly companies are integrating the environment into all parts of their operations. Whatever the nature of the commitment, most companies follow a similar series of steps when addressing their environmental impact.

Environmental Policy: Companies committed to reducing their environmental impact usually create a set of environmental principles and standards, often including formal goals. At minimum, most such statements express a company's intentions to respect the environment in the design, production and distribution of its products and services; commit the company to be in full compliance with all laws, and to go beyond compliance whenever possible; and establish an open-book policy whereby employees, community members and others can be informed of any potential adverse impacts the company might have on the environment. Environmental policy statements typically are endorsed by the company's CEO or owner, or by its board of directors.

Environmental Audit: Before a company attempts to reduce its environmental impact, it is important to first gain a full understanding of it. For most companies, this usually involves some kind of environmental audit. There is a wide range of audits, some simple, others quite complex. The goal of audits is to understand the type and amount of resources used by a company, product line or facility, and the types of waste and emissions generated. Some companies also try to quantify this data in monetary terms to understand the bottom-line impact. This also helps to set priorities for where a company can get the greatest return on its efforts.

Employee Involvement: Leadership companies recognize that to be effective, an environmental policy needs to be embraced by employees throughout the organization, not just those in an environmental function. To do that, companies engage in a variety of activities, especially education, to help employees understand the environmental impacts of their jobs and to support their efforts to make positive changes. Some companies go further, helping employees become more environmentally responsible throughout their daily lives, helping them build a true environmental ethic. Beyond education, many companies create incentives, rewards and recognition programs for employees who demonstrate their environmental commitment.

Toxics Reduction: At the heart of many companies' environmental commitments is the reduction or elimination of toxic chemicals throughout their operations. Many engage in pollution prevention, which seeks to reduce chemical waste and emissions by redesigning manufacturing processes that involve these chemicals and implementing safe disposal methods. Others are eliminating problematic chemicals by redesigning products or substituting nontoxic alternatives. Even nonmanufacturing companies are finding they can eliminate or reduce the use of toxics found in office machines, printing processes, cleaning materials, building products, office furnishings, or in the repair and maintenance of vehicles, among other things.

Energy Efficiency: Energy is another resource that environmentally responsible companies try not to waste. That is, they seek to ensure that every gallon, therm or kilowatt of energy they pay for is used as wisely as possible. Many companies conduct energy audits to assess their potential energy and financial savings from upgrading to more energy-efficient lighting or equipment. Others purchase "green" energy from renewable energy sources, promote telecommuting or the use of public transit by employees, purchase or lease fuel-efficient or alternative-fueled vehicles, and employ a variety of other energy-efficient management techniques.

Waste Minimization and Recycling: Leadership companies promote the idea that "waste" represents something that they bought but could not sell, and had to pay to get rid of—in other words, lost profit. Minimizing or eliminating waste involves a wide range of initiatives to ensure that materials are not used needlessly, and that all processes—from the front office to the loading dock to the shop floor—are examined for their potential to reduce trash sent to landfills. Many leadership companies have set ambitious "zero-waste" goals, meaning that they intend to virtually eliminate dumpsters and other trash receptacles, opting instead to ensure that everything is reused or recycled. This can involve avoiding wasteful products, donating surplus furnishings and equipment, renting equipment that is used only occasionally and disposing of waste materials through waste exchanges, among many other techniques.

Green Procurement: To help ensure that their products and processes are environmentally responsible, many companies are seeking to buy greener products and materials from their suppliers. This includes buying everything from recycled paper for office use to products or packaging that reduce waste but do not compromise costs, reliability or quality. Some companies participate in buyers' groups in which they leverage their collective buying clout to push suppliers to consider alternative products or processes.

Green Design: Green design applies to the design of both products and facilities:

Many leadership companies are designing and building environmentally conscious buildings in which the life-cycle costs—the total cost of building, owning and maintaining the structure—are equal to or lower than that of a conventional building. Techniques include incorporating daylight to reduce reliance on electric lighting, installing energy-efficient materials and equipment, and including performance-assurance language in building design/construction contracts to ensure that the building's environmental goals are met.

Green product design includes a variety of techniques and strategies, including reducing the raw materials that go into a product, increasing a product's recycled content, eliminating problematic ingredients, or creating a system to take back a product or its packaging for reuse, refurbishing or recycling at the end of its useful life. This includes designing products that can be easily upgraded, rather than replaced, when they become outmoded, or that can be easily disassembled for reuse or recycling.

Measuring Progress: Realizing that "what gets measured, gets addressed," many companies are committed to regularly measuring, evaluating and disclosing data about how well they're achieving their environmental goals. Increasingly, leadership companies are recognizing the need for reliable and scientifically sound information, are arranging for independent third-party auditors to verify their data, and are using corporate environmental reports or sustainability reports to communicate this information to internal and external stakeholders.

Community Involvement: Many companies, especially manufacturers, actively work with their communities on environmental issues. Some do this by inviting community leaders and the public into their facilities to see the environmental safeguards and to hear firsthand the company's commitment. Others send employees into the community to participate in any of a wide range of environmental projects, such as: setting up recycling programs, cleaning up streams or parks, refurbishing homes of those without the resources to do so themselves, talking to school groups, etc. Companies perceived by their neighbors to have potential environmental problems often set up community-involvement groups, bringing community leaders, citizens, activists and others together with company management and employees to openly share concerns and solve problems collaboratively.

Leadership Examples

These "leadership" practices have been chosen as illustrative examples in the area of corporate social responsibility addressed by this topic overview. They are intended to represent innovation, higher than average commitment, unusual industry practice or a comprehensive approach to this issue. . . .

IKEA adopted a systematic approach to its environmental policies starting in the early 1990s. After performing environmental audits to identify its areas of greatest impact, IKEA developed an environmental action plan, which includes environmental training for all IKEA coworkers. IKEA believes the best ambassadors for the environment are the coworkers who interact with customers face-to-face. IKEA also sees its suppliers as partners in meeting its environmental commitments. All IKEA suppliers are required to have an environmental policy, establish measurable targets for reducing environmental impacts, and develop a plan for meeting those targets. IKEA monitors suppliers' compliance with its environmental requirements by having them self-report progress, and by performing site visits and product testing to verify their claims. In addition, IKEA's buyers take training courses to learn more about the environmental impacts of the materials they specify. Because wood accounts for 75 percent of the material used in IKEA products, IKEA has committed not to use solid wood from intact natural forests unless they are certified to be sustainably harvested.

Fetzer Vineyards evaluates all business decisions based on a triple bottom line of economics, environment and social equity. Fetzer farms over 700 acres of organic wine grapes, but because the company currently grows less than 10 percent of the grapes it uses for its wines, it developed a training program to help its growers meet its increasing demand for organic grapes. From 1991 to 1999, Fetzer reduced its waste going into landfills by 93 percent, while from 1994 to 1999 their profits and revenues grew at a 15 [percent] annual compounded rate. The company is committed to using 100 percent organic grapes by 2010 and producing zero waste by 2009. Fetzer's environmental commitment extends to its buildings: its office building is constructed of rammed earth obtained from the building site, and the roof is made of recycled wood and steel. An onsite photovoltaic array supplies three-quarters of the building's energy needs, and all other power used by the winery is from renewable sources. The company's commitment to sustainability has established it as a leader in its industry and has encouraged other, larger wineries to meet or exceed what Fetzer has accomplished.

British Petroleum (BP): BP Amoco has committed to assessing its business activity against a "triple bottom line" that embraces economic prosperity, environmental protection and social equity. The company's business plans include measurable health, safety and environmental performance targets. The company has taken an aggressive stand on global climate change, pledging to reduce its emissions of greenhouse gases by 10 percent from a 1990 baseline over the period to 2010. Its CEO, John Browne, has been highly visible in making speeches on the topic. BP Amoco has launched an internal carbon-dioxide trading scheme among its numerous international divisions to help them meet targets for reducing emissions, and managers are evaluated on not only their financial performance but on how well they do at cutting emissions. The company is the world's largest solar energy producer and plans to achieve solar energy sales of $1 billion by 2007. The company is developing a low-sulfur gasoline as part of an effort to cut vehicle pollution and plans to completely convert its more than 14,000 U.S. gas stations to lower-sulfur fuel by 2004. BP Amoco makes its policies, speeches, practices and technology available to other companies that are addressing similar issues.

Nortel: The company's position as an environmental leader dates to late 1991 when it became the first global electronics company to eliminate ozone-depleting CFCs [chlorofluorocarbons] from its manufacturing process. Since then, Nortel has set quantitative targets for reducing its environmental impacts below 1993 levels by the year 2000. Between 1993 and 1998, the company made significant progress toward achieving these goals, including: a 28 percent reduction in total annual pollution releases (against a target reduction of 50 percent by 2000); a 21 percent reduction in solid waste sent to landfills (target 50 percent); a 33 percent reduction in paper purchases (target 30 percent); and a 29 percent reduction in energy consumption (target 10 percent). Nortel uses an Environmental Performance Index that integrates 25 performance parameters into a single numeric score that shows overall progress from year to year. The company is implementing a life-cycle management program to reduce its products' environmental impacts and is a leader in design-for-environment initiatives. For example, it eliminated 99.9 percent of the lead in its printed circuit boards to make the world's first lead-free telephone. Nortel actively supports telecommuting, realizing benefits including reduced requirements for land, raw materials and energy; increased employee satisfaction and productivity; and decreased automobile emissions.

United Parcel Service: As part of its commitment to reduce vehicle emissions while cutting operating costs, UPS operates the largest private fleet of compressed natural gas (CNG) vehicles in the U.S. In addition, UPS built California's largest public-access CNG fueling station, and shares this station with local school bus companies, area cities, and community groups to promote favorable environmental practices. UPS is in the process of testing hybrid electric vehicle technology, which offers the potential to provide higher fuel economy while reducing vehicle emissions and maintenance requirements. The company's search for environmentally friendly technologies led them to reduce aircraft noise pollution and boost fuel efficiency, making them the "quietest" major air carrier in North America, with 100 percent of their jet fleet meeting federal noise regulations three years before required by law. In an innovative partnership with the nonprofit Alliance for Environmental Innovation, UPS developed an action plan to dramatically reduce the amount of natural resources needed to make its packaging. It boosted the post-consumer recycled content of its letter envelopes to 80 percent, and introduced an overnight envelope designed to be used twice, resulting in a 50 percent reduction of source material. The packaging plan is saving the company an estimated $1.6 million annually and reducing shipping material waste by an average of 13 percent.

AB Electrolux: Influenced by The Natural Step, and one of the first companies on the market with chlorofluorocarbon (CFC)-free refrigerators, Electrolux has a proactive strategy to move ahead of environmental regulations in incorporating sustainability into its business plan. Two of the primary areas of concern for the company are global climate change and ozone depletion. To address these issues, Electrolux's product development strategy involves developing highly energy-efficient appliances, a near phase-out of all CFC and HCFC coolants and insulators, and the introduction of Freon-free products. Another area of concern for Electrolux is resource use. In response, the company has introduced pilot programs offering customers free take-back services, and continues to work toward recyclability of products and components, and refurbishment and resale of used products. In Sweden, Electrolux has partnered with an energy utility company to start a pilot program in which customers are offered a pay-per-wash option for their laundry needs, which allows them to pay for only the function of clean clothes rather than purchasing the appliance. Electrolux's environmental strategies are an integral component of the company's overall business plan and operations, and have led to improved profitability and greater shareholder value. In 1996 its most environmentally sound European "white goods" (major household appliances) product area accounted for 5 percent of sales and 8 percent of profits. By 1999, the corresponding figures were 21 percent of sales and 31 percent of profits.

Design Tex: Design Tex, a subsidiary of Steelcase Inc., manufactures textiles for commercial use. In developing its William McDonough Collection of upholstery textiles, the McDonough Braungart Sustainable Design Protocol trademark was used. Under this strict set of design principles and criteria, all components (including materials, chemicals and production processes) of the collection were analyzed to eliminate any characteristics problematic to human or ecological systems. The effectiveness of natural systems is used as a model. The product line contains eight upholstery styles that are fully compostable after their useful life, leaving behind no carcinogens, persistent toxic chemicals, heavy metals or other toxic substances. Thus the end product is intended to return to soil as nourishment for living organisms.

Interface, Inc.: In 1994, Interface Chairman and CEO Ray Anderson spearheaded a movement to turn the carpet manufacturer first into a sustainable corporation, and eventually a restorative operation that helps improve the environment. The company has made significant progress on its path toward sustainability. Modeled on the energy and matter cycles found in natural systems, the company's sustainability efforts can be broadly divided into seven major components: 1) zero waste; 2) benign emissions; 3) renewable energy; 4) closing the loop; 5) resource-efficient transportation; 6) sensitivity (stronger connections to the community, co-workers, suppliers and customers); and 7) the redesign of commerce (including a shift from selling products to providing services). Since 1994, Interface companies around the world have been reexamining their sources of waste and finding ways to reduce and finally eliminate them. For example, through changes to product construction and many small waste-reduction steps, Interface Flooring Systems saved 2.5 million pounds of nylon from being purchased. InterfaceAR eliminated more than 500 gallons of solvent waste a year by modifying the adhesive application process for one of its products, while doubling productivity. The company's Evergreen Lease program enables customers to lease flooring from the company, essentially buying the service of a carpet, and allowing Interface to take back old or damaged carpeting for recycling. Through its sustainability initiatives, the company has cumulatively taken $90 million out of their costs since 1994 by eliminating waste. Additionally, as Interface spreads its efforts across the spectrum of suppliers, customers, employees and other stakeholders, its role as a leadership company increasingly enhances its image.

S.C. Johnson & Son, Inc.: A family-owned and managed company for the past 112 years, S.C. Johnson's sustainability initiatives date back to 1935. It conducted the first sustainability audits on record to determine the ongoing availability of carnauba from Brazil, a key ingredient in the company's wax products at the time. In 1975, S.C. Johnson unilaterally and voluntarily eliminated CFCs from its aerosols worldwide and set higher industry standards which governments years later enacted into law. Responsible environmental management continues to be a focus of the company's operational directives. In 1990 the company formalized its environmental programs and established specific waste reduction and elimination targets and a five-year plan for achieving them. Within the ensuing five-year period, combined air, solid waste and water effluent from manufacturing operations were cut virtually in half, virgin packaging reduced by 28 percent and solvent use reduced by 15 percent. More stringent sustainability targets and refined metrics have been established to guide the company's environmental actions through the year 2000. Already the company has gained significant value from its investments in sustainability. Since 1992, by eliminating over 420 million pounds of waste from products and processes, the company has saved in excess of $125 million. S.C. Johnson's Sustainable Progress Report also reflects its active commitment to local and international communities behind a policy which ensures charitable giving of 5 percent pre-tax profits, four times that of the average of most corporate giving programs. To address the equity component of sustainability, the company's community initiatives range from developing strategies to incorporate environmental protection into economic policy in the Ukraine, to catalyze multi-stakeholder sustainable community decision-making systems in its headquarters city of Racine, Wisconsin, to programs to help African street children.

Stonyfield Farm, Inc.: One of the earliest sustainability initiatives undertaken by Stonyfield Farm, the fastest growing yogurt company in the U.S., was an energy audit and retrofit of its facilities, providing a rapid payback on the initial investment while reducing energy consumption. Analyzing product packaging for environmental impacts is an ongoing company effort and, in recent years, the company underwent two eco-audits, conducted by an independent firm, which examined environmental impacts of all of Stonyfield's activities. The company also engages its suppliers on a product-by-product basis to find the best environmental products and processes. One of Stonyfield's goals, as stated in its mission, is "to serve as a model that environmentally and socially responsible businesses can also be profitable." The company's market research showed that its environmental mission is an important reason why people buy its products; the current annual growth rate of 35 percent bears this out. Sustainability measures have had tangible results: energy savings and waste reductions directly save the company money. Stonyfield's carbon offset program has resulted in offsetting 100 percent of its carbon emissions from its facility energy use through a reforestation project in Oregon and other projects. The company has also written a guide for other businesses interested in decreasing their impact on climate change titled "Reversing Global Warming through Carbon Offsets." In 1998, the company began to base part of its profit-sharing on environmental performance. If energy use and solid waste generation can be reduced by 10 percent, the money saved will be turned over to shared bonuses.

19

Ngos and the Environment
From Knowledge to Action

Sheila Jasanoff

An increasingly important player in the field of developing and implementing sustainable solutions is the nongovernmental organization, or NGO. In this chapter, Sheila Jasanoff details three principal ways that NGOs can help advance sustainable solutions: they can serve as important critical voices to shake up accepted environmental knowledge and policy; they can play a major role in bringing knowledge into the realm of practice; and they are key to disseminating new information to the public and to policymakers. In addition, for many individuals concerned about environmental issues, involvement in the activities of NGOs provides a way to take direct action and thus contribute to eventual solutions.

Sheila Jasanoff is a professor of science and public policy at Harvard's John F. Kennedy School of Government, where her research program centers on the relationships among science, technology, law, and politics in democratic societies. She is particularly interested in the mechanisms by which scientific claims and ideas influence public decisions affecting health, safety, and the environment.

The place of non-governmental organisations (NGOs) in international governance seems nowhere more securely established than in the field of environmental action.[1] Within the United Nations system, NGOs have been recognised as essential contributors to environmental protection for well over a decade. The 1987 report of the World Commission on Environment and Development, *Our Common Future*, urged governments 'to recognise and extend NGOs' right to know, and have access to information on the environment and natural

From Sheila Jasanoff, "NGOs and the Environment: From Knowledge to Action," *Third World Quarterly: Journal of Emerging Areas* 18, no. 3 (September 1, 1997): 579–94. Table omitted. Reprinted by permission of Taylor & Francis Ltd. (www.tandf.co.uk/journals).

resources; their right to be consulted and to participate in decision making on activities likely to have a significant effect on the environment; and their right to legal remedies and redress when their health or environment may be seriously affected.'[2] The 1992 United Nations Conference on Environment and Development (UNCED), held in Rio de Janeiro, confirmed by numbers alone that NGOs had taken their place beside states and intergovernmental organisations (IGOS), in particular, those of the United Nations (UN) system, as rightful participants in environmental management. The Global Forum for NGOs held concurrently with the official Earth Summit drew representatives from some 7000 organisations, outnumbering governments present by about one hundred to one.[3] More importantly, the intense preparatory activity in the non-governmental sector leading up to and through the Rio conference showed that environmental NGOs had developed extensive skills in scientific and technical exchange, policy making and policy implementation, which supplemented their more traditional roles in campaigning, activism and ideological consciousness raising.[4]

Although the centrality of NGOS in environmental action cannot be doubted, systematic assessments of their role, especially in relation to other governing institutions, are scarce. In part, the explosive growth of environmental activism over the past few decades confounds analysis. The term 'NGO' can be applied in principle to an enormous range of environmental actors, from tiny, grassroots coalitions of conservationists or pollution victims to mature, well funded, technically expert multinational organisations possessing many of the characteristics of state bureaucracies, but without their political accountability.[5] Some of these groups coalesced from the start around environmental concerns, while others have incorporated environmental objectives into broader agendas of social development. Some NGOs, like Europe's staid nature conservancies, have been in action for more than a century, with practices shaped by culture, place and history; others, like the daringly entrepreneurial Greenpeace, have won a place at the international policy table after less than a quarter-century of world-wide environmental advocacy.[6] Major 'nongovernmental interest groups'[7]—political parties, labour unions, industries and trade associations—have spun off a host of specialised NGOS and NGO coalitions to deal with the environmental matters that specifically concern them.[8] Scientific societies and committees, including those established under international regimes, constitute still another class of environmental NGOs with strong claims to political neutrality. Together, these groups display a bewildering diversity of form, function, style and expertise, with missions ranging from research to litigation, from lobbying to community education, and from monitoring to natural resource protection. Clearly, environmental NGOS conform to no simple taxonomy;[9] arguably, the only structural feature they have in common is their formal independence from the state.[10]

Function, then, seems more promising than structure as a starting point for teasing apart the possible lines of collaboration between NGOs and IGOs in the environmental domain. At the heart of environmental decision making is an attempt to connect knowledge about the world (expressed often, but not only, as scientific knowledge) with actions designed to advance particular visions of natural and social well-being. It is this link between knowledge and action that provides environmental NGOs their primary point of political intervention. The proliferation of such groups in recent years can be seen in large measure as a challenge to the perceived shortcomings of governments and industry in acting on the world's growing repositories of environmental knowledge. How can NGOs most effectively fulfil their appointed role, and how in particular can their work usefully complement or extend that of IGOs?

NGO activity in building, or rebuilding, the knowledge-action link can take three major forms, each of which carries different opportunities for collaboration with IGOs. First, and perhaps most familiar, is the role of NGOs as critics of accepted frameworks of environmental knowledge and regulatory policy. The NGOs that most visibly serve this function in the international arena have usually established their credibility through technical expertise and apparent lack of economic interest. A less structured but no less significant role is played by the thousands upon thousands of grassroots organisations whose criticism of dominant scientific and policy frameworks is founded on long-standing experiences in resource management and local environmental knowledge.

A second way in which NGOs can influence the transition from knowledge to action is by creating more inclusive 'epistemic networks' around nationally or internationally defined environmental objectives.[11] Environmental policy networks are most often conceived in the literature as the work of like-minded technical and administrative elites.[12] In many areas of environmental protection, however, success is contingent on the willingness of ordinary citizens to accept the validity of official policy framings and to participate in their implementation. NGOs may be able to facilitate such consensual action because of their experience in integrating environmental concerns with other aspects of community life, such as development, rural poverty, rights of indigenous people, women's emancipation or children's welfare. The ability of environmental NGOs to bridge the lay-expert, activist-professional and local-global divides thus emerges as a particularly important resource in their co-operative arrangements with IGOs.

The third route by which NGOs can take part in the construction of effective knowledge-action links is through information dissemination and technology transfer. IGO-NGO collaboration with respect to such activities can help compensate for the lack of capacity in state institutions. NGO involvement in monitoring and enforcement, for example, is widely recognised as essential by students of international environmental regimes.[13] The three forms of NGO activity in constituting the knowledge-action link are discussed in depth below. A theme throughout is participation, which relates to questions about the accountability of environmental NGOs.

Criticism and Reframing

Science is one of the pillars on which modern environmentalism was founded; yet, paradoxically, scientific controversy has proved to be one of the most intractable problems confronting environmental policymakers. Since Rachel Carson's stirring call to action in *Silent Spring*,[14] NGOs have recognised that scientific knowledge is potentially one of their strongest allies—and sometimes an obdurate impediment—in the struggle to protect the environment. On issues as disparate as whaling, oil spills, ocean dumping of chemical or radioactive wastes, the safety of nuclear power, river-valley development or climate change, disputes among environmentalists, industry and frequently the state have centred on different assessments of the probability and magnitude of adverse environmental effects. In such exchanges, NGOs may usefully open up the debate either by questioning prevailing expert opinion or by expanding the available information base with relevant bodies of local knowledge.

Questioning the Boundaries

Although science is environmentalism's favourite battleground, decades of research on environmental controversies indicate that clashes over science are often the surface manifestation of deeper political or cultural commitments that predispose actors to downplay some sources of uncertainty about nature and to emphasise others.[15] The framing of environmental problems, in other words, incorporates more basic social and political as well as scientific judgements.[16] In turn, conflicts that are ostensibly about scientific facts turn out on closer inspection to reflect underlying differences in the framing of the problem— around its causes, severity, boundaries, distribution and possible solutions—by opposing interests. Standing outside the peripheries of official, usually state-sponsored, knowledge production, NGOs are particularly well-situated to observe the limitations of dominant expert framings, to question unexplained assumptions, to expose tacit value choices, and to offer alternative interpretations of ambiguous data.

Scientific experts frequently protect their authority to deal with uncertain science through a sociological mechanism known as 'boundary work'.[17] This is the process by which expert committees assign the vast array of issues lying between the two ideal-typical poles of 'pure science' and 'pure policy' to one or the other side of the science-policy boundary. Issues deemed to be 'scientific' in this process can then be resolved by experts without need for full political or legal accountability.[18] Such boundary drawing is virtually indispensable in environmental decision making, where total paralysis results unless institutional means are found to cope with uncertainty.[19] Yet continual questioning of established boundaries is equally essential in order to increase the transparency of expert decision making and allow, as needed, for the incorporation of ethical perspectives and new social or scientific knowledge.

Participation in international environmental regimes provides a formal and much needed avenue for policy criticism by NGOs. Stairs and Taylor present a compelling account of productive boundary testing by Greenpeace in the implementation of the London Dumping Convention (LDC).[20] Scientific groups operating under the LDC must deal with a host of problems that involve judgement and interests along with science: the interpretation of monitored data, the definition of 'significant' harm, the assessment of comparative risks, and the development of multimedia assessment frameworks. To insiders in these groups it becomes almost axiomatic that what they are doing is strictly 'science'. Efforts by Greenpeace and other NGOs to highlight the value-laden character of such determinations have proved effective in removing the blinkers of governmental expertise, although it has also produced 'some backlash as the "old guard" have tried to reassert dominance with accusations that the debate has now degenerated because "policy" has been brought into science'.[21] Such defensive boundary work, as noted earlier, is altogether typical in environmental controversies, where challenged experts seek to defend their turf, and therewith their right to speak for science. Stairs and Taylor also credit NGO participation under the LDC with highlighting the extent to which predictive models had failed to account for the complexities of marine ecosystems and thereby initiating a 'paradigm shift' from prediction to precaution. This highly consequential move shifted the burden of proof from those who favour caution to those who wish to undertake potentially damaging activity.

It is reasonable to expect sustained policy criticism and reframing such as has occurred in the LDC from those NGOs that most closely resemble government agencies in their grasp of resources, technical expertise and political capacity. Greenpeace, for example, is known for specialist skills in the field of marine pollution, as are other large environmental NGOs, such as the Worldwide Fund for Nature (WWF), Friends of the Earth and the Sierra Club, in their respective areas of environmental involvement. The assimilation of NGOs to statelike status increases their influence but may bring with it the same problems of partial vision and ideological excess that befall experts serving states and IGOs. Thus Stairs and Taylor point to an ethnocentric bias in Greenpeace's opposition to sewage dumping world-wide.[22] This policy, which is appropriate for northern states disposing of industrially contaminated sewage, may be unnecessary as well as unacceptably costly for less industrialised southern states with different economic and pollution problems. Yearley, as argued below, provides another example in connection with the protection of endangered species.[23]

One of the institutional strengths of NGOs is that they can, when needed, pursue their goals outside the relatively inflexible channels of (inter)governmental communication and negotiation. NGOs' skill in manipulating symbols and grabbing media attention has helped move issues up on official policy agendas and tilted public opinion in favour of precautionary environmental action. But the downside of symbolic politics is that it substitutes the shortcut of emotion for the longer but more durable pathway of reason. For example, effective use of the media overcame corporate and government resistance when a determined campaign by Greenpeace led to the 1995 decision by Shell, UK to postpone the planned deep-water disposal of the Brent Spar oil storage tanks. Some have seen this as an important victory for the precautionary principle, since the effects on the marine environment could not be precisely known. Others, however, believe that Greenpeace's strategy placed an essentially ideological vision of the purity of the seas ahead of reasoned selection between alternative frameworks of risk perception and risk management—and perhaps weakened the NGO's credibility in the eyes of marine scientists.

Local Knowledge

Environmental controversies occur not only through structured confrontations between government and non-governmental experts but also when the impartial and authoritative problem framings offered by science seem to contradict people's lived experience of their environment. Thus, popular distrust of ruling institutions, rooted in historical experience, often gets translated into uncertainty about the government's scientific assessments.[24] Similarly, localised knowledge of nature gained through non-scientific activities such as farming or grazing may come into conflict with assumptions built into generic scientific models.

Scientific studies, in particular, may presume a homogeneity in environmental conditions or people's relationship with nature that is belied by the experience of local residents. Precision in science is often achieved by narrowing or simplifying the field of inquiry, at times with serious loss of accuracy with respect to local conditions. Thompson et al. offer an instructive example in discussing the causes of flooding in the great river basins of northern India. The problem, they say, can be localised at one level in a long, narrow strip of land extending from Kashmir in the west to Assam and Burma in the east. This picture, however, is profoundly misleading, since the 'cause' is not in reality evenly distributed throughout the region:

The convolutions of the Himalayan landscape, and its underlying geology, render some localities particularly prone to mass wastage and others virtually immune. And some localities are actually subject to mass deposition; that is where the Kathmandu valley came from. Far from the cause being evenly spread, ninety percent of the 'damage' may result from ten percent of the land. . . . What is needed is a rejection of homogenizing generalizations and their replacement by a sensitivity for local contexts.[25]

It follows that failure to recognise heterogeneity within the affected territory can lead to highly divergent, and hence controversial, predictions of risk to specific localities—as indeed has happened in India.

Brian Wynne offers a similar example of conflict between scientific homogenisation and local heterogeneity in connection with predictions of radiation risks made by British authorities in the wake of the Chernobyl nuclear accident, which deposited heavy but variable quantities of radioactive cesium over parts of Cumbria.[26] In this case, government experts wrongly estimated the likely risk of cesium uptake in the upland grazing environment because their model failed to account for variations in the acidity of the soil in different parts of Britain. Official policies shifted erratically when actual radiation measurements in Cumbrian soil and plants did not conform to predictions issued from London offices. Sheep farmers might perhaps have compensated for the faulty scientific estimates, and resulting policy uncertainty, with adaptive grazing practices, but their knowledge, based on a lifetime of raising sheep on the affected terrain, was not 'scientific' and hence not deemed relevant by the expert policymakers. Such examples make a persuasive case for closer collaboration between local actors and scientists attached to states or IGOs in building a secure knowledge-base for environmental action.

Science after Disaster

Conflicts between science and local knowledge can occur with special intensity after disasters that disrupt established frames of knowledge and understanding. A telling case arose in December 1984 in the central Indian city of Bhopal, when a runaway chemical reaction at a Union Carbide pesticide plant released a deadly cloud of methyl isocyanate (MIC), killing some 3500 people and injuring at least 150,000 others. The sheer scale and unexpectedness of the catastrophe paralysed government relief efforts and produced unimaginable administrative chaos, compounding the tragedy for survivors.[27] Fortunately for the citizens of Bhopal, NGOs from all over India trooped into the city, bringing vital stores of energy and expertise to supplement the government's limited resources. A number of victims' groups quickly formed and some remained active for many years, at first aggressively pursuing litigation and later campaigning for just compensation and other forms of relief.

Without the help of these organisations, both the Indian government and the state of Madhya Pradesh would have been completely overwhelmed, but cooperation between the private and public sectors proved to be anything but straightforward.

A particularly divisive controversy arose around issues of medical diagnosis, monitoring and treatment. NGOs, led by the Medico Friends Circle, spearheaded one set of efforts to document the victims' health, while the Indian Council of Medical Research coordinated the official epidemiological studies. State and non-state investigators parted early on in their strategies for registration as well as treatment. While government officials sought to limit their task by narrowing the definition of potential 'gas victims' (for example, by excluding 'malingerers'), NGOs understandably took a more expansive view, according greater weight to victims' subjective accounts of their condition. Besides reflecting institutional self-interest, the divergent state and non-state medical assessments pointed to fundamental differences between the government professionals' mechanistic understanding of disease causation and the more holistic and systemic views of illness espoused by NGOs.[28]

Adherents of different medical world-views clashed sharply over treatment decisions. Physicians associated with NGOs generally accepted the subjective testimony of many victims that they had been helped by treatment with sodium thiosulfate, a recognised antidote to cyanide poisoning;[29] autopsies performed on dead victims appeared to some to provide pathological evidence of cyanide exposure. Yet, after a brief initial consensus, state medical experts vehemently denied the victims' contention, arguing that there were no objective signs of cyanide poisoning. The situation turned ugly when officials decided to enforce their scientific conviction through strong-arm tactics. The police were ordered to break into volunteer clinics, confiscate available stores of thiosulfate and prevent physicians from dispensing the drug.[30] These methods deepened the victims' already considerable distrust of the authorities and erected almost insurmountable barriers against the possibility of a mutually acceptable settlement.

In retrospect, the 'thiosulfate controversy' as it came to be called could only have been avoided through orderly cooperation and accompanying negotiation of epistemic commitments between state experts and local organisers and activists. When disaster struck in Bhopal, little was known about the toxicological properties of MIC other than the fact that it was extremely irritating and even fatal at very low doses. The human health effects of sublethal doses had never been studied in detail; what little information was available had mostly been produced by Union Carbide and hence was proprietary in nature. Bhopal became in effect a gigantic, if unwitting, natural laboratory where MIC's real impacts on human beings could be studied for the first time. Careful record-keeping and systematic follow-through would have helped to identify and document the reported ill effects, to chart their progress, and eventually to resolve the victims' medical and legal claims. But the mix of sympathetic expertise and perceptive local engagement needed to translate medical knowledge into action in the disaster's wake was sadly absent. Instead, the state's professionalised (and far from institutionally coherent) understandings of 'what the medical science said' about MIC clashed unproductively with the victims' equally unsystematic attempts to make scientific sense of their subjective health experiences.

The failure of organised science to take advantage of unorganised local knowledge remains one of the less well-comprehended legacies of Bhopal. Although methyl isocyanate may never be implicated again in a tragedy of similar scope, the generic problem for science and medicine disclosed in Bhopal is likely to persist, unless better mechanisms are developed to integrate the varied knowledges that constitute the full meaning of disasters.[31] Large-scale releases of toxic substances, in particular, create the preconditions for health, environmental and socioeconomic effects that may never have been investigated, or even imagined, in contained, laboratory-based research. As we know from the Chernobyl nuclear plant explosion, the *Exxon Valdez* oil spill, and a multitude of less consequential tragedies, the impacts of such events can cross political boundaries, endure over long periods of time, and affect ecosystems as well as human beings. To understand these complex effects in detail requires a combination of observation, recording, interpretation and communication—possibly of several years' duration—that could appropriately be conceptualised as 'scientific relief'. Such sustained monitoring, moreover, is nearly impossible to carry out without securing the trust and willing participation of affected populations—a task which states or IGOs may be unable to accomplish without support from NGOs. These considerations furnish a strong argument for IGO-NGO collaboration in post-disaster scientific relief. Some possible costs are discussed below.

Epistemic Networks

NGO involvement in the implementation and enforcement of environmental obligations has long been sanctioned under both domestic and international law. Most U.S. environmental legislation, for example, provides for citizen suits against violators in situations where public officials, upon notification, have failed to prosecute offences. Internationally, the status of NGOs is somewhat less clearly defined and often unofficial, though no less crucial. In a review of major developments in global environmental governance, Peter Sand observes that, while formal supranational regulation could be accounted a failure, convergence towards higher standards of performance was occurring through more decentralised means, such as mutual recognition of national obligations, diffusion and cross-national learning, and the spread of epistemic networks.[32] NGOs have much to contribute to all of these informal processes, not only through knowledge creation, as noted above, but also by bridging conceptual and political divides from the local level to the supranational. Their role in protecting wildlife, most particularly through monitoring and enforcement under the Convention on International Trade in Endangered Species of Wild Flora and Fauna (CITES), exemplifies some of the positive and negative aspects of such bridging work.

CITES was signed in March 1973 and went into effect in 1975; by 1995, 131 parties had ratified the convention. The treaty's core consists of a permit system regulating the export, import and re-export of plant and animal species (and products derived from them) that have been listed in one of three appendices, each requiring a different level of protection. The regime depends on reciprocity, with each member state agreeing to recognise the permits issued by any other. Species threatened with extinction, listed in Appendix I ('black list'), and those that could face extinction if trade were not controlled, listed in Appendix II ('grey list'), must be agreed to by a two-thirds vote of the parties. Appendix III, by contrast, consists of species controlled in any member state and notified to the CITES secretariat. There is no international duty to honour or enforce such unilateral restrictions, but it had become standard practice by the late 1980s for member states to include Appendix III lists in the enforcement instructions given to national trade-control authorities.[33] In general, responsibility for enforcing CITES rests with the parties, who are required to develop 'appropriate measures' to discourage illegal trade.

NGO participation in the implementation of CITES has long been seen as one of the regime's strong points, partly compensating for the secretariat's inability to act against reported violations.[34] The treaty specifically provides for NGOs to participate in the meetings of the parties, where they are entitled to express their opinions and lobby for their positions, although they may not vote. They also play a central role in monitoring compliance. The World Conservation Monitoring Unit is responsible for the computerised tracking of trade in endangered species and reporting data to the CITES secretariat. TRAFFIC, a division of the Worldwide Fund for Nature, is also active in monitoring illegal trade. In addition, NGOs in many countries have been involved in gathering data for scientific studies and are officially represented on the panel that gives advice on the downlisting of the elephant.

Even when states are fully committed to implementing CITES, they cannot hope to achieve compliance solely through the vigilance of domestic customs agents, who are rarely equipped to detect forged permits or false assertions by smugglers, let alone to identify actual examples of protected species.[35] Community awareness, rather than top-down command and control, offers greater promise of effectiveness. Here again active collaboration between IGOs and NGOs could promote the desired results.

There are as well some hidden costs in placing heavy reliance on NGOs for species protection. Some strategic choices made by NGOs in their efforts to preserve wildlife, both under CITES and elsewhere, have raised questions about whose values they represent and whether their judgement in setting priorities is consistent with the regime's objectives, let alone with current scientific knowledge. The increasing power of NGOs under CITES is resented by national governments when resulting policies threaten domestic economic or political interests. African countries seeking the downlisting of elephants, for example, have not welcomed NGO support for maintaining the animal's black-listed status. Nor are alliances between NGOs and state governments guaranteed to be unproblematic. In one controversial episode, the WWF was discovered to have helped the government of Zimbabwe purchase a helicopter to protect the black rhino in spite of the authorities' shoot-to-kill policy against poachers.[36] This, together with the Fund's aid to Kenya in buying assault weapons and helicopter gunships to protect the elephant, underscored the tragic choices involved in protecting species in developing countries. People's lives were worth less, it appeared, than the charismatic megafauna cherished by northern environmentalists and publics. Disturbingly, the Fund seemed willing to support abroad policies of violence that would have seemed abhorrent at home.

A similar controversy about possible blindness to cultural values arose when Greenpeace and the International Fund for Animal Welfare launched a campaign to ban seal culling in Canada in the 1970s and 1980s. Confronted by evidence that seal hunting was important to indigenous people, these international NGOs argued that the use of modern technology, such as guns and snowmobiles, rendered the hunters' activities non-traditional and hence not worthy of protection.[37] As anthropologists and community activists pointed out, this assessment was based on an overly static understanding of 'traditional' culture, which could only be maintained in the contemporary world by allowing some room for technological adaptation. Ironically, this dispute turned the normative question of what should count as 'traditional' into a scientific problem and revealed substantial differences between local and non-local NGOs' interpretations of the issue.

Technology Transfer: A Role for NGOs

Environmental action often demands the transfer of knowledge, skills, technology or other material resources from places where they are readily available to places where they are in relatively short supply. NGOs of all kinds have demonstrated that they can participate constructively in such dissemination, although the skills and capabilities of particular organisations constrain their spheres and modalities of influence. Thus, the more professionalised multinational NGOs—such as Greenpeace, WWF and Friends of the Earth—have been able to influence the politics of national and international environmental agenda-setting by combining information available from official sources with additional information that they themselves have compiled or generated. By contrast, smaller, community-based NGOs are more likely to stimulate activity at the local level than to initiate sweeping policy change. These groups are especially adept at simplifying and, if necessary, translating difficult technical information for non-expert users, adapting generic emergency response measures to fit local circumstances, and mobilising direct action against local polluters or hazardous facilities.

Given the striking discrepancies in environmental knowledge and policy preparedness around the world, NGOs can make a sizeable difference simply by publicising the environmental performance of leading countries so as to exert pressure on laggard countries.[38] Strategic use of policy comparisons allowed the Natural Resources Defense Council (NRDC), a leading U.S. environmental organisation, to influence the 1990 negotiations leading to the revision of the Montreal Protocol on ozone depletion. Before the meeting of government officials in London, several of the leading international environmental groups had held press conferences and distributed informational brochures to the press, the public and officials. NRDC went a step further by compiling from existing government proposals a composite set of target reductions for ozone-depleting chemicals, incorporating the maximum reduction proposed for each by any government.[39] Demonstrating actual state support for each target in the proposal allowed NRDC to avoid the charge of impossibility conventionally levelled against any effort to tighten up environmental regulation. The skills that NRDC drew on were as much political as technical. Decades of experience in complex regulatory negotiations were brought to bear in repackaging publicly available information into a form calculated to have maximal policy impact.

Indeed, political imagination and experience in moulding public opinion have proved to be at least as important in NGO lobbying efforts as issue-specific technical knowledge. The NGO-led campaign to remove lead from petrol in Europe in the 1980s provides one illustration. In this case, NGOs pointed to the U.S., where catalytic converters had been standardly required on motor vehicles since the 1970s, to argue forcefully that the European automobile industry could afford to meet the same requirement without severe economic loss. Greenpeace, in particular, dramatised the point in the UK through a poster campaign that played on one of the Ford Motor Company's favoured slogans ('Ford Gives You More'); turning the message back on the company, the posters argued that a British Ford car gave customers more pollution than its U.S. counterpart.[40]

Examples like these suggest that aggregating information from states and making it freely available is one of the most promising avenues for cooperation between IGOS and NGOS. According to one count, the United Nations currently manages some nine separate programmes designed to provide member nations and other interested parties with information about environmental and industrial hazards.[41] But mere availability of information provides no guarantee that states will have the expertise or inclination to use it effectively. NGOS enjoy some conspicuous advantages over states as users of international databases: they are less hampered by inertia, more dedicated, more focused on pragmatic (and hence attainable) environmental objectives, and often more knowledgeable about the issues they have targeted for action. Better access for NGOS accordingly should promote the objectives of information transfer programmes managed by IGOS.

In an age marked by massive accumulations of information and by instantaneous electronic communication, NGOS can be expected to gain in importance as agents of knowledge transfer. Although the amount of environmental information in the public domain keeps growing, it is frequently available in forms that make unmediated use by lay citizens virtually unthinkable. Technical information remains inaccessible in practice unless it is translated into user-friendly forms. It is no surprise, for example, that the right-to-know provisions of the U.S. Superfund law proved most efficacious in those communities where an environmental NGO worked with residents to interpret the data reported under that programme.[42] On the international level, the linguistic competence provided by NGOS can prove to be a critically important asset, given the increasing importance of English as the world's primary medium of technical communication.[43]

Learning and the Politics of Sovereignty

In a model of global governance that looks like the circulatory system, NGOS are sometimes thought to function very much like capillaries, carrying out the same mandate as the major blood vessels, but on a smaller scale. It seems clear from the foregoing examples that environmental NGOS, both large and small, are especially well-suited to performing repeated, on-the-ground 'micro' functions, such as collecting samples, taking measurements, mobilising against environmental violators, educating people at the grass roots and providing interim relief. Even these community-based activities, however, may link up with global policy and politics in a variety of ways: by supplementing existing scientific theories about environmental phenomena with local knowledge; by disseminating, and if necessary translating, environmental information from national and international databases; by disclosing systematic patterns of violations and shortfalls that ought to be addressed at the international level; by reframing dominant policy paradigms to take account of social and scientific uncertainty; and, less benignly, by reinforcing specific, culturally conditioned tilts—even pathologies—in environmental regimes (for example, the emphasis on charismatic megafauna in the implementation of CITES). In all these respects, NGOs function proactively as creative policy initiators, not merely as passive agents of principals situated higher up in the political hierarchy.

The analogy with the circulatory system breaks down more completely when one inserts the state into the picture, since, on many issues of environmental management, the interests of NGOs run counter to those of state authorities. With the globalisation of environmental politics and knowledge, there is more than a negligible likelihood of IGOs and NGOs lining up on one side of an environmental issue and national governments on the other, so as to create possible arenas of conflict. The cases discussed above provide some insights into how this happens. In their efforts to educate, mobilise or lobby for policy change, NGOs frequently enlist support from IGOs to battle indifference at the national level. Even the collection of supposedly neutral scientific and medical information by NGOs can become a charged affair because it discloses state incapacity; creates obligations (for example, compensation claims) that the state does not wish or does not have the resources to honour; interferes with entrenched economic interests that are in league with the state; or opposes the scientific orthodoxy of state-sponsored expert institutions, as happened in Bhopal in connection with the thiosulfate controversy.

All this suggests that there is room for improvement in the institutional framework for NGO-state-IGO collaboration in the field of environmental action. Waiting for more coherent authority to develop at the supranational level, as Sand emphatically argues, is not a plausible solution.[44] A more promising avenue is to engage the full range of institutional resources—governmental as well as non-governmental and intergovernmental—to increase the prospects for learning and reduce the potential for interorganisational conflict. What are some steps that can be taken in pursuit of this goal?

Decentralised Learning

The past two decades of experience with global environmental management have generated extraordinary interest in the theme of learning.[45] This preoccupation reflects in part an awareness that our framing of environmental problems and related understanding of causes and effects are still embryonic and likely to change rapidly with massive new investments in knowledge creation. In part, as well, the proliferation of international environmental accords, and the associated disclosure of deeply divided environmental views and values, prompts an interest in learning. The realisation has grown in many parts of the world that the prospects for peaceful coexistence may well depend on how effectively human societies learn to manage their environmental interdependence.

As catalysts for environmental learning, NGOs offer an important alternative to the standard top-down model of knowledge-making and knowledge diffusion in the natural sciences. They supplement in crucial ways the more widely acknowledged role of technical and managerial elites in building epistemic communities and fostering international policy coordination.[46] NGOs in principle can gain access to domains of localised experience and understanding, and offer alternative models of environmental health or sustainability, that currently remain outside the purview of organised science.[47] They thus constitute a vehicle for scaling knowledge up from the grass roots—a necessary task, in view of the extreme heterogeneity of ecosystems and human-environment linkages.

Knowledge gathered by NGOs, however, will have to pass through processes of validation and standardisation, including perhaps translation into mathematical or statistical language, in order to achieve authority outside its places of origin.[48] This is where IGOs (along with state institutions) may be in a position to offer decisive help. Performance standards and technical guidance may often have to be developed on an *ad hoc* basis in response to particular challenges, as in the aftermath of disasters. IGOs could play an important part in legitimating the scientific activities of NGOs if they remain alert to some generic problems and have methods of responding to them. For example—given the importance of institutional boundary work in building scientific credibility[49]—collaborative arrangements for environmental monitoring could require the creation of an expert advisory body to guide protocol development, assist in data collection and storage, provide peer review, and help in the interpretation and dissemination of findings. IGOs could also maintain, make available and periodically revamp relevant databases of experts and expert services, such as organisations of scientists and physicians in the public interest. Finally, IGO support can partially compensate for the resource shortfalls that contribute to wavering leadership and unreliable performance by most of the world's smaller and less experienced NGOs.

Beyond Sovereignty

The rise and influence of epistemic networks or communities at the substate level has been remarked upon by many observers of international environmental regimes.[50] For the most part, however, the analysis of epistemic communities has sidestepped the challenge that such actor constellations may pose to state sovereignty. It has been widely assumed that ecological epistemic communities will include both national bureaucracies entrusted with environmental responsibilities and NGOs subscribing to a shared set of values and problem definitions. Experience of NGO activities to protect the environment paints a less comforting picture. Both expert, multinational NGOs and NGOs organised at the grass roots level have encountered at times violent opposition from state authorities. Their alliances, if any, with chronically weak national environmental agencies offer insufficient protection.

Strengthening the ties between IGOs and NGOs may enhance the latter group's voice and authority, as well as institutional stability and steadiness of purpose; but it will not solve the problem of conflict between NGOs and the states in which the great majority of them operate. The reality is that NGOs, at least in the short run, need states to act upon and legitimate their knowledge, world-views and preferred policies. Assisted by the fax and the Internet, and relatively unhampered by competing ideological commitments, environmental NGOs have achieved enormous success in building networks across state boundaries. But these developments reaffirm to varying degrees the proposition that 'all politics is local'. The international spread of India's famed Chipko movement provides an instructive example. Here, pre-eminently, was a local environmental initiative, organised to protect local natural resources, whose commitments seemed to spread throughout the world.[51] The movement generated actions that could be reinterpreted as symbols of global thinking by actors pursuing different political agendas in places far from India; yet it arose out of characteristically Indian political oppositions and had to succeed in its immediate context in order to achieve wider influence.

If bypassing states is not the answer, then what can IGOs do to encourage cooperation between state authorities and NGOs on environmental issues? Improved communication and formal participation, preferably built into the design of environmental regimes as in the case of CITES, is undoubtedly part of the answer. In such fora, more states may come to appreciate what U.S. environmental regulators, for example, have recently begun to acknowledge: that effective systems of environmental governance require constant recalibration among national policy commitments and emerging local and translocal problem frames. Scientific analysis of environmental risks, according to a 1996 report of the U.S. National Research Council, should therefore be integrated with forms of deliberation that directly engage citizens and NGOs. Top-down analysis, without horizontal deliberation, may end up all too often addressing the wrong problems.

According to one recent analysis of environmental learning, a necessary precondition is 'the absence of irreconcilable political differences among the dominant member countries'.[52] If this were not already a daunting goal, the addition of intractable epistemic conflicts among state and non-state actors makes action that much more difficult.[53] The explosion of environmental science in recent years, and its diffusion to more and more new actors, has if anything exacerbated the intensity of technical conflict. Greater knowledge seems only to reveal previously unsuspected areas of uncertainty, so that increased scientific understanding turns back and undermines science's own authority. The German sociologist Ulrich Beck refers to this self-destructive phenomenon as 'reflexive modernisation' in his influential thesis that risk—rather than, say, class or race or family—now functions as the dominant organising force in contemporary societies.[54] The quest to build Anderson's 'imagined communities'[55] against this backdrop of contestation is a perilous undertaking for environmentalists, who must compete with states and industry lobbies that command substantially greater resources and often deploy them to profoundly different ends. Collaboration with IGOs can help rectify these inequalities and give NGOs structured opportunities to interject their critical, but essential, voices into the emerging discourses of a global civil society.

Notes

1. See Peter Sand, *Lessons Learned in Global Environmental Governance*, Washington, DC: World Resources Institute, 1990; Kevin Stairs & Peter Taylor, 'Non-governmental organizations and the legal protection of the oceans: a case study', in Andrew Hurrell & Benedict Kingsbury (eds), *The International Politics of the Environment*, Oxford: Oxford University Press, 1992, pp 110–141; and Laurence Susskind, *Environmental Diplomacy: Negotiating More Effective Global Agreements*, Oxford: Oxford University Press, 1994.

2. World Commission on Environment and Development, *Our Common Future*, Oxford: Oxford University Press, 1987, p 328.

3. See Marvin S Soroos, 'From Stockholm to Rio and beyond: the evolution of global environmental governance', in Norman J Vig & Michael E Kraft (eds), *Environmental Policy in the 1990s*, Washington, DC: Congressional Quarterly Press, 1997.

4. Steven Yearley, *Sociology, Environmentalism, Globalization*, London: Sage, 1996.

5. See Stairs & Taylor, 'Non-governmental organizations'; and Jessica T Mathews, 'Power shift', *Foreign Affairs*, Vol 76, No 1, 1997, pp 50–66.

6. Andrew Jamison *et al*, *The Making of the New Environmental Consciousness*, Edinburgh: Edinburgh University Press, 1990.

7. Susskind, *Environmental Diplomacy*, p 51.

8. Some business interests have created NGOs to serve as fronts to pursue the founders' economic interests on issues such as wetlands and climate change (see, for example, Susskind, *Environmental Diplomacy*, pp 51–52). Greenpeace has published a list of over 50 such organizations in 'The Greenpeace guide to anti-environmental organizations' in Yearley, *Sociology*, p 90.

9. Peter Uvin, 'Scaling up the grassroots and scaling down the summit: the relations between Third World non-governmental organisations and the United Nations', *Third World Quarterly*, Vol 16, No 3, 1995, pp 495–512.

10. Even this independence may be a matter of degree. Autonomy is tempered in states where NGOs receive substantial funding or other supports from the state. In addition, regular participation in formal policy proceedings, such as regulatory hearings, can bring about a convergence of interests and outlook between NGOs and state agencies, with consequent loss of critical capacity.

11. Sand, *Lessons Learned,* p 29.

12. See Peter M Haas, *Saving the Mediterranean: The Politics of International Environmental Cooperation*, New York: Columbia University Press, 1990; and Sand, *Lessons Learned*, p 29.

13. Haas, *Saving the Mediterranean*; Stairs & Taylor, 'Non-governmental organizations'. See also Peter M Haas, Robert O Keohane & Marc A Levy (eds), *Institutions for the Earth: Sources of Effective International Environmental Protection*, Cambridge, MA: MIT Press, 1993; and Susskind, *Environmental Diplomacy*.

14. Rachel Carson, *Silent Spring*, Boston: Houghton Mifflin, 1962.

15. See Mary Douglas & Aaron Wildavsky, *Risk and Culture*, Berkeley: University of California Press, 1982; Sheila Jasanoff, *Risk Management and Political Culture*, New York: Russell Sage Foundation, 1986; and Stairs & Taylor, 'Non-governmental organizations'.

16. See Donald A Schön & Martin Rein, *Frame Reflection: Toward the Resolution of Intractable Policy Controversies*, New York: Basic Books, 1994; and Sharachchandra Lele and Richard Norgaard, 'Sustainability and the scientist's burden', *Conservation Biology*, Vol 10, No 2, 1995, pp 354–365.

17. See Sheila Jasanoff, *The Fifth Branch: Science Advisers as Policymakers*, Cambridge, MA: Harvard University Press, 1990.

18. For example, determinations characterised as 'scientific' through the boundary work of expert committees may be shielded from judicial and political review. Judges as well as policymakers generally defer to the findings of duly authorized scientific organisations.

19. Jasanoff, *Risk Management*, and *The Fifth Branch*.

20. Stairs & Taylor, 'Non-governmental organizations', pp 117–120.

21. Ibid, p 118.

22. Ibid, pp 133–134.

23. Yearley, *Sociology*.

24. See Brian Wynne, *Risk Management and Hazardous Wastes: Implementation and the Dialectics of Credibility*, Berlin: Springer, 1987; and Brian Wynne, 'Misunderstood misunderstandings: social identities and the public uptake of science', in Alan Irwin & Brian Wynne (eds), *Misunderstanding Science?* Cambridge: Cambridge University Press, 1996.

25. See Michael Thompson, M Warburton & T Hatley, *Uncertainty on a Himalayan Scale,* London: Ethnographica, 1986, pp 46–47.

26. Wynne, 'Misunderstood misunderstandings'.

27. See Ravi S Rajan, 'Rehabilitation and voluntarism in Bhopal', *Lokayan Bulletin*, Vol 6, Nos 1/2, 1988, pp 3–31; Sathyamala, 'The medical profession and the Bhopal tragedy', *Lokayan Bulletin*, Vol 6, Nos 1/2, 1988, pp 33–56; and Sheila Jasanoff, *Learning from Disaster: Risk Management after Bhopal*, Philadelphia: University of Pennsylvania Press, 1994.

28. Sathyamala, 'The medical profession'.

29. Ibid.

30. See Michael R Reich, 'Toxic politics and pollution victims in the Third World', in Jasanoff, *Learning from Disaster*, p 189.

31. See, for example, Kai Erikson, *Everything in Its Path: Destruction of Community in the Buffalo Creek Flood*, New York: Simon and Schuster, 1976.

32. Sand, *Lessons Learned*.

33. Ibid, p 29.

34. Susskind, *Environmental Diplomacy*.

35. Donald G McNeil, Jr, 'Madagascar reptile theft hits rarest of tortoises', *New York Times*, July 1996, p 61.

36. Yearley, *Sociology*, p 138.

37. Ibid, p 137.

38. Stairs & Taylor, 'Non-governmental organizations', p 129.

39. See Richard E Benedick, *Ozone Diplomacy; New Directions in Safeguarding the Planet*, Cambridge, MA: Harvard University Press, 1991, p 166.

40. Yearley, *Sociology*, p 88.

41. See Frank N Laird, 'Information and disaster prevention', in Jasanoff, *Learning from Disaster*, pp 204–224.

42. Susan Hadden, 'Citizen participation in environmental policymaking', in Jasanoff, *Learning from Disaster*, pp 91–112.

43. Stair & Taylor, 'Non-governmental organizations'.

44. Sand, *Lessons Learned*.

45. See Dean E Mann, 'Environmental learning in a decentralised world', *Journal of International Affairs*, Vol 44, 1991, pp 301–337; Martin Jachtenfuchs & Michael Huber, 'Institutional learning in the European Community: the response to the greenhouse effect', in J D Liefferink, P D Lave & A P J Nol (eds), *European Integration and Environmental Policy*, London: Belhaven Press, 1993; Haas *et al, Institutions for the Earth*; and Peter M Haas & Ernst B Haas, 'Learning to learn: improving international governance', *Global Governance*, Vol 1, No 3, 1995, pp 255–285.

46. Haas, *Saving the Mediterranean*; and Haas & Haas, 'Learning to learn'.

47. Irwin & Wynne, *Misunderstanding Science?*

48. See Bruno Latour, 'Drawing things together', in M Lynch & S Woolgar (eds), *Representation in Scientific Practice*, Cambridge, MA: MIT Press, 1990; and Theodore M Porter, *Trust in Numbers: The Pursuit of Objectivity in Science and Public Life*, Princeton, NJ: Princeton University Press, 1995.

49. Jasanoff, *The Fifth Branch*.

50. Sand, *Lessons Learned*; Haas, *Saving the Mediterranean*; Haas et al, *Institutions for the Earth*; and Jessica T Mathews, 'Power shift', pp 50–66.

51. Luther Gerlach, 'Thinking globally, acting locally', *Evaluation Review*, Vol 15, No 1, 1991, pp 120–142.

52. Haas & Haas, 'Learning to learn', p 255.

53. Schön & Rein, *Frame Reflection*.

54. See Ulrich Beck, *The Risk Society: Towards a New Modernity*, London: Sage, 1992. This book, which has been described as a sociological manifesto for the German Green movement, sold hundreds of thousands of copies when it was first published, showing that it had struck a deeply responsive chord among German citizens.

55. Benedict Anderson, *Imagined Communities*, London: Verso, 1991.

20

The Real Impacts of Household Consumption

Michael Brower and Warren Leon

Can you, the reader, make a difference? Certainly. One of the great paradoxes about environmental change is that individual decisions ultimately drive the unfortunate changes described in earlier chapters in this book. This apparent paradox should give us great hope; while individual choices cause damage, they can be part of the solution to global problems. The key to making a difference is knowing how our own actions are most effective. In the final chapter in this volume, the authors suggest areas where we can contribute to the long-term health of the planet. At the same time, the chapter indicates that there are some decisions over which we agonize that have no net impact on the environment. The book from which this selection is drawn, The Consumer's Guide to Effective Environmental Choices: Practical Advice from the Union of Concerned Scientists, *is highly recommended as a personal guide to responsible consumer action.*

Dr. Michael Brower is a physicist and nationally known expert on energy and environmental issues. Until 1994 he was director of research for the Union of Concerned Scientists, the country's leading public-interest science organization. Warren Leon is executive director of the Northeast Sustainable Energy Association, a regional membership organization that promotes the understanding, development, and adoption of energy conservation and nonpolluting, renewable energy technologies.

From Michael Brower and Warren Leon, "The Real Impacts of Household Consumption," *The Consumer's Guide to Effective Environmental Choices: Practical Advice from the Union of Concerned Scientists* (New York: Three Rivers Press, 1999), 43–80. Figures omitted. © 1999 The Union of Concerned Scientists. Reprinted by permission of Three Rivers Press, a division of Random House, Inc.

Americans spend their money on many different things—from apples and armchairs to zinnias and zip drives. Which of all these things cause the greatest problems for the environment, and which are relatively benign? . . . American consumers need more and better information about the actual impact of their various activities on the environment. That's what we will try to provide in this chapter.

We will divide all consumer spending into categories and show which cause serious problems and which do not. In perhaps our most striking finding, we will show how just seven spending categories are responsible for most of the environmental damage attributable to consumers.

The first step in reaching this conclusion was to determine which environmental problems pose the greatest threat to human health and the Earth's ecology. We have chosen to focus on just four problems. Here they are in alphabetical order:

**The Leading Consumption-Related
Environmental Problems**

Air pollution
Global warming
Habitat alteration
Water pollution

How did we arrive at this list? . . . To summarize [the process] briefly, we relied mainly on two comprehensive environmental studies, or risk assessments, one conducted by the EPA, the other by the California Comparative Risk Project.[1] These studies collected all available scientific data on the health and ecological impacts of a wide range of human activities and ranked them according to severity (high, medium, or low). We selected only the problems that ranked as medium or high risks in either study. We then whittled the list down further by excluding problems not linked to *current* household consumption or activities. That meant dropping, in particular, pollution from inactive hazardous waste sites and mines, as well as from chemicals such as PCBs that have already been banned or whose use is greatly curtailed. It also meant excluding stratospheric ozone depletion, since most of the chemicals that damage the ozone layer are being phased out under international treaties and are no longer sold in the United States. Of course, we do not mean to imply that these problems are insignificant, but decisions made by consumers from this day forward will do little either to alleviate or exacerbate them.

The resulting list of environmental problems is deceptively short, as each category actually includes a wide variety of impacts and sources:

Air Pollution

Two common outdoor air pollutants, ozone and fine particulate matter, pose an especially high risk to public health.[2] Most are generated directly or indirectly by the burning of fossil fuels, such as gasoline in cars and coal in power plants. The California report estimates that as many as three thousand deaths each year in California alone are caused by particulate matter, with an additional 60,000 to 200,000 cases of respiratory infections in children and up to 2 million nonfatal asthma attacks due to both particulates and ozone. A more recent national study indicates that fine particles with a diameter of less than 10 micrometers (PM_{10}) cause about 64,000 extra deaths every year, corresponding to an increase of about 31 percent in the mortality rate from cardiopulmonary causes in the most polluted cities.[3]

Certain highly toxic air pollutants, although not as widespread as ozone and particulate matter, also pose a serious health risk. The toxic pollutant category includes many chemicals not under federal regulation, such as evaporated pesticides and emissions from chemical plants, metallurgical processes, and sewage treatment plants. Although the health effects of most of these chemicals are not well known, the EPA risk assessment estimated about two thousand cancers a year nationwide from just twenty of the unregulated substances.

Although we think of it mainly as a scourge of densely populated cities, air pollution also affects plants and wildlife in rural areas. Pollutants such as ozone, nitrogen oxides, and sulfur dioxide are known to damage coniferous trees and may harm other plants as well. A closely related problem that occurs mainly in the East is acid deposition ("acid rain"), which arises when sulfuric and nitric acids are formed in the atmosphere and precipitate as rain or snow. These chemicals affect trees and change the acid balance of lakes and streams. About twelve hundred lakes in the United States, or 4 percent of vulnerable lakes, have become fully acidified because of acid rain, and little can now live in them. Another 5 percent are sufficiently acidified that some aquatic life is threatened.

Global Warming

Scientific data indicate that the Earth has gotten warmer over the past 100 years. Not only have global average temperatures increased, by an average of 0.5 to 1.1 degrees Fahrenheit, but glaciers have retreated, the mean sea level has risen, and other unmistakable signs of warming have been detected. Have these changes been caused, at least in part, by human emissions of greenhouse gases, most notably carbon dioxide? Are even more dramatic changes in store for the future?

Ten years ago hundreds of scientists around the world began to work through the Intergovernmental Panel on Climate Change to evaluate all the research that has been done on global warming and to reach conclusions about what is known and what remains to be determined. Over time they have become more confident in their projections. Although no one can predict the future with absolute certainty, the scientists believe that the climate has very probably already begun to change because of human activities and they expect a temperature rise of a few degrees in the coming decades.[4] For this reason many climate experts have called for strong international action to reduce human emissions of greenhouse gases. This view has been supported by the world's leading senior scientists, including the majority of living Nobel Prize winners in the sciences, who in 1997 called global warming "one of the most serious threats to the planet and to future generations."[5]

A temperature change of a few degrees may not seem like a lot, but it could be enough to alter the range of natural habitats and affect the distribution of the species within them. It would also likely cause changes in precipitation patterns, resulting in more summer dryness in some places but less in others, for example. Rising sea levels caused by melting glaciers and thermally expanding sea water would inundate coastal areas and harm coastal wetlands. Under the best scenarios these changes will occur gradually, but there is a risk of abrupt shifts in climate that could have catastrophic results not only for plants and wildlife but also for the global economy.

Scientists are only just beginning to assess the potential impacts of global warming on human health. A recent study by the World Health Organization, the World Meteorological Organization, and the UN Environment Programme points to a variety of potential health concerns, including increased heat stress, higher air pollution (because heat promotes certain pollution-forming chemical reactions), and increased incidence of certain waterborne and food-borne infections.[6]

In addition, a sense of fairness to the citizens of other countries should dictate that a high priority be given to reducing U.S. emissions of greenhouse gases. With only about 5 percent of the world's population, the United States produces about 20 percent of global emissions from human sources. Furthermore, it is the poorest developing countries that are likely to suffer the greatest health consequences because they have less institutional capacity and fewer financial resources to adapt to changing climate.

Habitat Alteration

Although poaching and the trade in endangered species are significant concerns, the greatest threat to wildlife by far is the human destruction or alteration of natural habitats. Within the United States the most serious habitat disturbances arise from activities such as logging, mining, agriculture, marine fishing, diversion of water for agriculture, and suburban sprawl.

As an example, in the past few decades in many areas, wildlife biologists have observed a decline in the numbers of neotropical migratory birds. At first it was assumed that this decline was caused mainly by deforestation of the birds' winter habitats in Central America and the Caribbean. But research has found that land development in the United States may be as much to blame. As people move into formerly wooded areas, for example, they are usually accompanied by cats, raccoons, squirrels, chipmunks, blue jays, cowbirds, and other animals that harass and kill smaller birds. In one study using fake nests, "[t]he eggs were raided constantly by a dozen or so different types of predators . . . most of them animals that live near human communities, feeding on garbage or handouts."[7] For other types of birds, such as prairie warblers, agriculture is to blame for disrupting their habitats. Still others, such as vultures and eagles, are threatened by toxic chemicals that are present in the food they eat and cause problems such as sterility and embrittled eggs.

When it comes to the alteration of freshwater habitats, hydroelectric dams, reservoirs, and water diversions of all kinds are often to blame, as they can radically change the salinity, sedimentation, and other characteristics of rivers. This can affect many threatened species, as well as migrating fish. For instance, water diversions caused the winter run of Chinook salmon in the Sacramento River system to drop from nearly 120,000 in 1968 to an estimated 100 in 1991.

Preserving natural habitats is not only good for plants and animals, but it also directly benefits people. In recent years scientists have become increasingly conscious of the many valuable services these ecosystems perform, including purifying air and water, controlling floods, detoxifying wastes, pollinating crops and natural vegetation, and helping to control potential agricultural pests.[8] The economic value of these services to humans is large and doesn't even count the emotional and psychological benefit many people feel they get from coming in contact with nature.

Water Pollution

The category of water pollution covers many different chemicals and compounds from a variety of sources. Despite tightened regulations over the years, some industries still discharge toxic chemicals into water, which can contaminate drinking water, kill plant life, and contaminate fish. Leading examples include mercury, cadmium, and other heavy metals released in mining and various industrial activities, numerous organic compounds discharged from petrochemical factories, and pesticides washed off agricultural fields and urban yards.

In addition to such highly toxic pollutants, various more common water pollutants can be harmful to humans and wildlife in substantial quantities. For example, soil eroded from cropland, range land, recently logged forest land, and construction sites frequently winds up in lakes, streams, and coastal waters, affecting the penetration of sunlight and choking off plants. Fertilizers that are washed off of cropland, as well as wastes from livestock, also frequently contaminate water bodies. (In one shocking case, according to a U.S. Department of Agriculture report, "a dike around a large hog-waste lagoon in North Carolina failed, releasing an estimated 25 million gallons of hog waste—twice the volume of the oil spilled by the *Exxon Valdez*—into nearby fields, streams, and a river. The spill killed virtually all aquatic life in a 17-mile stretch of river between Richlands and Jacksonville, North Carolina."[9]) Improved treatments notwithstanding, discharges from municipal sewage facilities and storm drains can cause elevated bacteria and nutrient levels.

The Consumer's Role

After determining the environmental problems to focus on, we created a set of environmental indexes so we could quantify the contribution of various activities to each problem area. The indexes included the number of tons of greenhouse gases, common and toxic air pollutants, and common and toxic water pollutants emitted each year. To represent sources of habitat alteration, we created indexes of consumptive water use (in gallons per day) and of "ecologically significant" land use (in acres, adjusted to take into account the relationship between different types of land use and species endangerment patterns).

Then we set about investigating how the environmental impacts are linked to household purchases and activities. We created a model of the U.S. economy that traces environmental impacts from all kinds of industrial and agricultural activity down through the production chain to individual consumer products and services. We added the direct effects of household activity, such as air pollution produced by home furnaces. We then used this model to calculate the impacts of household spending in 134 categories, including items as diverse as cheese and carpets. These categories were aggregated into fifty major categories (e.g., dairy products, furnishings), and then into ten broad activity areas (e.g., food, household operations). . . .

We discovered that just seven out of the fifty major categories account for a majority of the environmental impacts (except toxic water pollution) linked to consumer behavior. The list of the seven most damaging kinds of consumption is given in the box below, in rough order of decreasing importance. Through the rest of this chapter, we will show you why these seven categories are so significant and why other items don't make the list. We will also give you an overall picture of how the spending of the average American impacts the environment.

The Most Harmful Consumer Activities

Cars and light trucks
Meat and poultry
Fruit, vegetables, and grains
Home heating, hot water, and air conditioning
Household appliances and lighting
Home construction
Household water and sewage

The Big Picture

Before we discuss some of the most important and interesting findings, we want to give you an overview of the relationship between consumer spending and environmental problems. The percentages in Table 1 show the fraction of environmental impacts due to each of the ten broad activity areas: transportation, food, household operations, housing, personal items and services, medical, yard care, private education, financial and legal services, and "other." Again, they are listed in rough order of decreasing overall impact.

Table 1. Environmental Impacts per Household

ACTIVITY AREA	Global Warming GREENHOUSE GASES	Air Pollution COMMON	TOXIC	Water Pollution COMMON	TOXIC	Habitat Alteration WATER USE	LAND USE
Transportation	32%	28%	51%	7%	23%	2%	15%
Food	12	17	9	38	22	73	45
Household operations	35	32	20	21	14	11	4
SUBTOTAL	80%	77%	80%	67%	59%	86%	64%
Housing	6	7	4	10	10	2	26
Personal items and services	6	7	6	7	12	6	5
Medical	6	6	6	4	13	3	3
Yard care	0	1	2	9	3	3	0
Private education	1	1	0	0	1	0	0
Financial and legal	1	1	1	1	1	0	1
Other	1	1	0	2	1	0	0

You will notice a surprising degree of variation in the impacts of the ten household activity areas. Transportation and household operations (heat, hot water, lighting, and appliances, among other things) account for thirty times as much common air pollution as yard activities or education expenses, for instance, while food purchases cause five times as much common water pollution as transportation.

The variation is important because it shows that how households spend their money does indeed matter. Nothing would be more discouraging than to discover that no matter what we do (short of living in a cave), about the same amount of environmental damage will result. This table demonstrates, on the contrary, that some kinds of consumption are *much* worse for the environment than others.

Furthermore, just three of the household activity areas—food, household operations, and transportation—account for the majority of environmental impacts. The reason is not simply that people spend more money in these areas than in others. We spend as much on medical care and personal items as we do on household operations, yet the latter produce six times the emissions of greenhouse gases. Rather, something about the way these services are provided or used results in a much greater impact on the environment.

Now let's look at some of the details behind the numbers. What are the main contributors to environmental harm in each area? And why? For example, within household operations, how do air conditioners stack up against refrigerators, wood stoves, electric lights, and furniture? We will focus on six of the ten areas on the table: transportation, food, running a household, housing, some personal items and services, and yard care. We will not talk about the impacts of medical expenses, which although substantial are not something over which consumers have very much control. The impacts of the other expenditure categories (private education, financial and legal, and other) are too small to bother with here.

Transportation

We have all heard something of the evils of the automobile—pollution, the blight of highways, junkyards filled with wrecked cars and tires. But when analyzed objectively, how does it stack up against the other sources of environmental harm?

For the most part, unfortunately, transportation, particularly automobiles, deserves its bad reputation. Our findings indicate that household use of transportation, ranging from recreational boating to cars to passenger air travel, is responsible for 28 to 51 percent of greenhouse gases and air pollution and 23 percent of toxic water pollution. Our use of transportation even poses a significant threat to wildlife through the use of land for roads and highways.

To see how these problems are distributed among different modes of transportation, we can divide the transportation sector into the following broad categories:

- Personal cars and light trucks (including minivans and pickup trucks)
- Personal aircraft, recreational boats, and off-road vehicles
- Passenger air, intercity rail, ferry, and intercity bus travel
- Other (includes motorcycles, trailers, mass transit)

The impacts in each case include both vehicle operations and manufacturing. (As in other consumer categories, impacts from the disposal of cars, tires, batteries, and similar items by households are not counted here, but are folded into the impacts of household solid waste.) . . .

Not surprisingly, among the transportation modes, automobiles and light trucks, including minivans and sport utility vehicles, dominate every sector, mainly because they account for the vast majority of personal vehicle travel (about 84 percent, measured by passenger miles[10]). Because this is such a significant category, it is instructive to look at the kinds of impacts cars and trucks produce and how they are distributed between manufacturing, maintenance, and fuel use.

In terms of greenhouse gases, the average new car is responsible for about 2 metric tons of carbon emissions each year. But because many households own more than one vehicle, and when emissions in the production of maintenance items (fuel oil, batteries, and so on) are counted, the average emissions per household amount to 3.7 tons per year, just over one-fourth of all greenhouse gas emissions linked to household purchases. About 15 percent of the emissions can be traced to the manufacturing of the vehicles and maintenance items, while the remaining 85 percent is caused by their use (primarily from the burning of gasoline).[11]

The data on common air pollution tell a similar story. Household ownership and use of cars and light trucks account for about a quarter of all such emissions; the impacts of driving contribute about four-fifths of the automobile total. An even greater proportion of *toxic* air emissions—over 45 percent—comes from cars and light trucks, with all but 10 percent of the automobile contribution attributable to driving.

The automobile's impact on water pollution is more intriguing. What could be the source of the large toxic chemical releases? Here the problem lies squarely with car manufacturing, in particular with the production of steel, batteries, paints, plastics, aluminum, lubricants, fluids, and other items. When the manufacturing of items for car maintenance is included, batteries become easily the most important source of toxic water pollution. Indeed, our analysis suggests that about 4 percent of toxic chemicals released into water come solely from factories manufacturing batteries for household vehicles.

About a third of the automobile's contribution to common water pollution is from runoff of salt and other chemicals applied to roads. The substantial automobile share of land use is also due to the damage caused by roads and highways to ecosystems. This is one case where the impacts are clearly not in the consumer's direct control, so it is tempting to ignore them. We need to recognize, however, that the tremendous emphasis on automobiles in our society is behind much road construction, and that roads have a major impact on wildlife in one way or another. Including the effects of roads in our analysis helps remind us of our responsibility for how our society meets its transportation needs.

All of the other categories of transportation make a fairly small contribution to our environmental problems overall. This is not to say that every one of these alternative modes of transportation is better than automobiles for the environment; it's just that they are not used nearly as much. To make a head-to-head comparison, we can divide the impacts of each mode by the number of miles passengers traveled. Table 2 shows this comparison using intercity bus travel as the baseline.[12]

The data in this table have to be treated with some caution, since the emissions and passenger mile data come from different sources and may not be entirely consistent. Also, we don't have passenger-mile data for subways and urban light rail systems, personal boats and aircraft, off-road vehicles, and ferries and cruise ships. Nevertheless, the table suggests that overall, intercity bus travel is the winner, while motorcycles and automobiles have the greatest impacts in most categories relative to the service they provide.

The finding for motorcycles is perhaps surprising at first glance. Although motorcycles get over twice the average fuel economy of cars and light trucks, their small engines have no catalytic converters or other pollution controls, resulting in high air emissions. Also, the proportion of steel and other metals in motorcycles is high compared with their total weight, resulting in relatively high toxic air and water pollutant emissions. In addition, motorcycles usually carry only one passenger, which raises the impact per passenger mile.

The high common air pollution emissions from intercity passenger rail service (meaning Amtrak) is a consequence of two facts: most passenger trains are pulled by diesel engines that have few emissions controls,[13] and ridership is relatively low on many train routes.[14] The extensive track network, which is not as heavily used as highways, also makes land use impacts relatively high. Nevertheless, in most categories, intercity rail travel, as well as air and intercity bus travel, have lower impacts than automobiles and motorcycles. This may be particularly surprising for air travel. However, modern jet aircraft are relatively efficient in fuel use, while average aircraft load factors are quite high—65 percent. By comparison, cars carry an average of only 1.9 passengers, which for a five-person car implies a load factor of just 37 percent.

Table 2. Impacts per Passenger Mile by Transportation Mode, Compared with Bus Travel

Transport Mode	Global Warming Greenhouse Gases	Air Pollution Common	Toxic	Water Pollution Common	Toxic	Habitat Alteration Water Use	Land Use
Cars and light trucks	3.0	1.6	4.2	1.8	2.7	1.2	4.4
Motorcycles	3.0	3.3	9.1	3.9	11.1	4.2	5.9
Passenger air travel	1.7	0.7	0.6	1.0	0.8	1.0	3.5
Passenger rail travel	1.2	2.2	0.2	0.6	1.5	0.7	7.8
Intercity bus travel	1	1	1	1	1	1	1

Although we could not include personal aircraft, recreational boats, and off-road vehicles in this table because of a lack of passenger-mile data, all of them are well known to generate disproportionately large amounts of air pollution. Off-road vehicles, including snowmobiles, dirt bikes, go-carts, and the like, have small, uncontrolled engines and are often operated under conditions (slow speeds, up and down hills) that greatly increase their emissions. EPA data suggest that the emissions rate for two-stroke off-road vehicles may be as much as ten times that of four-stroke on-road motorcycles and fifteen times that of ordinary cars.[15] Recreational boats—and to a lesser degree, personal aircraft—have similar characteristics. Expensive toys, both for the consumer and the environment!

Food

Food production has a pervasive impact on the environment. About 60 percent of our country's land area is devoted either to crops or to livestock grazing, often greatly diminishing its ability to support natural wildlife. Then there are the effects of fertilizers, pesticides, animal wastes, and erosion on water quality, not to mention methane emissions from rice production and ruminant livestock and air pollution and greenhouse gas emissions from energy use. All of these factors combine to make food second perhaps only to transportation as a source of environmental problems.

To analyze the consumer's role in these impacts, we've divided food purchases into the following broad categories:

- Meat and poultry
- Fruit, vegetables, and grains
- Dairy products
- Other (including seafood, alcohol, soft drinks, specialty foods, and tobacco)

All four categories include food purchased for consumption outside the home. . . .

Meat and poultry consumption has a large impact on common water pollution, water use, and, most important, land use. About 800 million acres, or 40 percent of the U.S. land area, is used for grazing livestock, most of which is for household food consumption. An additional 60 million acres is used to grow grain for feeding livestock. Although cropland can support some wildlife, and range and pasture can support considerably more, our index of ecologically significant land use nonetheless indicates that household meat and poultry consumption alone is responsible for about a quarter of threats to natural ecosystems and wildlife.

Raising livestock for meat consumption has other impacts as well. Irrigating crops for feed production puts a major drain on water resources. (About 18 percent of total consumptive water use is attributable to feed for livestock.) Animal wastes are responsible for about 16 percent of common water quality problems traceable to household consumption. The sheer quantity of animal wastes generated is astounding—some 2 billion tons of wet manure a year, over ten times the amount of municipal solid waste generation. The danger posed by such wastes to aquatic habitats and drinking water was highlighted by the case of the failed North Carolina dike we mentioned earlier in this chapter that released an estimated 25 million gallons of hog waste into the surrounding environment.

Among the different kinds of livestock, beef cattle appear to pose the most serious problem, with chickens coming in second and pigs third. In 1995, 103 million cattle (including about 10 million milk cows), 60 million hogs and pigs, 10 million sheep and lambs, and about 7 billion chickens were being raised in the United States.[16] The cattle account for about 45 percent, chickens for 34 percent, and pigs for 12 percent of animal waste production. The remaining 9 percent comes from turkeys, sheep, goats, and other livestock. Cattle are also responsible for most livestock land use.

Although raising cows to produce milk involves similar kinds of activities as raising beef cattle, the overall impacts on the environment are much smaller. According to our analysis, dairy production accounts for 4 percent of common water pollution and 7 percent of water use, whereas meat production is responsible for 20 percent and 18 percent of these impacts. The difference is especially striking when you consider how much more food energy and nutrition milk and milk products provide to the average diet. The average

American consumed 570 pounds of dairy products in 1995, nearly ten times the consumption of beef.

Growing fruit, vegetables, and grains also has a major impact on the environment, most noticeably in water use. Irrigated crop production for human consumption takes an enormous amount of water (about 30 percent of the total). Food crops in general also use substantial amounts of land and produce some water pollution, mainly because of fertilizer and pesticide use and soil erosion.

Our model does not show consumption of seafood ranking high in causing environmental damage, in part because Americans eat much less seafood than meat, dairy, fruit, vegetables, or grains. However, we need to acknowledge that our analysis did not factor in several serious problems with seafood production, including depletion of particular fish species from overfishing, the impact of excessive fishing on other sea life, and the environmental damage caused by unregulated fish farms in other countries. For that reason, it is hard to reach a general conclusion about whether it is better or worse for the environment to eat fish rather than something else.

We do know, however, that there are significant differences in the environmental impacts of eating different types of fish. Consumers should shun some fish species and instead choose from among those types that are not depleted, whose fisheries are managed well, and whose fishing does not cause major damage to ocean ecosystems. Various organizations have begun publishing information evaluating the relative impacts of eating different types of seafood. The National Audubon Society in the May–June 1998 issue of its magazine *Audubon* featured a useful guide to 21 species of fish and seafood. Although consumption of sharks, swordfish, and orange roughy should be avoided, squid, mackerel, and striped bass, for example, appear to be much less problematic.

How about food processing, transportation, and packaging? Do they cause substantial harm to the environment? Alan Durning's popular book *How Much Is Enough?* asserts that food packaging absorbs "mountains" of metal, glass, paper, cardboard, and plastic. It also stresses the environmental impacts of shipping food long distances from where it is grown to where it is sold.[17]

Our findings suggest that although food processing, packaging, and transportation play a significant role, they are not the leading cause of environmental problems due to food consumption. For the fruit, vegetables, and grains category, we broke out the environmental impacts of crop cultivation, food processing, packaging, transportation, and retail stores.[18] (The fruit, vegetables, and grains category includes both highly processed and packaged foods such as boxed cereals, and relatively unprocessed foods such as fresh vegetables and fruits.)

We find that in five out of seven environmental impact categories (and especially the dominant water-use category), the majority of the impacts come from the cultivation stage rather than the packaging, processing, transportation, and retail stages. Moreover, in those cases where packaging, processing, and transportation account for a significant share, the *total* impacts due to fruit, vegetables, and grains are modest. For example, although transportation accounts for 26 percent of greenhouse gas emissions from the fruit, vegetables, and grain category, it represents only 0.6 percent of all greenhouse gas emissions traceable to consumer purchases.

Household Operations

Running a household involves consuming many things, from heat and electricity to toilet paper and dishwashing detergent. All of these items entail some environmental impact, and cumulatively the impact from household operations is very large.

There are innumerable ways to divide up and classify the operations of running a household. We've adopted the following broad categories:

- Heating, hot water, and air conditioning
- Appliances and lighting
- Furnishings (including furniture and metal, glass, paper, and plastic products)
- Cleaning products, paints, and other chemicals
- Water, sewage, and solid waste disposal

Three areas of household operations appear to place by far the greatest burden on the environment: (1) heating, hot water, and air conditioning; (2) appliances and lighting; and (3) water, sewage, and solid waste disposal.

The first two categories contribute the most to greenhouse gas emissions (31 percent) and common air pollution (24 percent). Those emissions are the result almost entirely of fossil fuels burned either directly or in the generation of electricity. The share due to the manufacturing of furnaces, air conditioners, and ordinary appliances is small (around 1 percent of the total, according to our model). Manufacturing plays a greater role in toxic air and water pollution emissions, however, since the production of both metals and plastics used in appliances entails relatively high releases of toxic chemicals.

Within the first broad category of heating, hot water, and air conditioning, consumers use many different systems. For heat, they rely on either electricity, natural gas, oil, or wood. For hot water, they use electricity, natural gas, oil, or solar power. And only some of them have air conditioning.

Interestingly, on a per-household basis, the most polluting option is wood heat.[19] The main reason is the very high emissions of particulate matter from uncontrolled fireplaces and wood stoves. Particulates are given a heavy weight in our air pollution index because of strong evidence that they cause serious health problems. On the other hand, wood heat produces very little in the way of greenhouse gases, and the water use and pollution it generates are also relatively low. (We would note that wood used to generate electricity can be an environmentally sound alternative to fossil fuels. Advanced technologies for using plant matter for electricity, including whole-tree combustion and biomass gasification, are especially desirable.)

Among the other heat sources, natural gas appears to be the best; in particular, it generates low emissions of air pollution and moderate amounts of greenhouse gases.

The third household category with substantial impacts on the environment is water, sewage, and solid waste disposal. The main source of trouble here is sewage. Despite many advances in sewage treatment, ordinary municipal sewage remains a major source of water pollution, especially in coastal areas and estuaries, and it accounts for about 11 percent of the total in our common water pollution index. Most of that is directly attributable to households. Of course, short of taking themselves off city sewer systems and installing septic tanks in their backyards, there is nothing consumers can do in their personal lives to reduce this form of pollution—it is up to government to improve waste treatment. Individual citizens can, however, prod their local governments to take action.

It may surprise readers to note that home water use accounts for only about 5 percent of total water consumption. As we have seen, the vast majority of water consumption actually goes to irrigated agriculture and livestock, not to households. However, high household water use can still be a serious problem in communities where water is in short supply.

Solid waste disposal contributes to environmental problems mainly through the air pollution generated by trash incineration. Before anyone leaps to blame commercial trash-burning facilities, however, it should be noted that about three-fourths of the pollution in this category comes from open trash burning by individual households.

Although household operations account for a relatively small share of toxic air and water pollution, some useful things can be learned from the data. Cleaning products and services turn out to be the leading sources of toxic air pollution in household operations and are responsible for about 9 percent of all emissions in this category linked to consumer purchases or activity. This finding may be surprising but is easily explained. First, dry-cleaning establishments—which sell most of their services directly to households—emit more than ninety thousand tons of toxic compounds into the air each year (out of a total of around 3.5 million tons from all sources). Second, the evaporation of commercial and consumer solvents (which are used mainly for cleaning but also in paints and other household chemicals) contributes an additional 500,000 tons, of which perhaps a third is due directly to household use.

Cleaning products and services contribute much less to toxic water pollution, probably because most of the chemicals poured down household drains get removed in sewage treatment plants. It should be stressed, though, that the risks to family members, especially children, from direct exposure to solvents and other potentially toxic chemicals can be significant but aren't counted in our environmental indicators.

The main sources of toxic water pollution are the manufacturing of appliances (4 percent) and furnishings (3 percent). In the case of appliances, the pollutants are mostly generated in steel production, the manufacturing of printed circuit boards and electron tubes, wiring, plastics, copper drawing and rolling, and surface coatings. In the case of furnishings, it is the manufacture and application of preservatives, adhesives, paints, dyes, and other chemicals used in wood furniture and carpets, drapes, and other fabrics that are mostly to blame.

Housing

Buying a home is the largest single investment most of us will ever make, and renting a home or apartment is one of the largest expenses. We're extremely conscious of the financial implications of these decisions, but what about their environmental implications?

Overall, housing as a category—which includes rental and owned housing—is not one of the most important sources of environmental damage, primarily because the most environmentally harmful activity, the construction of new homes, involves only a relatively small share of the population in any given year. Nevertheless, housing has a significant impact in a few areas, particularly water pollution and land use, because of the wood, stone, and other materials, as well as energy, used in its construction and upkeep. To investigate those impacts we divided housing into the following categories:

- Home construction
- Maintenance and repair
- Mobile homes

The home construction category includes new houses and apartments for both rental and individual ownership. Everyone who lives in a house or apartment shares responsibility for the impacts of home construction, even if we don't actually own the dwelling we occupy. You can't escape the environmental responsibility of living in a mansion just because you rent it.

The maintenance and repair category includes remodeling and additions as well as exterior and interior repairs paid for both by homeowners and by landlords on behalf of renters. The mobile homes category covers only the impacts of manufacturing, not of driving the homes around. Land occupied by housing lots is included in the home construction category; indirect land use (such as forest land harvested for wood for home construction) is distributed among all categories as calculated by our model.

About 26 percent of ecologically significant land use is linked to home construction, or, put another way, this category is the source of about a quarter of threats to wildlife and natural ecosystems from land use. Some of this impact is due to the direct use of land for housing lots. Roughly 36 million acres of land in the United States are devoted to residential use, or a third of an acre per household on average.[20]

But the materials that go into home construction also play a significant role. Building a house takes an enormous amount of wood and wood products. In 1991 about two-thirds of the timber harvested in the United States went to structural lumber of one kind or another, and most of that was for home construction. Of course, houses last a long time, so it is appropriate to spread the impact over many years.[21] Residential construction is also the leading source, within the housing category, of greenhouse gases, air, and water pollution. Where common water pollution is concerned, the main cause is soil disturbance in construction, with forestry operations (to produce the wood) a distant second. When land is cleared, a lot of erosion often results, and the sediments eventually find their way into lakes and rivers, where they can affect plant and fish life. Road construction and clear-cutting produce similar effects in forests.

Toxic water pollution is produced in the manufacture of materials that go into new houses, including steel, paints and preservatives, plumbing, plastics, paperboard, and copper wiring. Another source is landscaping for new homes, which uses abundant amounts of fertilizers. (The fertilizers themselves are not counted as toxic, but toxic chemicals are produced in their manufacture.) As for air pollution and greenhouse gases, electricity used in the production of materials for new houses, trucks bringing materials to housing sites, and construction vehicles such as backhoes and bulldozers are the largest sources.

The maintenance and mobile homes categories appear to be much less important. That is mainly because expenditures in these areas are much smaller than expenditures for new home construction. When compared on an equal footing, however, the impacts of mobile homes in particular can be substantial. Although a typical mobile home is responsible for only one-sixth the common water pollution of the typical single-family home, its manufacture causes a third the greenhouse gases and common air pollution and over half the toxic air and water pollution.[22] The explanation for these differences lies in the different mix of materials in each type of construction. Single-family houses are built mainly of wood and wood products, stone, or brick, while mobile homes (like cars) are constructed mainly of metal and plastics. The manufacturing of metal and plastic materials produces relatively more toxic air and water emissions but uses relatively less land.

A key difference between the two, however, is that single-family homes provide a great deal more living space than mobile homes. If the comparison were made on the basis of comparable living space, single-family houses would probably come out better than mobile homes in almost all categories.

Personal Items and Services

This category of expenditure is far more diverse than the others we have looked at so far. Thus, although its impacts overall are quite significant, no single item within the category is terribly important, and indeed none of them appears in our top seven list. Nevertheless, we will take a look at a few of the items, since some of the results are surprising.

We've divided this category into four broad groups:

* Clothing
* Personal services
* Paper products
* Other

Clothing includes boots, shoes, handbags, luggage, and leather goods. The personal services category spans a wide array of things, including the U.S. Postal Service; religious, civic, and business organizations; photographic studios and developers; beauty and barber shops; and child care agencies. Also included are sports clubs, golf memberships, race tracks, and other entertainment. Newspapers, magazines, books, notebooks, stationery, greeting cards, and sanitary products are covered under paper products. Under "other," we have placed jewelry, clocks and watches, toys, musical instruments, and small arms and ammunition.

Among these categories, purchases of clothing have consistently the most serious impact, followed closely by personal services. In one or two categories, paper products and "other" are significant, though never dominant. This general distribution reflects, in part, the relative expenditures for these categories. The largest expense category is clothing, for which consumers spent roughly $230 billion a year, or $2,400 per household in 1995. That is followed by personal services ($207 billion), entertainment ($103 billion), jewelry, toys, and instruments ($87 billion), and paper products ($79 billion).

These categories are still so broad, however, that it is difficult to know where the impacts come from, so it is useful to consider smaller subcategories. . . . Under clothing, for example, apparel is the leading source of environmental damage. The production of these products is surprisingly energy intensive, and perhaps because unfinished cloth and finished apparel take up a lot of space for their weight, motor freight transportation also ranks high on the list of pollution sources. One reason clothing contributes to toxic water pollution is that the production of synthetic fibers from petroleum products and the dyeing and bleaching of cloth result in substantial releases of toxic chemicals. But cloth from natural fibers is perhaps no better, since the use of cotton and other plant fiber leads to impacts on water pollution and land use and a rather heavy consumption of water for irrigation.

Yet even though apparel leads the impacts, shoes and leather goods are responsible for a relatively large share of water pollution and land use. This is because leather comes from cattle. On a per-dollar basis, shoes and leather goods are considerably more damaging in this respect than ordinary apparel.

Entertainment has a significant impact, particularly on water pollution. There are two main factors behind this: golf courses, which use large quantities of pesticides and fertilizer to keep their grass green; and dams and reservoirs for recreational purposes (either fishing or boating).

Considering how much consumers focus on recycling newspapers, it is interesting to note that, among the paper products, the largest impacts come from sanitary paper products. The fact that a large fraction of newsprint is recycled probably lowers the relative impacts of newspaper production. In addition, the paper that goes into sanitary products may require more bleaching and other processing than does newsprint.

Yard Care

Americans are renowned for loving their yards. The image of row upon row of neatly trimmed suburban landscapes is strongly associated with the American middle-class dream. However, those landscapes are highly unnatural, and a considerable amount of effort is required to keep them looking nice. Grassy lawns grow easily only in damp, temperate parts of the country; elsewhere they require large amounts of water and fertilizer to maintain their greenness. They are also prone to weeds and pests, with the result that homeowners frequently apply relatively large amounts of pesticide to them.

How do these impacts stack up against other sources of environmental harm we have examined? Overall, they are fairly modest, primarily because total spending on yards is much smaller than for some of the other categories we have looked at. In this case, we have divided the category into the following main elements:

- Fertilizer and pesticide use
- Water use
- Lawn and garden equipment and use
- Other (including landscaping services and materials)

Fertilizers and pesticides include those purchased by households or applied to residential yards, whether by the homeowner, a landlord, or a landscaping service. Water use is that portion of household water consumption that is used outdoors to water lawns and gardens. The lawn and garden equipment category (which includes lawn mowers, weed wackers, chain saws, and the like) covers both the impacts of manufacturing and the air pollution generated during their use. Landscaping materials include mainly stone and concrete products for such things as patios, walkways, and retaining walls.

The most serious problem linked to yard care is water pollution (both common and toxic) from fertilizers and pesticides. Rainfall tends to wash chemicals applied to lawns and gardens into streams and rivers. This urban runoff accounts for about 14 percent of common water pollution on our index, and just over half of that, or 9 percent, is due to residential use of fertilizers. Pesticides are the main factor in toxic water pollution, as residential use of pesticides accounts for about 8 percent of all pesticide applications. (The impact on human health is probably larger than this low number indicates, since people frequently come into close contact with common yard pesticides.)

Direct use of water in the yard, of course, dominates water consumption for yard care. (Other, minute water use is mainly for manufacturing fertilizers and pesticides.) On average, about 35 percent of household water use goes to tending yards, and the proportion may be as high as 50 or 60 percent in hot, arid climates such as the Southwest.[23] Most of this is for watering lawns. Simply switching from a landscape dominated by grass to one dominated by trees and shrubs could reduce outdoor water use by as much as 80 percent. Still, water use in the yard is a fairly small fraction of total water consumption, since the great majority of water is used in agriculture.

Another finding to consider is that, within the yard category, lawn and garden equipment is the main source of common and toxic air pollution. The reason the overall share is so small is that lawn and garden equipment is very seldom used. An EPA study indicated that leaf blowers, for example, are used by homeowners an average of just nine hours a year, and homeowners run their lawn mowers only one-sixteenth as often as professional landscaping services do.

The air pollution generated per hour of use of such equipment is actually very high, since the equipment has nothing in the way of pollution controls. The EPA estimates that running a new lawn mower for an hour produces the same emissions as driving a used car fifty miles, while running a new chain saw for an hour has the same impact as driving two hundred miles. These figures may well understate the case, as there is evidence that in-use emissions from lawn mowers and similar equipment are at least twice as bad as emissions from new equipment.[24]

Notes

1. U.S. Environmental Protection Agency; *Reducing Risk: Setting Priorities and Strategies for Environmental Protection*, Report of the Science Advisory Board to William K. Reilly, Administrator (September 1990). California Comparative Risk Project, *Toward the 21st Century: Planning for the Protection of California's Environment*, Summary Report, Submitted to the California Environmental Protection Agency (May 1994).

2. Several other pollutants are important precursors in the creation of ozone and particulates, however. A large fraction of fine particulate pollution is made up of condensed aerosols from both volatile organic compounds and sulfur; and ozone is created through photochemical reactions involving volatile organic compounds and nitrogen oxides.

3. Natural Resources Defense Council, *Breath Taking: Premature Mortality Due to Particulate Air Pollution in 239 American Cities* (New York, May 1996), 1, 55–56.

4. The Intergovernmental Panel on Climate Change concluded that "the balance of evidence from changes in global mean surface air temperature and from changes in geographical, seasonal, and vertical patterns of atmospheric temperature suggests a discernible human influence on global climate." The various findings and conclusions of the Panel's most recent major assessment were published in three massive volumes—*Climate Change 1995* (Cambridge, UK: Cambridge University Press, 1996) and are available via the Internet at www.ippc.ch. See also Chap. 8, this volume.

5. Union of Concerned Scientists, "World Scientists Call for Action at the Kyoto Climate Summit" (September 1997).

6. A. J. McMichael et al., eds., *Climate Change and Human Health* (Geneva: World Health Organization, 1996), xvi, 57.

7. Malcolm W. Browne, "The Decline of Songbirds," in Nicholas Wade et al., eds., *The New York Times Book of Scientific Literacy: The Environment from Your Backyard to the Ocean Floor*, vol. 2 (New York: Times Books, 1994), 51.

8. Gretchen C. Daily, "Introduction: What Are Ecosystem Services?" in Gretchen C. Daily, ed., *Nature's Services: Societal Dependence on Natural Ecosystems* (Washington, DC: Island Press, 1997), 4–5. See Chap. 16, this volume.

9. U.S. Department of Agriculture, Economic Research Service, *Agricultural Resources and Environmental Indicators: 1996–97*, chap. 2: "Water" (July 1997), 91.

10. Passenger-mile and vehicle-mile data are from *National Transportation Statistics 1997*, 222 and 225, and are for 1995.

11. Table omitted.

12. The actual amounts of pollution for our baseline of one passenger mile traveled by bus are 35.7 grams of greenhouse gases, 2.0 grams of common air pollutants, 0.1 gram of toxic air pollutants, 0.5 gram of common water pollutants, 0.0 gram of toxic water pollutants, 0.1 gallon of water used, and 1.9 acres of land used per year. To find out the actual amounts of the other forms of transportation, you can multiply these baseline numbers by numbers in Table 2 for the other methods of transportation.

13. Emissions controls on locomotives will be phased in soon. The EPA is promulgating emissions standards and associated regulatory requirements for the control of emissions from locomotives and locomotive engines as required by the Clean Air Act. The primary focus of this rule is the reduction of emissions of oxides of nitrogen (NOx). The standards will take effect in 2000 and, according to the EPA, will ultimately result in a more than 60 percent reduction in NOx from locomotives. U.S. EPA, *Locomotive Emissions Final Rulemaking* (December 1997).

14. The average Amtrak train has nine cars and carries eighteen passengers per car, a very modest loading indeed. *National Transportation Statistics 1997*, 238.

15. U.S. Environmental Protection Agency, Office of Air and Radiation, *Nonroad Engine and Vehicle Emissions Study*, EPA-21A-2001 (November 1991), xii. (Available from the National Technical Information Service.) Compare with *National Transportation Statistics, 1997*, 191.

16. *Statistical Abstract of the United States 1995*, table 1140, 690, and table 1145, 692.

17. Alan Durning, *How Much Is Enough?* (New York: W. W. Norton, 1992), 69–77.

18. Table omitted.

19. Our definition of wood heat includes both casual use of fireplaces and the use of wood as a principal source of heat in wood stoves.

20. It is difficult to estimate residential land use precisely. The Economic Research Service of the U.S. Department of Agriculture estimates there were 58 million acres of urban or built-up land in 1992 (*Agricultural Resources and Environmental Indicators, 1996–97*, chap. 1: "Land," 3). However, some of this land was occupied by roads, rail lines, utility lines, shopping centers, parks, golf courses, and other uses. From data on the distribution of urban land in fast-growth counties, we estimate that about 62.5 percent of such land, or 36 million acres, was actually occupied by residential housing (including farmsteads). This works out to 0.39 acre per household. For comparison, the average lot size of new single-family houses built in 1985 was about 0.25 acre. See Marlow Vesterby, Ralph E. Heimlich, and Kenneth S. Krupa, *Urbanization of Rural Land in the United States*, USDA, Economic Research Service, AER 673 (March 1994), 18, 59.

21. A simple way to do this, since we don't really know the life span of houses being built today, is to divide the land-use figure by the total number of existing households. Measured that way, the land used to produce wood and other materials in homes is about 1.75 acres per household per year, or five times the land physically occupied by the housing. When you adjust for ecological significance, the construction share shrinks to about 18 million acres, or 0.2 acre per household per year.

22. To compare the impacts of building a typical single-family house with those of manufacturing a typical mobile home, we started by gathering some basic cost figures. In 1995 the average new single-family home cost $170,000, while the average price of a mobile home was $33,500. When we ran these figures through our model, we got estimates of the one-time impact of the construction of each. But a single-family home usually lasts much longer than a mobile home. We assume that an average new house will last one hundred years and a new mobile home thirty years. Table omitted.

23. The average rate of yard use is inferred from data on average indoor use (without conservation measures) and total household use. See American Water Works Association, *1990 Residential Water Use Summary*, at http://www.waterwiser.org. Surveys on individual communities indicate outdoor water use fractions as high as 50 or 60 percent.

24. U.S. EPA, *Nonroad Engine and Vehicle Emissions Study*, vi, viii–ix.

Suggested Readings

Blumberg, Louis, and Robert Gottlieb. *War on Waste: Can America Win Its Battle with Garbage?* Washington, DC: Island Press, 1989.

Brower, Michael, and Warren Leon. *The Consumer's Guide to Effective Environmental Choices: Practical Advice from the Union of Concerned Scientists.* New York: Three Rivers Press, 1999.

Brown, Lester R., Michael Renner, and Christopher Flavin. *Vital Signs: The Environmental Trends that Are Shaping Our Future.* New York: W. W. Norton, various years.

Callendbach, Ernest. *Ecology: A Pocket Guide.* Berkeley: University of California Press, 1998.

De Villiers, Marq. *Water: The Fate of Our Most Precious Resource.* Boston: Houghton Mifflin, 2000.

Durning, Alan Thein. *How Much Is Enough?: The Consumer Society and the Future of the Earth.* New York: Norton, 1992.

Easterbrook, Gregg. *A Moment on the Earth: The Coming Age of Environmental Optimism.* New York: Viking, 1995.

Ehrlich, Paul R. *Human Natures: Genes, Cultures, and the Human Prospect.* Washington, DC: Island Press, 2000.

Ehrlich, Paul R., Anne H. Ehrlich, and Gretchen C. Daily. *The Stork and the Plow: The Equity Answer to the Human Dilemma.* New Haven: Yale University Press, 1995.

French, Hillary. *Vanishing Borders: Protecting the Planet in the Age of Globalization.* New York: Norton, 2000.

Gelbspan, Ross. *The Heat Is On: The High Stakes Battle over Earth's Threatened Climate.* New York: Addison-Wesley, 1999.

Gore, Albert. *Earth in Balance: Ecology and the Human Spirit.* Boston: Houghton Mifflin, 1992.

Hawken, Paul. *The Ecology of Commerce: The Declaration of Sustainability.* New York: HarperBusiness, 1993.

Hawken, Paul, Amory Lovins, and L. Hunter Lovins. *Natural Capitalism: Creating the Next Industrial Revolution.* Boston: Little, Brown & Co., 1999.

Intergovernmental Panel on Climate Change. *The Regional Impacts of Climate Change: An Assessment of Vulnerability: A Special Report of IPCC Working Group II.* R. T. Watson, M. C. Zinyowera, R. H. Moss, eds. Cambridge, UK: Cambridge University Press, 1997.

_____. *Second Assessment: A Report of the Intergovernmental Panel on Climate Change.* Geneva, Switzerland: IPCC, 1995.

National Research Council. Board on Sustainable Development; Policy Division. *Our Common Journey: A Transition toward Sustainability.* Washington, DC: National Academy Press, 1999.

Ponting, Clive. *A Green History of the World: The Environment and the Collapse of Great Civilizations.* New York: St. Martin's Press, 1991.

Postell, Sandra. *Last Oasis: Facing Water Scarcity.* 2d. ed. New York: W. W. Norton, 1997.

_____. *Pillar of Sand: Can the Irrigation Miracle Last?* New York: W. W. Norton, 1999.

Reisner, Mark. *Cadillac Desert: The American West and Its Disappearing Water.* New York: Penguin Books, 1993.

Schneider, Stephen H. *Global Warming: Are We Entering the Greenhouse Century?* San Francisco: Sierra Club Books, 1989.

Shabecoff, Philip. *Earth Rising: American Environmentalism in the Twenty-first Century.* Washington, DC: Island Press, 2000.

.